MW00816899

The Insurmountable Darkness of Love

The Insurmountable Darkness of Love

Mysticism, Loss, and the Common Life

DOUGLAS E. CHRISTIE

OXFORD
UNIVERSITY PRESS

OXFORD
UNIVERSITY PRESS

Oxford University Press is a department of the University of Oxford. It furthers
the University's objective of excellence in research, scholarship, and education
by publishing worldwide. Oxford is a registered trade mark of Oxford University
Press in the UK and certain other countries.

Published in the United States of America by Oxford University Press
198 Madison Avenue, New York, NY 10016, United States of America.

Library of Congress Control Number: 2021056058
ISBN 978–0–19–088516–8

DOI: 10.1093/oso/9780190885168.001.0001

1 3 5 7 9 8 6 4 2

Printed by Sheridan Books, Inc., United States of America

For the community at Redwoods Monastery.

Before today, what darkness
did you let into your flesh? What stillness
did you cast into the soil?

—Mary Szybist

I am the night.
Then I am no one.

—Idea Vilariño

Contents

Acknowledgments

Spiritual darkness: not a subject to which everyone warms easily, and not something lightly broached among friends and colleagues. Still, as I come to the end of this project, I smile in amazement and gratitude to think of all those who have tolerated, engaged, accompanied, and encouraged me in this work. Who have opened themselves to my questions and shared with me their own. And who have entered with me into the silence that is the very ground of this work.

I want to offer particular thanks to those who accompanied me and my family during the two years we lived in Córdoba, Argentina, from 2013 to 2015, who demonstrated through their gracious and unstinting hospitality what it means to welcome the stranger, who helped us navigate the sense of bewilderment and unknowing that was such a prominent part of our experience there, and who invited us into such a rich, transformative experience of community. The ideas and questions that have come to form the heart of this book first arose in their company and could not have come to expression without them: Martin Maldonado, our colleague and friend whose boundless energy, good humor, and improvisational flair helped keep our program Casa de la Mateada afloat and our spirits buoyed when we could not do it ourselves. Diego Fonti, a philosopher who embodies in his thinking and his life the spirit of the "organic intellectual" and who has taught me so much about the true meaning of dialogue. Ariel Ingas, writer and language teacher who brought to life for me, our students, and everyone involved in our program the deep currents of Argentine language and culture, and who, with his partner, the late Alfredo Brunori, generously hosted us in wild, beautiful La Bolsa. Juan Carlos Stauber, who so beautifully expressed, in his life and his thought, what it means to be a contemplative in action. Also Santiago Bunce, Bianca McNeill, Michelle Lally, Vivian Valencia, Michelle Almanza, Jake Wild Crea, Amanda Montez, Catherine Goggins, Abbey King, and Alex Gaynor, who helped lead and shape the program in such important ways. A special thanks also to Joe LaBrie, our colleague and friend at Loyola Marymount University who did so much to envision what a program rooted in the Jesuit ideal of "education for solidarity" could be and who faithfully supported the work from beginning to end. Our friends at La Luciernega, Barrio Argüello, El Gateado, and Nuestro Hogar III welcomed us and created a space for us to share their lives and experience the richness and depth of the common life.

I have also been blessed to be part of a community of writers and scholars who take seriously the work of thinking about the way mystical and contemplative traditions of thought and practice can be read, retrieved, and brought into conversation with our own concerns. Ongoing exchanges, friendly but often challenging, with Rubén Martínez, David Albertson, Greg Boyle, Lynda Sexson, Leah Buturain Schneider, Charlotte Radler, Ralph Black, Laurie Kutchins, Gary Paul Nabhan, Dennis Apel, Jules Pretty, Jared Lindahl, Peter Lynch, Maria Clara Bingemer, Bernard McGinn, Barbara Newman, Rachel Smith, Trish Zimmerman, Steven Chase, Michael O'Laughlin, and Sharon Duggan have helped me think more carefully and critically about the questions at the heart of this book than I ever could have done without them. I also want to express my appreciation to Louise Nelstrop, John Arblaster, Rob Faesen, and my other colleagues in the "Mystical Theology Network" who demonstrate both the highest level of scholarly integrity and an extraordinary imaginative reach in thinking about the ongoing possibilities for mystical theology. The two conferences Mark McIntosh and Eddie Howells convened to help contributors to the *Oxford Handbook of Mystical Theology* think through the challenges of that project were also so helpful in opening up the critical, imaginative challenges of understanding the possibilities for mystical theology in the current moment.

I am grateful for the invitations I received to speak about the questions and ideas that eventually became central to this book. I want to thank Fred Bahnson and the late Gail R. O'Day of Wake Forest Divinity school; Steve and Pat Ahearne-Kroll of the University of Minnesota; Richard Topping of the Vancouver School of Theology; Alan Kolp of Baldwin Wallace University; Mark Wallace of Swarthmore College; and Harold Roth, Mark Cladis, and Susan Ashbrook Harvey of Brown University, for the rich, challenging dialogue that emerged from their invitations, something which immeasurably deepened and clarified what I was trying to say in the book.

Loyola Marymount University has proven to be such an open and nourishing environment in which to teach and think and write, and I am grateful to my friends and colleagues there who have supported this work. My colleagues in the Theological Studies Department graciously accepted my absence (in Argentina) and created room for me, then and upon my return, to pursue the questions that mattered to me most. My dean, Robbin Crabtree, offered me encouragement and support and time at a moment that was critical to the work of finishing the book. I want also to thank my students, especially those who left home to live and study in Argentina, and who opened themselves to the challenge of our shared life there with such grace and courage; but also those in Los Angeles, in particular those students who took the course "Into the Desert," and who risked exploring with me (and my colleague Rubén Martínez) the depths of the apophatic tradition and the wild, silent spaces of the eastern Mojave Desert. They have consistently inspired and challenged me to keep it real.

The thinking and learning that unfolded in conversation with living monastic communities has also been critical to the work of this book. I want to express my gratitude for the hospitality these communities have offered me and for their invitations to dialogue with them about the meaning of silence, stillness, and darkness in their lives and my own: especially Sr. Kathy DeVico, of Redwoods Monastery, California; Fr. Peter McCarthy, of Guadulupe Abbey, Oregon; Sr. Rebekka Willekes, of Klaarland Priory, Belgium; and Mother Máire Hickey, of Kylemore Abbey, Ireland. Also the communities at St. Antony's, St. Paul's, and St. Tawdros monasteries in Egypt; Gaudiam Mariae Abbey, near Córdoba, Argentina; the Abbey of Saint-Martin du Canigou, in southern France; and the Monastero di Bose in Italy. These communities helped me grasp more fully than I would have been able to do otherwise what it means to enter and inhabit silence. This living tradition of monastic practice is facing serious challenges in the present moment, but I have witnessed and been moved by the integrity with which members of these communities attend to the silence and yes darkness at the heart of their lives; by their openness to the difficult questions that so often arise there; and by the vibrant community life that unfolds within that space.

I also want to express my deep appreciation to those at Oxford University Press who helped bring this book into being: Cynthia Read, editor extraordinaire, for her original interest in the book, her careful attention to its slow unfolding, and her patience; Rachel Gilman, for her care in shepherding the book across the final threshold; and to Nandhini Thanga Alagu for her skillful and perceptive work throughout the entire editing and production process.

The idea of "the common life" is central to this book. It is such a simple idea, an evocation of the common ground that makes the giving and receiving of life possible. But it can be so challenging to realize in practice. I hope that my acknowledgment of those who have accompanied me in this work gives at least some sense of how much this idea and those who embody it have come to mean to me. Nowhere is this more powerfully present for me than within the circle of my own family, in the company of my wife Jennifer, and of our children and stepchildren, Julia, Samantha, Jessica, Adam, and Bennett, in whose company the joy and challenge of showing up, being present, remaining open to whatever unfolds next (and revising as needed) is always readily at hand. And where this long-term writing project on "spiritual darkness" has come to occupy an ambiguous and sometimes humorous place: mostly tolerated, sometimes gently mocked, often forgotten completely, but in the end accepted as something that moves and is important to me. The work of this book has been nourished and sustained by our common life. I owe a particular thanks to Jennifer, whose openness in sharing my life and whose generosity and insight in thinking with me about the questions at the heart of this book (which are so often close to the questions at the center of our shared life) have made all the difference.

December 8, 2021

Introduction

We lift our foot from the solid ground of all our life lived thus far, and take the perilous step out into the empty air. Not because we can claim any particular courage, but because there is no other way.[1]

—Han Kang

"This is the dark silence in which all the loving are lost." That is how the fourteenth-century Flemish mystic John Ruusbroec described the immensity in which the soul finds itself moving at the furthest reaches of language, thought, and experience.[2] An evocation of a space where loss, darkness, silence, and love all move together as part of a mysterious whole; and where a sense of participating in an encompassing, communal reality that he calls "the common life" begins to take hold. This radical vision of community arises from sense of shared loss and manifests itself in an experience of wordless, loving union with others.

What does it mean to enter these depths? To acknowledge the extent of your own loss and the reality of the loss you share with others? And to consider how or whether the recognition of your shared vulnerability with others can help open a space where love can grow and flourish?

These are old questions. But they have a surprising and continued resonance as we struggle to respond to the immensity of loss unfolding around and within us. The pandemic's terrible toll. Chronic racial violence. The devastation wrought by climate change. And so much more. To speak of such things, or even try, can be painful. Not only because it brings close what we would rather not acknowledge or face, but also because every attempt to express such loss, as well as the suffering bound up within it, is bound to fail: it is and always will be ineffable. Still, the loss remains. So too the sense of absence that arises in the aftermath. The question of how to live in this absence and what if anything we can say about it—to ourselves or to one another—remains one of the most pressing concerns of this historical moment. And in

The Insurmountable Darkness of Love. Douglas E. Christie, Oxford University Press. © Oxford University Press 2022.
DOI: 10.1093/oso/9780190885168.003.0001

at least some of its contemporary expressions, it has also become a question about the meaning and possibility of faith: whether it can survive amid such acute loss and absence. Or whether, paradoxically, emptiness and relinquishment will come to be seen and felt as somehow necessary to the deepening of faith. And to the cultivation of community.

In the traditions of spiritual thought and practice known variously as apophatic mysticism, negative theology, or the way of unknowing, these questions surface most often through images—darkness, desert, abyss, and void—that both honor the depth of loss at the heart of experience and open up a space for considering the potential power of renewal that lay in those depths. Especially in that immensity mystical writers sometimes refer to as the "abyss of love"—a space of terrible emptiness that can also become a space of intimate encounter with the beloved other, and with all those souls moving through this darkness.

Can these traditions of mystical darkness help us grapple with and respond more deeply and honestly to our own losses and darknesses? And can our understanding of these mystical traditions of darkness and unknowing be deepened by reading and thinking about them in light of our own dislocations? Also, can faith and the meaning of faith be renewed by acknowledging and making room for the depth and extent of unknowing that so often grounds it? And can community, and the very possibility of intimacy and love, be rekindled through an acceptance of our shared vulnerability in darkness? These are the primary questions of this book.

* * *

When I consider how these questions arose for me and why, I find myself returning to a cold October day in 2013, a few miles from Córdoba, Argentina—at La Perla, once an infamous detention center during the period of Argentina's dictatorship, now a site of memory. I was standing in a court-yard with a small group of students and colleagues, listening to stories of those had been arrested, imprisoned, tortured, and disappeared, struggling to take in the immensity of this loss. Impossible. The stories themselves were fragmentary, broken, unfinished. So much remained unknown, beyond recovery. But this was the stark reality of *los desaparecidos:* the lost bodies, the eclipse of memory, the ache of absence. I scanned the faces of the others gathered with me here on this day. I could feel the weight of this absence descending upon us. On the drive home, there was only a shared, stricken silence.

It took some time before we were able to speak of what happened that day. Even then, our conversations were filled with uncertain pauses and half-thoughts, a sense that we were bumping up against something mysterious and ineffable that could only be brought to language with difficulty, in fragments and whispers. Or perhaps not at all. We gradually came to accept this ineffability as necessary and important, part of what it meant to face an immensity whose meaning could never fully be encompassed in language. But it was not only that day at La Perla. Almost all of our experiences in Argentina had something of this character. We were *extranjeros* and found ourselves continuously moving through a world that was only partially comprehensible to us. Our own cultural, social, and linguistic displacement brought home to us again and again a growing sense of all we could not say or know—including an awareness of the distance that often separated our experience from that of our Argentine friends.

I had arrived here in the summer of 2013 with my wife and four of our five children in response to an invitation to help establish an immersive study abroad program based on the Jesuit ideal of "education for solidarity." It did not take long for me to realize how little I understood this ideal or what it would mean to live it. I began to see that the only way forward was to learn to open myself to the daily, moment-by-moment, unfolding of life in this place, to accept my own dislocation and to listen carefully to the witness of others who were themselves moving through their own profound experiences of loss and dislocation. Also to acknowledge the necessity of silence and darkness to the work of deepening my own awareness of this reality. And to reckon with the significance of the unknowable and unsayable to my own emerging life and to the lives of those who shared this place with me.

The questions I found myself facing were not only personal, rooted in my own sense of insecurity and displacement; they also arose in response to the daily encounters—my own and those of the students and colleagues who had come here to join us—with those with whom we lived and worked in Córdoba. What would it mean for us to locate ourselves within the complex reality of our life in this place and participate in it, however partially and provisionally? And could we learn to navigate the questions of incommensurability that shadowed almost all of our experience here: the growing recognition that, even as we opened ourselves more and more to share in the lives of our Argentine friends and invited them to share our lives, the social, cultural, and political gaps between us remained profound and not always bridgeable. What would it mean for us to acknowledge, with genuine humility, the limits of what we can know about the lives and experiences of others? To accept and make room for the radical unknowability of experience? But also to recognize how our own unknowing could help open us to genuine vulnerability, to the possibility of receiving and giving love?

Thinking about these questions in the company of ancient mystical writers, who were themselves so sensitive to the presence of darkness and unknowing in their experience, proved immensely helpful. I found myself thinking in a new way about the significance of the invitation to accept and embrace what Pseudo-Dionysius calls *agnosia*, or "unknowingness," an attitude or disposition born of a recognition of the vast field of mystery in which you find yourself moving.[3] And that cautions against trusting too much in your limited knowledge of things; or imagining that you can manage or control everything that happens to you. Instead, there is an insistent invitation to face and open yourself to what Simon Ortiz calls the "vastness beyond ourselves."[4]

"Nobody knows anything."[5] This disarmingly simple teaching from the early desert tradition captures this sensibility with such eloquence and force. And it suggests a way of thinking (and praying) that gives precedence to what Meister Eckhart calls "potential receptivity," a capacity to remain open to what is emerging in the depths of the night.[6] Gradually, this sensibility came to inform my own practice and became central to the unfolding conversations with others with whom I was now living and working in Córdoba.

I found myself drawn to consider especially how to absorb experience that cannot be fully grasped or known and to resist the temptation to analyze or explicate it or reduce it to something it is not, a habit of thought that so often results in the diminishment of the original experience. Also thinking about what it means to remain open, pay attention, listen, allow silence to gather. There was, I began to sense, an ethical imperative at work here, rooted in a growing awareness of the need to respect the mysterious otherness of the world through which I was moving and the lives of those with whom I shared this world. Increasingly, I felt compelled to re-examine certain aspects of my own life in light of these ideas, inquiring, more deeply than I had done before, into places of darkness and loss within my own experience. And paying attention to the reality of loss in the lives of those around me, and all those elements of experience that could never be brought to adequate expression in language. I began wondering especially how the practice of silence might help me acknowledge the vast unknown within which I now found myself moving and serve as the ground of my ethical obligations toward others.

This was a particular moment in time, shared with my family, students, and Argentine colleagues and friends who joined us in our work in Córdoba. Still, the questions that emerged from that moment have continued to reverberate for me long after—especially questions about the meaning of absence and darkness at the heart of human experience, and about the potential value of apophatic spiritual traditions to the work of reconstituting community. One particular question took hold within me and became a focal point for the work of this book: can the unexpected but necessary dialogue between these ancient spiritual traditions and our own diverse and complex discourses of loss can help in the creation of a new and vital mystical theology of darkness?[7]

To speak of mystical theology in these terms can seem too far removed from the complex social, political, and environmental realities that characterize so much contemporary existence, too dependent on ideas of radical transcendence, too disengaged from historical reality and experience, to have much meaning for us within the gritty, mundane often-fractious reality of our lives. These are serious and important challenges to the idea that apophatic traditions of spiritual thought and practice can be integrated into contemporary thought and practice and inform the complex social realities that shape our lives. Still, the language and images of *apophasis* are increasingly surfacing within contemporary accounts of dislocation and loss, sometimes explicitly, other times more implicitly. Loss, exile, darkness, and emptiness reverberate through such accounts and invite, I think, a reconsideration of the meaning and significance of *apophatic* thought in light of them.

In March 2020, as the global pandemic was just beginning to take hold, Pope Francis stood alone in the rain in St. Peter's square and gave expression to a feeling was just in that moment beginning to take shape in the minds of so many around the world: "Thick darkness has gathered over our squares, our streets and our cities," he said. "It has taken over our lives, filling everything with a deafening silence and a distressing void, that stops everything as it passes by. . . . We find ourselves afraid and lost."[8] The almost complete absence of any language of consolation or hope in this address is so striking, and reflects the force of the fear and loss of ground that was already gathering momentum and casting its long shadow over the world. Something similar can be seen in the way the language of shadows and darkness and emptiness and abyss are being employed to describe the depth and extent of the environmental crisis, as well as our experience of it. "The Cloud of the Impossible," "The Dark Night of the Planet," and "Dark Ecology" have now entered our shared discourse, in response to the unspeakable losses—of species, places, cultures and peoples—that are at the heart of this crisis, but also as a gesture toward the creative possibilities that may yet emerge from thinking and practice rooted in the rich world of the night.[9] There is also renewed attention being given to the myriad ways the language of darkness has been employed to exclude and erase, including the ambiguous and often racialized meaning of darkness within religious and mystical thought, and to the recurring power of darkness as a crucial dimension of spiritual identity and a resource for liberative practice.[10] It is time, suggests Judith Schalansky, for an "inventory of losses."[11]

Increasingly, it seems, we *need* the language of darkness and abyss and emptiness; nothing else is strong enough to help us address or respond to the acute and encompassing losses that mark the world in which we are currently living. Still, it is not easy to describe the effects of such darkness upon persons or communities, especially the deepening sense of psychological and spiritual precariousness that seems to be such a crucial part of this experience. Sometimes this takes the form of an inchoate sense of absence or affliction or displacement, an emptying out of meaning and the very possibility of meaning; or a sense of utter bewilderment, an experience Fanny Howe has described as "an enchantment that follows a complete collapse of reference and reconcilability."[12] Timothy Morton speaks of an "elemental anxiety" or an "existential Ganzfeld effect" as becoming increasingly critical elements of contemporary experience. This idea draws upon the "visual experience that comes upon one during a blizzard," and creates an effect that "renders *here* and *there*, *up* and *down*, *foreground* and *background* quite meaningless."[13] There is, Morton suggests, a growing sense that we are drifting, with almost no coherent frame of reference, though a great immensity.

Within more explicitly spiritual discourse, there is a comparable reimagining of the possible meaning of darkness and unknowing. Constance Fitzgerald, in her important essay "Impasse and Dark Night," revises and deepens St. John of the Cross's notion of "dark night of the soul" in response to our deepening growing sense of being overwhelmed by increasingly complex and often unresolvable social and political crises. She notes the sense of utter "impasse" that so often characterizes such experience, but also the potential for creative, transformative, and subversive practice that can arise from it.[14] Barbara Holmes, seeking to reclaim the idea of contemplative practice as a force for liberation and transformation, articulates a vision of "crisis contemplation" arising from the violence and suffering of slavery and its long aftermath.[15]

These are only a few of the ways the language of darkness and unknowing is being employed to respond to the growing sense of bewilderment at being caught inside an abyss of loss and uncertainty. With this, new questions are emerging about the meaning of human identity, community, and the very possibility of hope.[16] Some of these questions have an inescapably personal character: Where do you end up when all reference and reconcilability has collapsed, when you find yourself dis-languaged, unable to give voice to your loss? When you suddenly find yourself working at the very edge of language to give voice, haltingly, in fragments, to your experience? Still, it should not be imagined that these deeply personal experiences are or ever can ever be separated from the larger, collective losses that sweep over us. At the heart of the idea of the common life is an ethical-spiritual commitment to listen to the voices of those whose losses too often escape our attention altogether, and to ask what it will mean to honor those voices and to incorporate them into a vision of the whole.

* * *

The significance and particular shape of this communal, dialogical work will, I hope, be evident in what follows. But I want to underscore it here in relation to the improvised, open-ended, and sometimes fragmentary character of this book, something that is in no small measure due to the central place these diverse voices have come to occupy in in my thinking about darkness and unknowing and my commitment to listen to and honor them. This also helps account for the conceptual fluidity of these reflections. The question of how to distinguish among and between different kinds of darkness, for example, surfaces continually in these pages. I hesitate to make such distinctions; often, it seems to me, the darkness is too deep and impenetrable and the possibility of distinguishing between different kinds of darkness is simply not possible. Still, moving through the night can mean such different things.

There is the near universal sense of being "at a loss," of being brought face to face with what W. G. Sebald refers to as "Night, the astonishing, the stranger to all that is human."[17] The feeling of coming to the end of something in yourself; a Joban sense of displacement that is opaque, unknowable, endless. The recognition that, as Alejandra Pizarnik says, "sometimes we suffer too much reality in the space of a single night."[18] But there is also the idea, memorably expressed by John of the Cross as "the dark night of the soul," of darkness as a space of an ineffable but also ambiguous and sometimes painful

encounter with God, the very ground of love.[19] This idea has had a long afterlife, even if in much modern and contemporary writing its meaning has
become more fluid, less certain. Thomas Merton, writing to Czeslaw Milosz
in June 1961, describes his need to reimagine the meaning of this idea in light
of his growing sense of absence and loss: "My darkness was very tolerable
when it was only dark night, something spiritually approved. But it is rapidly becoming an 'exterior' darkness. A nothingness in oneself into which
one is pressed down further and further . . . [though] perhaps here in this
nothingness is infinite preciousness, the presence of a God who is not an answer, the God of Job, to Whom we must be faithful above all, beyond all."[20]
There is little sense of assurance here, or confidence that darkness will yield
a meaning that can be fitted into a larger pattern of meaning. And in this, it
echoes the way darkness, void, and abyss have increasingly come to be employed in the twentieth and twenty-first centuries to evoke an awareness of
collective loss and absence so deep and far-reaching that every linguistic
or conceptual strategy for responding to it fails and the prospect of finding
meaning or resolution feels impossibly distant. "All Absence means presence
to nothingness," says Edmond Jabès, "means awakening to the void."[21]

These are not the same kinds of experience, nor should they be included
within a single frame of meaning. Again, the question of incommensurability.
But often the boundaries between these different ways of conceiving the night
are not so easy to locate, and the language and images used to describe and
respond to them seem to inhabit a shared semantic field. Reckoning honestly
with this ambiguity and fluidity and thinking critically about both difference
and shared meaning is part of what it means to think about and respond to
darkness in the contemporary moment. And it is critical to the effort to articulate a mystical theology of darkness that can move within and respond to
this ambiguous, uncertain space of emptiness and unknowing.

What does it mean to inhabit or endure such emptiness? Or to incorporate
it into a conscious spiritual practice? It is not easy to say. In much modern
and contemporary discourse, emptiness evokes a radical loss of ground, a
profound uncertainty about the possibility of any meaning or purpose and
an attendant sense of despair or hopelessness. The precise source of such
feelings is not always easy to describe or understand, but often they carry
within them a deep and nameless sense of absence. "Fluid, absent, inessen-
tial, I lose myself as if I were drowning in nothing" says Fernando Pessoa,
evoking a feeling that has become all too common in the late twentieth and
early twenty-first centuries. Here is a feeling of weightlessness that is also,

paradoxically, the heaviest burden imaginable.[22] This sense of emptiness as loss and abandonment also surfaces continuously in the writings of mystics and contemplatives and occupies a central place in the discourse of what it means to relinquish those limited and limiting ideas about God, self, and the world that undermine the possibility of arriving at a place of true spiritual freedom. Often this means facing a terrible abyss where all meaning seems to have been emptied out and lost. In Hadewijch of Antwerp's writings, for example, "Despair in darkness," "noble unfaith," and "affliction" become elements of a profound grammar of emptiness that both describes and mediates a space of abandonment and encounter.[23]

These ideas find echoes in the vocabulary of other spiritual traditions—*Sunyata* in Buddhism, *Xu* in Daoism, *Ein Sof* in Judaism, and *Takhliyah* in Islam—that also evoke in different ways the significance of "emptiness," "nothingness," "purity," "stillness," or "withdrawal" within spiritual practice. And that give voice to the profound challenge of opening oneself to becoming emptied of all particular objects and images and capable of inhabiting a space of undifferentiated unity. Still, it is not always easy to distinguish between and among these different expressions of emptiness or to say where despair leaves off and freedom begins. Nor is it possible to say with certainty whether or how the deep sense of relinquishment, detachment, and spiritual honesty that one encounters in mystical texts can help us grapple with all that has been lost to us in our own time. But the idea of emptiness or relinquishment as a *practice,* as found, for example, in Meister Eckhart's idea of *Abgeschiedenheit,* or detachment, offers one important way of thinking about these questions. To ask what it means to face emptiness, to practice it, to *stay* with it (here I think of Donna Haraway's powerful idea of "staying with the trouble"), and to consider what it might have to say to you or where it might lead you, is often the first and most significant question.[24]

It is because of this that Meister Eckhart, for example, urges those who wish to know themselves (and God) truly: "stand still and do not waver from your emptiness." Here is a reminder of the critical importance of discovering a space beyond thought and images where a more clear-eyed vision of things can take hold. So too with Marguerite Porete, who, in her *Mirror of Simple Souls,* points repeatedly to the need for a self-annihilation so radical and so complete that one becomes "pure Nothingness," capable of being suffused by divine love. And with John Ruusbroec, who places such importance on becoming "a person [who] possesses God through bare love in emptiness of self, above and beyond all exercises."[25] At the root of these teachings is the invitation to risk a vulnerability that makes it possible to begin realizing true spiritual freedom (what Porete calls the life of the "unencumbered soul") beyond crippling fear and anxiety. A simple practice of "bare love in emptiness" that makes it possible to draw closer to others, to feel the depth of the bonds that connect your life to the lives to others: emptiness as the ground of the common life.

To invoke ancient spiritual texts in this way and to suggest that they can help us engage and respond to the loss and emptiness of our own historical moment calls for at least a brief comment about how I understand these traditions of thought and the language they use to describe experience. It is important to acknowledge at the outset that there is a certain fluidity among and between the ideas of spirituality, mysticism, and contemplative practice, both in contemporary discourse and in the pages of this book. Spirituality is the most encompassing category, evoking both the experience of self-transcendence and the work of critical, interdisciplinary reflection on that experience. In the context of this book, its primary significance lay in its expansive, inclusive character, which allows spiritual meaning to be considered in relation to both explicitly religious contexts and non-religious or religiously indeterminate contexts. Mysticism and mystical thought refer here to a particular expression of spirituality: the longing for or realization of a unitive experience of divine presence (and, by extension, a sense of unity with all living beings) but also, in many cases, the destabilizing experience of emptiness and loss and absence. It is a particular way of speaking about such experience that evokes, in dense, dynamic, and paradoxical language, a sense of what it means to move through a space of unknowing, beyond language, images, or ideas. Contemplative practice as I use it here refers primarily to those practices and sensibilities—especially those rooted in attention and stillness and silence, but also including the reality of struggle and relinquishment—that facilitate and open the mind to the very possibility of such unitive awareness and that also mediate it. It is also important to note that the always-embodied social-cultural-political reality out of which such thought and practice arises and to which it so often addresses itself is critical to understanding its meaning and significance. Spirituality, mysticism, and contemplative practice are never solely the domain of the individual but always open out onto and address the life of the larger community. Finally, I would note that mystical and contemplative writing is often characterized by an extraordinary sense of risk, an awareness that becoming open to the immensity within and without requires real vulnerability.

This sensitivity to vulnerability has also shaped my approach to writing this book, which has, little by little, taken on an inescapably personal character for me. In thinking about the meaning of darkness, I have found myself increasingly drawn to locate myself honestly within the questions I ask and to allow these questions to come to expression through my embodied experience. This has meant facing my own losses and risking opening myself to my sense of where and how darkness has shaped my experience. But it has also meant listening carefully to the experience of others, especially those experiences where meaning seems to empty out entirely, where hope becomes difficult or impossible to access. Experiences of suffering, dislocation, exile. "We sail on in darkness," says Amma Syncletica, a reminder of how old and persistent these anxieties are.[26] And how challenging it can be to address them honestly and openly.

* * *

When I arrived in Argentina in 2013, I was still carrying with me the pain of particular losses. The death of my mother just a few years earlier. The end of a long marriage. And the gradual, almost imperceptible reckoning with how much of my life now lay behind me (I was fifty-nine years old when I left Los Angeles for Córdoba). These experiences marked me deeply but not in ways that I could easily articulate. And now this uprooting and this new world, almost completely unknown to me. I became less confident than I once had been about the categories of meaning I used to understand and account for things. My sense of prayer became more wordless, imageless, and empty.

When words did begin to emerge, I found myself drawn to language, images, and ideas in the apophatic spiritual tradition that open out onto immensity: the night, the desert, the void, the abyss. I was learning to speak with language that arises from and returns to silence. Sometimes not speaking at all. Living with these images in a space of stillness and emptiness. Thinking with them about my own experiences of unknowing—thinking that I gradually came to understand as part of a contemplative practice.

The thought that is expressed in these pages emerged in response to particular experiences or intimations of bewilderment or impasse that claimed my attention but also resisted my efforts to grasp or comprehend in ordinary discursive thought. This included experiences in which my own sense of unknowing often grew acute and painful, and which compelled me to struggle with the limits of my capacity to locate or understand myself; that invited a radical relinquishment into unknowing—something close to what Luca Di Santo refers to as a "kenosis of the subject."[27] These threads of experience, around which certain apophatic images insistently gathered, gradually became incorporated into the personal narratives that frame much of the thinking in this book: my own night, desert, void, abyss. My own emptiness. These personal narratives, provisional, unfinished, and open-ended, in turn became nested within larger stories centered on the experience of others. A sense of shared, communal unknowing began to take hold of me, a growing sense that I could not easily consider my own experience of lostness apart from the experience of others—something I attend to throughout the book in relation to the idea of "the common life." I have tried to follow the promptings leading me into this place of unknowing as honestly and faithfully as I can, for my own sake but also for the sake of those whose thought and practice has so deeply informed my own.

These notes about the personal character of this work open up onto questions of language and manner of address. Whenever possible, I speak for myself, using the first-person pronoun to locate myself within the narrative structure of the work and in relation to the central ideas and questions I am exploring. Sometimes I use the second-person pronoun: I address *you* the reader in a more direct way. Or you and I together in a moment of imagined simultaneity, in the way that sometimes happens when *you* becomes tentatively inclusive: "You find yourself facing a situation far beyond your capacity to endure or comprehend." Here, *you* can and sometimes does include you and me both. The *you* is expansive, open, and moving within a space of possible dialogue. Elsewhere I use the first-person plural, *we*, usually as a way of asking whether some experience or idea is or might be shared. To ask, for example, whether the question of darkness or unknowing is something to which *we*, or many of us anyway, are now turning our attention? Whether *we* can say this is something that is part of a shared experience? Whether I may include you the reader in my questions? My use of these different pronouns carries with it, I hope, a sense of courtesy and respect and retains a tentative character that does not assume too much or implicate the reader in a way that he/she/they would not wish to be implicated. It is a delicate matter that rests once again on the question of the commensurability and incommensurability of experience. The use of language here has ethical implications: especially the obligation to respect difference and not to move too quickly to assume or claim common ground. But I want to avoid as much as possible the pseudo-objectifying and risk-averse *one*. Instead, I hope to open up a space where the questions and ideas at the heart of this book are allowed to come alive with all the risk and danger and possibilities they bring with them: for me certainly, but also for you, for us.

* * *

I want to address briefly the temporal and geographical range represented in the chapters of this book. The year 2013 in Argentina represents a kind of axis point, a moment when my life and thought began unexpectedly to converge around questions of loss and darkness and unknowing and love. Later, certain experiences that seemed at first not to have much to do with one another gradually began to gather around that unexpected axis point. As I reflected on them, I began to notice how many questions and concerns they shared. And what it might mean to think about them in relationship to one another.

The end of my marriage in 2006 was one of my most significant and painful encounters with this reality. And this is where the book begins: on Christmas Eve at Redwoods Monastery, in the company of old friends, as I was struggling to absorb a loss of unutterable depth and reach. The second chapter takes place a year earlier, in late fall of 2005 in Egypt, where I traveled, ostensibly to participate in a dig at the White Monastery in Sohag, but which also became a moment when I began to face my deepening sense of loneliness and emptiness—something of which I was mostly unaware at the time. The narrative of Chapter 3 unfolds in the summer of 2007, on the Lost Coast in northern California, a place of wild, remote beauty where I came seeking solace and healing after the end of my marriage. The remaining chapters take place a few years later. Chapter 4 is set in Córdoba, Argentina, and in the Argentine altiplano northeast of Salta and Jujuy where I traveled with my friend Rubén Martínez in 2013. Chapter 5 describes a journey I made in October and November 2016, with my friend Ralph Black, across Germany and into eastern Poland, to seek out the site where his great-grandmother Sabina had been killed by the Nazis in 1944. Chapter 6 also takes place in 2016, in California and Idaho, and traces my experience of accompanying my father during the final year of his life. The last chapter is again set in Córdoba, in the spring of 2015, toward the end of my time in Argentina, a moment that helped bring home to me in a new way the power and meaning of community.

The questions that I engage in these pages unfolded over many years, often in response to the experiences I have described, but also in relation to the reading and thinking toward which I was drawn along the way. Darkness emerged in unexpected places in both my experience and my thinking, and I followed it where it took me. My interlocutors also surfaced at various moments and in serendipitous if challenging combinations. Mystical writers who courageously opened themselves to the abyss, including Marguerite Porete, Meister Eckhart, Hadewijch of Antwerp, and John Ruusbroec, became central to my effort to articulate and understand the meaning of Christian apophatic thought for myself. And certain modern and contemporary writers, like Simone Weil, Edmond Jabès, Anne Michaels, Thomas Merton, Simon Ortiz, J. M. G. LeClezio, and others, for whom the desert, the void, and the night became critical for thinking about and confronting immensity also came to occupy a significant place in my thinking. There were also artists, such as Agnes Martin, Eric Orr, and those mostly unknown companions with whom I once created beautiful *alfombras* on the streets of San Salvador, for whom absence and emptiness became the necessary ground for artistic expression. I have looked to these figures, along with other kindred spirits, to help me think carefully and deeply about the myriad ways we traverse and struggle with darkness. And about how these struggles mark and change us and open up a space in which we can begin to meet the most challenging experiences of our lives with honesty, integrity and heart.

* * *

The abyss of love: this image, so deeply cherished within the medieval Christian mystical tradition, stands at the very center of this book. I may have sensed this all along. But the significance of this idea only became apparent to me as the work unfolded, as my own questions about loss and unknowing took deeper root within me. And as I gradually began to discover for myself the potency and beauty of this space of unimaginable immensity where the uncontrollable wildness of love flourishes. This image has become an emblem of the empty, open space comprising the center of this book, and a reminder of how love and the unknown depths of our lives, including those places where things fall utterly apart, can be mutually nourishing and sustaining. "Love's deepest abyss is her most beautiful form," says Hadewijch.[28]

There is always a danger of romanticizing such ideas or underestimating the potency and danger of love. Which is one of the reasons I find myself returning to the writings of the mystics, and why I believe their work retains its significance in an historical moment when the very idea of love as something that can knit us together often feels remote, foolish, or simply impossible. Hadewijch asserts: "To be reduced to nothingness in Love / Is the most desirable thing I know."[29] There is nothing sentimental or romantic about this idea. Still, its potential meaning for us in this particular moment is not easy to grasp. "Reduced to nothingness" can feel too much like a condition, born of violence or neglect or carelessness, that many human beings know too well already. But this is, I think, a different kind of nothingness, something both hopeful and necessary: an empty, open space where the narrow, restrictive categories of identity that so often impoverish existence fade from view and the dark abyss of love opens up before us. It is, says Hadewijch, "the most desirable thing I know."

And yet. Loss and darkness can never be completely resolved or known, even in a mystical vision of love. This also is part of the testimony of the mystics, who are often surprisingly frank about how devastating it can feel to be lost beyond your capacity to comprehend, to find the way back blocked or shrouded in shadows.

The image on the cover of this book is taken from one of the most beautiful and compelling depictions of loss and grief I know. I first saw this painting on a trip to Paris in 2009. I knew nothing about it or how it had come to be created. Wandering through the halls of the Louvre late one afternoon, I suddenly found myself standing in front of the image of a dead woman and those who loved her lost in grief—held by its raw, fearless gaze into the abyss of death. And seized by the visceral, tactile sense of loss that entered me as stood looking up at the image of that dead woman and her friends, sunk in wordless mourning. I thought of my own mother and those terrible moments after she drew her final breath. But I also felt a sudden, rushing sensation of every other loss I had known, of *loss itself.*

I was looking at Caravaggio's *The Death of the Virgin*. In formal terms, it is a depiction of a religious subject. But something about its stark rendering of death is so unguarded. Faith and hope feel distant. Only later did I learn the story about how those who had commissioned this painting rejected it. Its depiction of the Virgin was, they felt, unseemly. Her sprawling figure was too vulnerable, her death too raw, too real, too human.[30] Perhaps the trouble with the painting was also seen in the stark, uncompromising depiction of those who knew and loved her. Mary Magdalen, who sits closest to the Virgin, shudders with grief, utterly lost to herself. There is a mood of almost hopeless bereavement among all those gathered around the dead woman. Looking at this image, it is difficult not to find yourself drawn into the utter darkness, finality, and unknowability of death. No wonder those who commissioned the painting gave it back. It is so potent, so honest. But it is also so tender in its depiction of love and the unutterable loss we so often feel in the face of death. The darkness here is so deep. And it does not admit of any easy resolution. Whatever meaning is to be found in the face of death must be found in the wracked figures of those mourners, those who knew and loved this woman who now lies lifeless before them. Who love her still. And who are perhaps coming to know something of what it feels like to be lost in that immensity that Hadewijch calls "the insurmountable darkness of love."[31]

1

The Night Office

California, 2006

In late night hours
work on the soul is the way.

—Fanny Howe[1]

Cold. Dark. Bitter. That is how it feels on this winter evening as I make my way slowly, haltingly through these woods. I have walked this path many times before. But tonight it is more difficult. There is no moon. And I have forgotten my flashlight. But it is not only that. I have come to the end of something in myself. I find myself suddenly, unexpectedly alone. Lost.

I raise my hands and wave them in front of me—an awkward gesture that I employ to keep from running into trees. I take a few more tentative steps forward. Still, I am disoriented, all sense of depth and direction and dimensionality gone. Where to put my foot next? I have no idea. I stop to listen: the sound of the creek rises from below and a little to the left. Good. I am still on the path. I continue walking. My eyes begin to adjust and, looking up, I can just make out the faint outlines of oak branches overhead. Beyond, somewhere in the deeper darkness, are the giant redwoods. I cannot see them. But I sense their presence.

Christmas Eve 2006. I am making my way toward the night office at Redwoods Monastery, a small Trappistine community in northern California. My long marriage has come to an end. And this community has offered me refuge. Still, I am having a hard time locating myself, in my experience or on this night. What am I doing here? What has become of me? My usual confidence in being able to put one foot in front of the other, to get where I am going, to make my way through the world, has come undone. Grief washes over me. Anxiety at the unknown opening up before me pierces me. I catch a glimpse of myself: a scared child groping in the dark.

The Insurmountable Darkness of Love. Douglas E. Christie, Oxford University Press. © Oxford University Press 2022.
DOI: 10.1093/oso/9780190885168.003.0002

A bell is ringing up ahead. At the edge of the woods, I see a faint light coming from the chapel. Relief. I enter and take my place on one of the long pine benches that encircle this space, settling into the silence and stillness. The chapel is dark except for single candle flickering before the crèche and the tabernacle light. Behind the crèche stands the altar and just beyond, barely visible through a large window, a giant redwood tree. One by one, members of the community enter the space, white cowls rustling, and take their places along the benches. We stand, bow deeply, and lift up our voices in prayer: "O God come to my assistance, O Lord, make haste to help me" (Ps. 70). The ancient prayer. How often have I uttered these words in just this setting and felt myself reassured by them (the prayer will of course be answered)? Or not considered, as I do now, the depth of my need for help? I do not really want to acknowledge this or open myself to the brute force of it. I am afraid of the dam bursting. But it has already burst. I know this. "The waters have come up to my neck" (Ps. 68). Or, as the King James Version puts it: "the waters are come into my soul." Sitting in the dark silence, I begin to feel these words as my own.

These floodwaters. I do not feel equipped to defend myself against them. Better, I think, to flee. But where? There is nowhere to go. We begin singing again:

> Is your mercy proclaimed in the grave,
> your faithfulness among those who have perished?
> Are your marvels declared in the darkness
> your righteous deeds in the land of oblivion? (Ps. 88)

The utter bleakness of these words. The world scoured clean of hope. Loss pushed out to its furthest edge. But how true and honest, as the Psalms so often are, to the experience of desolation. This is what it *feels* like. On this night, it is strangely comforting for me to hear God addressed with such mournful defiance. To align myself with this fierce, unadorned prayer. But it is not only this. It is also the depth of longing I feel in these words, nostalgia for something that once was but is no longer. A vision of myself as whole and safe. Uninjured. Free of the knowledge of having injured another. Will all that has become fragmented ever be knit together again? There is no way to know. For now all I can do is stand in my own emptiness and helplessness.

A long silence. Then we continue singing: "You shall not fear the terror of the night / Nor the arrow that flies by day" (Ps. 91:5). I have always loved this Psalm. "You shall not fear." Never in my life have I felt so deeply the need for the Psalmist's assurance. But the terrors of the night are real. And I am struggling not to succumb to the fear and anxiety they bring with them. I listen to these words and repeat them with as much conviction as I can summon. Still, it is not only the words. It is the silence out of which the words arise and to which they return. The ground of silence and emptiness and darkness beneath the words. I am trying to open myself to this darkness, trust it, allow myself to be carried by it.

One of the sisters reads from Karl Rahner's meditation on Christmas: "We should feel as we do on a clear winter night, when we walk under the starry sky: far away the lights of human nearness and the security of home are still calling us. But above us stretches the sky, and we feel the silent night, which may at times impress us as uncanny and frightening, like the quiet nearness of the infinite mystery of our existence that is at once sheltering love and wide expanse." An alluring vision of the night, filled with grace and hope. Sitting here in the silence of this chapel with these women, I almost believe it. But the terrors of the night are tenacious. They keep coming for me. In this moment, I feel so deeply my own poverty and helplessness. This night feels threatening, empty, and cold. The reading continues: "The meaning of Christmas is that the emptiness of death is filled with the 'nameless incomprehensibility of God.'"[2]

An astounding idea. I feel the strange force of it, even if I cannot say what it means for me or might mean. We descend again into silence, and I sit with this idea turning it over in my mind. Candles burning. Faint light dancing on the crèche before the altar. Outside, the wind is picking up. A low roar moving through the giant redwoods. Inside, all is still. I think about those words: the emptiness of death is filled with the "nameless incomprehensibility of God." This is not an answer or a resolution to anything. It feels more like a gesture toward what it might mean to stand within darkness and loss. And listen.

Sr. Kathy stands to offer a prayer: "Christmas is an invitation for us to open ourselves ever more deeply to the power of love in our lives. May we not fear doing so, may we open ourselves boldly to the presence of love in our lives and in so doing open ourselves to the possibility that love may come to flow through us more and more." Piercing, beautiful words. I have lived in fear for too long. I know this. Can I learn to let it go? Can I respond to this invitation to open myself to love?

We bow and depart the chapel in silence. I wander out into the night. Across the clearing I notice a small Christmas tree aglow in the corner of the guest dining room. I am content for the moment to be moving alone in this darkness. But I am also aware of my loneliness, my hunger. The cold winter air cuts through me. I shiver and walk back inside.

Sr. Veronique finds me in the kitchen. "Come here," she says, smiling. She needs help preparing for the Christmas Eve gathering. Can I please hold the pitchers of eggnog while she pours in the brandy? She is struggling to measure out the right amount. Finally she gives up and begins sloshing the brandy generously into the pitchers. "What do we have it for?" she asks, smiling. We both burst out laughing. I feel the kindness in her gesture: she is doing what she can to help pull me out of the morass. It is what old friends do for one another. And it works. For a few minutes I forget about my situation. I help her pour out the brandied eggnog into little mugs. We place them on trays to be carried into the community room where the others are waiting to begin the celebration. We join them, and soon we are standing around the tree lifting our glasses in honor of the mystery of this night: the deep joy of this birth, the light that has come into the world. I look around at the faces of these old friends. I have known them for almost forty years. How honestly and beautifully they themselves have faced and struggled in the night. How often they have created a space for me here, invited me to share in their life, in the silence of this place. Now again, at one of the lowest ebbs of my life, they have welcomed and embraced me.

Later that night, back in my room, I look again at the little mimeographed sheet on which that day's liturgy has been printed. There I read the words of the German Dominican mystic Meister Eckhart: "I need to be silent for a while, worlds are forming in my heart." Words. Silence. Worlds forming. I am so used to navigating the world with words, language, concepts. How else to make sense of experience? Still, in that moment, I begin to sense that there is something wordless in my own longing—now shaped by grief and loss—something I have long been aware of but have never known how to respond to or access. Not fully anyway. But here in this place I begin to feel the power of that silent ground. Worlds are forming in this moment, born of my fragility and need.

I walk outside and stand alone in the empty field breathing in the cold night air. All is still. Tiny grasses glisten in the moonlight. The fir trees on the hill loom silently above me. Everything in my life has brought me to this moment. I am empty, open, waiting.

* * *

During those December days I spent at Redwoods Monastery, I was only just beginning to reckon with the depth of my loss and was far from being able to imagine any resolution or healing. Nor did I find it easy to speak of what had happened to me. I had thoughts, mostly fragmentary, about what had happened, what had led to the collapse of my marriage. But they were not coherent. I had lost the thread of my own story. Perhaps it is this more than anything else that drew me into silence and darkness. And into a wordless, imageless space of prayer. I cannot say now, anymore than I could at the time, why I found that small cinderblock chapel in the forest so necessary and important. Yes, I felt the deep blessing of being able to share that space with others. And I was consoled by the painful honesty of the psalms which, in the absence of any words I could form for myself, became a way of expressing the unsayable, of crying into the immense space of loss and longing.

Something as yet unknown to me was gestating within, and I had to give it time and space to grow in the dark. But how? Without realizing it at the time, my sense of prayer and spiritual practice was already beginning to shift, gradually becoming more wordless and empty. And it was in part because of this that I found myself drawn toward to those apophatic traditions of spiritual thought and practice, shaped by great respect for the vast unknown and the unknowable, inflected with emptiness and silence, nourished by doubt and uncertainty, and rooted in loss so far beyond our capacity to express or understand that all that remains is "darkness, bareness, and nothingness."[3]

These ideas have long been part of Christian spiritual thought and practice, finding a home both in the stillness of monastic spaces and in moments of acute social crisis and displacement. So too is the language of darkness, absence and negation becoming indispensable to the work of describing and responding to the often-bewildering sense of loss and dislocation that characterizes so much contemporary experience. And as questions about God and the very ground of meaning grow more acute and difficult. Edmond Jabès asks, "As for truth, is the abyss all we shall ever have glimpsed of it?"[4] An old and difficult question is reemerging: What will it mean to respond to and learn to live within the very darkness of God?[5] Or to face absence and loss so deep that no language or prayer will ever be able to express or encompass it?

Still, what kind of loss is this? What kind of darkness? What absence? And what happens when the experience of loss is so intense and overwhelming that language fails, and you are plunged into a silent and fathomless abyss? Is this the end of all hope? Or can we, as Emily Dickinson suggests, "grow accustomed to / the Dark / When Light is put away"?[6]

Such questions often have a deeply personal character rooted in particular losses mostly hidden from others. Certainly this has been true for me. But these personal questions are themselves often nested within and reflective of larger, more widely shared concerns arising from immense losses rooted in acute social, political, economic, and ecological dislocations. Increasingly, the language of *apophasis*, or something very close to it, is being employed in response to these accounts of loss, exile, darkness, and absence. Not as a way explaining or illuminating them, but as part of the larger work of bearing witness to all we cannot say or know.

Reading and responding to these ancient apophatic traditions in light of our contemporary experience of loss is immensely challenging. Not only because the thought worlds and social realities out of which they arose are often so different from ours. But also because the questions and assumptions about God found in these ancient texts often differ significantly from those found in so much contemporary discourse, including the question whether it is even possible to speak of God—even a God beyond language and concepts. The question of language, its limits and possibilities, recurs continuously in this discourse. The root meaning of *apophasis* (away from the image) suggests a skepticism regarding how much trust one can place in images to mediate the mysterious reality beneath or beyond these images. It also suggests a skepticism about the capacity of language to encompass or evoke the depths of spiritual experience. Still, apophatic traditions make generous use of both images and words—night, desert, ocean, abyss, void, ground—to evoke what can never be fully grasped in the imagination or in language. These and other comparable images recur continuously in the apophatic traditions of thought, often serving to subvert limited and limiting ideas about God. One effect of this language is to create an open, expansive space where the mind can move freely, unbound by the conceptual categories that too often constrain or overdetermine what can be known and said about God.

The openness and indeterminate character of this space is part of what accounts for the appeal of these ideas in a moment when the very possibility of God's existence has become so problematic for so many. And when ideas and language about God that both reflect and contribute to an unjust social reality have lost so much of their credibility. Still, most Christian apophatic thought arises from and is reflective of a strong conviction about the mysterious presence of God at the heart of human experience. It is also extraordinarily sensitive to the inadequacy of all efforts to speak of God and to the feelings of loss and absence that so often characterize spiritual experience. There is a deep trust in silence. Because of this, there is significant room here for expressions of doubt and uncertainty, as well as a recognition that sometimes the most honest response one can make to the question of how to think of or express the experience of God is to say nothing.

These are more than ideas, more than systems of thought. They are also expressions of experiential awareness rooted in practice. Personal practice, certainly, but also communal practice. Because of this, it is important to give careful attention here to the way these ideas arise from and return to spaces of practice. My own reading of these traditions has been profoundly influenced by time spent with Christian monastic communities, in the Egyptian and Judean deserts, on Mt. Athos, with the ecumenical community of Bose in Italy, and with the Redwoods community in California. And with other communities of practice, including those communities in Argentina who taught me so much about what it means to enter silence for sake of deepening and strengthening the practice of solidarity. To think about and meditate on the night in such spaces, in the company of others who are opening themselves seriously and deeply to this reality, is to find oneself called to risk what Richard R. Niebuhr calls a "deep reading" of this apophatic tradition (or what the monastic traditions often refer to as *lectio*). With such reading, Niebuhr says, "we do not have a text 'before' us as much as a 'presence' of voices, of living words and symbols, around us."[7] To engage and respond to these voices within a context of communal silence can deepen and extend their meaning in unexpected ways. And it can challenge the reader to risk more, to ask new questions about our own experience in response to these voices and the ground of silence from which they arise.

* * *

The next day, I wander over to the guest dining room to make a cup of tea before Vespers. It is a simple, uncluttered space—two long tables, a dozen wooden chairs, a piano, a small wood burning stove in the corner, a few books—but also warm and inviting. There is a portrait hanging on the wall, a large black-and-white photograph of a young woman, maybe twenty-three or twenty-four years old, black hair pulled back, dark, quiet eyes. Utterly arresting. I have noticed this photograph before but never looked at it closely. Tonight I do. I look up, scanning her eyes, her face. It is not easy to hold her gaze. Yet, I am unable to look away. What is it? I cannot say. But I stand there in the stillness of that room for several long minutes, held by her face.

Later, I ask Sr. Veronique about the portrait. "She was a prisoner of conscience," she tells me. "Originally from Uruguay, she was arrested by the Argentine military during the period of *la dictadura*. And disappeared." I look carefully at the woman who is telling me this. Her words are simple, unadorned. But I see the anguish in her eyes. The pain of this loss, now many years past, is still sharp and strong. It fills the silence between us.

After a few moments, she continues, describing how the Redwoods community, through its work with Amnesty International, had committed itself to advocate for her, to stand with her. Not only by writing letters on her behalf, something that was part of their practice at that time, but also in the silent work of prayer. They have long understood the work of accompaniment as essential to their contemplative practice and entering the silence as necessary to the work of deepening their commitment to accompaniment. Her fate is unknown. But her portrait remains, as a reminder.

A reminder of what exactly? For the community, it seems, the portrait stands as reminder of the fundamental commitments that have drawn them to the contemplative life and to their life in this place. Especially the commitment to pay attention. A long-cherished value in contemplative traditions stretching back to fourth-century Egypt and beyond, the practice of *prosoche*, or attention, has long been understood as the very ground of the life of the monk and the shared life of monastic communities. To learn to pay attention, to oneself, to one's brother and sister, to God, to the wider world, is the heart of contemplative practice. So too with this work of attending to the most forsaken, of entering and inhabiting places of loss and brokenness.

I feel chastened by this encounter. In this moment, I am so preoccupied with my distress that I can hardly see beyond the closed circle of my own pain. Still, this woman's face and her story, and the community's response to her, pierces the fog of my grief and helps me begin to consider my own lostness as part of something larger. This seems so elementary: the simple practice of empathy and openness to others. And in a way it is. Still, I have to find my own way there. Part of this means taking seriously my own vulnerability, not denying it or fleeing from it, but opening myself to it honestly and deeply. But the practice of attention, I know, needs to become more expansive and encompassing. Which means not closing myself off from others but opening myself up, risking myself. The community's commitment to this work moves me and emboldens me to consider whether I might participate in it with them and make it my own. Entering the silence and darkness not only to face myself but also to become more sensitive to the pain of others. To acknowledge our kinship, our shared lostness.

* * *

Much of this, for me, is embodied in the space and practice of what is called in the monastic tradition vigils, nocturns, or the night office.[8] Not only as it unfolds within monastic life but also as an emblem for the kind of spiritual practice that attends to all that cannot be seen, known, or fully spoken. Increasingly, I find I cannot live without this practice. Even so, the explicitly monastic context of these reflections is significant and shapes the approach to thinking and practice that is reflected everywhere in this book. For one thing, the practice of living in silence, embodied in the lives of particular women and men, has given rise to so many of the spiritual texts and traditions upon which I draw here. I want to inquire into the potential fruitfulness of this context for considering the meaning of contemplative thought and practice in broader terms, beyond this distinctively monastic context and beyond the Christian spiritual tradition.

The space and practice of the night office can, I believe, provide a context for thinking about an entire range of contemplative practices that rely on darkness, stillness, and silence for their meaning. Many of these practices cannot be easily or simply located on conventional maps of religious thought and practice. And this is part of their value. Contemplative space is a kind of terra incognita that, precisely because it cannot always be discovered employing our usual categories of description and analysis, offers us an invaluable imaginative resource for navigating the alluring but often bewildering terrain of spiritual experience. "We are measured," says Simon Ortiz, "by vastness beyond ourselves." If, that is, we can risk opening ourselves to this vastness and allow ourselves to be drawn into it, moved by its force and depth. This is not easy. Often, Ortiz suggests, we find ourselves facing a "vastness / we do not enter."[9] A vastness we cannot bear to enter. The night office is a ritual space that invites consistent, unwavering attention to this reality, and that acknowledges both the immense difficulty of looking out into this vastness (especially the fear of becoming lost in it) and its allure and beauty and significance. It makes room for honest struggle—in solitude and in community—with the vastness of the night.

This ritual practice also suggests a way of thinking that is, like *lectio*, less about acquiring a deeper certainty or clarity than it is about slowly meditating upon things and giving them time to open up within us. "I repeat things in order to feel them, / craving what is no longer there," says Henri Cole.[10] Simple repetition is at the heart of the monastic practice of *rumination*: repeating things in order to feel them. To feel their fecundity, their disturbing power, their elusiveness. To learn to stand within the things that call to us most deeply in the night even if we cannot find them or locate ourselves within them. Including, perhaps especially, absence and loss.

Paying attention in this way means learning to attend to the often-ambiguous character of darkness—in its diverse linguistic and aesthetic expressions, and in the ineffable space of silence. In ordinary language, it sometimes arises as an emblem of absence, loss, or evil; but other times, it evokes the hidden depths of cherished experience that can only be discovered in the stillness of the night. Often the experience is deeply personal. But it also comes to expression in response to larger, shared experiences—historical trauma, social-political upheaval, or environmental catastrophe. Something similar can be observed regarding writing about darkness that arises within explicitly religious or spiritual contexts: entering the night, the desert, or the abyss is necessarily painful, in part because of the incommensurability of human experience and language and the encompassing, infinite reality of the God. Also because of the often-bewildering sense of God's alternating presence and absence. But the night can also become a refuge, a vastness in which one can move freely, without encumbrance and discover again what Thomas Merton has described as the "hidden ground of love" at the heart of existence.[11]

One of the challenges of this way of listening is its unpredictability, the sense of surprise and sometimes consternation that comes from encountering a word that seems to be directed at you. The uncanny feeling of such an encounter. One evening, sitting in the chapel, I listen as someone reads these words from Issa, the great Japanese haiku master:

> Loneliness already
> planted with each seed in
> morning glory beds

The spare, simplicity of these words. But also such intense feeling. "Loneliness already planted" in morning glory beds. In everything. Later, reading *The Spring of My Life*, I learned of Issa's deep losses. His loneliness. His first son surviving only a month; his daughter, dying of smallpox after only a year; his second son surviving only a few months; his wife, dying shortly after the birth of their third son, their son dying not long after; remarriage, divorce. His poetry, often so joyful and responsive to the limpid, ephemeral beauty of the world, is also tinged with a deep sadness. "*Haya sabishi*" (the loneliness is already there), Issa says.[12]

Here in this place, amid silence and stillness, I suddenly feel my own loneliness. Has it always been already there? I wonder. It moves me to hear these words. And I know I need to consider them carefully, struggle and think with them.

* * *

The work of *lectio* continues to deepen and expand. And with it comes a growing awareness of the sheer extent of loss, its distinctive expressions, and the pathos of each particular experience. I am listening.

"I wondered if you thought we were lost. / We weren't lost. We were *loss*," says Robin Coste Lewis, reflecting on the centuries-long history of violence against black bodies.[13] Here loss is not a temporary condition or an inconvenient predicament. It is reality itself—rooted in history, written on the body, possessed of a tenacious capacity to continue inflicting harm. I think too of Spanish poet Vicente Aleixandre, writing in the aftermath of the Spanish Civil War and Franco's violent repression, who speaks of the enduring reality of "that profound darkness where weeping doesn't exist."[14] Or the stark space Bolivian writer Jaime Saenz calls "the other side of the night . . . a night without night, without / earth, without shelter, without rooms, without furniture, / unpeopled."[15] A sense of loss and bewilderment so profound that no way forward or around or through it can be found. Not now. Perhaps not ever. Aracelis Girmay asks: "What could she do / but swallow loss?" When everything has been stripped away, what remains can barely be brought to language or accounted for in thought: "They live. There is nothing left / to do . . . but live."[16]

What are these spaces of lostness and darkness? What does it mean to inhabit them, feel them, struggle with them? And is it possible for one person feel and share the loss of another? Or must there always be a recognition, born of respect and awe, of the gulf that separates the experience of one from another—an awareness that "no one's darkness can truly be shared and no one's light works in someone else's darkness?"[17] It seems important to acknowledge the particularity, even privacy, of loss, the distinct places, histories, and cultures from which it arises, and the acute difficulty of accessing the experience of another. Perhaps the only meaningful way of proceeding in such testimony is to adopt an apophatic practice of attention: listening carefully, respectfully, and humbly to the experience of the other, and allowing silence to gather and hold the immensity. Still, sometimes it feels critical and necessary to struggle at the very limits of language to find a way to express and imagine and stand within what Forrest Gander calls the "loss that every other loss fits inside."[18] Even if the ground of that sharing is silence in the face of what is and must always remain unsayable.

And what of God? Is it still possible to speak of God in light of all that has befallen us? Can we still pray? "You ask me how to pray to someone who is not," says Czeslaw Milosz, addressing himself to an unnamed interlocutor, words that reflect a painful, fundamental loss that seems to underlie and encompass so many others.[19] The sense of negation here—"someone who is not"—is, or seems to be, unequivocal. What can prayer possibly mean amid such absence? For some it means honoring the absence and recognizing the limits of what can be said or known in light of it, practicing radical relinquishment: "Say goodbye to everything. With a wave of your hand, say goodbye to all you / have known."[20] This emphatic farewell, suggests Carolyn Forché, stands at the very heart of prayer. Perhaps in the end, it is a matter of practicing spiritual honesty, of accepting the unavoidable truth of our situation. As it is for R. S. Thomas: "Why no! I never thought other than / That God is that great absence / in our lives."[21]

God as the great absence in our lives. A startling, disturbing idea that seems impossible to reconcile with certain traditional notions of faith, especially the idea of faith as grounded in a profound sense of God's presence. Still, there are so many places—in the biblical tradition, in the mystical writings in Judaism, Islam, and Christianity, and in contemporary philosophical and theological work—that honor absence and doubt and unknowing as necessary to faith, that conceive of faith as a radical relinquishment of all ideas and language about God for the sake of God. That trust more in what we can perceive in the night than what we apprehend in the light of day.[22]

The sense of an abyss opening up is sometimes palpable. But how to respond? In despair at the prospect of having to face and live within this stark, empty, endless night? Or with a sense relief at finally being able to move through a space not defined by hopelessly inadequate words and ideas, an open, empty space full of possibility and hope?

"In a dark time, the eye begins to see," says Theodore Roethke.[23] There is something quixotic and defiant in this idea, a sense that, in spite of the unrelenting pressure of the darkness pressing down upon us—associated for so many with an ongoing global pandemic, a deepening social crisis, and impending environmental collapse—we may yet learn to see more clearly and deeply and honestly. We may yet cultivate a way of seeing that is simple and penetrating but rooted in openness and courage, that calls into question narrow and constricting categories of thought to arrive at a more capacious and compassionate vision and practice. To see in this way is to relinquish control, to open oneself to beholding the other honestly and openly.

This brings us close to the heart of how Christian mystics have long understood the task of seeing, especially the seeing that becomes possible in darkness. Gregory of Nyssa refers to this as the "seeing that consists of not seeing."[24] Dionysius the Areopagite speaks of the "brilliant darkness" that one enters "through not seeing and not knowing."[25] And John Ruusbroec refers simply to a "modeless" way of seeing and knowing—boundless, beyond thought, uncontainable.[26] The contemplative gaze nourished in the night is open, receptive, and free. Darkness subverts the all-too-common inclination to determine (or overdetermine) reality to fit our own narrow understanding of things. It invites instead a way of seeing rooted in simplicity, humility, and awe.

Is this perhaps a kind of faith? Not simply a denial of faith or an assertion of faith's impossibility, but a way of thinking about and struggling with the most difficult questions, especially those arising from fragility, pain, and absence? We are, it seems, struggling to find a new language for faith nourished in the depths of unknowing. "To believe is to believe you have been torn from the abyss, / yet stand waveringly on its rim" says Christian Wiman.[27] There is something undeniably stark and forbidding in this orientation, an eschewing of all objective certainty for something more difficult and demanding. Close to what Søren Kierkegaard describes as "holding fast the objective uncertainty so as to remain out upon the deep, over seventy thousand fathoms of water, still preserving my faith."[28] This idea of faith honors the abyssal, the unknown and unknowable, and creates space for meeting and struggling with the most ambiguous, anomalous, and paradoxical elements of experience. It also pushes back against the idea that God can ever be encompassed in our limited categories of thought and opens the mind to consider what it might mean to seek what Meister Eckhart calls the "God beyond God."[29] It acknowledges and accepts that the structures of meaning we create to comprehend reality or account for the reality of God or fend off suffering and loss and grief are wholly inadequate to the task. What emerges instead is an awareness that we must let them go and learn, as the author of *The Cloud of Unknowing* puts it, to "rest in darkness."[30]

This sounds, perhaps, too simple. As if such rest can be found without difficulty, or that all the night asks of us is to let it surround us with its gentle, healing presence. There is little in our experience to suggest that this is so. Nor does the witness of those writers, poets, and mystics who speak to us out of the darkness give us any reason to believe this. The experience of the night can be terrifying, bewildering, less a place to rest and heal than a dispiriting struggle with pain and absence. Still, there is also something about the enveloping darkness, its silence and stillness and depth, its inscrutability and ineffability, that comforts and soothes, that releases us from our compulsive need to account for everything, explain everything. What Antoine de Saint-Exupéry calls: "Night, the beloved. Night, when words fade and things come alive."[31]

* * *

I sit in the darkened chapel listening as the space slowly fills with cries of anguish and longing. Low booming base notes, slowly building to a huge, powerful crescendo: organ, drums, cymbals. And a chorus of voices crying out from and into a space of what seems to me to be some unspeakable loss. *De profundis clamavi ad te, Domine.* It is, I learn later, a recording of Arvo Pärt's setting for the ancient Psalm: "Out of the depths I cry to you O Lord" (Ps. 130). There is such deep feeling in this music, a sense of prayer arising from and returning to an ineffable depth. The urgent need to cry out for help, and the uncertainty about whether the halting, broken speech that emerges has any meaning or can help us. The struggle to find language adequate (or at least not wholly inadequate or dishonest) to the experience of acute suffering and loss, and the recognition that sometimes refuge can only be found in the deep ground of silence.

Lying awake in my room that night, I think about how it felt to be drawn by this music down into those depths, and my sense of trepidation at feeling that abyss opening up within me. The wild force of the music pulsing through my body that somehow carried within it the embodied loss and longing of so many others. And the dawning awareness that I both want and do not want to open myself to these depths. I also wonder: Is this prayer of another, on loan to me, really part of my own soul's longing? Can I claim it as my own? Can I discover the necessary grace to relinquish myself to it?

The presence of those gathered with me on this night—some of whom are surely traveling through their own darkness and loss and uncertainty and also wondering about how or whether to stand within these words of prayer—is so encouraging to me. I may never know what these words do for me or to me. But there is something consoling about this simple, heartfelt expression of vulnerability and need, and in sharing it with others. Also recognizing that this is only a moment within a much larger, deeper space of prayer, grounded in silence. Slowly I am learning to trust that silence, open myself to it, get lost inside it.

* * *

I think of those figures who long ago withdrew into the silence and stillness and darkness of the desert, who also struggled with these questions, often long into the night. The call to enter solitude, for example: "Sit in your cell and your cell will teach you everything" said Abba Moses.[32] How many of the early Christian monks took this saying to heart I wonder? St. Antony certainly: the image of the monk alone in his cave, struggling with the demons, undergoing a painful, bewildering baptism of solitude, became emblematic of the fierce hunger that drew so many to the desert—in the fourth century and long into the future. So many of the questions in the later Christian mystical tradition trace their origin to the darkness of that cave.

But the solitude was never absolute. There was also a deep conviction among those who undertook this way of life that the work of the cell is always undertaken in the context of and for the sake of community. "Our life and death is with our neighbor," says Antony. "If we gain our brother [or sister], we have gained God, but if we scandalize our brother [or sister], we have sinned against Christ."[33] Words spoken out of the depths of his own long sojourn in solitude. *The cell. The neighbor. Solitude. Community.* A fundamental paradox of desert monastic practice. Solitude, silence, and darkness as elemental, the very ground of this practice. But also emerging from that ground: simple, unwavering attention to one's neighbor. Love born of solitude, silence, and darkness.

The later Christian contemplative tradition would make much of this intuition, locating the heart of love's transformative work in the darkness of the abyss. John Ruusbroec, in his *Spiritual Espousals*, describes the ultimate end of the spiritual journey as "being lost in the darkness of the desert."[34] Marguerite Porete cherishes "the bottomless depths," "the nakedness," the "nothingness" into which love leads those courageous enough to open themselves to such relinquishment.[35] John of the Cross, in his *Dark Night of the Soul*, exults: "O night more lovely than the dawn! / O night that has united / the Lover with His beloved / Transforming the beloved in her Lover."[36] And Hadewijch of Antwerp speaks of the "deepest abyss" as "love's most beautiful form."[37]

There is no denying the allure of this vision of love: the dark silence, the night more lovely than the dawn, the endless reach and depth of the space in which love flourishes. Who would not want to enter such a space? Still, the initial allure of the night is deceptive. It gives way eventually to something more difficult and painful. John of the Cross reports that on that mysterious night, in the presence of his beloved, he experiences a "wounding of his neck." For Ruusbroec, there is the mournful, aching reality of loss: in the dark silence, he says "all the loving are lost."[38] Marguerite Porete testifies that souls embarking upon the spiritual path must continuously struggle with the "love by whom alone they are exiled, annihilated and forgotten."[39] And Hadewijch claims that "to founder unceasingly in heat and cold, / In the deep, insurmountable darkness of love, /... outdoes the torments of hell."[40]

What is this love born of and nurtured in darkness? Why does love require darkness, silence, and space to grow and deepen? And what to make of the acute sense of wounding, loss, and exile that haunts these accounts of love and that seems both inevitable and necessary to the work of love? These are impossibly difficult questions. But I take comfort in knowing that others, including many of those whose voices can be heard here, have also found them to be immensely difficult; also unavoidable, necessary, fundamental.

It is not easy to speak of such things without falling into clichés or slogans. Is there any word in the English language that has been more debased and trivialized than love? To engage this subject honestly and deeply requires a willingness to acknowledge that our understanding is always partial and incomplete, that we may never be able to say what it means. That we, like the characters in Raymond Carver's strange and beautiful short story "What We Talk about When We Talk about Love," may need to talk and listen and contend with one another for a long time, cry out in anguish, and fall silent in wonder and incomprehension before the wild force of this reality we think we know so well.[41]

So it is for many of the mystics whose work figures so importantly here: silence and emptiness and darkness lay at the center of their struggle to say what love is and how it takes root in the soul; this ground is what gives love its power to move and undo and alter the soul. I have already alluded briefly to Hadewijch of Antwerp, the thirteenth-century Flemish mystic whose work occupies a significant place in this book. A figure of immense intellectual and spiritual originality in the late medieval world, her writing and thought occupy a critical place in the history of Christian mysticism, not least because of her courage in facing the reality of absence, exile, and despair for the sake of love. And her willingness to enter and live within what she calls "the deep, insurmountable darkness of love."[42]

There is something undeniably strange in this way of speaking of love. Why is it dark? Deep and insurmountable? Hellish even? What kind of love *is* this? And why would one want anything to do with it? Addressing these questions seriously will require listening carefully to those who thought about love in this way, and trying to understand what it meant to them. It will also mean thinking about how such language, and the spiritual sensibility underlying it, might help us reimagine the place of darkness, silence, and loss within spiritual practice in our own historical moment. Especially significant is the insistence of so many in this spiritual tradition that loss, uncertainty, and fragility are essential to the work of love.

As Michel de Certeau has painstakingly documented, the reality of loss and absence has had a significant impact on the production of Christian mystical discourse, especially in the sixteenth and seventeenth centuries. But it was there from the beginning: "Christianity," he says, "was founded upon *the loss of a body* . . . A founding disappearance." So much of the subsequent mystical tradition, he suggests, is marked by "haunting questions of an impossible mourning: 'Where art thou?' These questions stir the mystics."[43] Absence elicits desire. And desire, born of absence, grows and deepens until it encompasses all of reality. Certeau gave much attention to the sense of loss and desire embedded in the particular social, cultural, and political upheavals of the sixteenth and seventeenth centuries. But it is not difficult to see how apt this insight is for thinking about other historical moments, whether fourth-century Egypt, fourteenth-century Antwerp, or our own historical moment.

Here darkness is a kind of absence. Or a reflection, an expression of that absence. Perhaps a way of touching into loss so far beyond our capacity to express or understand that what remains is, as Ruusbroec says, only "darkness, bareness, and nothingness." So it is with prayer, which in this context becomes a practice and an awareness marked by kind of "negative capability" nurtured in silence. Absence, silence, and darkness become the very ground of prayer.

* * *

Marguerite Porete long ago noted: "God is none other than the One of whom one can understand nothing perfectly . . . about whom one does not know how to say a word."[44] So it is with so much of our own experience, especially in those places of loss, darkness, and unknowing that haunt our lives. Sometimes it seems clear that to speak at all is to risk distorting or confusing the very things about which we are speaking. Ordinary language, concepts, and symbols simply cannot encompass such immensity. Still, we do speak of these things, often haltingly and tentatively. And we listen to what others say, often in the hope that some of what we hear, or hear ourselves saying, might help us navigate the darkness. But the invitation to practice silent attention remains, and it is this ground of silent attention that makes it possible to listen and locate ourselves within that ground. This tension between speaking and silence surfaces continuously in apophatic spiritual thought and practice. And it has also become a prominent element in much contemporary thought, especially in relation to experiences of loss and dislocation.

The mid-twentieth-century work of Maurice Blanchot, Fernando Pessoa, Simone Weil, and Edmond Jabès, among others, bears witness to the severe limits regarding what we can know—or say—about the world, about our own path through the world, about God.[45] Entering silence and darkness becomes a critical gesture of respect toward and awe before the immensity in which we move—what Pessoa calls "the formless Night, mother of the origin of the world"—and humility before a reality that we know radically transcends our capacity to grasp or understand.[46] It signals also a willingness to face and respond to the depths of suffering and loss that have become such an inescapable part of our experience of the world, our own and others.

How, for example, to engage, respond to, and speak of places of acute loss that reflect and embody what W. G. Sebald describes as the "the marks of pain which . . . trace countless fine lines through history?" This is the very challenge facing the narrator of Sebald's magnificent and disturbing novel

Austerlitz, as he struggles with the severe limits of his own capacity to see or absorb or express the weight of suffering that transpired at and still emanates from the infamous Nazi fortress prison at Breendonk. Standing in the presence of this gruesome, hunched, and misshapen place, he admits that "the longer I looked at it, the more often it forced me to lower my eyes, the less comprehensible it seemed to become." Still, this does not prevent him from describing, over the course of several pages and in painstaking detail, the execution ground, the labor site, the places of torture, and the dank, pit-like cells where the prisoners were held and often perished. Even so, he confesses that his memory of the place has clouded over the course of time and he wonders whether this is at least in part because "I did not really want to see what it had to show." The obscurity seems only to deepen over time.

> Even now, when I try to remember . . . when I look back at the crab-like plan of Breendonk and read the words of the captions . . . the darkness does not lift but becomes heavier as I think how little we can hold in mind, how everything is constantly lapsing into oblivion with every extinguished life, how the world is, as it were, draining itself, in that the history of countless places and objects which themselves have no power of memory is never heard, never described or passed on.[47]

The very effort to remember and bear witness seems, in this telling, doomed to fail, "lapsing into oblivion" along with everything else. This darkness far exceeds our capacity to comprehend or express: "How little we can hold in mind," says the narrator. And it is dangerous: no one who travels down into this darkness can ever be sure of returning. Still, there is also a compelling sense of ethical-spiritual obligation here, a longing to pay attention, to summon the courage to look deeply at things, including those places where suffering and loss are most acute.

Tracy K. Smith writes: "I ache most / To be confronted by the real, / By the cold, the pitiless, the bleak."[48] It is not easy to account for such longing, or to know what it will mean to respond to it. But, as with Sebald, one can sense here a fierce desire not to look away from those places of stark emptiness, not to fall into spiritual blindness or moral complacency. Still, it is not easy to say whether what emerges from this confrontation can be expressed, even partially or provisionally. Language is not completely impotent; still, there are limits to what can be said. And what can be said will, it seems, always be held within the huge expanse of the unsayable.

This paradox is at the heart of so much of our thinking and experience about darkness. And it points to a challenge at the heart of these reflections: the effort to respond thoughtfully and respectfully to a reality that seems always to be moving out beyond thought, beyond language, but which nevertheless surfaces continuously in images, words, and practices. A reality that challenges our very notion of what language can and cannot do and opens up a space where silence often seems to be the only honest or adequate response. Or perhaps language arising from the depth of loss, shaped by its ineffability and respectful of the need for silence, but giving voice nevertheless to the often-raw, halting, uncertain thoughts and feelings pouring forth from it.

Theodor Adorno, in his 1949 essay "Cultural Criticism and Society," articulated what was then and remains now among the most significant responses to the question of how or whether to speak in the face of the horrors and violence that have so dominated life in the modern world. "To write poetry after Auschwitz is barbaric," he said.[49] This utterly uncompromising statement has served as an important caution for many against the idea that language can somehow address or offer a meaningful response to such horror. Still, Adorno himself revised this comment in his late work *Negative Dialectics* ("Perennial suffering has as much right to expression as the tortured man has to scream" he said), acknowledging that his earlier comment was perhaps too categorical. But even in doing so, he deepened his original critique, asking what it means for anyone who has escaped—purely by accident—the fate of Auschwitz to go on living.[50] Here is a fundamental existential-spiritual question regarding our relationship with the dead, and our moral obligation toward all those who have fallen silent forever.

The question of whether or how to speak has remained, for many, an open question. The French-Egyptian writer Edmond Jabès offer an important counterpoint, addressing Adorno specifically, but also responding to all those who wonder whether it is ethical to say or write anything: "I say that after Auschwitz, we must write poetry but with wounded words."[51] Jabès spent a lifetime probing the unutterable losses of the Holocaust in light of what he called "the book of our silence, the desert"—which was for him the only place empty and wild enough to do this work. His own experience of exile from Egypt marked him deeply and informed his lifelong struggle to respond to the larger and deeper losses of the twentieth century. Is it possible to continue speaking at all? he asked. Or is silence the most appropriate and respectful, the only possible response? Here we encounter a central paradox of much twentieth- and twenty-first-century response to suffering, loss, and exile. There are no words sufficient to express such experience. Therefore an ethic and practice of silence is necessary. But there is also a longing to bear witness, to say something (however inadequate) about it. For Jabès, as for many others, the only possible response is to continue working to create a poetry and literature of "wounded words." Which also means cultivating a practice of attention to and relinquishment into the desert, the void, and the night.

Something comparable can be seen in the witness of Mexican poet Javier Sicilia, who, in response to the brutal murder of his son Juan in 2011 (an innocent victim of the so-called narco wars), wrote: "The world is not worthy of words / they have been suffocated from the inside / just as they suffocated you." Then he embraced silence and vowed never to write another word. "Poetry doesn't exist in me anymore," he told friends at his son's funeral. Still, he did not fall completely silent. He came to see that his son Juan's death put a name and face to the more than 40,000 who have died because of the violence afflicting Mexico. And he recognized too his own grief had not only a personal but also a public meaning. "In speaking openly about my pain," he says, "I've been speaking about the pain of all the families who have lost loved ones." This sharing of loss, pain, and grief has helped kindle solidarity, and community and political action to end the violence of the drug wars that have long ravaged Mexico. At the heart of this experience, a kind of faith remains. "I still believe," Sicilia said when asked about the effect of his son's death on his faith, "but these days it's a naked belief, it's a belief that's in a very dark place."[52]

In the face of such loss, silence is sometimes the only possible response. Not the silence of complicity or evasion. Rather a silence that refuses to explain or even give voice to something that is, after all, beyond our capacity to understand or express, a silence that becomes part of an ethical response that honors this immensity, this absence, this darkness. In the presence of such painful absence, language collapses and loses its capacity to signify. There is nothing to say. And if one does choose to speak, there are only "wounded words."[53]

* * *

The night office, I begin to see, creates a space where such words, and the silence surrounding them, can move together. A space of solitary and communal prayer open to the endlessness of what moves within and beyond us, which does not constrain how we think about or speak of these things, but is open, expansive, and indeterminate. It creates a space for struggle and grief and loss to surface but also sometimes embodies solace, refuge, balm. It is not easy to account for this apparent contradiction, except to note that the image or symbol of darkness remains so fecund and elastic in its possible meanings that it cannot be easily or simply contained. It continues to say more—or less—as needed.

So it is for Louise Gluck, for example, who turns to the night as a space of healing and freedom:

> At last the night surrounded me;
> I floated on it, perhaps in it,
> or it carried me as a river carries
> a boat, and at the same time
> it swirled above me,
> star studded but dark nevertheless.[54]

Pure exhilaration. The sense of being carried, enveloped. The feeling of being inside of something immense, unknowable, comforting. So too for Henri Cole: "When I close my eyes and hold / my breath, I can stay in one place, / detoxifying experience like a kidney . . . the night feels / so indispensable, soothing."[55] There is nothing explicitly religious or spiritual about such accounts; no mention of God or any struggle with belief. Rather, there is something simple and elemental: contact with and openness to an immensity that reassures, delights, heals. Even in contexts where the religious meaning of darkness is referenced more explicitly, it sometimes happens that religion itself, or at least the conventional understanding of religion, begins to fade from view. Thomas Merton, writing in 1963 to his friend Herbert Mason, spoke of the onset of darkness as a kind of grace that defies any attempt to categorize or explain. "God has given Himself completely to us already. Completely. But we have to enter into the darkness of His presence. Not tragic darkness, just ordinariness: but above all what does not appear to be religion."[56] Learning to "rest in darkness" becomes in this sense a simple, if also hard-won, acceptance of ordinary existence as graced, expansive, endless. A posture of openness toward what is and must always remain beyond rational explanation or understanding but which can enter the soul as a gift.

I think too about how such questions come to expression in the work of certain visual and performance artists and filmmakers sensitive to the night and the desert. The prominent place of darkness, silence, and emptiness in this work is striking, varied, and often paradoxical. The effort to "represent the unrepresentable" seems on the face of it quixotic, even absurd. But this aesthetic gesture—even though it is bound to fail—is important, not least because of how it opens up the possibility for the experience of depth and immensity that for many can be found nowhere else. Agnes Martin, for example, in her "Statement about Her Work," notes: "I want to draw . . . that quality of response from people when they leave themselves behind. My paintings . . . [are] about merging, about formlessness. . . . A world without objects, without interruption."[57] Many of those who have encountered her work, myself included, can testify to the uncanny power her grids have to draw you in and open you up simultaneously, to quiet discursive thought and invite a kind of relinquishment into a space of stillness and emptiness; to mediate a sense of transcendence. Not with reference to any particular religious symbol system, but rather within an open, unencumbered space that invites the kind of aesthetic-spiritual response that Martin herself describes. And while the responses provoked by such artistic spaces are often deeply personal in character, they also provoke searching questions about the need, amid the often fractured and wounding social, cultural, and political landscape we currently inhabit, for more expansive and inclusive sacred spaces.

I think here also of Patricio Guzmán's haunting film *Nostalgia de la Luz*, in which the vastness of the Atacama Desert in Chile and the endlessness of the heavens observed through the giant telescopes of the Atacama converge to create an unexpected imaginative and political space—for the subjects of the film and for its viewers. The desert itself becomes a space where those whose family members were disappeared under Pinochet's dictatorship can gather to mourn and deepen their commitment to resist all efforts to erase or distort this history.[58] The film becomes its own non-discursive space that invites, even demands, a serious reckoning with this history and with other comparable histories. A participation in and evocation of the still-unfolding narrative of loss and (potential) recovery. That such work cannot be mapped easily or simply onto any recognizable spiritual landscape makes it challenging to interpret or understand in terms of classic religious symbols and ideas. But this is also part of its appeal: the indeterminate, non-discursive, and open space that such work opens up invites renewed attention to the emptiness that encompasses and grounds and often enlivens and gives meaning to ordinary human experience, especially the experience of acute suffering and loss. And it can inform and deepen our sense of how the apophatic surfaces, continuously and boundlessly, in contemporary thought and imagination.

This space of unknowing—imagined as night, desert, abyss, void—often has deep theological meaning within the Christian tradition; but it also opens possibilities for engagement with dimensions of experience beyond or outside of the explicitly religious. Darkness and silence and unknowing here play a creative and often subversive role, undermining the false sense of certitude the mind often attaches to the categories and symbols of faith. In their place, a more simple, open, and expansive of knowing begins to emerge. Even so, darkness often mediates a relationship with the spiritual traditions and their symbols that, far from denying their truth, opens a more capacious way of understanding their meaning. Similarly, apophatic thought and practice may well prove helpful for interpreting the emerging contemporary reality of "non-religious spirituality," precisely because it so often resists and questions strong claims for the meaning of particular religious symbols and concepts. For those who have experienced the oppressive and alienating power of a religious tradition, or who find the persistence of historical suffering and loss too great to allow for any simple theological affirmations, the open, indeterminate character of silence can be liberating. Still, even within the complex and shifting postmodern spiritual landscape we currently inhabit, apophatic thought and practice can also help to create a space where a more thoughtful engagement with the ancient symbols of spiritual traditions—and a more creative relationship between the discursive and non-discursive—becomes possible. This dialectical tension—at once calling into question the limited categorical meaning of so much discursive thought and opening a critical space where it can be reimagined—is one of the most significant contributions of apophatic thought and practice to the contemporary challenge of responding to emptiness and loss.

* * *

To suggest that spiritual thought and practice can emerge and thrive both within and beyond the bounds of recognizable religious traditions is not a new idea. But it remains difficult and challenging to describe and understand the ever-shifting shape of contemporary spiritual experience broadly speaking, especially considering the complex and often-competing realities of religious pluralism, spiritual eclecticism, and secularism. Nor is it easy to know how, in light of this cultural climate, contemporary persons and communities can stand within their own traditions and retrieve and reimagine ancient spiritual sources as part of a meaningful practice. Both questions are important to the work I am undertaking here.

This complex relationship between spirituality and religion in contemporary experience is sometimes framed in terms a deepening, perhaps irreconcilable, divide between them. Clearly there is a growing hunger for a spirituality free from the tyranny of tradition and dogma and symbols. And those who respond to questions about their religious identity by responding "I am spiritual but not religious" or who identify themselves simply as "nones" (none of the above) are coming to be seen as an increasingly significant part of the contemporary religious landscape.[59] But the larger social-cultural meaning of this phenomenon is difficult to name or describe, much less map or analyze. It may well signal a deep and irrevocable decline in the power of religion to shape human consciousness and culture. Or it may suggest a shift of religious thought and feeling into new and less easily definable spheres, even an intensifying of such thought and feeling.[60] It is not easy to say. Still, the distinction or divide between spirituality and religion is sometimes oversimplified, and the enduring fact of their interdependence and complementarity remains one of the most significant dimensions of contemporary religious experience.[61] Scholarship in both spirituality and lived religion is helping to provide us with a more textured and nuanced understanding of the shifting spiritual landscape than we have had before, highlighting the complexity and ambiguity of the relationship between practice and belief in the current historical moment.[62]

The question of how to retrieve ancient spiritual thought for contemporary use is also complex and challenging, especially in an historical moment that feels so culturally, spiritually, and politically fractured. Charles Taylor's *A Secular Age* has cast a long shadow over much recent thinking about how or whether faith and spiritual experience, including spiritual experience rooted in ancient sources, can be reimagined (or recovered) in light of the intense "cross-pressures" that are such a prominent part of our so-called secular culture.[63] Some have questioned Taylor's sharp distinction between the secular and the religious, his nostalgia for a particular idea of the past, and his vision of a restored whole.[64] But the question remains: Is it still possible for the secularized and "buffered" self to engage and retrieve ancient spiritual traditions, even if partially and imperfectly? Or has too much changed for us to find meaning there?

I have already signaled, through my expression of regard for monastic spaces and culture, that I think it is possible to listen deeply to and be shaped by ancient spiritual traditions. Still, the challenge of struggling with the gaps and contradictions and silences of our own historical experience remains. Postmodern spiritual experience is, for many, deeply fragmented and marked by profound loss. The work of retrieval needs to take this reality seriously. One possible approach to this question has been articulated by David Tracy, who (following Simone Weil and Walter Benjamin) speaks of the inevitably fragmentary character of such retrieval—and the need to attend carefully to what he calls the "saturated images," or "fragments," of ancient spiritual traditions, fragments that cannot be fitted easily into any totality system but that retain a capacity to become "events opening to Infinity." Partial, provisional, and open, these dynamic fragments can help us recover and reimagine, in terms that acknowledge how uncertain and bewildering so much of our own experience has become, what Tracy describes as "the very excess of intelligibility in infinity and excess of intelligence in the radical incomprehensibility of God."[65]

Such work need not, I think, be rooted in nostalgia for a lost past. Rather, it can be understood as part of a creative, constructive project of reimagining premodern and early modern contemplative and ascetic traditions in terms that are faithful to their own distinctive lifeworlds, but that also help us think more deeply about the challenges we face in our own historical moment. At its best, this work takes seriously the historical specificity of particular spiritual expressions, but also remains open to their capacity to reveal something new and unexpected to us, to move and change us.[66] There is also a more explicitly practical and constructive dimension to such work, aimed at retrieving and reinterpreting traditions of ancient contemplative thought and practice for contemporary use.[67] A significant feature of much contemporary writing on contemplation is the serious attention given to the social, political, and cultural context in which contemplative practice unfolds and to which it is always responding.[68] And there is important if not easily categorizable work, drawing upon philosophy, literature, and art, that also sheds new light on how thinking about contemplative practice is changing and developing in the contemporary moment.[69]

I want to take careful note here of spiritual thought and practice that thrives in the absence of any particular tradition or idea of religion or that creates an eclectic, dynamic bricolage out of old and new; as well as spiritual thought and practice that is rooted in a strong, if also critical, engagement with the symbols and language of a tradition. This is especially important when seeking to understand and interpret the work of Christian contemplatives and mystics whose work is profoundly influenced by the Christian symbol system and is almost always deeply theological, even as these symbols and theological ideas remain subject to significant critical questioning that often seems to reframe or call into question their original meaning.

* * *

What will it mean, in this moment, to "think with the night?" I am paraphrasing and adapting here Levi-Strauss's oft-quoted and suggestive dictum: "animals are good to think with." Thinking *with* the vast, knowable darkness (or the abyss or desert) can also be "good," allowing us to perceive and experience things not easily accessible to us in the more cramped, orderly spaces of ordinary discursive thought.[70] Even though what we perceive and experience so often transcends our capacity to comprehend. Even though thought itself turns out to be something very different than it initially appeared to be: not thinking about this or that, not overly analytical, but open, receptive, and responsive to the presence of mystery. But first, perhaps, there is a need to let go of certain habits and assumptions regarding thinking itself. As Ellen Bryant Voigt puts it: "Whoever said that I should count on mind? / *Think it through, think it up*—now that I know so much, / What's left to think is the unthinkable."[71] Not an absence of thought. But the mind working in a different way, entering and inhabiting an empty, dark stillness. Thinking nothingness.

This is how Ray L. Hart articulates this idea in his brilliant analysis of apophatic thinking:

> To think nothingness is not to go in quest of discovering something in some state of affairs; nothingness is not in the inventory of what is there or what there is. Whatever this "something" is as *die Sache* [the thing] of thought, it is not there as things are there in any state of affairs. Nothingness is there as the accompaniment, underside, or penumbra of states of affairs, more strictly of human life-situations (as, for example, their "limit," contingency, figuring in their determinateness, and so on). Nor is this accompaniment itself something that lies in wait for discovery by thought; "it" has always and already escorted life-situations without itself ever having become a life situation.[72]

Such thinking (or awareness) is not uncritical. But neither is it the kind of thinking we so often associate with the effort to understand or analyze something. "Nothingness" cannot be fitted into ordinary categories of thought. It cannot be comprehended. It is the very ground of thought, or perhaps its horizon. This is especially true of contemplative and mystical thought, which invites a relinquishment of the narrow and confining perspective of the grasping ego and a gradual acceptance and realization of something both simpler and more encompassing: thinking within a space that Marguerite Porete describes as "unencumbered."[73]

To "think with" the unencumbered soul or mind means opening yourself to the night or the desert with radical honesty and courage. It means thinking *in* the night, asking questions about what emerges *within* this empty, open space. At the heart of this approach is an ethic of attention to a range of voices for whom thinking with the night has become a crucial means of navigating and responding to the deeper currents of reality—the abyss of God or the ineffable depths of ordinary experience. It also means attending carefully to the silences that gather around loss and darkness. Such thinking often has a recognizably theological, spiritual, and ethical character and can be meaningfully placed within the category of what is often referred to as "negative theology," or contemplative thought. But it can also help us become more sensitive to the myriad (and sometimes contradictory) ways darkness, loss, and absence emerge within ordinary human experience, perhaps help us cultivate an "apophatic poetics" that can encompass this entire chorus of voices, all the while retaining a deep respect for the silence out of which it arises.[74]

There is so much about this apophatic work that remains unfinished, syntactically unstable, and inconclusive, so much that strains against the edges of what we can say—about God, about ordinary experience, about the world. Still, it seems increasingly evident that we need this beautiful, complex, paradoxical language to help us navigate the depths of our own often bewildering experience. I think here of the question Jeff Sharlett asks toward the end of his extraordinary and compassionate book *This Brilliant Darkness*, about the sense of absence and emptiness that haunts the lives of so many. "What to call an absence of something that was hardly ever there? Not any kind of certainty. It's an emptiness that feels alive. It needs no name."[75] I agree. What feels most important is listening carefully and deeply to these soundings and asking what they have to teach us about the challenge of inhabiting and responding to the darkness that has now become so deeply woven into our lives. A space we inhabit together.

Increasingly, we are coming to recognize that loss, affliction, and vulnerability are deeply shared, are part of our common condition and that any response to this reality will also have to be shared. Entering the darkness enables us to acknowledge and embrace our shared vulnerability and to open ourselves to the prospect of meeting and standing with the lost and forsaken other (who is also oneself). It encourages us, challenges us, as *Laudato Si'* puts it, "to become painfully aware, to dare to turn what is happening to the world into our own personal suffering and thus to discover what each of us can do about it."[76] This statement of Pope Francis startles with its directness and moral force, especially its refusal to succumb to the temptation to imagine that the concerns and suffering of others have nothing to do with us. Or to imagine that we are not moving through the night together.

It also creates a climate that can contribute to the work of reimagining community life. Experiences of loss and abandonment can be utterly isolating, cutting us off from ourselves, others, and God. This is reflected both in the often-raw character of dislocation found in so many accounts in the Christian mystical tradition, and in the stories of loss that have become so pervasive in our own time. The sense of loneliness and abandonment expressed in these accounts is often deeply personal. Still, such experiences almost always arise within a particular social, cultural, political context and often reflect the deep erosion of the social fabric and the loss of community, something Michel de Certeau's work on the rise of mysticism in the early modern period has so clearly demonstrated.[77] Because of this, one can discern in many accounts of apophatic thought a profound concern to respond to this loss and to understand what it might mean to reconstitute community.

Here the utterly personal character of each person's journey into the night becomes joined to the fate of others and to the question of how the life of the community can be reimagined and rekindled. The relinquishment of all security in the night becomes bound to a commitment to stand with others in their loss and dislocation. It reveals, in the depths of the night, the sense of shared vulnerability and shared participation in what John Ruusbroec and other late medieval Christian mystics called simply "the common life." Openness to darkness and silence can nourish an ethic of accompaniment and become a resource for helping us recover a more vibrant and durable sense of community.

* * *

I think often of that week at Redwoods Monastery: the darkness within which I found myself moving; the intimate silence I was invited to inhabit with others; and the kindness I received. Also the difficult, ambiguous questions that surfaced in that moment and that remain with me now: Is darkness a threat? Or a balm? Annihilation? Or solace? Is it an absence, a void, empty of meaning? Or can darkness, as well as the loss that is always embedded deep within it, yield something meaningful? Can it become, as improbable as this might seem, the ground of love, the source of hope? Can an honest recognition of the shared reality of darkness help us reimagine the possibilities of community?

I think also of the commitment of the Redwoods Monastery community to enter the darkness and not look away. To carry with them into the space of prayer the lives and concerns of others, to stand with the lost and forsaken. To provide hospitality to those struggling and alone. To open themselves generously to the work of love. This remains an important reminder to me of what contemplative work is fundamentally about: the cultivation of an awareness that the moral fabric that joins us one to another is continuous and unbroken. An awareness, as Salvadoran poet Roque Dalton says, "that my veins don't end in me but in the unanimous blood of those who struggle for life, love, little things, landscape and bread."[78] It seems important to think more about how such intimacy is born within us, and what it will mean to take seriously the challenge of responding to and inhabiting with others the dark silence that makes such intimacy possible.

* * *

New Year's Eve. It has been nearly a week since I crossed that bridge over Thompson Creek and entered alone into the dark silence of this place. My young daughter is here with me now. Two long days of driving to pick her up and bring her back here so that we can spend a few days together at the end of the year. She is sitting in her room reading, a miniature Christmas tree shining with light and color, presents strewn on the floor. Only a bare cinderblock wall between us. We do not speak of all that has happened these

past months, of all that has been lost to us. Not yet. For now we move together through a silence that cannot be filled. Still, I cling to an uncertain
hope. I think of the reading from from earlier this evening at Vespers: "And
now we welcome the new year, full of things that have never been."[79] It is almost time for the New Year's vigil. I knock on her door. She joins me on the
path and we walk out together into the night, making our way slowly through
the dark forest.

2

The Inner Mountain

Egypt, 2005

It was as if there were no names here, as if there were no words. The
desert cleansed everything in its wind, wiped everything away.[1]

—J. M. G. Le Clézio

I depart Luxor at dawn. A muezzin's call to prayer sounds in the distance.
Shadowy figures moving through the streets. The smell of coffee. A donkey
braying. The bus rumbles north for a few miles along the Nile toward Quena.
Feluccas are cutting silently through the water. Then we turn east, leaving the
green valley behind and begin climbing slowly through a stark landscape of
dun-colored mountains and dry wadis. Faint traces of pink appear in the sky.
Warm air is pouring through the windows. Emptiness all around.

Somewhere ahead lies my destination: Deir el Quaddîs Antwân—the
monastery of St. Antony, or the Inner Mountain. This is how the place has
been known since at least the late fourth century, when Antony first arrived
here after his three-day journey from the Nile Valley. A remote, wild place
located at the far edge of the eastern Sahara Desert, under the shadow of tall,
rugged mountains, fed by a small spring and dotted with date palms. A place
of stark beauty and profound silence, where, according to the stories told of
the early Christian monks, Antony lived, in almost complete solitude, for the
greater part of his life. Hidden away in a cave inside a mountain. Listening.
Struggling with his demons. Descending into the depths. And emerging
from those depths to engage the wider world.

I first encountered the figure of Antony many years ago in Helen Waddell's
translation of the *Verba Seniorum*. Those short, sharp sayings standing
naked on the page, without adornment or explanation, awoke something in
me. Two in particular I never forgot. "The Abbot Antony said, 'Fish, if they
tarry on dry land, die: even so monks that tarry outside their cell . . . fall

The Insurmountable Darkness of Love. Douglas E. Christie, Oxford University Press. © Oxford University Press 2022.
DOI: 10.1093/oso/9780190885168.003.0003

away from their vow of quiet. As a fish must return to the sea, so must we to our cell: lest it befall that by tarrying without, we forget the watch within.'" And also this: "The abbot Antony said: 'Who sits in solitude and is quiet hath escaped from three wars: hearing, speaking, seeing: yet, against one thing shall he continually battle: that is, his own heart.'"[2] I did not know at the time the Greek word *hesychia* that lay behind Waddell's rendering of quiet or how important this idea was to early Christian monasticism. But the power in that word "quiet" reached me anyway. So too the centrality of the "heart" and the potency of desire. The sense of a space of inner stillness and self-knowledge, but also the reality of vulnerability and struggle. And the idea of a practice—remaining in the cell, keeping watch within—that can help lead one deeper into that mysterious space.

There was also something about the wild otherness of that desert place that captivated me and drew me in—especially the "hollow mountain" in the remote eastern desert where Antony entered solitude. Sometimes, it seems, without knowing where he was going or why: "Antony continued to travel through the region he had entered upon," one of the early accounts relates, "now gazing at the tracks of the wild beasts, and now at the vastness of the broad desert: what he should do, wither he should turn, he knew not." What were these wandering monks doing out in this vast, remote place? The stories and sayings provided hints. But often it was their gestures that carried the most weight: "All night long," one account relates "[Antony] spent the darkness in prayer."[3]

Strange, powerful ideas, arising from an ancient, distant culture, that somehow sparked a sense of recognition in me. Here was something precious, worth seeking, cultivating, safeguarding. I sensed that something was at stake for me here, even if I could not articulate what it was. I began dreaming of the Inner Mountain. I bought a map of Egypt, laid it out on my table, ran my fingers down the long blue thread of the Nile River, south almost as far as Beni Suef, then east across the North Galâla Plateau, past the Wâdi Sannûr, the Wâdi Abu Rimth, the Wâdi Irkâs, following the ancient path to that remote, obscure place. I said the names aloud. Strange, beautiful names. But as I looked over the map, I noticed that most of it was blank, unnamed, empty, unknown. I returned to that map often during the next several years as my engagement with ancient desert traditions deepened. Wondering about those places, thinking about them. Now I was on my way there.

There is a sharp sound of grinding metal as the bus driver shifts gears and begins a steep ascent. The low murmur of conversations around me. The smell of diesel, sweat, and a pungent fragrance I cannot identify. The heat is building. I reach into my bag for an apple. Thoughts drifting. Also feelings of anxiety spiking. I am far from home, traveling alone, making my way across this empty, open space. Going where exactly? And why? I cannot say. Not completely anyway.

I am here in part because of an invitation. Several months ago, a colleague contacted me about the possibility of participating in a dig at the White Monastery at Sohag on the west bank of the Nile—an exciting project that was already unearthing beautiful artifacts and shedding new light on the life of this early Christian community. Others had recently uncovered cells at St. Antony's monastery dating from the fourth or fifth century. And the restoration work on the ancient frescoes at St. Antony's and St. Paul's, a long, painstaking project of cultural recovery, had now been completed.[4] The same team of Italian conservators who brought these images back to life were now at work at the Red Monastery in the Nile Valley, not far from the dig in Sohag. There was a possibility of meeting and talking with them about their work, an exciting opportunity for me to deepen and extend my long-standing research on ancient Christian monasticism. But it was more than this. I had reached a place of impasse in my life and was struggling to respond to the deepening sense of loss I now found myself facing.

My mother had died the year before, following a long struggle with cancer. I stood by her bedside as she took her last breaths. Later, together with my father and brothers and sister and other family members, I took a handful of her ashes and scattered them out onto the rushing waters of the Wood River in Idaho's Sawtooth Mountains. The awful finality of that farewell. Later that year, I read Micheline Aharonion Marcom's novel *The Day Dreaming Boy*, pausing especially over the narrator's account of his lost mother: "Why can't you speak to me? I will go to the desert to find you. Here in this handful of dust. Here in this handful of dust." A very different loss from mine, rooted in a terrible experience of historical genocide. But I recognized the deep longing to hear her voice, to somehow find her again. Also the sense of having entered a silent, lonely country. And the truth of these words: "The man who has no mother's form to form him is a sad man, unanchored man, vile and demoniac."[5] Too extreme? I don't think so. I was now motherless. And falling into an abyss of grief and loss.

But that was not all. I had also begun to lose my way in my marriage. And I feared that I would not be able to find my way back. My heart felt raw and unsteady, not quite ready for what I knew I must eventually face. Which was also, I suspect, a big part of why I had come to this place: to face my own vulnerability and need, to struggle with my own heart. And to face my own long practice of evasion, the idea that I can seek or find refuge or solace on the surface of things.

Sometime around midday, the bus pulls into a small lean-to shelter perched improbably and precariously at the edge of a cliff. Everyone piles out to stretch and move around for a few minutes. There is strong, sweet tea, warm bread, and dates; animated conversation among my traveling companions; then we are on our way again, cutting through this arid, rugged landscape, wending our way east. For the next several hours, I drift in and out of sleep.

Suddenly, I am jolted awake by the sound of screeching brakes: we have arrived at the shores of the Red Sea. I gaze out at the deep, blue expanse. My body is soaked with sweat; but there is a cool breeze drifting in off the water. We pause a few moments before turning north, traveling along a mostly empty highway, the sea to the east, the desert to the west. At Râs Az 'farâna, the bus stops to refuel before continuing north toward Sinai. But to reach St. Antony's I must travel west, so I climb down, bid my traveling companions goodbye and begin searching for a way back into the desert.

There is no way. At least none that I can work out in this moment. I have made inquiries, but no one is heading west. I do not have any good options. So I decide to walk a short ways down the road and sit for a while. Perhaps a car or truck will come. I drop my bag and begin waiting. There is nothing else to do.

I think about my predicament and wonder what I will do next. I am not sure. For the moment, I am stuck here at the edge of this unknown immensity, feeling more than a little anxious about what will happen or not happen next. I know it cannot be helped, that there was only so much I could do to plan or map out this journey ahead of time, that somehow this was as far as I could get. Still, it feels like my own fault, that if I was a just little bit more resourceful I would not have ended up here on the side of this road. A familiar feeling that arises when things fall apart. This is a challenge all travelers face I know: accepting the fact that map is not territory, and the possibility, even the likelihood, that at some point you will get turned around, or stranded, or completely lost. It has happened to me before. The upending of my expectations about what I was doing and where I was going. The sudden need to revise or scrap my plans. The relinquishment of control. Yes, I know this. But in this moment, these ideas are scant comfort to me.

I have been reading Renée Daumal's *Mount Analogue* and find myself thinking again about the small band of seekers who searched obsessively for that remote, possibly mythical, place. And their sense of triumph when they finally discovered it: "How it was proved that a hitherto unknown continent really existed with mountains much higher than the Himalayas . . . how it happened that no one detected it before . . . how we reached it." A "hitherto unknown" place: hiddenness and obscurity at the heart of its allure. And the moment of discovery: "How we *reached* it," the narrator says. A deceptively simple phrase that hardly begins to account for the immense difficulty, near impossibility, of doing so. Nor was the difficulty primarily geographical or topographical; these were seasoned, well-tested travelers who knew how to read maps. No, the fundamental challenge was, if anything, philosophical or spiritual in nature. "To find a way to reach the island," the narrator of this strange tale relates, "we must assume on principle, as we have always done, the possibility and even the *necessity* of doing so. The only admissible hypothesis is that the 'shell of the curvature' that surrounds the island is not *absolutely* impenetrable—that is, *not always, everywhere,* and *for everyone. At a certain moment,* and *a certain place, certain people* (those who know how to and wish to do so) can enter."[6]

I take this as a warning but also as an encouragement: to think carefully about what I am doing, and why I am doing it. But also to hold lightly to my own ideas about this journey. To remain open and responsive to what is unfolding before me. What am I hoping to find in this remote place in the Egyptian desert? Shelter? Healing? A reckoning? Why is it *necessary?* And why now? I cannot say, not with any certainty. All I know in this moment is that I need to withdraw for a time into this silent, obscure place.

I think again of that figure who came here long before me, who knew what it meant to traverse the depths, who risked everything for the sake of that hidden work of *hesychia.* I look out at the empty highway stretching endlessly ahead of me and continue waiting.

* * *

How much of the lives of the early monks consisted of just this—sitting and waiting? Listening carefully and deeply in the silence and darkness of the cell. "While staying in the cell," Antony says, "collect your mind: remember the day of your death . . . but remember too the day of your resurrection."[7] The work of the cell: intensely focused and sobering, a descent into the depths.

Memento mori: the remembrance of death, a clarifying, grounding practice, long understood by the monks as necessary for waking up to one's
own existence, to God. "Always keep your death in mind," says Evagrius,
"then there will be no fault in your soul."[8] The stark recognition of your
own mortality, in light of which other, more superficial concerns can be
seen for what they are. Still, it is not only your death upon which you are
invited to meditate; it is death itself. Including its apparent capriciousness,
its cruelty, its injustice. "How is it that some die when they are young, while
others drag on to extreme old age?," asks Antony. "Why are there those who
are poor and those who are rich? Why do wicked men prosper and why are
the just in need?" These questions pulse with the ache of unresolved loss.
Often they possess a Joban character—arising from the naked confrontation with those painful, mysterious, and intractable realities that can never
be resolved theologically or philosophically, that threaten to engulf, even
annihilate, everything and everyone.

Such questions surface continuously in the darkness of the cell and
are suggestive of a struggle with death that includes but also transcends
questions of one's personal mortality. In the ancient monastic world, such
questions arose from a complex, difficult social-political reality—in particular the crushing force of the Roman Empire on the lives of ordinary
men and women living in towns and villages along the Nile Valley—that
was critical to the formation of the ancient Christian monastic movement.
An honest meditation on death, in light of this reality, leads inevitably toward an uncomfortable but necessary consideration of one's relationship
to all those who have died early or unnecessarily or unjustly. A meditation that raises questions about one's relationship to and participation in
the social and political structures underlying and contributing to those
deaths. And that can bring with it a painful awareness of the invisible
threads that bind each one of us to every other being, living and dead, a
recognition that "what one of us lives through, each must, so that this, of
which we are / part, will know itself."[9] The work of the cell requires and
makes such awareness possible.

Still, such work also—unexpectedly and paradoxically—invites meditation on resurrection: on life, presence, hope. Not only a future hope but a
present reality. Emerging from within this painful awareness of death. Not its
antithesis, not answering or resolving it, but somehow bound to it, including
it. Part of a strange, unexpected equation or paradox that somehow becomes
visible in this place: "Death = night = desert = rebirth."[10]

This paradox permeates *The Life of Antony* and so much of the ancient desert tradition. I suspect this is no small part of why I have found myself drawn into this world. And walking this road. I need and want the purifying power of this silence, even as I hesitate at the prospect of opening myself to it. I recall the warning of another desert sojourner, Edmond Jabès:

> It is very hard to live with silence. The real silence is death and this is ter-rible. To approach this silence, it is necessary to journey into the desert. You do not go to the desert to find identity, but to lose it, to lose your personality, to become anonymous. You make yourself void. You *become* silence. You must become more silent than the silence around you. And then something extraordinary happens: you hear silence speak.[11]

A warning. But also an encouragement. Silence as an immensity that opens out onto the immensity of death, that invites, demands a confrontation with death. A relinquishment of old ideas about the self, identity, meaning, which are subverted, reconfigured, reimagined in the ground of silence. Learning to listen in silence. Part of the work of the cell.

"Listen with the ears of your heart," counsels *The Rule of St. Benedict*. A beautiful and inviting idea that nevertheless holds within it a difficult pros-pect: opening yourself with a wholehearted and uncompromising attention, opening your soul to its deepest, furthest reaches. A relinquishment into si-lence. Into the void. Into God.

Many have traveled this road before me, and no doubt others will follow after me. I am not alone on this path. But for the moment, it is my own de-scent into silence that I must attend to.

* * *

I was in my early twenties, living in Santa Cruz, California, when I first encountered the literature of the desert. Soon I was reading voraciously anything I could find on the ancient Christian monastic tradition: The *Apophthegmata Patrum*, the *Conferences* of John Cassian, *The Life of Antony*, the *Praktikos* of Evagrius, the *Life of Melania*. These texts had a strange and unsettling force on my thinking and my life. At the time, I had nothing more than intuitions of what this world was about or what it might come to mean for me. But I was moved by the silence and stillness, the purity of solitude, and the sense of endless depth. These dimensions of the desert tradition, obscurely grasped but deeply felt, seemed to correspond to something that was coming alive in me. Something I wanted to understand better, take hold of more firmly, live into. It was enough to set in motion a years-long dialogue with the places, figures, and teachings of the ancient Christian desert monastic tradition. Also an encounter with silence, darkness, and emptiness—the very ground out of which this tradition arose. I had only the faintest understanding at the time of what it would mean for me to open myself to this world. Or where it might take me. But I knew I had to pay attention to it. And I did.

The vision of prayer I discovered in these ancient monastic texts—wholehearted and unstinting—was especially moving to me. John Cassian describes it this way: "The whole purpose of the monk and indeed the perfection of his heart, amount to this—total and uninterrupted dedication to prayer. He strives for unstirring calm of mind and for never-ending purity, and he does so to the extent that this is possible for human frailty."[12] Evagrius says: "If you seek prayer attentively you will find it; for nothing is more essential to prayer than attentiveness. So do all you can to acquire it."[13] Here was both a sense of the ultimate aim of prayer—"unstirring calm of mind"—and a way get there—"attention." I had not yet encountered Pierre Hadot's lucid account of the work of *prosoche* or attention that was central to both ancient Greek philosophical thought and early Christian thought and practice.[14] But I could sense already the importance and power of this teaching. Attention as the ground of all spiritual practice. And critical to the creation of community.

In his treatise on prayer, Evagrius offers this strange and beautiful description of what it means to commit oneself to the practice of prayer in the desert: "A monk is one who is separated from all and united with all"—the work of prayer inviting a simultaneous and continuous attention to the mystery of God and to one's kinship with and responsibility toward others.[15] A beautiful reminder of the inescapable and creative, critical tension between solitude and community, born of the recognition that paying attention means not only listening in silence for a word from God but also thinking carefully about the life you share with others. There is an uncanny echo of Evagrius's teaching on prayer in the writings of the French philosopher and mystic Simone Weil, written almost fifteen hundred years later: "Not only does the love of God have attention for its substance; the love of our neighbor, which we know to be the same love, is made of this same substance."[16] Attention—rooted in and coming to expression in love. Attention as a way of practicing love.

These ideas were of more than academic interest for me. I began to feel myself drawn beyond the page toward the question of what it would mean to engage in contemplative practice. And how I might apprentice myself to contemplative practitioners. But how? And where? I soon discovered a small community of Poor Clares, contemplative nuns whose tradition stretches back to the thirteenth century and the origins of the Franciscan movement, whose convent was just a few miles away, near Highway 1 in Aptos, California. I began joining them once or twice a week for their 6:00 a.m. mass, rising in the dark in my dorm room, and driving the ten or so miles south in my 1964 Chevy Malibu convertible, mostly in silence. Not a normal practice for a college student I know, but something I found compelling, and necessary. The silence and stillness of that place soon became woven into my thinking and reading and wondering. And my hunger for the immensity that I sensed was at the heart of that place and that practice deepened. I began venturing further out—spending time in the stark solitude of New Camaldoli Hermitage on the coast in Big Sur and at Redwoods Monastery near the Lost Coast in northern California in the company of small community of Cistercian nuns. I was coming to know the living witnesses of the ancient desert tradition and beginning my own practice of entering the silence, paying attention, praying.

This practice impacted deeply how I read and thought—especially about *hesychia*, or stillness, which in many sayings of the desert monks seemed to hold the key to so much else. "An elder said, 'In the same way that no plant whatsoever grows up on a well-trodden highway, not even if you sow seed, because the surface is trodden down, so it is with us. Withdraw from all business into *hesychia* and you will see things growing in you that you did not know were in you, for you were walking on them.'"[17] Hesychia: space of emptiness and silence, but also a condition of the mind. Nourished by solitude, but always unfolding within and responsive to the needs of the community, bound to the question of what it meant to cultivate intimacy with others. Above all, necessary to any hope of "see[ing] things growing in you that you did not know were in you." My own initial attempts at practice had already given me intimations of this truth. But it was fleeting and elusive and I found I could not easily hold onto it. Nor could I see more than a faint trace of the things growing in me.

"What knows to do so dives deep as it can."[18] I was only a beginner. But I could sense a new awareness of this depth taking hold within me, and needed to find out if I could enter that space and give myself to it. And so I embarked upon a long journey into silence. After graduating from college,

I spent the better part of a year wandering, spending time with monastic communities on Caldey Island off the coast of Wales, at Mont des Cats in northern France, at Camaldoli in the forests above Arezzo, Italy, and on Mt. Athos in Greece, eventually reaching the remote stillness of St. Catherine's monastery at the foot of Mt. Sinai. This long sojourn in silence proved hugely influential for me and came to inform my thinking and my life in unexpected ways. Not least by giving me a concrete sense of what it meant to inhabit such deep stillness as part of the rhythm of daily living. But also by giving me a taste of how such practice was stitched into the entire life of these communities: manual labor, shared meals, common prayer, hospitality, and love of place all bound together as part of a mysterious whole. Also struggle. It took me awhile to notice and understand this: how the simple practice of paying attention, listening, and opening yourself to the vastness of the silence also meant allowing yourself to become vulnerable. Allowing the silence to work on you, open you up, touch you, especially those unhealed parts of yourself. I witnessed this in different ways among those who welcomed me into their lives in these places: the pain of disappointment, suffering, and loss. The struggle to learn how to face and live with it, and the invitation to bring this pain into the silence. Still, there was also the experience of feeling yourself held, in the midst of uncertainty and loss, in the shared life of community.

This brief monastic apprenticeship touched something in me and opened me up to an awareness of the untrodden ground that had always been there but which I had hardly ever taken the time to notice: my inner life. And it helped me to see what I was seeking was less an ersatz idea of spiritual enlightenment than a deepening of my own humanity. The simple practice of entering the space of silence with others, following a rhythm of liturgical prayer, sharing common meals, working with my hands, walking in the fields, dreaming, struggling, feeling things helped so much with this. In all of this, I was beginning to discover for myself what John Climacus describes as the "inviolable activity of the heart."[19] Something utterly personal and often hidden but also shared with others.[20]

In the years to come, the desert and the cloister became touchstones—actual places where I withdrew from time to time to create room for this mysterious and still-emerging dimension of my life. But they also became emblems of the kind of awareness I was seeking within the flow and rhythm of everyday life where my life was unfolding—marriage, parenthood, work. The practice of silence and solitude, I began to see, was both more expansive and inclusive than I had imagined it to be and more diverse in its meanings and expressions.[21] The desert and the cloister had undeniable power—places set apart where the mystery of silence could gather and deepen. But these places were not ends in themselves and certainly not the only places where the work of prayer could be undertaken.

I took to heart Meister Eckhart's caution against imagining that radical openness of spirit is only possible in certain rarefied places or circumstances. As he notes, for example, in one of his *Talks of Instruction*: "I was asked, 'Some people shun all company and always want to be alone; their peace depends on it, and on being in church. Was that the best thing?' And I said, 'No!' Now see why . . . if a man truly has God with him, God is with him everywhere, in the street or among people just as much as in church or in the desert or in a cell."[22] A radical reimagining of what it means to enter the desert or the cell, and one that democratizes and demystifies it in a way that allows it to become incorporated into the fabric of ordinary life, an expression of what Ariel Glucklich calls "everyday mysticism."[23] Even so, sometimes you have withdraw for a time to the desert and listen deeply in silence.

* * *

This was true for me in 2005. By the time I arrived in Cairo, I was frayed and worn. The period leading up to my departure had not been easy. The tensions, uncertainties, and distances within my marriage were growing more acute; and I felt helpless to respond to or resolve them. I was at an impasse. Perhaps time in the desert would help. But upon arriving in Egypt, I was quickly drawn into a blur of activities: several days of meetings with scholars at the American University, five days at the White Monastery in Sohag helping with the dig, and two days spent with the Italian conservators who were restoring ancient frescoes at the Red Monastery. Only after arriving in Luxor, on the eve of my departure for St. Antony's, did I finally find myself alone with a chance to gather myself a little. I decided to leave the city and walk out alone into the desert. Friends in Sohag had told me of a small community of Coptic nuns living out at the foot of the Theban hills and said that I should try to visit them if I could.

I have only the roughest of directions to guide me as I set out along a dirt road leading into the desert. But I decide to try. I have been walking now for more than half an hour. It is getting close to sunset. In the distance I see the hulking form of the great necropolis of Medinet Habu, but nothing I can identify as a monastery. I keep walking. Two dogs intercept me, circling, barking. I pause and back away slowly, just in case. They soon lose interest in me and run off down the road. Up ahead I notice a walled enclosure and decide to investigate. Just above an old wooden gate are written the words "St. Tawdros." This is it. I ring the bell and wait. Nothing. I ring the bell again. Still nothing. Maybe it is too late for visitors. Then I hear the sound of a bolt sliding and the gate swings open. A nun dressed in black is standing just inside. She greets me, invites me to enter and motions toward the church. It is almost time for Vespers. The church is plain and simple. Arched porticos. Carpets lining the floor. Paint peeling from the wall. Candles burning. A few icons. A large banner of St. Tawdros (El-Mohareb the Warrior) astride his white horse. A deep quiet.

It is a relief to be here. But also a little unsettling. I have been on the move almost the whole time I have been in Egypt; and I now find myself entering a stillness against which I have no protection. I am suddenly aware of my weariness, my fragility, and my deep uncertainty about what is happening to me and where I am heading in my life. Have I even begun to reckon with the depth of the sadness I carry within me or its sources? I know I have not. But here in this place I begin to realize that I must open myself to these questions, that this is part of why I am here. I think again about something I read in Evagrius's *Praktikos*: "Sadness tends to come up at times because of the deprivation of one's desires."[24] I remember feeling surprised at encountering this idea in the *Praktikos*. Here at the heart of his discussion of the "eight principle thoughts," his perceptive taxonomy of those places in the soul where we are most vulnerable and susceptible to attacks from the demons, Evagrius places *lupe* or sadness. And he connects it to desire, especially desire that has somehow become frustrated or thwarted. And to anger.[25] How accurately this describes my own condition. I have been sunk, for longer than I can say, inside an unnamable sadness. And a sense of acute loneliness that I cannot seem to shake. It has followed me to this remote place in the Egyptian desert and this evening it comes rushing in. A heaviness. The sense of being caught, unable to move.

The singing begins. Simple, beautiful, rhythmic chanting. I drink it in, let wash over me, through me. I do not know what they are singing. But tonight it is enough to drift inside the rhythms, the repetitions, the feeling of this singing. It touches me, carries me out somewhere beyond myself. Also deep within. I find myself weeping.

After the final prayers, I move toward the door to take my leave. It is getting late. And I feel like I have come to the end of something in myself. But one of the sisters catches me and motions for me to follow her. I accompany her to an adjoining room where the community is gathering for a simple meal. On a small table, I see some traditional dishes: *ful medames, kushari, aish baladi*. And sweet tea. "Please sit," she says, smiling. "Eat." And I do.

What an unexpected gift—to be invited into this space of silence and stillness, to slow down, enter into the simple beauty of this prayer, and to receive the hospitality of these women. I experience it as a kind of embrace. Without knowing it, this little community has helped me catch up with myself, begin facing my loss, and perhaps open myself to my own desire. A little while later, walking along the road in the dark, I think also about the fragility of their life in that place out on the edge of the desert. Poor, largely hidden from view. But also simple and honest and vibrant. A life in common born of silence and emptiness and love. And for me, in this moment, a place of unexpected solace.

In his late journal *Woods Shore Desert*, Thomas Merton writes: "Not to run from one thought to the next, says Theophane the Recluse, but to give each one time to settle in the heart."

> *Attention*: Concentration of the spirit in the Heart.
> *Vigilance*: Concentration of the will in the heart.
> *Sobriety*. Concentration of feeling in the heart.[26]

This awareness comes and goes. Not only in my ordinary, daily existence, with its many competing demands for my attention, but also here in this open, silent space, where my capacity for attention and awareness also seems to vary so much. Preoccupations enter in and cloud my vision. And then, for brief moments or sometimes longer, they lift and fade, and I am back inside my own life. To come away to this place, even for a short time, is a gift, a chance to reorient myself around my deepest center. To recover, again, that ground I depend on to give my life meaning and value. To become more open and honest. The silence and solitude are a balm. But they also challenge and open me up in unexpected ways. I notice that it is not so easy to hide from myself here. In the stillness, my fragility and vulnerability begin to surface. And turn, tentatively and with some trepidation, to face them, considering what they have to say to me about my life, my relationships, everything. I turn again toward my own practice of *anachoresis*: engaging solitude in search of clarification and deepening, but also opening myself to struggle with loss and absence.

* * *

Loss and absence are at the heart of Antony's story, something I have become more sensitive to now than I was when I first read that story many years ago.[27] When he is still a young man, Athanasius relates in *The Life of Antony*, his parents died suddenly, and he and his sister were left orphaned. This loss changed everything. In the crisis that followed, he withdrew into the emptiness of the desert, where he spent the rest of his life moving through that immensity in a kind of exile, often finding himself struggling at the very edge of himself, reduced to almost nothing by the sheer force of his struggle with the demons. The demons were essential characters in the narratives of the early monks, for whom the empty space of the desert became a kind of breeding ground for these shadowy figures who, it turned out, were part of the monk's own psyche. Here was a way of expressing and bringing to language those deep places of vulnerability, fear, and lostness in one's life that could not, it seems, be expressed in any other way.

For Antony and the early monks, to speak of confronting the demonic in solitude was another way of talking about confronting the self. It meant facing all those anomalous forces at work in the depths of the psyche, forces usually kept at bay by the noise and distractions of everyday life but which, in the space of solitude, made their presence felt with alarming intensity. Peter Brown suggests that the monk in the desert was, above all, a person grappling with his own personality. For the monks, he says, the demonic was "sensed as an extension of the self. A relationship with the demons involved something more intimate than attack from the outside: to be 'tried by the demons' meant passing through a stage in the growth of awareness of the lower frontiers of the personality. The demonic stood not merely for all that was hostile *to* [the human person]; the demons summed up all that was anomalous and incomplete *in* [us]."[28] This intensely interior understanding of the encounter with the demons is confirmed by the monks' own testimony. They knew full well how intimately bound up the demonic was with their own complex, often-conflicted inner lives. One day Abba Abraham asked Abba Poemen: "How do the demons fight against me?" Poemen responded: "The demons fight *against* you? . . . Our own *wills* become the demons, and it is these which attack us in order that we may fulfill them."[29]

Antony's story can be understood in similar terms, as an account of a person shaken to the core of his being, stripped bare by the rigors of solitude, brought to the very edge of his capacity to say or understand what is happening to him. In this, Antony's experience captures something essential to that of many of the early monks and to the experience of many seekers since then—the sense of profound uncertainty and doubt that comes from confronting oneself in solitude. There is a strong sense in the early monastic literature that the solitary did not always understand where he or she was going. The mysterious, unfinished character of the experience is part of what makes it so compelling: there is only a solitary human person standing naked before God seeking to be remade in God's image.

Athanasius includes this struggle in his account of Antony's journey into the desert. But he mutes it considerably. The reason is clear: Athanasius wanted and needed a heroic Antony to help carry the banner of the Nicene theological cause. Because of this, he notes continuously that it was Christ living in Antony that led the ascetic to overcome the devil. So too the light that pours down into his monastic cell suggests nothing less than the presence of the Divine—the Nicene Christ for whom Athanasius fought, "light from light, true God from true God"—lifting and sustaining the weary monk.[30] Athanasius's ascetic hero must, with the help of Christ, triumph in the end and he does. But not before we catch a glimpse of the monk, "lay[ing] upon the earth, speechless from the tortures." This image of Antony brought to the very edge of himself, frightened, alone, mute, deeply uncertain about the meaning of his experience and about where he is going, entered deeply into the consciousness of later generations of Christians, becoming a kind of emblem of what it is to open yourself honestly and deeply to solitude and silence.

Antony persevered and, with the help of friends, he survived this ordeal and eventually emerged from his solitude purified and transformed. He became a person capable of holding and responding to the pain and bewilderment of others and of offering healing and solace. But he kept moving deeper and deeper into the emptiness, journeying east from the Nile Valley into the wild and remote Red Sea desert, arriving eventually at the Inner Mountain, a place he came to consider as "his own home." His life there remained precarious and uncertain, the sense of absence and loss that haunted his early life continuing to shape his experience in this remote desert place. But the Inner Mountain also became a kind of paradise where he learned to open his heart in love to all those souls who came seeking healing and hope.

These are the bare outlines of the story only. But a pattern emerges: an opening to and withdrawal into emptiness. A descent into the depths. And an awakening to love. *Anachoresis, askesis, agape.*

Anachoresis—the sense of being called to withdraw into the silence and vastness of the desert to seek something as yet unknown and perhaps unknowable—is central to Antony's story and to the meaning of the Inner

Mountain. This idea stands at the very beginning of *The Life of Antony* and of the ancient monastic tradition more generally and grounds everything that follows. Whether the withdrawal is momentary or more protracted, this idea signals the importance of space and depth within contemplative practice, the need to create what Henry David Thoreau called a "broad margin" to our lives.[31] Nor does the work of *anachoresis* ever cease or stop having meaning or significance: it becomes part of the rhythm of life, an openness that allows for thought and practice to breathe and deepen. It also signals a willingness to become open to your own vulnerability and the vulnerability of others. And it creates the necessary conditions for the costly work of *askesis*: the monk's long, painful struggle with himself in the solitude of the tomb in the heart of the desert—symbolized by that moment when Antony finds himself lying alone on the bare earth, uncertain and afraid, reduced to a condition of utter need. The moment when he risks everything in darkness; when he suddenly finds himself drawn into a place where nothing is certain or known any more except pain, loss, and absence. This confrontation with the very end of things, the end of meaning, at least as you have always constructed it, cannot be resolved or explained. It can only be lived through, endured. And while Athanasius insists that it is grace that carries the monk through this darkness, there is also an undeniable sense of utter loneliness, uncertainty, emptiness. Still, Antony emerges from the darkness and opens himself to all those fragile souls he finds present in that place. Who reach out to him and who seek his healing touch. *Agape*.

Already in the fourth and fifth centuries, Antony's story exercised a profound hold on the imagination of many who read or heard it. Athanasius notes dramatically, if also hyperbolically, that it was the witness of Antony that led to the "desert becoming a city"—the wild solitary expanse now teeming with those seeking to emulate the practice of the great monk. Augustine memorably attributes the turning point in his own conversion to a moment when he heard the story of Antony of Egypt; it pierced him, and he was no longer able to think about his life in the same limited terms that he had before. The *Golden Legend* recast the story of Antony for a medieval audience; it took on new and unexpected life, including in the work of artists such as Matthias Grünewald and Hieronymus Bosch, who looked to the monk's solitary struggle with the demons as a necessary and significant emblem of what it meant to grapple with the deepest human suffering.[32] Nor have modern and contemporary writers and artists been able to resist the arresting force of this story: Gustave Flaubert, Salvador Dali, Bernice Johnson Reagon, and Robert Wilson, among many others, have looked to this ancient story as a way of asking searching questions of their own historical moments about what it means to plumb the depths in solitude, how to contend honestly and courageously with abandonment and loss. Also how to seek renewal and hope in a space beyond language and concepts and form. How to listen in silence.

Many of those who have taken up the monastic or contemplative vocation have also been shaped by this story, directly or indirectly. I have already alluded to my long friendship with the community of Cistercian nuns at Redwoods Monastery. Their witness to the power of silence and stillness to open up a space for contending with the deepest and most difficult questions of faith and to the possibility of kindling community in that space of emptiness traces its own lineage back to the fourth-century Egyptian desert, by way of Bernard of Clairvaux, Beatrice of Nazareth, William of St. Thierry, and so many others. This is also true for many other contemplative practitioners, both those who have withdrawn to the wilderness and those who have chosen to inhabit the margins with the dispossessed. In myriad different contexts, the story has kept renewing itself, inviting creative and often-courageous responses to questions of personal meaning (and loss of meaning), as well as responses that contend with larger questions of social, political, and cultural loss, that ask how this solitary figure in the desert can speak to this reality. When Peruvian theologian Gustavo Gutierrez asks, for example, what it will mean for us to "drink from our own wells," he is drawing on this ancient tradition of contemplative practice to articulate a vision for living with hope and tenacity and courage in the face of the most abysmal poverty and chronic social injustice.[33] Entering the desert, contending with the night, drinking from one's own well—in this context, these images become resources for resisting violence and injustice, for reimagining life and community. The city becomes a desert, and the work of listening and responding to the deepest impulses of the Spirit for the sake of life and community becomes critical to desert spiritual practice.

My own reading of this ancient desert story and my struggle to understand what it might mean to live in response to it has been deeply informed by these and other witnesses. They are present to me as I make my way through the silence and stillness of this desert landscape. I carry with me especially that saying of Antony's: "[The one] who stays in the desert in *hesychia* is released from fighting on three fronts: hearing, speaking and seeing. He has only one to contend with: the heart."[34]

* * *

I recall the feeling I had when I first encountered this teaching: it seemed to me hopeful and reassuring. I *wanted* to contend with my own heart. I *wanted* to live more wholeheartedly. Here was an approach to spiritual practice, rooted in the idea of purity of heart, that suggested a way into such a life. More recently, though, the idea of contending with my own heart has begun to feel more daunting. It has been a little over a year since my mother died. The stabbing grief of the days and weeks immediately following her death has begun to subside. But I am still having trouble focusing, finding it difficult to locate myself in my own experience. Unable to access my own feelings. I cast about looking for her. But there is only absence. And I cannot in this moment find a way through or around it.

A little over a month after she died, I receive a note from a friend who told me about an opera being staged at the Brooklyn Academy of Music, based on Gustave Flaubert's *La Tentation de St Antoine* (1874).[35] The fourth-century hermit on the stage in New York. Amazing. This production, conceived of by Robert Wilson and Bernice Johnson Reagon, and based loosely on Flaubert's nineteenth-century meditation on the life of Antony, retells the ancient monastic tale through the lens of the long history of slavery and the music of African American spirituals. An unexpected and risky recasting of the story of the monk in the wilderness, contending with his own heart, yes, but also with ominous forces far beyond his capacity to encompass in language or thought, perhaps beyond his capacity to endure. I check my schedule, scan the internet for a cheap flight, and make the decision to travel to New York. I call my niece, my sister's eldest daughter, who is living in the Bronx, to see if she wants to join me. A week later, I find her waiting for me on the steps of the theater in Brooklyn. Soon, we are sitting together in the darkened theater as the curtain rises and the actors slowly make their way onto the stage.

Reagon and Wilson's retelling of the ancient monastic story is faithful to the spirit of the original fourth-century account, and to Flaubert's idiosyncratic rendering of the tale. Still, this dramatic production brings into bold relief elements of the story that, on the page, often feel elusive or inaccessible. The sight of the monk standing alone in the dark, struggling with an impossibly complex and withering constellation of demonic forces arrayed against him is utterly unnerving. He paces back and forth, gesturing, crying out, other times falling silent—so clearly weighed down by the nameless fears and anxieties that afflict him. He is unable to wrest himself free. These struggles feel timeless. Still, as both the music and lyrics make clear, the forces arrayed against the monk here are not in fact timeless but arise within and reflect a particular social, historical, cultural reality: the long history of racism. In a deep, mournful voice, Antony sings:

> I be troubled, I be troubled
> I be troubled 'bout my time
> done long gone . . .
> In the morning, in the morning
> don't feel like seeing
> the sun come shining.

The utter bleakness of these words, a response to the specter of a violence so potent that it threatens to eclipse all meaning, all hope. But it is the voice that carries all the feeling: the slumped figure crying out with his whole body, expressing affliction that rises to a howl. This solitary soul, laboring under an unseen weight, cannot move from this space. There is, it seems, no resolution, no escape. At least not in this moment. But this is not the only note that sounds in that desert place. The chorus of figures who visit the monk in his solitude break forth in the raucous, pulsing, joyous spirit of gospel rhythms, a necessary and important counterpoint to the stark emptiness that characterizes so much of the monk's experience. He is not, after all, alone. Still, even this company cannot shield him completely from the crushing weight of loss that afflicts him: "In the morning, in the morning / I don't feel like seeing the sun come shining," he cries.

The lonely struggle of the monk touches something in me. His sorrow, emptiness and grief feel so raw, alive, embodied. Sitting there in the darkness, I feel his words, his trembling voice, his grief-stricken eyes pierce me, tear something open in me. The monk is lost in his own darkness, and he is traveling through places of emptiness and pain that I can hardly imagine. Still, in this moment, some part of his pain reaches me. And it touches something in me that I have long tried to keep at bay: not only the growing sense of my own vulnerability and the need to face myself in solitude. But also my own part in the larger story of loss that Antony's story reveals.

The deep currents of this story continued working on me long after I left the theater. Especially the way the story of this solitary figure is given new meaning by recasting the place of the struggle, by asking new questions and by looking for different patterns of meaning. Perhaps this meaning was always implicit in the story, waiting to be lifted up. Violence and chronic social dislocation were, after all, endemic in Late Antique Roman Egypt. Racism, slavery, forced labor. Whatever else it meant to struggle with demonic forces in the desert, these fundamental social realities of violence and exclusion were part of it. This is part of what make's Flaubert's nineteenth-century retelling of Antony's story, on which this play is based, so disturbing: the phantasmagoric array of forces against which the monk struggles in the desert can only be understood against the backdrop of the deep social and political fragmentation that gave rise to them, which now manifests itself in currents of darkness and violence against which it feels impossible to stand. In Flaubert's telling, "They become frightful—with lofty plumes, eyes like balls, fingers terminated by claws, the jaws of sharks. And before these gods men are slaughtered upon altars of stone, others are slayed alive in huge mortars, crushed under chariots, nailed upon trees. There is one all of red-hot iron with the horns of a bull, who devours children."

At the sight of all this, Antony can only exclaim: "Horror."[36]

It is difficult to miss here the echoes of Bosch, Grünewald, and others who drew upon the obscure terror of the original story to create vivid, disturbing images of a fragmented, broken world. Or the sense of horror we often feel at the depth of violence coursing through our own world. Wilson and Reagon saw this and created a dramatic and musical idiom that situates Antony's struggle with demonic forces within the long history of racialized violence. And that asks hard questions about the continuing presence of that violence in our own historical moment.

The long tradition of reflection on demonic temptation points to the depth and potency of the struggle against "principalities and powers"—something that continues to have unexpected resonance for us. Such language also provides a necessary counterpoint to the often-superficial explanations for the immense power of what is unleashed within and beyond us, and for the immensity of the darkness through which we so often find ourselves moving: "Darkness starts inside of things / But keeps on going when the things are gone," notes Christian Wiman.[37] So it is in the ancient monastic tradition, where there is a serious, sustained, and psychologically astute analysis of how demons (or passions as they were often called) lodge themselves within the soul, touching on all our deepest fears and anxieties. And that acknowledges how, left unchecked and unaddressed, they pour forth from us, often chaotically, coming to expression in myriad forms of violence and recrimination. The personal demons with which we struggle are also embedded within and come to expression in the social-political body.

In Reagon and Wilson's production, the haunting presence of all those souls who have fallen victim to this violence is made sharply, disturbingly visible. The mournful song of the desert ascetic carries within it the immensity of this loss. It asks us to listen, to look, not to turn away from it. To look closely at our own complicity in perpetuating a culture of racialized violence.

In the days and weeks after I saw the performance, I found myself thinking again of James Byrd. It had been less than five years since he was chained by his ankles to the back of a pickup truck in Jasper, Texas, and dragged three miles along an asphalt highway, tearing him to shreds. The following day, law enforcement officials found parts of Byrd's body scattered in at least seventy-five different places. A grotesque, racist hate crime in late twentieth-century America. Hardly isolated but devastating in its brutality and cruelty—part of the long history of racialized violence that now includes the names of George Floyd, Ahmaud Arbery, Breonna Taylor, and so many other victims of systemic racism and white supremacy. And critical to the historical climate out of which Wilson and Reagon's retelling of the ancient monastic story has come into being.

This work plumbs the depths of our seemingly endless capacity for racialized violence. The story of the solitary monk struggling to withstand the violence afflicting him, within and without, here reimagined in a contemporary idiom, challenges us to grapple with the depth and extent of all that has been lost. And with our own complicity in perpetuating racist violence. The imaginative space this work opens up for thinking deeply about the abyss of loss in which we now find ourselves living, and asking new questions about the meaning of this abyss, feels so important and necessary. Especially, in this context, with regard to what it means to see, and what we are willing and able to see. And how the very idea of contemplation and contemplative practice will, perhaps need to be reimagined in light of these questions.

I think here of the bold and courageous work of Barbara Holmes who argues that it is time to take seriously what she calls "crisis contemplation"—taking contemplation beyond the confining constraints of religious ideas and expectations to, as she puts it, "reach the potential for spiritual centering in the midst of danger." This will mean, among other things, setting aside the idea of contemplation as something only accessible in moments of safety and security and considering anew its significance amid encounters with violence, suffering, and loss.[38] We are close here, I think, to a "mysticism of the abyss" that Maria Clara Bingemer argues has become so characteristic of late twentieth-century and early twenty-first-century spiritual practice and which surfaces, increasingly, not in cloisters or religious orders but in so-called secular places, and in the marginal, often-hidden lives that unfold in factories, prisons, and in the hell of lagers and gulags.[39] Close also to what Johann Baptist Metz describes as a "mysticism of open eyes," a capacity for awareness that "makes visible all invisible and inconvenient suffering, and—convenient or not—pays attention to it and takes responsibility for it."[40] It is not easy to say what such seeing will mean, or what it will cost to take on such responsibility. But the ethical imperative to do so is, it seems to me, inescapable.

Learning to see this way is immensely challenging. But sometimes you catch a glimpse of what it might look like. I am thinking here of the work of Eula Biss, whose *Notes from No Man's Land* reads as a sustained meditation on the question of what it means to see deeply and honestly. She describes how an old man she met one day in Bed-Stuy advised her to "keep your eyes on the world . . . pay attention to what is going on . . . write it all down, every single detail . . . but don't forget that what you have to capture is the unseen, the imponderable."[41] I think too of the work of Sara Uribe, whose *Antígona González*—a harrowing account of loss and violence in contemporary Mexico—provides such compelling insight into what it means to become vigilant and learn how to pay attention, especially to "all the gaps, all the absences no one notices and yet are there."[42] What are these gaps and absences? What will it mean to attend to them with all the care and courage we are capable of? Apophatic thought and practice require careful attention to these questions.

My own absences and losses are, I know, mostly personal, hidden, and small scale. But they are mine, and I know I must attend to them honestly. Still, the further I descend into the silence of Egyptian desert, the more I begin to sense how these personal questions cannot be separated from the questions of others who have been drawn into their own desert places and who are also present with me in this place. I find myself thinking again about the relationship of solitude and community, about how to understand the meaning of *anachoresis* both as a way of responding to the deepest concerns my own life and as a response to needs of the world. And whether the withdrawal into the desert can perhaps be understood as part of an ecology of solitude and silence that will help us address this entire range of concerns. This feels not unlike what the environmental encyclical *Laudato Si'* means in speaking of an "integral ecology"—the call to pay attention to the beauty and fragility of the living world understood to be always bound deeply and irrevocably to the call to attend to the beauty and fragility of the human community. Not two separate spheres or realities, but a single integral ecology. So it is, I begin to see, with the work of solitude.

* * *

Here in the solitude of this place, this wild, emptiness of the eastern Sahara, I consider again what has brought me here. The sense that somehow, by setting out on this path, I might find a way to resolve the impasse in which I find myself. I am aware that there is a danger of mistaking the act of walking this road for the work of seeking, and that if I do not remain vigilant, I will miss what I most need to see. This is one of the occupational hazards of being a pilgrim—and a question that has been part of the debate around pilgrimage from the earliest centuries of Christianity: Isn't what you are seeking already before you, *within* you, *around* you? Must you leave home to find the presence of God? The ancient arguments against pilgrimage are strong and compelling.[43] Even so, the impulse to set out into the unknown to seek and perhaps find something necessary to your life retains a powerful allure. I feel this myself. And even if I cannot say with certitude what I am seeking or hoping to find, I sense that this is where I need to be in this moment: standing on the side of this desert road, looking out into this immensity, opening myself to what is emerging before me.

This is a solitary path. But I am aware of the presence of those who are accompanying me—including those Christian mystics for whom the language of desert, ocean, night, and abyss opened up a space for expressing and inhabiting the unimaginable depths of their own experience, for encountering the wild otherness of God.[44] Thinking with them about what it means to relinquish everything for the sake of a more honest, open-hearted response to my own life. And to the life of this world. Often, living far from any actual desert, they found themselves drawn into a vast, untracked emptiness. Something in their own experience of God, utterly boundless and ineffable, called them out beyond themselves, beyond all expressions, all categories, all thought, into an unspeakable silent depth.

In one of her stanzaic poems, the Flemish Beguine Hadewijch gives expression to her conviction that the call to love leads to the desert:

> I do not complain of suffering for Love:
> It becomes me always to submit to her,

Whether she commands in storm or in stillness.
One can know her only in herself.
   This is an unconceivable wonder,
   Which has thus filled my heart
And makes me stray in a wild desert.[45]

In *The Spiritual Espousals*, John Ruusbroec describes how "the sublime nature of the Godhead is examined and beheld: how it is simplicity and onefoldness, in accessible height, and unfathomable depth, incomprehensible breadth and eternal length, a dark stillness and a wild desert."[46] And Meister Eckhart speaks of the soul who, "delving deeper and ever seeking . . . grasps God in His oneness and in his solitude . . . seizes Him in His desert and in His proper ground."[47]

It is not easy to say what this desert is or what it means to inhabit it. Nor do these different accounts of the desert evoke the same experience or idea of God. For Hadewijch, the desert is a part of a strange, often-bewildering, and ceaseless search for love; it is where love leads the soul and where the bereft soul must travel, alone and often without any consolation. For Ruusbroec, the desert is a place vast and deep beyond imagining and, like the night and the fathomless sea, expansive and empty enough to allow the soul to behold, even if partially and imperfectly, the "sublime nature of the Godhead." And for Eckhart, the desert is a place where the soul encounters God's "oneness and solitude," God's "proper ground"—a hidden, solitary place beyond every category of thought or imagination where God is somehow mysteriously grasped. There is a sense of vulnerability here, a feeling of exposure to a presence whose reach and depth and purity is both alluring and forbidding, and that subverts every effort to control or explain or comprehend it. A sense of becoming lost inside an immensity. Utterly transformed by it. An experience Paul Bowles describes as the "baptism of solitude."

For Bowles, as for these mystics of the desert, the experience of finding yourself immersed in a space of silence and solitude is, potentially, a moment of great risk and reckoning. His account of becoming lost inside the "incredible, absolute silence" of the Sahara echoes the sense of raw, unfettered abandonment found in the testimony of these mystics, including the feeling of having the very ground of your identity dissolve. "Here, in this wholly mineral landscape lighted by stars like flares, even memory disappears; nothing is left but your own breathing and the sound of your heart beating. . . . A strange, and by no means pleasant, process of reintegration begins inside you," he says, "and you have the choice of fighting against it, and insisting on remaining the person you have always been, or letting it take its course. For no one who has stayed in the Sahara for a while is quite the same as when he came." Bowles acknowledges the immense difficulty of facing yourself in such extremity, and the understandable reluctance to venture out so far beyond the structures of language and identity. But for some, this vast emptiness is irresistible, necessary. The person who "has been there and undergone the baptism of solitude," he suggests, "can't help himself. Once he has been under the spell of the vast, luminous, silent country, no other place is quite strong enough for him, no other surroundings can provide the supremely satisfying sensation of existing in the midst of something that is absolute."[48]

The stillness of the desert at night. Silence. The erasure of memory. The disintegration and reintegration of the self. The intense allure of the absolute. These are elements of experience—potent, beautiful, and difficult—shared by desert travelers and pilgrims of the absolute. And they are also emblems of a hunger that often accompanies such experience, a hunger to inhabit an open, unencumbered space. To live with freedom, and without fear. This is something recognizable to me, from my own sojourns in the desert, from time spent in monastic spaces, and from my efforts to attend carefully to ordinary domestic life, and the daily work of learning to become sensitive to the depths opening before me in every moment.

Still, I hesitate before the challenge of opening myself to this baptism, of allowing myself to be drawn down under those waters. I both want and do not want to risk myself this deeply. But here in this wild, solitary place, I begin to wonder how much longer I can resist doing so. The impulse to guard and protect myself has already cost me so much. It has kept me from living freely and openly. It has kept me from opening myself to love. And I have grown weary of the effort it takes to keep myself safe from harm. I am no longer certain whether this is what I most deeply want or need. These personal concerns often preoccupy me and keep from even noticing where I am. But I begin to see that they are also part of what has drawn me to this place and that allows me to see and feel and respond to it. And begin to open myself again to my own desire.

"What does the lonely and absurd man have to teach others?" Thomas Merton asks. "Simply that being alone and absurd are not things to be feared. But these are precisely the two things that everybody fears. . . . Everybody remains secretly absurd and alone. Only no one dares face the fact. Yet facing this fact is the absolutely essential requirement for beginning to live freely."[49]

An unexpectedly consoling word in a moment when I am being brought face to face with my own absurdity and loneliness. It is painful to see how deep they run in me and how much energy I have devoted to avoiding this fact. Nor can I say in this moment what it will mean to do so. But I am beginning to realize how much harm I have done to myself and to others, by evading and ignoring it; by allowing fear to dictate too much of my thought and behavior. And how necessary it is for me now to stand, as honestly as I can, in the truth of my own life. Not only for my own sake, but for the sake of learning to respond honestly and with love toward others. I think again of that saying of Abba Antony: "against one thing shall [the solitary] continually battle: that is, his own heart." So it is for me. I am trying to learn to be more honest about the condition of my own heart. And about all that keeps me from opening myself more freely in love, from practicing radical self-honesty.[50] What will it mean for me to become less guarded, more open? To learn to live out of my deepest desire? Here in the solitary place, these questions reverberate with unsettling power.

I begin to see that my attraction to wild places and to those mystical writers who are so responsive to the wild immensity of their own experience has much to do with my long history of shielding myself from this part of my own experience and with a deepening hunger for it that has only grown in me over time. A hunger for touch and intimacy and love. I bring these "biases of openness"—that are surfacing with particular force in this moment of my life—with me into this place.[51] And I am trying to pay attention to them, learn from them, risk myself in and through them. In my own embodied experience here in the desert. And in my imaginative life, in the company of those witnesses who express so honestly and deeply the possibility of living an unguarded life, open to the lives of others, grounded in love.

What is it about moving through the desert that makes this begin to feel more possible? What is it that elicited something so compelling among those monastic seekers who first withdrew into that silent immensity and continues to elicit it even now? I am not sure. But I have come to feel myself the truth of Susan Brind Morrow's words about the power and mystery of this desert landscape:

The desert's pure air was a prism separating the harsh light into bands of intensely articulated color. Vision there became a joy. The eye in the desert could see with such clarity that something as subtle as an animal track, which in the city would be lost, stood out distinctly . . . I have sometimes thought that this quality of light in the Egyptian desert is what inspired the monasticism of the early Christians . . . who spoke of an intoxication of the spirit there. To see it is enough, is like falling in love.[52]

This, I begin to realize, is at the heart of my own work in this place: learning to see. It is a slow work. And costly. But here in this place I begin again to open myself to this vision and practice of unguarded love.

* * *

I cannot remember how long I sat out on the edge of the road that day in the Eastern Desert, hoping for a ride to St. Antony's. No one ever came. Eventually I gave up. It was getting late, and I was out of ideas. I wandered back to the rest stop by the highway at Râs Az 'farâna and made some inquiries. It seemed no one was heading west into the desert that day. But there was a driver who was going south: the direction I had just come from earlier in the day. He could take me as far as the junction to St. Paul's, the other great monastery in the Eastern Desert. From there I could walk.

I was moving backward. Perfect. But I had no other choice, and I accepted the offer gratefully. I tossed my bag into the cab of the eighteen-wheeler and climbed up after it. The driver laughed at the sight of me and handed me a stalk of sugar cane. Then he put the truck in gear, and we embarked for the south, raucous Egyptian dance music pulsing from the radio. I do not remember much about the journey that evening along the Red Sea. Thoughts drifting as I gazed out at the mountains rising up to the west, the long narrow ribbon of highway opening up ahead of us; thrumming music, sweet sugar cane, and the low roar of the engine. After an hour or so, the truck began to slow and, brakes screeching, came to a sudden halt. I looked over at my companion. He was smiling, handing me more sugar cane, and gesturing toward a dirt road across the highway: keep walking and I would eventually arrive at St. Paul's. I climbed down from the cab, made a wordless gesture of thanks, and began walking. It was dark when I arrived at the gate of the monastery.

The next morning, I am awakened with a knock at the door of my little cell. A young man tells me that one of the elders of the monastery, Abba Sarabuman, has asked to see me. I do not know why. But soon I am ushered out past the gate of the monastery and into the open desert. We walk together for twenty or thirty minutes over a rise and down into a little wadi, eventually arriving at an old wooden gate. I pass through the gate and am led around the corner where I find myself standing in front of a makeshift hut built into the side of the hill. This, it turns out, is Abba Sarabuman's hermitage. My companion disappears inside to summon him and soon he emerges from within, a beaming smile lighting up his face. He embraces me warmly. "Welcome. You are most welcome."

He puts a kettle on the stove for tea and invites me to join him outside under a simple shelter made of palm fronds. I sit in a plastic chair, gazing out to the east. Soon he brings the tea and joins me. For the next couple of hours, we engage in a meandering conversation, talking about his life in that place, my life in California, the larger world beyond. Visitors come and go, sometimes with requests for help or advice, sometimes, it seems, just to check in on him. He also makes requests of those who come to see him, once or twice sending one of the young men back to the monastery to retrieve something. From time to time, he steps outside to take a call on his cell phone. He notices me looking at him when he returns from one of these calls. "That was from the Nile Valley," he says. "An old friend. He is in trouble." This, it turns out, is quite common. Friends of the monastery calling to seek help or just needing to talk. Reaching out to the hermit in the desert. Connecting.

During my stay in Cairo, I had become aware of how difficult life was becoming for many in the Coptic Christian community in Egypt, the deepening political, cultural, and religious divides in the country pushing many of them close to the edge. In the monasteries close to Cairo, like St. Macarius in the Wadi Natrun, I had witnessed how many Copts made their way out to the monastery on Sundays to sit and spend time with the monks, whole families sharing food and drink and conversation, children often playing nearby. There was such solace in being welcomed into that space. Even here, in this remote corner of the Eastern Desert, there was a sense of community between those living in solitude and silence in the desert and those living in Cairo or along the Nile Valley. The monks in the desert, I began to see, had come to play a key role in accompanying those struggling to meet the challenges of their increasingly difficult and fragmented lives in Cairo and in towns and villages along the Nile Valley. These phone calls were part of this practice of accompaniment—separated by distance and time but joined in a shared commitment to stand with one another. Abba Sarabuman, and who knows how many others, accepted this challenge as part of what it meant to enter and inhabit the solitude of this place, as part of their responsibility to the larger community.

I thought again about that saying of Antony's: "Our life and death is with our neighbor." The relationship between monks and solitaries and the larger community has always been complex. The idea of a firm and clear boundary between monastery and world, enshrined in the discourse of "flight from the world," was one part of the story. But there was also the continuous call to tend carefully to the needs and concerns of those who came seeking help and solace in the desert. "Abba/Amma, speak to me a word." This was the cry from the heart that those seeking help from the desert elders so often uttered. An entire world of longing contained in this simple expression. To which the elders, listening carefully and deeply, would respond, sometimes with a word of their own, sometimes with a gesture, sometimes with silence, always paying attention to the particular circumstances of the person posing the question. Always engaging that person with tenderness. Solitude and community bound up together in the complex spiritual ecology of the desert.

My host asks me if I am hungry. I have lost track of time but realize it is past noon and that I have not eaten anything that day. He calls to one of the young men and indicates what he needs from the monastery. Half an hour or so later, the young man reappears, bearing onions, garlic, tomatoes, carrots, a few herbs, and fish. "We are going to have fish stew," Abba Sarabuman declares, smiling. He pulls out a small wooden board and begins chopping the vegetables, sautéing them slowly in olive oil, then adding the fish, the herbs, and some water for broth. The stew begins to simmer. We return to our places and resume our conversation. He looks at me intently and asks: "Why have you come here?"

The directness of his question catches me off guard. Also the tenderness in his voice. I am struck by a sense that we have been moving toward this moment for the past few hours. But now it has arrived, and I do not know how to respond. Or perhaps it is that I am afraid to respond. I have held my grief and loneliness at bay for so long. What will happen to me if I acknowledge it, open myself to it? Still, I know I must not evade or deflect his question. Strange, this unexpected reversal of the old pattern: the abba is asking *me* to speak to *him* a word. An honest, sincere word. I feel so grateful for the invitation. And so, after a few moments, I begin, haltingly, to tell him what has brought me here. Yes, the longing to touch and be touched by these wild, solitary places of ancient monasticism, something that has been alive in me as long as I can remember. But also a desire to open myself more honestly and deeply to my own life, a desire to face my own loneliness, to stop hiding from myself. A hope that I may find healing in this solitude. He listens carefully but does not say anything in response. Not in that moment. We let the silence gather. Then he leans over and tests the stew to see if it is ready. He ladles up two bowls and passes one to me. Also some bread, a few olives and two more cups of tea. We sit and eat together in the warmth of this desert afternoon. It is delicious.

I remained at St. Paul's for several more days. The time felt spacious, porous, open. I spent my days sleeping, eating, working with my hands, and wandering in the open desert around the monastery. At night I sat alone in the courtyard under a sky pulsing with stars, immersed in a deep silence. Catching up with myself a little. The questions that had brought me here, arising from my acute sense of loss and loneliness, were still very much with me. But they receded a little during these days, became less pointed, diffused within the silence and stillness of this place.

I had almost forgotten about my desire to get to St. Antony's. But one afternoon, word came to me that a visitor would be departing soon and could take me there. My flight home from Cairo was departing in a few days. Perhaps it was time to go. We departed the monastery in an old Volkswagen Beetle and tore down a rutted dirt road toward the Red Sea, clouds of dust trailing behind us. At the highway, we turned north toward Râs Az 'farâna, then eventually traveled west back into the desert toward St. Antony's. It was dusk when I arrived at the Inner Mountain.

* * *

Buried under moss
and ivy leaves but from within
the tomb, a faint prayer.

—Basho

The next day, I seek out the cave where Antony lived. From the monastery below, it appears as a tiny smudge of dark on the mountain side. But arriving at the opening of the cave, I realize that is deeper than I imagined. Much deeper. Now that I am inside, it feels bottomless. A thin film of perspiration forms on my neck and arms. I struggle for breath. Is it the temperature? Or anxiety? I am not sure. After a few minutes crawling along in the dark, I reach what I take to be the heart of the cave. I notice that the space has opened up a little to form a kind of bowl. Before me stands a small, simple altar upon which several candles are burning. Dark red carpets line the floor. The smell of melted wax. Behind me, I glimpse the faint glow coming from the cave opening. The way out.

I sit and lean my back against the cold, hard stone. My mind is blank. But I am feeling so many things. Uneasiness at having descended so far down into this dark, empty place: like being in a tomb. A sense of absurdity too: What am I doing here? Still, it feels good to be down inside this mountain, held in the warm stillness. Slowly, I begin to let go of my expectations. Just be here I think. I close my eyes, entering further into the dark stillness of the place. This is enough.

I open my eyes and scan the walls of the cave. There is a small niche in the rock stuffed with tiny pieces of paper. I pull one out and unfold it: words scrawled in Arabic. Another: the same. And yet another. Dozens of and dozens of these little pieces of paper crammed into this cleft in the rock. Later, I ask my host about this, and he confirms my hunch: they are prayers left for the saint. Prayers, expressing who knows how much hidden grief and longing, still-unrealized desires and hopes, written on scraps of paper, carefully placed into a niche in this cave in the heart of the Egyptian desert.

I consider all those souls who have journeyed to this place before me, and who felt moved to unburden themselves in the presence of the saint, who allowed themselves to become vulnerable in this way. Who allowed themselves to hope. Who believed that the one who disappeared into this mountain all those years ago was somehow alive and present to them and held their lives and their concerns close. Who perhaps sensed what Athanasius had long ago noted in his *Life of Antony*, how the monk, "While sitting in the mountain . . . kept his heart alert," how he "sympathized and prayed with those who suffered." And how he responded to those who came to him in distress, lending "his support to victims of injustice so avidly that it was possible to think that he, not the others was the injured party . . . who came to him tempted by a demon and did not gain relief? And who came to him distressed in his thoughts and did not find his mind calmed? . . . It was as if he were a physician given to Egypt by God."[53]

The solitary life: I begin to wonder if I have any understanding of this at all. Or what it means to enter solitude and feel the presence of others moving and thrumming within you. Here in this place, I recall another solitary figure, Musō Soseki (1275–1351), the great Rinzai Zen Buddhist monk, calligrapher, poet, and garden designer, who found himself, in the solitude of his lonely mountain hut, surrounded by a great host.

In this small hut
    are worlds beyond number
Living here alone
    I have endless company
Already I have
    attained he essence
How could I dare
    to want something higher.[54]

Worlds beyond number present in this small hut; alone but surrounded by an endless company. There is something at once whimsical and utterly serious about this meditation. "Already I have / attained the essence. How could I dare / to want something higher?" There is no striving, no obsession with accomplishing anything. The whole idea of accomplishment, with its shadow of ego and insecurity, fades in the light of the simple awareness of self and other that arises in this deep stillness. Simple, joyful awareness of life, spirit, community. Worlds beyond number.

Just a few days earlier, looking out into the desert from Abba Sarabuman's little hut and eating that fish stew, I felt myself blessed by such awareness: seen and held in an open, spacious field of love. That simple gesture of hospitality, the gift of that meal, the tenderness of the elder's gaze. I think of the promise that moment held for me: "You will love again the stranger who was your self."[55] And the call to open myself to that promise. In this moment, it still feels beyond me, ungraspable, unknowable. But also unexpectedly close at hand.

This, it turns out, has become a significant element of my own ongoing journey into the desert: my inability to understand or say—at least in anything approaching adequate terms—what it means or what it means to me. "Nobody knows anything."[56] I smile now to think of the force of this little saying from the desert tradition. This used to frustrate me. Increasingly, I accept it as necessary to the work of entering and inhabiting this space of emptiness.

I think (and do not think) of these things as I slowly make my way out of the cave. Outside, I pause for a few moments to adjust my eyes to the late afternoon light. There are hints of pink and blue along the horizon. Silence. Purity. Emptiness.

I am still living with a deep sense of uncertainty about the way ahead, and what I am facing upon my return home. But something has begun to be clarified. Words come to me unbidden: "less fear, more honesty." This, I think, is the gift of this place, something precious I will take with me as I turn for home. I make my way slowly down the path and back to the monastery. I do not pass anyone along the way. It is quiet and still. I walk across the courtyard, reach my little cell, and close the door behind me. I lay down on my bed and fall fast asleep.

3

A Wild, Wide Oneness

California, 2007

In this wild, wide oneness
The poor in spirit live united.
There they find nothing but emptiness,
Which answers always to eternity.

—Hadewijch of Antwerp[1]

Stone by stone it rises, this little house by the sea. Soft, damp sand for mortar, moss for the garden, little pieces of driftwood for the roof. A tiny stone wall made from pebbles encircles the yard, a path constructed from bits of glistening seaweed winds toward the front door. I am on my belly, my young daughter beside me, working to bring this little dwelling into being. A breeze from the Pacific Ocean cools us. All around us: the pounding surf, cormorants diving, an osprey circling high overhead. We began building this miniature house here in Bear Harbor on a whim; but now we are going at it in earnest. We want to make it strong and beautiful. A place to make a life. Pausing from time to time to consider our creation, we talk and laugh and exchange stories. We imagine the lives of the inhabitants of this place, where they came from, what they do all day, what they care about. Slowly, imperceptibly, we enter their world, becoming tiny people wending our way down the path and through the driftwood door. Disappearing inside. Gradually, a whole cosmos comes into being. And for a time we lose ourselves inside it.

My daughter is grown now. And that little house, surely, is no longer. The tides and winds here on the Lost Coast would have brought it down long ago, disassembling its lovingly gathered elements, carrying them off into the ocean, and perhaps returning them sometime later to that very place. Or to some unknown place miles to the south.

The Insurmountable Darkness of Love. Douglas E. Christie, Oxford University Press. © Oxford University Press 2022.
DOI: 10.1093/oso/9780190885168.003.0004

I think often of this moment, as well as other moments like it, unfolding over many years here in the Sinkyone Wilderness. Walking for hours along those vast, empty, black sand beaches in the presence of terns, pelicans, and gray whales. Lying in an open field atop the gnarled, bleached-white trunk of a fallen Eucalyptus tree, listening to the sweet song of a white crowned sparrow, rising and falling, rising and falling. Cresting a ridge and finding myself suddenly enveloped by a herd of Roosevelt elk. A world whole unto itself, complex and intricate and beautiful beyond my capacity to imagine or say. Hospitable, welcoming me in, offering me a place to dwell. But also wildly other, not centered on me and my concerns, continuously inviting me out beyond myself.

So it is here in this remote harbor where I spend a day building this little dwelling with my daughter. My own house has come apart. And I find myself full of longing for something I cannot easily name. Refuge? Healing? I am not sure. In this moment, these feel impossibly distant, beyond my reach. I can still hardly say what has happened to me, or how I lost my way. But for now I am here, gazing out at the vast, churning ocean. Its mesmerizing rhythms hold me and draw me in. Thoughts drifting up and out into this immensity. For a moment, I forget about myself and all that has happened to me; a relief. I turn my attention back to the simple, satisfying work of building this house with my daughter. We have two weeks together in this place, precious time that I do not mean to squander. But neither can I say exactly what the time is for—or if it is *for* anything. I smile to think of this, my instinctive impulse to assign a meaning and purpose to everything. And the resistance of this place—with its expansive, open, trackless character—to my designs. I need this.

I recall the sense of astonishment and wonder I felt when I first happened upon the Sinkyone in the fall of 1977. I was staying at Redwoods Monastery, and one of the sisters mentioned a beautiful, wild place just a few miles away: "The road is steep and treacherous. But you should visit if you can." A few hours later, having picked my way slowly down that narrow, rutted dirt track, I found myself standing on a bluff overlooking Needle Rock, an enormous crag rising up out of the surf, breathing in the ocean air. Behind me, a steep slope covered in fir trees. Below, miles of black-sand beaches. Ahead, that immense blue expanse. A deep silence washed over me. And with it, a spasm of giddy delight at having stumbled upon this hidden, solitary place. The solitude stirred something in me and drew me in.

After a few minutes, I noticed a trail, almost completely overgrown, pointing northward, and set off walking. The trail hugged the cliff top, passed through a grove of Eucalyptus trees and descended into a deep ravine, then rose sharply up the steep slope of Chemise Mountain. I kept walking until I reached a small clearing near the top of the mountain. I sat there for a long while, gazing out over the blue Pacific, thoughts drifting this way and that. The place enveloped me, held me close; but I also felt strangely exposed, vulnerable. The thin scrim that usually mediates reality had somehow been stripped away. Instead, raw, unfiltered contact. It was not a comfortable feeling, but I was enthralled. And I remained sitting in my perch until the light began to fade. Finally, I turned and made my way back down the mountain and south toward Needle Rock. It was dark by the time I reached the monastery.

As a child growing up in the Pacific Northwest, I moved within a world that felt numinous and alive: the snow-capped Olympic Mountains, endless gray skies, the fragrance of fir trees, storms pouring in off the North Pacific, the presence of bald eagles circling high overhead, swimming and fishing in Puget Sound. That sense of wonder so familiar to children—what Edith Cobb calls "the power of perceptual participation in the known and un-known"—was deeply woven into the ecology of my imagination.[2] It never left me entirely. But somehow, after I moved away, the vibrant reality of this world faded from view. A world that had once been alive and stitched into my consciousness became distant and external to me. And something in me became diminished. That afternoon on Chemise Mountain, I felt something of that old awareness returning, or at least the possibility of it. In that moment, I could not have said exactly what it was or what it might mean to me. But it felt important and worthy of my deepest regard: a feeling of awe and joy at finding myself immersed within this immensity. Slowly, and with the help of others who were more sensitive than I was to the power of the wild world, I began opening myself again to this mysterious reality. And tentatively giving myself over to a new form of spiritual practice, something I eventually came to understand as "the practice of the wild."[3]

At the time, I was unaware of the long reflection on wildness in the Christian mystical tradition, an idea that many mystical writers associated with darkness, the desert, the abyss, and emptiness, and which became a critical part of expressing the radical otherness and unknowability of God. This would come later. But for the moment, I found myself drawn, in a way I had not felt since childhood, to pay closer attention to the wild world. To listen to, notice, and feel the presence of other living beings and consider the meaning of my own life within that mysterious web. I apprenticed myself to teachers who were willing to accompany me on this path and help me to see again what I had long forgotten how to see.[4]

Many years later, I received an invitation to return and spend a few weeks living in the old ranch house above Needle Rock, to tend and care for the place. I happily accepted. For the next several years, I returned every summer to live in that little house—sometimes alone, sometimes with my family. Living for a few weeks without electricity or cell service and walking out every day into the vast, open space of the Lost Coast. Gradually, the life and rhythms of the place revealed themselves to me: the shifting tides, the movement of animals, the flight patterns and nesting habits of particular birds, the swirling fog—for days standing far offshore, then suddenly rolling in and blanketing the coast—the scorching winds pouring down over the mountains from far inland, the pulsing stars.

I also came to see more clearly than I had upon my first visit the wounded character of this place. One night, sitting outside the old ranch house with some friends, I heard for the first time the story of the Needle Rock massacre that occurred in this very place sometime in the 1850s. Sally Bell, a member of the Sinkyone community and the lone survivor of the attack, later recounted what happened, describing how a group of white men came and killed her grandfather, her mother, her father, and her baby sister, and how she escaped and hid in the woods for several months, sleeping under logs and in hollow trees until her brother found her and brought her to safety. This was not an isolated event, but part of a much larger and more extensive history of violence and genocide that decimated indigenous communities all across California during the nineteenth century, and it is a critical part of the meaning of this place.[5] So too is the long history of industrial logging that has left nearby fields strewn with giant stumps, torn by ragged ditches caused by erosion, and marked in some places by a strange, troubling silence: the absence of birdsong. Still, there is also a remnant stand of old-growth redwoods, sacred to the Sinkyone people, hidden in a remote and barely accessible ravine far down the coast—trees that survived in no small part because of the work of a coalition of indigenous and local community members who organized to resist Georgia Pacific's plans in the 1980s to clear-cut them.[6]

My awareness of this history deepened and complicated my sense of the place and my own spiritual-ethical relationship with it. I found myself rethinking what it meant for me to be here, and whether I could learn to see the place in a way that encompasses this entire, ambiguous reality. There was also something else at work in me that I was just beginning to notice: a hunger to lose myself in this immensity, to be buffeted and torn open by it, to overcome my long habit of keeping a safe distance from things.

Something similar began taking hold of me during the time I spent in the contemplative space at Redwoods Monastery. The monastery was just a few miles inland from the Sinkyone Wilderness; once a week I would travel up the road and enter the space of prayer with the community, reciting the Psalms, listening in silence, sometimes sharing the Eucharist and a simple midday meal, before eventually returning to that little dwelling near the ocean. A kind of tidal rhythm that slowly returned me to myself and to the beautiful wild world. And that helped alter my sense of what it means to become open, vulnerable, and responsive to ineffable, unnamable mystery, what it means to pray. I found myself considering again the witness of those mystics who traveled far out onto the edge of existence, who struggled to relinquish narrow categories of identity and inhabit an open, porous space where the borders among and between things are no longer clear. Who, for the sake of love, allowed themselves to become lost inside what Hadewijch called a "wild, wide oneness." And to reimagine within that ineffable, unbounded unity what it might mean to reknit the whole.

Here in this place, I consider what it might mean for me to lose myself within this wild, wounded beauty. Whether I can learn to slow down, listen, and pay attention; feel my way back into my body; immerse myself in the rough black sand, the salt air, the cry of gulls; thrill to the pulsing vitality of this place. Also confront the losses that are part of this place. And face my own losses. I look over at my daughter carefully arranging small driftwood pieces into a pattern along one side of our little house on the sand. A garden enclosure perhaps? I am not sure. It does not matter. In this moment, we are dreaming, lost to ourselves, adrift within this wild immensity.

* * *

This simple awareness of myself moving in and through the living world: a small and insignificant thing in itself. But it is connected, I am beginning to see, to wider, deeper questions about how we can learn to reimagine our place in the natural world, and come to inhabit the world with a greater sense of humility and openness toward other living beings. Questions about how the transformation of awareness and identity can and must form the ground of meaningful ethical practice, in particular our ethical relationship to the natural world.

Aldo Leopold long ago noted the fundamental character of this relationship: "No important change in ethics was ever accomplished," he said, "without an internal change in our intellectual emphasis, loyalties, affections, and convictions. We can be ethical only in relation to something we can see, feel, understand, love or otherwise have faith in."[7] For Leopold, these ideas were rooted, at least in part, in a painful encounter with a dying wolf (a wolf that he himself took part in killing). This experience revealed to him his own distance and alienation from the natural world, his scant knowledge of the intricate relationship among and between living beings, and how little he had allowed his own affections to be touched by the presence of these beings. It also made clear to him the devastating impact of such inattention and lack of feeling—especially when considered as part of a more widely shared cultural sensibility—on the natural world.

This experience, and the process of reflection it provoked in Leopold, initiated him into a long process of "internal change" that altered forever how he understood himself in relation to other living beings. Gradually relinquishing the idea of himself as the principal actor in the world, and the narrow conception of knowledge as a form of power or control, he asked instead what it would mean to cultivate the empathy and imagination and humility necessary for learning how to "think like a mountain." What it would require for him to listen deeply to the voice of the living world, allowing that voice to speak on its own terms. How he might learn to place the earth and its needs at the center of his own ethical practice. And whether he could learn to live in a way that reflected this emerging awareness of himself as part of an intricate immensity.

His articulation of what he called "the land ethic" was deeply informed by his encounter with the dying wolf, and the radical sense of relinquishment that emerged from it. And it altered dramatically the course of environmental thinking and practice, here in the United States and elsewhere. Not least because of his clear call to rethink human identity and to ask what it will mean for human beings to decenter themselves, to become small, humble, and responsive to the mysterious presence of other living beings. So too, his insistence on the importance of grounding our ethical relations with others in terms of what we "can see, feel, understand, love or otherwise have faith in," which stands as an enduring reminder of the critical place of deep affective and spiritual change to in our efforts to become more fully part of things.

Still, learning to see this expansively and deeply is not easy. It requires a willingness to question the categories and assumptions that shape your particular way of seeing the world and which, in many cases, render certain persons, things, and places invisible. This was certainly true for Leopold. He saw so much. And his commitment to reconsider his own subject position and his way of beholding the world led to a bold reimagining of the boundaries of community in a way that re-centered soils, water, plants, animals and the land. But his vision was limited. And, as Lauret Savoy notes, in her admiring but critical reassessment of Leopold's legacy, race and the pernicious impact of racism were rendered largely invisible in his understanding of the land ethic. "What I wanted more than anything," she says, "was to speak with Mr. Leopold. To ask him. I so feared that his 'we' and 'us' excluded me and other Americans with ancestral roots in Africa, Asia or Native America. . . . Did Aldo Leopold consider me?"[8] Savoy's question opens up the horizon of ecological thinking and the question of community far beyond where Leopold was able to take them.[9] And it helps reframe the question of what the land ethic, as an inclusive and just vision of community, must always include: attention to "the high percentages of people of color and the economically poor" who live and die next to degraded environments, and the resulting "losses of relationships with land or home, losses of self-determination, and losses of health or life."[10] Something Rob Nixon describes as the "slow violence" of chronic environmental degradation.[11]

This way of thinking about environmental ethics is close to the idea of "integral ecology" that is so central to Pope Francis's 2014 encyclical on the environment, *Laudato Si'*—a way of understanding ecology that refuses to separate our relationship with and obligation toward the natural world from our relationship with and obligation toward our fellow human beings, especially the most marginalized. Any attempt to understand the scope and extent of what we often refer to simply as the "environmental crisis," notes Pope Francis, will require recognizing that we are facing not two separate crises, one social and the other environmental, but rather "one complex crisis, which is both social and environmental."[12] The cultivation of such awareness, it seems increasingly clear, will require a radical rethinking of our identity and our place in the world. A relinquishment of long-held ideas of subjectivity, agency, and control for the sake of a more holistic way of seeing that is essential to the work of healing. Not unlike what Aldo Leopold had in mind when he spoke of learning to "think like a mountain"—a way of beholding the world from *within* the world, as part of the world. A recognition of the imperative to decenter the human proclivity to overwhelm the field. And part of reconsideration of what it will mean to become small, humble, receptive, open. Something that can only come about through an "internal change in our intellectual emphasis, loyalties, affections, and convictions." It echoes also Lauret Savoy's vision of what a more encompassing, inclusive land ethic might look like. "I could imagine it possible," she says, "to refrain from dis-integrated thinking and living, from a fragmented understanding of human experience on this continent. Possible to refuse what alienates and separates."[13]

To refuse what alienates and separates. This is not only a powerful ethical imperative. It also describes a way of seeing that arises from an apprehension of reality as variegated and whole and that resists every attempt to "dis-integrate" things or to render invisible what ought to remain visible and knitted into the whole. This is part of what I am trying to open myself to here on the Lost Coast, slowly learning to behold the rich complexity of this place and listen as carefully as I can to its mysterious rhythms, to a language not my own. Taking the time necessary to reconsider who I am beyond the limited identity markers that have for so long defined my existence. Working to locate myself within a complex ecology that includes not only the flora and fauna endemic to this part of the northern California coast but also its long, fraught human history. Rethinking the artificial and harmful distinctions between our obligations to the natural world and to one another that have so often undermined our capacity to know and love and care for both the places we inhabit and one another. And becoming more attentive to the hidden, obscure, often incomprehensible sources of my own feeling for the living world.

The question of love, I am coming to see, is fundamental. Not only for those, like Leopold, who consider love to be indispensable to the work of coming to tend and care for the living world. But also for those who understood the call to relinquish themselves to the wild force of love to be at the very heart of spiritual practice, of prayer. And for those who understood this relinquishment to be essential to the possibility of cultivating a durable and lasting sense of community. Here in this wild, solitary place, I begin to consider again whether I am capable of or willing to become small, poor, empty, and open, to risk the relinquishment of identity necessary for entering and participating in this larger, shared reality. Whether I can learn to respond to and care for it with honesty and courage and love.

* * *

It is evening. I am standing in the kitchen of the little house in the Sinkyone, looking out at the ocean. Swallows are circling. The light is slowly fading from the sky. The wind is beginning to pick up. I have water boiling for pasta. A few tomatoes, some garlic, and olive oil on the counter before me. On one of the nearby shelves, I spot a blue plastic wind-up radio someone has left in the house. I pick it up and crank it four or five times to see what will happen. A faint crackling of a signal. I spin the dial slowly. On the AM side, I find a Giants game, then a talk radio show from Reno filled with rancorous commentary on the decline of our country. Not what I am looking for. I switch to FM. There is mostly silence and static. Then I find a signal and hear someone speaking: "Abruptly stripped of light, of heat, of company, you seemed to be walking disembodied into who knows what unearthly sort of limbo. And with mounting anguish you looked backwards toward that happy corner, those bright days, now irretrievable. . . . You yourself were the widower of your lost love, the loser and the lost one, all at the same time."

Someone is reading. But who is reading and from what text? I do not know. Still, this voice touches something in me. And the predicament of the writer is recognizable: "those bright days, now irretrievable." There is such melancholy in these words: the irretrievable past, the depth of loss, the sense of anguish. I am suddenly aware of feelings that have been lying dormant within me for much of the past year: my own anguish at all that has been lost to me, all that I cannot retrieve. My failures at love. It is painful to face this in myself. But I am grateful to be in the presence of someone who can speak so honestly and clearly of his loss. And I feel the invitation to attend more carefully and deeply and honestly to my own.

The radio cuts out and I sit in the silence absorbing these words: "You yourself were the widower of your lost love, the loser and the lost one, all at the same time." Yes.

I crank the radio to life again and continue listening. The writer, it turns out, is Luis Cernuda. And the speaker Stephen Kessler, who is sitting in a studio in San Francisco reading from his new translation of Cernuda's prose poems: *Written in Water.* This piece is called "Regreso a la Sombra," or, in his rendering, "Return to Darkness." It is my first encounter with Cernuda, and I cannot place him in any meaningful context. Still, the simple honesty and openness and pathos of his writing moves me, and I make a note to myself to seek him out later. A few weeks later, having closed up the house and departed from the Lost Coast, I stop at City Lights Bookstore in San Francisco and purchase a copy of the book. It is then that I begin to understand more about the painful ground from which Cernuda composed so much of this work. As a poet and a gay man living in mid-twentieth-century Spain, he wrote openly about his sexuality long before it was morally or politically acceptable to do so. Along with many other poets and dissidents of his generation, he became suddenly vulnerable during Franco's rise to power, and left Spain under duress in 1938, imagining he would be away for only a few months. But he never returned home. His lyrical evocations of place, so many of them meditations on his home place, were all written in exile. Cernuda's poetry was rooted in the solitude of loss; but he also considered it a great gift: "Between others and you, between love and you, between life and you, lies solitude," he writes, clearly addressing himself, but also anyone else who has entered and spent time in this solitary space, anyone who will listen.[14]

I am listening. And I am gradually settling into my own solitude, beginning to pay closer attention to this place and to the questions surfacing for me here. Thinking especially about my own lost love, why I have so often shrunk from love's upending power, and whether I can still open myself to it. I walk out onto the front porch of the little house and sit for a long while on the wooden steps. The call of gulls, the fog swirling, the slender, quaking grasses in the field before me, the dense green forest above, black sand beaches below. The sense of "all this life going on about my life, or living a life about all this life going on."[15] There is something so intimate, so tender in this embrace. For a moment, I forget myself and drift out into this immensity.

* * *

At the heart of these reflections is the question of what it means to relinquish control and open yourself to the life of another. What it means to allow yourself to be addressed by the life of another. What it means to *enter and share* the life of another. To fall into an immensity so far beyond your capacity to grasp or comprehend that you lose yourself completely. Become part of that immensity. To consider how it sometimes happens that, in our contact with other living beings, we "grow larger" by participating in a shared lifeworld.[16] And, paradoxically, also become smaller, humbler, perhaps disappearing altogether.

Such questions surface continuously in mystical literature, where the boundaries between self and other become blurred, sometimes eclipsed entirely. Where the habitual tendency to say "I" and to think of yourself as somehow distinct from the other often gives way to something more fluid and mysterious and encompassing. Here, there is a radical relinquishment of identity for the sake of love. This is not always easy or without pain. Lovers of God, says Marguerite Porete, become "exiled, annihilated, forgotten," a forbidding prospect that few can face without trepidation. Still such lovers, she suggests, eventually come to discover a way of living that is open, transparent, and unencumbered—free from the compulsive habit of making claims for the self too closely bound to the restrictive needs of the ego.[17] This mysticism of self-effacement creates the space necessary for perceiving reality from the depths, from *within*, not unlike what Aldo Leopold meant when he spoke of learning to "think like a mountain." It is, potentially, to discover and inhabit a profound shared reality, rooted in love.

It is this insight that helps to account for the central place of mystics and contemplatives—St. Francis of Assisi, St. Bonaventure, St. John of the Cross, St. Therese of Lisieux, Ali al-Khawas, and others—in the vision of "integral ecology" articulated in *Laudato Si'*. These spiritual seekers, who committed themselves deeply and honestly to facing and responding to reality in all its complexity and ambiguity, and who risked allowing the fixed boundaries of the self to become open and diffuse, serve as critical witnesses to the possibility of inhabiting the natural world with humility, openness, and love. Their presence serves as an important reminder that at the heart of the difficult and complex challenge of rethinking our relationship to the natural world arises the question of what it means to see, and whether we have the capacity to renew how we see ourselves in relation to other living beings—a question that for many in the present moment have taken on a distinctly spiritual, even mystical, character.[18]

Ali al-Khawas, the ninth-century Sufi mystic and poet, figures importantly in *Laudato Si's* mystical vision of integral ecology: "The universe unfolds in God, who fills it completely," he says. "Hence, there is mystical meaning to be found in a leaf, in a mountain trail, in a dewdrop, in a poor person's face."[19] St. Bonaventure, the thirteenth-century Franciscan theologian and mystic, offers this reminder of what can happen when we learn to look long and carefully at the living world: "Contemplation deepens the more we feel the working of God's grace within our hearts, and the better we learn to encounter God's creatures outside ourselves."[20] And St. Francis of Assisi (1181–1226), whose presence deeply infuses the encyclical's vision, places the question of kinship with other living beings at the very center of what it means to seek God with integrity and depth.[21]

The sense of awe and wonder that characterized Francis's attitude toward all living things—his ecstatic response to the sun, the moon, the air, fire, water, birds, wolves, the entire living cosmos—is fundamental to his witness. Still, it is easy to underestimate the challenge that this vision presents us. St. Francis—in history and memory—is so much more than a friendly backyard saint who loved animals; he is a strange, unpredictable, wild figure, someone who felt the living world coursing through his veins, and who understood the cost of this all-involving relationship with the living world. Yes, he saw and felt the presence of other living creatures as manifestations of God's presence in the world. Francis dwelt in a paradisal world where the capacity to communicate with and be touched by the presence of other living beings was, if only for a moment, fully restored to us. As he expresses so powerfully in his *Canticle to the Creatures*, praise and adoration of God cannot be conceived of as arising within us in any other way but *in and through* the living world. This joyful sense of communion with all living beings can also be seen in the *vitae* of St. Francis by Thomas of Celano, Bonaventure, and others; and in Giotto's light-infused rendering of Francis's sermon to the birds.[22] There is, in the witness of this saint, a radical displacement of the narrow bounds of the self for the sake of a more encompassing, inclusive vision of community.

Still, Francis's practice of relinquishment also meant reckoning honestly and deeply with suffering, darkness, and loss, and this too influenced his mystical vision of unity. The embodied character of this practice is striking and significant, seen especially in his intimate encounter with lepers early on in life, something that utterly transformed his sense of what it meant to be a follower of Christ; in the intense physical suffering he endured late in life (malaria, trachoma, and a gastric ulcer so acute that it caused him to vomit blood); and in the final harrowing experience at La Verna of receiving the stigmata—the wounds of Christ.[23] His capacity to behold and delight in all beings in the living world as his kin was bound up with his embodied commitment to touching and being touched by the lost and forsaken. This deeply ethical vision of life was rooted in an ever-deepening understanding of what it means to see. Not in a detached or possessive way, nor in a way that objectifies what one beholds; rather, by cultivating a gaze that makes it possible to become more responsive to the intricate bonds that connect us to one another and to all living beings. A way of seeing that helps us recognize how deeply bound our lives are with the life and welfare of all sentient beings.

To see and feel the presence of God in everything and everyone and to be-hold everything and everyone in God is potentially to arrive at the kind of transformative spiritual awareness—what *Laudato Si'* calls simply "loving awareness"—that enables us to share in the lives of others, helps us relocate our-selves in relation to the living world.[24] But as the witness of St. Francis makes clear and as the encyclical also insists, the practice of awareness must also in-clude suffering and loss. We must become "painfully aware" and "dare to turn what is happening to the world into our own personal suffering and thus to dis-cover what each of us can do about it."[25] Here we encounter an understanding of awareness that rejects the careless, objectifying, and utilitarian gaze that so often characterizes our way of being in the world. Awareness in this sense collapses the distance between us and other living beings and creates the conditions for a deeply empathetic response to them. It calls for a more intimate, embodied and involving way of seeing and inhabiting reality, born of love.

* * *

The coarse, black sand between my fingers, slightly sticky from the salt water. The feeling of my hand moving slowly along the surface, smoothing a place near our miniature dwelling. Back and forth my hand moves, a humble but functional tool. I pause from time to time to pick out bits of driftwood and kelp. Tiny pebbles. The simple sensual pleasure of this work. Also the pleasure of proximity. I have lowered my lanky frame down onto the ground; it is the only way I can do this work. This ground's eye view is a little strange: I am hardly ever down here anymore (though as a child I used to crawl around in the dirt more or less constantly). I have forgotten how it feels to be this close to things, to see things from this intimate perspective. Occasionally I pause in the work and roll over onto my back to gaze up at the sky; or lie on my side, face pressed hard against the sand and look out into the churning ocean; or scan the steep, thickly forested ridge overlooking this harbor.

These different ways of looking out at and into the world become part of the game. And the feeling of the earth upon my belly, the wind tousling my hair, my hands immersed in the beautiful texture of this dark, pulverized vol-canic soil, and the presence of my daughter laughing beside me—all of these things converge into a single, embodied perception of reality. Gradually, the habitual perception of myself as the principal actor in my own existence begins to shift. Yes, I am acting upon the world. But it is also acting on me.

I am in the world. But it is also moving in me. There is no inside and outside. There is only this mysterious whole within which I live and move and have my being (Acts 17:28).

This awareness, I begin to realize, is mediated through touch. The simple, visceral sensation of my own embodied self, immersed in this place, gives me a knowledge of myself as a living being among other living beings in the world that I can come to in no other way. A critical part of my own redis-covery of "vibrant matter"—the aliveness of things to which we are invited to attend and respond to and make room for within our embodied existence.[26] Or what the Christian tradition often refers to simply as sacrament. It also makes possible a renewed awareness of the depth of loss that marks this place. I am, I know, moving through an ecologically and morally compromised landscape: the stumps of ancient redwoods, long since cut down for timber, in their place vast stands of eucalyptus trees imported from Australia to provide wind breaks and firewood. Innumerable patches of scotch broom steadily encroaching on the native grasses. And, yes, the knowledge of those human beings who first inhabited this place, long ago killed or driven from their home.

How to hold all of this in my awareness? How to live in relation to this beautiful, solitary place I have come to love but which is also marked by our collective failure to practice paying attention to the lives of other living beings? I am not sure. I think again of *Laudato Si's* call to become "painfully aware," to allow the larger reality of what is happening in the world to become part of "our own personal suffering." Here is a moral-spiritual ecology that invites us to recognize how porous the borders are between our own lives and the lives of all other living beings. It is a call to *live* with greater awareness of the intimate bonds connecting us to others and to participate in the life of the world. At its root, this is a contemplative practice that echoes the teaching of many ancient spiritual traditions on the need to pay attention, to become more deeply aware of oneself as part of the whole fabric of being.

"Return to your material [body] and let your works blossom forth," says Hadewijch.[27] This is how she expresses and understands the deeply embodied ground of all seeing and the fruit that can come from it. I am coming late to this realization I know, but it has already begun to change so much for me. This day I spend laying on that black sand beach with my daughter at Bear Harbor brings with it a dawning recognition that I am being called to accept and live within the fundamentally sacramental character of my own spiritual tradition and to experience and revere the world itself as sacramental. Also to take seriously the fundamental Christian teaching on the incarnation—the idea that all matter shimmers with transcendent beauty and power by virtue of the Word of God having become "enfleshed" in a human body. And to feel what the early Christian community felt so intensely: the profound cosmic, or as we might say now, ecological significance of this idea.

My own practice has led me, increasingly, back into my body and into more consistent contact with the living world; toward a greater sense of immersion in and responsibility for the living world. I have now come to think of this in terms of what Michel de Certeau calls a "tactic," that is, a way of acting in the world that helps us preserve or recover elements of our basic humanity in the face of social, political, or economic structures that are always threatening to undermine or eclipse them. A liberating practice of resistance. Also, at least sometimes, a meaningful form of spiritual practice. Here in this moment in the Sinkyone Wilderness, it is a practice grounded in the senses that also alters and expands my sense of myself. Through such practice, the world within which I move gradually becomes less distant, less of an object and more of a living presence. I am growing into an awareness of myself as somehow *part* of the world, part of an indissoluble whole.

In his essay "The Sage and the World," Pierre Hadot describes the kind of consciousness of the whole that was once common among sages, philosophers, and contemplatives but which we have to a great extent lost. At the heart of this consciousness was an experience of what he calls "unitive contemplation" rooted in an intense awareness of the present moment. "In order to *perceive* the world," Hadot notes, the sages believed that "we must, as it were, perceive our *unity with* the world, by means of an exercise of concentration on the present moment."[28] A deceptively simple idea whose degree of difficulty is easy to underestimate, and whose potential cost to the one who practices it can be immense. It is a truth that many spiritual traditions affirm—without a capacity to dwell deeply in the present instant, to perceive and become immersed in what we perceive, and enjoy and delight in it, we risk losing the precious reality we seek to behold. We risk losing both ourselves and this reality under the flood of preoccupations and projects for the future that come to dominate our consciousness. And we end up living not in the present moment but in a future that may never come. "Only the present is our happiness," says Goethe.

How elusive the present moment can seem. How oppressed we often feel by the tyranny, the relentless pace of time. How much of our experience is eclipsed by, lost beneath the breathless, merciless power of *chronos*. Our capacity to engage in "an exercise of concentration on the present moment," to be present to what we behold, becomes lost to us. As does the world. The human gaze remains "so partial, dark and fragile."[29] We miss so much.

I lift delicate strands of seaweed and place them along the black sand leading to the doorway of the miniature house; then carefully arrange gnarled pieces of driftwood into a kind of fence—a paddock for horses perhaps or protection against the harsh winds pouring in off the ocean. The tide is coming in, gulls are passing overhead. I am breathing in this moment. Falling into a kind of wordless prayer. Beginning to learn how to become present to myself, my daughter, this place.

* * *

Thomas Merton came to the Lost Coast in May 1968. He was searching for a place to renew and deepen his own contemplative practice. And he spent time, both with the community at Redwoods Monastery and walking alone along the bluffs above Needle Rock, considering whether this wild, solitary place might become. A copy of his book, *Woods, Shore, Desert*—a spare, haunting meditation on silence and emptiness, written during the final year of his life and in part while he was moving through this landscape—is here in the house at Needle Rock. And I am slowly reading through it.[30] Thinking with him about what it means to let go of what is extraneous and unnecessary, to learn to listen in silence, without agenda or fear; about how to become more vulnerable and open in prayer; and about how to rediscover the purposeless wonder and joy at the heart of my own life.

It seems so simple. But there is a cost to such relinquishment. And I hesitate to open myself to this honest, difficult work. Still, I find Merton's approach to this work so heartening. He arrived in California from his home at Gethsemani Abbey in Kentucky at a critical juncture in his life, having come to the end of something in himself: "There is a need of effort, deepening, change and transformation," he wrote. "I do have a past to break with, an accumulation of inertia, waste . . . foolishness . . .[there is] a great need of clarification of mindfulness, or rather of no mind."[31] Having spent much of the previous ten years thinking and writing about the spiritual-ethical imperative to resist war, racism, and violence, he found himself increasingly drawn toward a deeper engagement with solitude and toward a contemplative thought and practice rooted in solitude. He had already been thinking and writing about how contemplative traditions of spiritual thought and practice—especially those rooted in the ancient monastic ideal of *anachoresis*—could inform a vital and durable ethic of concern for the world. And in 1965, he had begun living full-time in a small hermitage in the woods behind Gethsemani Abbey, giving himself over fully to what he called "the work of loneliness." His journals and essays from this time, including "Day of a Stranger," "Rain the Rhinoceros," and "A Life Free from Care," reflect his growing engagement with silence and solitude and with the question of how they could deepen the work of radical social and cultural critique.[32]

Woods, Shore, Desert is part of this ongoing work. But in both form and language, it is simpler and more distilled than so much of what had come before; and it reflects a growing sensitivity to silence and to the inevitable sense of loss that comes from abandoning yourself to the unknown and un-knowable. "I am the utter poverty of God," he writes. "I am His emptiness, littleness, nothingness, lostness." A dawning awareness of something for which he had long been yearning: the "self-emptying of God in me . . . a love without measure."[33] It is not easy to know what precipitated these thoughts. Or what he made of them. They were, it turns out, among his last reflections on these questions: just a few months after leaving California for Asia, he lay dead from an accidental electrocution in a Red Cross conference center out-side of Bangkok, Thailand. But the days he spent moving through the silence and emptiness of the Lost Coast seems to have given him new access to his own "emptiness, littleness, nothingness, lostness." And to the possibility of inhabiting this expansive, empty space as part of his own spiritual practice.

It also altered his sense of time and his understanding of the relationship of time to the life of prayer. Slowing down, paying more careful attention, allowing thought to gather and deepen, all critical elements of contempla-tive practice, began to come into focus around the question of time. He cites approvingly a statement by the Russian mystic Theophane the Recluse: "Not to run from one thing to the next . . . but to give each one time to settle in the heart."[34] The ancient work of *hesychia*; here reimagined in a cultural context where the most common impulse is often to run and not stop running. His reflection on this question became part of a talk he gave to the community at Redwoods Monastery during his stay with them.[35]

How to recover the fundamental simplicity of prayer as an open, empty, receptive space where love can take root and grow? Also: how to avoid re-ducing prayer to yet another activity governed by the tyranny of time and utility? These were the central questions preoccupying him as he engaged the community at Redwoods that day. "We were indoctrinated so much into means and ends," he says, "that we don't realize that there is a different dimension in the life of prayer."

> In technology you have this horizontal progress, where you must start at one point and move to another and then to another. But that is not the way to build a life of prayer. In prayer, we discover what we already have. You start where you are and you deepen what you already have and you realize you are already there. We already have everything, but we don't know it and we don't experience it. Everything has been given to us in Christ. All we need is to experience what we already possess.

We already have everything. An astonishing assertion that in its simple clarity serves as an indictment of long-held habits of spiritual striving and acquiring. Nor has our growing preoccupation with time as a commodity served us well in our effort to understand of what it means to pray.[36] "If we really want prayer," Merton observes, "we'll have to give it time. We must slow down to a human tempo and we'll begin to have time to listen. And as soon as we listen to what's going on, things will begin to take shape by themselves. But for this we have to experience time in a new way."

This fundamental insight is widely shared among monks and mystics throughout the Christian spiritual tradition, who recognize the fundamental simplicity of prayer and who also struggle against the inclination to think of prayer as an activity governed by the ideology of means and ends. A story from the early desert tradition illustrates this. "Abba Sisoes [one day] said to a brother, 'How are you getting on?' and he replied: 'I am wasting my time, father.' The old man said, 'If I happen to waste a day, I am grateful for it.'"[37] The deeper currents informing this exchange are not easy to identify. The brother's concern about wasting his time may reflect a worry expressed frequently in the desert tradition about the seeming impossibility of freeing oneself from certain obsessive thoughts or patterns of behavior, of continuously falling prey to feelings of listlessness or sadness or anger. The sense of being trapped with no way out. It is difficult to know. In any case, Abba Sisoes takes the question in a different direction that is reflective of the early monks' consistent hope that they might learn to live with *amerimnia*, or "freedom from care." In particular, Sisoes's words reflect a different way of thinking about time. Here, as so often in the early monastic tradition, there is an invitation to relinquish all plans, all projects, all designs for one's life, all concerns regarding progress—especially progress in the spiritual life. Instead there is a gesture toward the cultivation of an inner disposition of freedom and openness that allows one's relationship to time to take on a completely new meaning. *Chronos* gives way to *Kairos*.

Thomas Merton's awareness of this more expansive sense of time emerged with increasing force and clarity during the last few years of his life, especially after he moved into the hermitage in 1965. It was there, he says, that he began to become "attentive to the times of day: when the birds began to sing, and the deer came out of the morning fog, and the sun came up"—rhythms rooted in the cycles of the natural world. Life in the hermitage was less structured than it was in the monastery, more open, free, spacious. Also more demanding. The solitary life required greater honesty and commitment, less reliance on conventional structures of thought and practice. Here, he began rethinking the meaning of the contemplative life as a whole, especially the misplaced sense of purpose and direction and utility that too often undermines and compromises its essential meaning.

His study of Zen Buddhism was becoming more serious and focused during this time and this too provoked a questioning of certain assumptions about spiritual thought and practice that had, for him at least, too long gone unquestioned. "Nothing is allowed to be and to mean itself: everything has to mysteriously signify something else," he wrote. "Zen is especially designed to frustrate the mind that thinks in such terms."[38] He was becoming more alert to the danger of relying too much on certain conceptual categories, including the categories of self and God. So too with the idea of purpose, the sense that everything has to have utility, has to do or achieve something. In a letter to D. T. Suzuki in 1964, Merton wrote: "I am especially struck with the idea of the purposeless life 'filling up the well with snow.' I suppose all of life is just that anyway, but we are all obsessed with purpose."[39] The solitary life was teaching him to question these assumptions and to develop a more fluid, open, and expansive understanding of contemplative practice.

It also helped him deepen his commitment to be contemplative in the world and to respond thoughtfully and deeply to the to the world's suffering. His sustained writing against racism, violence, and nuclear weapons and on behalf of nonviolence in the early 1960s reflected his sense of what it meant to be a "contemplative in a world of action." He now found himself thinking more carefully about how he could continue to remain faithful to this commitment while also responding to what his solitary life was asking of him. His 1965 essay *Day of a Stranger* offers what is perhaps his clearest, and most compelling articulation of this idea.[40] Written, at least ostensibly, in response to a request from a South American editor asking him to describe a "typical day" in his life, Merton offers a whimsical demythologizing of monastic and solitary life that also invites a serious engagement with the question of what it means to be a contemplative witness. "This is not a hermitage—it is a house," he says. "What I wear is pants. What I do is live. How I pray is breathe.... Up here in the woods is seen the New Testament: that is to say, the wind comes through the trees and you breathe it."[41] This playful spirit is far from the triumphalist, apologetic, and hyper-Catholic tone of his famous autobiography, *The Seven Storey Mountain*, written almost twenty years earlier. That work reflected a relatively narrow and often-defensive reading of the theological and ecclesial categories the tradition had given him; and that understood "the world" as a place that he, as a monk, must flee and reject. He was now seeking to give voice to a very different vision of contemplative practice, less conceptually and structurally constrained and more transparent, free, and open. Also more involved in and responsive to the world.

He resists what he calls the "hot medium" of monastic life that is filled with words like "must," "ought," and "should" and that insists on making everything as clear as possible. In contrast, he says, "the hermit life is cool. It is a life of low definition in which there is little to decide, in which there are few transactions or none, in which there are no packages to be delivered." There is, however, time to pay attention—to the trees, the birds, the place—which he does assiduously and lovingly. Also to all those, living and dead, who accompany him in this solitary place and contribute to its distinctive ecology of spirit. But this expansive sense of time is not unambiguous. He also notices and names the wounds that afflict the world, a world of which he is very much a part: the SAC plane with its deadly payload flying overhead; the "way of blood, guile, anger, war" that courses through the country and the world. Nor is this a mere abstraction; it is close to home: "the way over the hills is blood, guile, dark, anger, death: Selma, Birmingham, Mississippi. Nearer than these, the atomic city, from which each day a freight car of fissionable material is brought to be laid carefully beside the gold in the underground vault which is at the heart of the nation." Attending to these realities, situating himself in relationship to them, and learning to respond to them, was becoming critical to the work of contemplative solitude to which he had committed himself, and to which so much of his late writing responds.

At the heart of this work is a commitment to make time to enter deeply into the night. "I am out of bed at two-fifteen in the morning, when the night is darkest and most silent. . . . I find myself in the primordial lostness of the night, solitude, forest, peace, a mind awake in the dark." A mind awake in the dark. Alone in the forest. Lost. These images evoke a life beyond all images, all understanding, but open and responsive to the presence of mystery that emerges in obscurity. It also suggests an approach to prayer willing to relinquish what Meister Eckhart refers to as "ways"—all those structures and strategies of evasion that keep us from opening ourselves fully and honestly to the "God beyond God"—for the sake of an ever-deepening encounter with the night.

The space he inhabits is not devoid of light or images or language. There is an icon in the corner. A candle burning. The Psalms. All have meaning and signify something important about the sacramental presence of God mediated through things. But he is especially attentive to "the secret that is heard only in silence." This, he gradually comes to see, is at the heart of this solitary work: "to preserve the stillness, the silence, the poverty, the virginal point of pure nothingness."[42] Such language depends for its meaning on the stillness of the night and on ancient traditions of practice that understood prayer to be nourished by and responsive to the night. Also responsive to the limits of language in expressing or encompassing the suffering and loss born of violence. Merton's correspondence from this time returns to this question often, and he shares the sense felt by so many of his friends of the impossibility of expressing, in ordinary language or in prayer, the depth of what is moving through them. This loss, this lack, becomes part of the very climate of prayer. Writing to his Jesuit friend Daniel Berrigan, who was deeply immersed in antiwar witness and who struggled, as many in that moment did, with a sense of profound uncertainty about the meaning of this work, Merton says: "There is an absolute need for the solitary, bare, dark, beyond-concept, beyond-thought, beyond-feeling type of prayer."[43] And addressing his friend Etta Gullick, in a letter composed around the same time he wrote *Day of a Stranger*, he comments: "The more I see of it, the more I realize the absolute primacy and necessity of silent, hidden, poor, apparently fruitless prayer."[44]

Bare, dark, silent, hidden, poor, apparently fruitless. This language, which itself arises from and turns back toward the deep silence of the night, draws upon a long tradition within Christian mystical thought. At the heart of this tradition is the idea that the call to relinquish all for the sake of All opens up within us a kind of abyss. "Keep yourself empty and bare," says Meister Eckhart, "just following and tracking this darkness and unknowing without turning back."[45] Marguerite Porete encourages those seeking God to cultivate in themselves the sensibility of a "transparent" soul, who "sees herself to be nothing in God and God nothing in her."[46] And Hadewijch exhorts true seekers to abandon themselves to a "naked love who spares nothing." To enter and get lost inside a "wild, wide oneness." To accept that "nothing is there except silent emptiness."[47] Such experience can never be brought fully to expression or completely understood. To enter such a space of prayer and dwell there requires a willingness to give up the need for clarity, security, knowledge. But there sometimes arises within this emptiness a freedom and openness and trust that can become the ground of solidarity with others who are themselves moving deeply through the night.

The call to practice relinquishment, letting go especially of a certain relationship to time that often prevents us from discovering the deep spaciousness of prayer, also forms an important part of Merton's talk to the community at Redwoods in 1968. "For each one of us time is mortgaged," he says. "We experience time as unlimited indebtedness. We are sharecroppers of time." It is sobering to recall that he uttered these words in 1968, long before the ubiquitous presence of the always-on internet or social networking or the twenty-four-hour news cycle. But the image is, if anything, even more poignant in this moment: whole hours, days, weeks already accounted for, already spent, long before we ever have the opportunity to live them. Time as endless indebtedness: that rich space closed up, lost to us forever. Seen from this perspective, the approach to time and prayer and knowledge found in contemplative traditions begins to seem both utterly radical and necessary. "We must approach the whole idea of time in a new way," says Merton. "We are free to live. And [we] must get free from all imaginary claims. We live in the fullness of time. Every moment is God's own good time, his Kairos. . . . We have what we seek. We don't have to rush after it. It is there all the time, and if we give it time it will make itself known to us."

It is not easy to imagine living this way. There is an inevitable sense of foolishness that comes with letting go so completely of the idea of purpose. Or perhaps it is something even more disturbing than this: the sense that here in this spaciousness, we no longer control anything: knowledge, existence, identity, anything. Still, this radical relinquishment of control is critical to the emerging sense of what it means to live more slowly, more openly, more fully. There is an intense vulnerability here that has always been central to the life of prayer, the awareness that "I am the utter poverty of God. I am His emptiness, littleness, nothingness, lostness."[48]

So it seemed to Merton in May 1968 out on the Lost Coast. He was already disappearing, traveling into an unknown country where the old boundaries between self and other were becoming open, empty, indeterminate. Becoming empty, little, nothing, lost. "Not to deny subject and object but to realize them as void."[49] Learning to accept this. Letting go of the "feeling that we have to keep moving," that it is better not to look too closely at or care too much about things. Refusing the impulse to turn every encounter or activity into something purposeful, useful, commodified. Letting time, plans, agendas, identity fall away. Learning to live for others.

These ideas, deeply rooted in the ancient contemplative traditions and given new life and meaning in this wild, solitary place, hold the promise of a more spacious understanding of community, where your own life is no longer separate and distinct from the lives of others. Where it becomes possible again to feel the mysterious unfolding of what John Ruusbroec called "an eternal now."[50]

* * *

These ideas have become part of my experience in a way they never were before. Especially the sense of emptiness and littleness and lostness—no longer an abstraction, but a visceral, embodied reality. The raw, hollowed-out feeling of my own life having come apart, my once-secure (or so I thought) identity fractured and frayed, scoured out. And yes, the sense of homelessness: the appalling feeling of waking up alone, far from home, having become a stranger to myself. And the recognition that there is no way back, at least no way that I can securely navigate.

What is left to me? What is left *of* me? I am not sure. I am still a father. And my daughter is here beside me. In this moment, it is enough. More than enough. And there is this beautiful, wild place: I look out at the sky, the trees, the silky, glistening kelp, cormorants, terns, gulls, the pulsing ocean and think: this is everything. And I am part of it. Here in this place, my preoccupation with who and what I am begins to fade from view. Something less solid and well defined, more open and expansive, is taking hold of me. I cannot easily name this something. But I find myself thinking in a new way about what Marguerite Porete calls the unencumbered self, or what Henry David Thoreau describes as the precarious self, a sense of self born of radical loss and nourished by grief. Empty, open, free, and susceptible to giving and receiving love. A vision of the self that takes seriously the emptiness at the heart of experience and seeks to reconstitute the very idea of community around this open space.

It was not until I read Branka Arsić's brilliant and original study of Thoreau, *Bird Relics*, that I began to grasp how deeply loss and grief figure into Thoreau's radical rethinking of identity, especially human exceptionalism. And how significant this idea is for our contemporary efforts to rethink the meaning of community. Arsić sheds new light on one of the most enduring and important aspects of Thoreau's work—his insistence that "no living form is more accomplished than another, and life doesn't therefore unfold hierarchically and progressively but, more democratically, moves simultaneously in a variety of directions."[51] For Thoreau, taking this idea seriously meant removing himself more and more from his own reflections on the natural world, in deference to those life forms toward which he was directing his gaze—a gesture of ascetic relinquishment for the sake of the world itself. Arsić argues that Thoreau was able to formulate what she calls "a complex materialist epistemology," leading him to radically rethink both the dualistic divide between mind and matter and the very idea of subjectivity. At the root of his work, she contends, was a way of thinking "predicated on radical dispossession and self-impoverishment verging on self-annihilation." This commitment to weaken the self, to cultivate a "precarious self," Arsić suggests, stands in stark contrast to the images of strong individualism so often associated with Thoreau's thinking. And it creates the ground for a radically egalitarian ethics and politics, a vision of community in which human beings participate in a shared world with other living beings but do not dominate or exert power over them.[52]

Loss, grief, and mourning occupy a central place in Thoreau's thinking about the precarious self and contribute significantly to his understanding about how we can come to cultivate a greater sense of belonging in and reciprocity with the natural world. The death of his brother John in 1842 has long been acknowledged as deeply impactful on Thoreau's thinking and writing about the natural world.[53] But Arsić offers valuable insight into a particular idea that arose from that terrible loss, something Thoreau came to think of as "perpetual grief"—an awareness that infuses all life with significance and becomes the ground of all knowing, including what we can know of the natural world.[54] This idea is also critical to understanding one of Thoreau's most important contributions to contemplative thought and practice: his sense that it is possible, even necessary, for us to "fuse with the natural." Arsić notices and lifts up the radical character of this idea but also interrogates it thoroughly: "Why exactly would a self wish to fuse with the natural?" she asks. "What kind of knowing would self-cancellation generate; what kind of self would be capable of enacting its own cancellation; and finally, *how exactly*, by what practices such a cancellation of the self or such a fusion with the natural might occur?"[55]

There are echoes here of questions that emerge in the testimony of the mystics, where the self seems to disappear or become annihilated in the presence of the Divine. The seriousness of these questions—what happens to the self that opens itself to an annihilating encounter with God? Does it still exist? Can it bear to be "forgotten," as Marguerite Porete puts it, even for the sake of love?—is also evident in Thoreau's thinking about the self that seeks to become united with the natural world. Arsić examines these questions in Thoreau's work with the help of Cora Diamond, in particular her investigation of "epistemological responses to experiences in which 'we take something in reality to be resistant to our thinking it, or possibly to be painful in its inexplicability.'"[56] Arsić's focus here is on what Diamond calls "the difficulty of reality"—"the pain and death of others, for instance—that is so intense that it instantaneously dismantles the analytical categories and concepts we typically use to mediate reality, filling reason with terror, leading it not toward the safety of abstract thinking but to the awe of embodied knowing."[57] How, she wonders, can we resist the temptation to respond to such difficult reality by "avoidance and deflection"—fitting or trying to fit such experience into recognizable categories of thought, something that risks reducing the complicated and bewildering experience of pain into a kind of argument.

This is precisely what Thoreau refuses to do, suggests Arsić, especially in response to his brother's death. He does not "deflect loss and pain into the safety of rigorous argument, even if they can unhinge us; or alternately . . . he accepts the risk of unseating 'ordinary modes of thinking' embedded in attending to the 'difficulty of reality.'"[58] He questions the validity of thought that allows the mind to become separated from the body and pushes through the prejudices of accepted and limiting categories of thought to open up the possibility of an encounter with *reality* itself. "Let us settle ourselves," Thoreau says, "and work and wedge our feet downward through the mud and slush of opinion, and prejudice, and tradition, and delusion, and appearance, that alluvion that covers the globe . . . through church and state, through poetry, philosophy and religion, till we come to a hard bottom and rocks in place, which we can call *reality*, and say, This is, and no mistake . . . . Be it life or death, we crave only reality."[59] To abandon such judgments, values, and traditions, Arsić suggests, is "in fact to abandon everything, to start thinking from scratch, in a different way, in a real way, in a way that would enable thought to settle in the real, in its own body and so to become embodied." And this is precisely what Thoreau seeks to do. Embodied knowing, in the sense that Thoreau understands it, is no vague romantic ideal, but an attempt to respond to what Arsić calls "a pressing epistemological crisis, a crisis generated precisely by the unspeakable loss that reality presses on us. Thoreau's response to the pressure of such loss—a pressure that is nothing other than grief . . . responds to what is unbearable in reality by bearing with it, not by deflecting it."[60]

It is this practice of radical honesty, born of loss and grief, that allows Thoreau to engage in what Arsić calls "an absolute renunciation of the 'I,'" a self-relinquishment that allows things to be what they are, freed from the "demands of our desires or the judgements of our identifications."[61] Here, again, we come up against the profound challenge of learning to behold and respond to the ineffable, a question Sharon Cameron probes with uncommon care in *The Bond of the Furthest Apart*. "How to regard aspects of the world that can't be grasped and that may even leave us speechless?" she asks. Cameron argues that this question possess real ethical significance, for it has the potential to radically reframe our sense of what it means to enter into relationship with other living beings. "What hangs in the balance in such a confrontation," she says, "is how to respond—how to be in relation—to aspects of the world with which we are not affiliated, but from which we are also not estranged, which call to us, the way voiceless things, or things that lack our voice, can be said to call to us to see them, unobstructed by the shadow of categories or ideas."[62] The "eroding boundaries of the personal mind" that result from such relinquishment make it possible to reimagine what it might mean to inhabit the world, or to "perceive our *unity with* the world" as Hadot puts it, without defining or appropriating or dominating it. Being present to experience in a simple, open-hearted way. Lost within it.

Toward the end of *A Week on the Concord and Merrimack Rivers*, a work that, more than any other, reflects the grief at the heart of Thoreau's experience, he recalls a moment he shared with his brother John: "As we sat on the bank eating our supper, the clear light of the western sky fell on the eastern trees, and was reflected in the water, and we enjoyed so serene an evening as left nothing left to describe . . . . All things are as I am . . . I am astonished at the singular pertinacity and endurance of our lives. The miracle is, that what is *is* . . . that we walk on in our particular paths so far, before we fall on death and fate . . . . So much only can I accomplish ere health and strength are gone, and yet this suffices."[63] This suffices. That simple phrase evokes so much: a moment in time that will not come again and that, even in memory, *suffices*. His brother's presence beside him. The clear light of the western sky falling on the eastern trees. The harsh realities of death and fate. There is nothing left to describe: what is *is*. All things are as I am. This suffices.

How much *difficulties* are present here? How much loss? It is not easy to say. Nor does Thoreau attempt to do so. Not directly anyway. Still, this recollection of a moment shared with his brother camping on the Merrimack near Hooksett is shadowed by grief, something Thoreau alludes to later in *A Week*: "our darkest grief has that bronze color of the moon eclipsed" he says.[64] Here grief and the beauty of the world mysteriously coalesce, become part of a unity that can never be fully expressed or understood. Still, it can be lived into, and this becomes the primary focus of Thoreau's attention. In this beautiful openness to the world, and to the life he has been given to live, arises a recognition that he is part of things and that the boundaries that distinguish his life from the life of everything around him cannot be fully known or described ("All things are as I am"). He gives himself over joyfully to what he calls simply a "*natural* life . . . a *purely* sensuous life. . . . Our lives," he says, "should go between the lichen and the bark."[65]

Is it really possible to become this small, this hidden, to disappear this far into the life of things? It is a difficult question. Still, the witness of both mystics and naturalists suggests that without such radical relinquishment, our lives and the life of the world will become utterly diminished. We will be incapable of feeling the life of the world pulsing through us or of responding to other living beings with care and affection. Perhaps this is why the testimony of Aldo Leopold, who opened himself to learning to "think like a mountain," continues to resonate so deeply. So too with Francis of Assisi's *Canticle of the Creatures*, with its beautiful expression of kinship among and between all living beings. And with Hadewijch's sense that we are deeply immersed within a "wild, wide oneness."

Here we find intimations of something long known to us but too often forgotten: it is possible to relinquish your own hard-won identity, to become lost within the wild world and open yourself to becoming part of things. It is possible to become what Freeman House calls a "mindful witness." There is an inescapably personal dimension to such work, rooted in the felt sense of being touched by and subsumed into the living world ("All things are as

I am"). But it is also more than personal: "As our individual mindful witness is turned purposefully outward," House suggests, "we are transformed; we become part of a piece of the planet's own memory. We find individualism, the holy grail of modernity, not diminished but grown into a mature inter-penetration of individualities; we grow larger." We become part of "the whole that promises relief from our unbearable isolation."[66] To become a mindful witness, enlarged by openness and relinquishment, part of the whole: what a powerful and compelling vision of what is possible and necessary for us in this moment. A kind of homecoming.

*　*　*

That day in Bear Harbor: it was a rare moment when I needed nothing, wanted nothing, except the simple enjoyment of the work I had been given to do, the place in which it unfolded—the black-sand beach, the crashing waves, the crying gulls, and the afternoon sunlight pouring down—and the sharing of this work with my daughter. It was, and is still, an emblem of par-adise. And that little house, over which we exercised so much care and im-agination, as if it mattered. Which of course it did and does. More than we knew, I suspect, we wanted to make something beautiful. To begin repairing something precious to us. To create a place where we could learn to live free from care. And open ourselves again to the wild world.

I think also of St. Francis and his own rebuilding project at San Damiano. How he responded so wholeheartedly to the call to rebuild that little church that had fallen into ruins. How, with wonderful naiveté and directness, he began reassembling the stones of San Damiano church: his own little house. And so began the larger work of reparation, including his joyful rekindling of relationship with all living beings. His *Canticle to the Creatures*, composed toward the end of his life, by which time he had spent himself completely on this work of restoration, stands as a powerful reminder of the deep inti-macy with the world that is still possible for us. With disarming simplicity, he invites us to pause and see and feel the truth that every living being is kin to us. And that we can only love and honor God fully *in and through* our love and care for the elements of creation—praise to you, O God, *through* brother sun, *through* sister moon, *through* brother wind and air, *through* sister water. Kinship: no distance between us and every other living being.

And I think of the place Sally Bell and her people called home, marked by blood, but still alive and real, especially among her descendants and among all those who have come to love and cherish this place. And that sacred grove hidden deep in the forest.

After finishing work on our house in Bear Harbor that afternoon, Julia and I decide to see if we can find the grove. It is maybe a mile or so down the Lost Coast trail from where we have been working. It is getting late, but we think we might be able to make it there and back before dark. We set off down the trail into the thick, dense forest, picking our way slowly through the tangled undergrowth. Sword ferns, moss, and lichen blanket the forest floor. All around us, wild orchids, trillium, and columbine. Tan oak, alder, and Douglas fir trees loom overhead, light just seeping through the canopy. It is slow going. But so beautiful and still. We walk along together in silence.

After an hour or so, we descend down a long, steep section of the trail into a kind of glen. Looking up, I realize we are surrounded by redwoods. This is the place: Sally Bell Grove. The trees were not hiding. But we were so focused on the trail in front of us that their sudden presence surprised us. It does not matter. We are here now, standing in this ancient grove, a tiny remnant of what was once a huge expanse of ancient trees along this part of the Pacific Coast. Almost all gone now. Except here in this place. I think of Wendell Berry's words: "There are no unsacred places / There are only sacred places / And desecrated places."[67] The challenge of learning to see everything, every place as sacred. Nothing as unsacred.

Standing here with my daughter, I share with her what I can recall of the story of this place: those who lived here originally, the age of the trees, and the struggle to protect this grove in the 1980s when it was in danger of being lost forever. The Georgia-Pacific Lumber Company had made plans to clear-cut the grove, one of the last stands of virgin redwoods on the North Coast, and an improvised coalition committed to preserving the grove intervened. At a critical juncture in the struggle to keep the clear-cutting plan from being implemented, and as part of a larger effort to recover the character and history of this place, it was decided to rename the grove in honor of Sally Bell. It was a strategic move, aimed at giving the grove a more meaningful and recognizable place in the history of the Lost Coast and inspiring devotion and resistance among those who might not otherwise have felt a stake in this struggle. It helped re-sacralize the place. But it was also part of an effort to bring back into clear view the history and presence of the Sinkyone people here on the Lost Coast. Their story once again became integral to the larger story of the place.[68]

Through a combination of direct action on the ground and in the community and deft legal maneuvering, the ancient grove was saved. An old friend of mine, Sharon Duggan, with whom I have celebrated New Year's at Redwoods Monastery for many years, participated in these efforts—as a lawyer, an activist, and a friend of the International Treaty Council, which represented the interests of the local native communities in this struggle. She described to me the sense of reverence among those who regularly visited Sally Bell Grove: "It was for us a sacred place," she said, "a place of solace and healing and we spent time there whenever we could. But it was also an island—the surrounding hillsides had been completely clear-cut. Loss and the threat of further loss haunted these visits. . . . We were grieving for what this place had once been and clinging to what we hoped this remnant stand still might be . . . . There was one tree in particular, one of the oldest, that drew us. We would gather around the tree in silence, sometimes offering sage for protection. I remember feeling how much meaning this place holds for so many people."

It was also meaningful to the community at Redwoods Monastery and an important part of their own contemplative witness. "The monastery was critical to the effort to protect the trees," Sharon told me. "We had no place to gather, so the sisters let us use their entrance hall as our office, a place to meet and organize and make phone calls. Also, many of the activists working to save the grove stayed at the monastery guesthouse. The community provided us with hospitality. They were in solidarity with our effort." She recalled one of the community members telling her: "This is where we live. This is our home. We need to care for it." But it was more than this: there was also something about the monastery and the way of life in that place that expressed their commitments so eloquently and deeply. "Their attention to the beauty and sacredness of the land was profound," she recalled. "It was so clearly part of their own spiritual practice."[69] Soo too with their practice of entering deeply into silence, into bare, dark, silent, hidden prayer. Prayer arising from a shared longing to rekindle intimacy, to become immersed within the whole, to give embodied expression to the reality of "our *unity with* the world."

That day in Sally Bell Grove, Julia and I stand for long time looking up into the canopy above us. A dense tangle of deep green blocks out almost all the sunlight. Here below it is dark and cool. I think about all that my time in this place has given me and opened up in me. I think also of all those who have come here before me: the Sinkyone people who have long called this place home, who were violently driven away, and who are only now beginning to return to perform the ancient ceremonies and reclaim this place as their own. And I think of those who—moved by their deep devotion to this place and by respect for the long history of the Sinkyone people here—entered this grove again and again and held fast to these trees, fiercely resisting the efforts of those who were seeking to destroy them. The gift I experience here with my daughter comes to me through them. How to respond? How to express my gratitude, my own devotion?

I glance over at Julia. What is there to say? This place and the stories of this place have taken hold of us. I move close to one of the trees near the trail and run my hand slowly along the soft, rough bark. Then, overcoming my own sense of foolishness, I reach out and wrap my long arms as far as I can around the enormous trunk, holding on tight, my face pressed close, breathing in the fragrance: sweet, mossy, and cool. I crane my neck and gaze up and up into that immensity. For a moment, I am lost inside this wild, wide oneness. *All things are as I am. This suffices.*

We remain standing there under those trees, held in the wild beauty of this place, until the light begins to fade. Then we gather our things and begin walking, making our way slowly homeward.

4

The Weight of Emptiness

Argentina, 2013

> There must be places that join pressing weight with emptiness.
> Their density and immobility lend themselves at the same time to
> penetration and to reflection. Thought merges with stones, with
> water, with light.
>
> —Philippe Diolé[1]

The black door. The threshold to *La Sala de Tortura*: the torture chamber. Part of a complex known as La Perla, an infamous detention center located a few miles outside of Córdoba, Argentina. Once a place of unspeakable horrors—many hundreds of human beings, perhaps thousands, were abducted, tortured, and disappeared from here during Argentina's so-called dirty war—now a site of memory and resistance.

The wounds are still raw. And the black door retains its own strange potency all these years later. A friend who was abducted and tortured in a different prison in Argentina tells me that even seeing an image of the door shocked and sickened her.[2]

I stand before the door on this cold autumn day for as long as I can bear it. Here in this place of abysmal suffering and loss, words fail. Thought fails. There is only silence and darkness.

I walk off into the rain that has been falling steadily all morning. Low, dense clouds hang in the sky. The hills are a saturated green, the trees just beginning to flower. It is beautiful. And yet. The utter weight of loss eclipses everything. Everything but grief and emptiness. I am a visitor here and had no part in the terrible events that transpired in Argentina during the period of *la dictadura*. No matter. I am implicated too. Yes, I am a citizen of a country that played a critical role in supporting the regime that perpetrated this genocide. But I am also thinking about what connects me to this place

The Insurmountable Darkness of Love. Douglas E. Christie, Oxford University Press. © Oxford University Press 2022.
DOI: 10.1093/oso/9780190885168.003.0005

now: friendship with those who lived through these events, who even now carry in their memories, in their bodies, the deep scarring that this violent history has left in its wake. Who feel so deeply the emptiness and absence that continue to mark the landscape, culture, and history of Argentina. This place where I now live and which has begun to lay its claim on me.

I am here with a small group of students, who have come from different universities in the United States to live and study in Córdoba, to immerse themselves in the life of the place, to open themselves to the work of accompaniment. Which is why we are here in this place today. One of our Argentine colleagues made it clear to us that we should come to La Perla, that we should open ourselves to this painful part of Córdoba's history. And so we have. But this is no mere history lesson. The residual pain that haunts this place ensures that not one of us is able to maintain a safe distance from what has transpired here. It is a visceral gut punch that has reduced us all to silence.[3]

We pause for a few moments near the entrance. Water is pouring off the roof. A cold, cutting wind. I look down at the glistening red tiles. "They were brought in *con los ojos vendados*" (blindfolded) our guide tells us. "Those who survived later spoke of looking down at the tiles beneath their feet. Just the tiles. They did not know where they were or why they were there. But later they remembered the tiles." Most who entered this space were left with no memories at all. They were disappeared, lost forever. Still, the work of memory persists. The gathering of names, the tiny artifacts left behind, photographs, stories. The work of bearing witness.

I make my way slowly over to the chain link fence that lines the property, where I notice hundreds of tiny, knitted flowers that have been placed there by visitors—emblems of a loss that can never be fully expressed, but also resonant with hope and love. I run my hands along the fence in an effort to locate myself here, if only for a moment. The damp, worn fabric of these little flowers steadies me, opens me up a little, connecting me to all those, living and dead, who have passed through this place.

Still the black door remains, eclipsing any attempt to make sense of what has happened here. I know I must respect this silence and resist the temptation to seek solace in words or stories. Or to assign meaning where there is no meaning to be found. I stand for long moments in that silence, breathing in the damp air looking out over this stricken landscape. Then I turn and rejoin the others.

* * *

What does it mean to enter the abyss, to feel everything known and un-known falling away into nothingness? To find yourself immersed in dark-ness, silence, the void? This was not the first time I had considered these questions. But that day at La Perla, I felt them pierce me in a new way. What possible response could I make to the loss and absence that lay at the very heart of this place? To the reality of the disappeared that had left such a deep wound on this country? I could not say. Still, I felt compelled to try to face this reality, initially out of respect for my Argentine friends who had lived for so long with the enduring effects of this historical trauma, but also as part of my effort to better understand my own place here. What would it mean for me to look into this darkness? Not only as a solitary act but as part of the work of accompaniment, the challenge of learning to stand with others in the darkness?

Struggling with these questions led me to turn my attention again to the work of the fourteenth-century Flemish mystic John Ruusbroec, for whom darkness and loss were indispensable for thinking about the depths and mys-tery of spiritual experience. Also to the work of Michel de Certeau whose writing expressed such sensitivity to the relationships among absence, bro-kenness, and mystical experience. And to the work of certain contemporary Argentine writers who were grappling with what it meant to live with the enduring sense of fragmentation and loss arising from the violence and dark-ness of *la dictadura*. These writers became my companions in thinking about what it meant to be lost in darkness.

Ruusbroec was the first Christian mystic I ever read with any real care or feeling. I was in my early twenties, staying with the Cistercian community at Redwoods Monastery, when I happened upon an English translation of his work in the library. I knew nothing about his writing, nor did I have any context for understanding his work. This, I have come to see, was a gift: I was able to read him with a naiveté and openness that did not constrain either my thoughts or feeling. I remember my growing sense of amazement, but also unease, as I read through *The Spiritual Espousals*, especially in those places where he speaks of the "wild, dark desert of the Godhead." It was strange and bewildering to me, and unlike anything I had ever heard anyone say about God. Later, encountering the work of Pseudo-Dionysius, *The Cloud of Unknowing*, and other writers for whom darkness was an essential part of the grammar of spiritual experience, I began to understand better how and why this language had emerged within the Christian spiritual tradition and why Ruusbroec employed it in the way he did in his own writing. In that moment, however, I was unable to make sense of it intellectually or absorb it in my consciousness in any meaningful way. Still, I never forgot it.

Many years later, living in Argentina, I suddenly found myself facing other darknesses, other losses. And I began thinking again about the darkness at the heart of Ruusbroec's mystical vision, feeling myself in need of its potency and depth. I found a copy of *The Spiritual Espousals* and began reading it again, following him along his mystical itinerary into the depths, and considering the steady, continuous relinquishments that are so integral to that path. Eventually, I reached the place, toward the end of the *Espousals*, where he declares: "This is the dark silence in which all the loving are lost."[4] Extraordinary. Darkness, silence, love, loss: all bound up together. But what kind of experience was he describing? And what happens to the soul who reaches this point of profound intimacy, only to find herself lost in a dark silence? At one time, such questions might have seemed abstract or remote from my experience. Now, they pulsed with urgency and significance. They were questions I was asking myself. About the meaning of the dark silence I had come to encounter here in Argentina. About losses too deep for words. And yes, about love, what it meant to relinquish control and become more open and vulnerable, more capable of sharing in the loss of others.

Such questions are not uncommon in the tradition of apophatic mystical discourse. Still, considering them in this moment, not long after my visit to La Perla, I felt their power in a new way. There was, it seemed to me, a deep resonance between Ruusbroec's vision of dark silence and the loss and darkness of that place, a comparable potency and depth and reach that bound them together. The depth of loss especially. I could not say what this resonance meant or if it meant anything at all. It seemed to exist right out on the edge of things, far beyond anything I could ever hope to understand. But that was part of what held and captivated me about his work. And part of what I sensed as I moved through that space at La Perla. The ineffable. The unsayable. Perhaps the unthinkable. "I'm after whatever is lurking beyond thought" says Clarice Lispector.[5] Yes. In that moment, I was already being drawn deep into a place of unknowing, beyond language, beyond thought.

Which is why Ruusbroec's work impacted me so deeply. It provoked me to search out what was "beyond thought," to consider what it might mean to inhabit this empty, vast space. Not only because of that evocative phrase at the end of the *Espousals*, but because of the way his fluid, densely layered Middle Dutch prose insistently opened up endless vistas, returning always to the dark silence beyond all thought. A place of utter lostness; but also, paradoxically, a place of "unfathomable love." The context in which I now found myself living provoked me to think and read differently, to grapple with the question of what it would mean to open myself to this dark silence. And to consider what it would mean for me to take seriously the idea of an "inward practice of love" that was at the heart of this mystical vision. I needed these apophatic texts in a way I had not needed them before. And not only for myself, but for the sake of the work I was engaged in with others, work that touched often on ineffable experiences of loss and emptiness.

Part of the reality of being *extranjeros* was learning to live with humility and openness and respect for the unknowable. Listening deeply to those with whom we were now sharing our lives. And relinquishing our own ideas about what things meant or whether there was any particular meaning to be found in our experiences. This was especially important in our work with those living in the *villas*, precarious places out on the edge of the social, economic, and geographic world of Córdoba, communities that were often rendered completely invisible and forgotten. It also emerged in our work with students, who sometimes found themselves struggling with their own sense of social-cultural dislocation; seeking to open themselves to their life here in Córdoba in spite of or perhaps through their own bewilderment. And yes, at La Perla, that place of acute, painful and incomprehensible dislocation, where the question of how to face and live in the shadow of absence and loss persisted.

This is also how I found myself drawn again to consider the work of Michel de Certeau, especially his acute analysis of the way loss and absence figure into the production of mystical discourse. In *The Mystic Fable*, he argues that Christianity was born from a sense of absence and loss: "Christianity was founded upon *the loss of a body*," he says. "A founding disappearance." So much of the subsequent mystical tradition, Certeau suggests, is marked by. . . "haunting questions of an impossible mourning: 'Where art thou?' These questions stir the mystics."[6] Certeau focused much of his attention on the losses embedded in the social, cultural, and political upheavals of the sixteenth and seventeenth centuries. But his analysis of loss and mystical thought can, I think, help us think about the convergence of absence and mysticism in other historical contexts, whether fourteenth-century Brabant or in our own historical moment. About whether darkness itself can be understood as a kind of absence or a reflection of that absence, a way of touching into loss or emptiness so far beyond our capacity to express or understand that what remains is, as Ruusbroec says, only "darkness, bareness, and nothingness." Haunting questions of an impossible mourning born of a radical loss of identity and security. A dawning awareness that whatever God might have meant before, whatever conceptual and existential clarity you had counted on to construct your life, you must relinquish it and travel far beyond yourself into an incomprehensible immensity. Absence elicits desire. And desire is endless in its reach and depth.

There is a danger of course of imposing our own sense of lostness, born of historical-political trauma, onto a time and place whose concerns and interests lie elsewhere. Still, it is worth recalling here that Ruusbroec and his little community at Groenendal lived through an historical moment of profound and devastating loss, during which the Black Death reduced the population of the region where they lived by almost half.[7] And while the literary and historical record does not allow us to say with any certainty how profoundly this devastation touched Ruusbroec and his community (there is a record of at least one member of his community having died from the plague), it is important to bear this in mind when assessing the possible meanings found in Ruusbroec's understanding of darkness, loss, and absence. And with the work of other mystics from this period—Beatrijz of Nazareth, Hadewijch of Antwerp, and Marguerite Porete, who also grappled courageously on the far edges of darkness.

A second important insight of Certeau's is his sense of the enduring dialectical tension between *order* and *gaps* in mystical itineraries. He is especially intrigued the way the ostensible order of mystical itineraries (the stages or steps) is always dissolving and giving way to the gaps, to the sense of an *elsewhere* that can never be fully known or possessed. How losing one's way becomes the way itself.[8] This dialectical tension plays out endlessly in Ruusbroec's work. The sense of order can be seen clearly in the itinerary laid out in *The Spiritual Espousals*, where he invites his readers to journey through the three stages of the *active life*, the *inner, exalted, yearning life*, and the *superessential or "God-seeing" life*. Still, the sense of dissolution and lostness that marks the highest or deepest stages of the mystical journey is striking. Here the itinerary gives way increasingly to darkness, the desert, the fathomless. There is no anchor or touchstone. It is an itinerary leading toward ever greater lostness: of those who embark upon this path and enter the darkness, Ruusbroec says: "they want to dwell there / And never come back, / Deep in that lostness."[9]

What is this space of lostness? And what does it mean to enter "the dark silence in which all the loving are lost?" For Ruusbroec, as for so many other mystics in the late medieval period, getting lost meant becoming vulnerable to the power of love, allowing yourself to become utterly overwhelmed by, even annihilated, in love. And discovering in this space a kind of communion, with "all the loving" who are also lost. It is such an unexpected but also compelling vision of community. And one that, here in this place, seemed to me to hold so much promise.

I began to wonder: Could the deep respect for the unsayable embedded in these mystical texts help open up a space for thinking about, encountering, and responding to the ineffable darkness of La Perla and all those other places of collective loss into which we find ourselves continuously descending? And could the witness of those who entered the darkness to stand with the disappeared provide a new way of thinking about the vision of love at the heart of this mystical experience? Could a recovery of this negative space help us kindle empathy for one another and the courage to reimagine and reinhabit what Ruusbroec calls the "fathomless abyss of love."[10]

The Christian mystical tradition has long acknowledged that descent into darkness has an inescapably personal and even solitary quality. Still, there is also a communal dimension to this work that surfaces whenever the question arises regarding what it means to share this darkness with others. And about how this shared loss alters and deepens the meaning of the night. Reading Ruusbroec in Argentina challenged me to think more deeply about these questions and to open myself more wholeheartedly to the darkness through which I found myself moving. It also challenged me to take more seriously the centrality of community, and what it meant to share darkness with others. And it challenged me to summon the courage to lose myself within the "incomprehensible love" pulsing mysteriously within that shared darkness.

* * *

For Ruusbroec, becoming lost is a demanding, dynamic, and often bewildering descent into "darkness, bareness, and nothingness," an annihilation of the self so profound that nothing remains. Nothing, that is, that can be compared to what came before. This descent is undertaken or endured for its own sake—so that one can come to know what it is to exist free and unencumbered in God—but also for the sake of a deep and abiding participation in what Ruusbroec refers to as "the common life." This return or reintegration of the annihilated/reborn self within community—the culminating moment in Ruusbroec's mystical itinerary—is in fact one of the most significant and compelling features of his mystical vision. Darkness, loss, and unknowing become the space within which compassion for and solidarity with the suffering of others is born and lives.

Still, how does this happen? In short, through an ever-deepening relinquishment of the self for the sake of love. In the *Espousals*, he traces this movement into darkness through three distinct moments in the mystical itinerary. In the "active life," there is an awakening to humility (*oetmoedicheit*). In the "inward yearning life," there is an experience of forsakenness (*gelatenheit*). And in the "God-seeing life," there is a descent into lostness (*verlorenheit*). The relationship between and among these ideas is complex and fluid, as is the experience being described. The awakening to *humility* is experienced and engaged at the earlier moments in the mystical itinerary. But what happens here can be understood, and is often experienced as, flowing into and creating the conditions for the deeper and more encompassing sense of *forsakenness*, and ultimately the utterly radical sense of *lostness* that unfolds in the depths of the mystical journey, what Ruusbroec calls "the abyss of namelessness."[11] The dynamic relationship among and between them is also necessary for understanding how the experience of lostness grounds the practice of the common life.

In the "active life," Ruusbroec suggests, one must give careful attention to the example of Christ's humility. How he chose "poor outcast people for His company . . . [and] was lowly and humble among them and among all . . . and was at the disposal of all, in whatever neediness they were." Also, how he "was betrayed, mocked and ridiculed, scourged and struck, condemned through false witness." How "he was," says Ruusbroec, "stripped mother naked [and] . . . endured shame, pain and cold before the whole world; for he was naked and it was cold, and the biting wind blew into His wounds."[12] Such exhortations to pay attention to Christ's humility and suffering were commonplace in late medieval Christian piety. Still, within the context of Ruusbroec's thought, the practice of gazing upon the image of Christ's humility and embodied suffering and considering one's own capacity for entering such suffering mark a critical moment in the contemplative journey. It is here, says Ruusbroec, that a person learns to stand "on his own littleness in the lowest part of himself and acknowledges that he has nothing and is nothing and can do nothing of himself . . . and acknowledges his poverty . . . neediness [and] . . . humility."[13] This awakening to one's own poverty and need, he notes, has other unexpected consequences, not least the deepening capacity to feel "compassion and a common shared suffering with all," or what he describes as "an inward movement of the heart for the bodily and spiritual needs of all."[14] It becomes impossible to think of one's own existence in isolation from others, or to stand aloof from their sickness, poverty, grief and loss. The common life begins to come into view.

How does this initial awakening deepen and grow? Ruusbroec takes up this question in the context of the second moment of the mystical itinerary, the "inward yearning life," by attending to the experience of forsakenness. One senses almost immediately the deepening psychological complexity of this experience in comparison to what has come before. He employs the metaphor of the seasons to trace the soul's journey into summer, where one experiences "sweetness," "blissfulness of heart," "delectable consolation," and "joy." The person who enters this summer of the spirit, says Ruusbroec, "believes himself to be interiorly enfolded by a divine embrace in affective love . . . that he neither can, nor ever shall, lose this well being."[15] But in high summer, as the work of love deepens, the soul experiences a "wounding," a "lasting affliction," "exile." Much of this experience is rooted in the sense of painful distance that remains between what one seeks—utter, modeless unity with God—and what one actually knows. This distance is intolerable.

Still, this sense of affliction becomes even more acute as one moves out of summer and into autumn. Here, Ruusbroec says, "the person goes out and finds himself poor, miserable, forsaken." The "fierce impetuosity of love" is, it seems, gone. Such loss is profound and destabilizing. "This is the farthest point where a person can remain standing without despair," he says. The soul in this place realizes that "he has nothing of himself but indigence . . . and will forsake himself in all things." He "should like as much to be in hell as in heaven."[16] There are echoes here of Hadewijch's audacious claim that "hell is the highest name of love."[17] Or of the exhortation attributed to the Russian monk Startez Silouan: "keep your mind in hell and despair not."[18] The sense of an undoing of the self so complete that no recourse or return seems possible.

There is a sense here of a fundamental realignment of the soul, a growing awareness that old certitudes—even certainty regarding the presence of God's love—are beginning to fall away; an emptying out of all that has previously guided and sustained you. What if anything remains? How, in light of this new reality, do you orient yourself? Where do you stand? Ruusbroec offers a partial response to this question in *The Spiritual Tabernacle*, where he describes how, "according to the manner of humility, which is deeper than all virtues," we "go down, by self-renunciation, to the ground of humble forsakenness. And this ground is empty and one-fold. And in this ground we ourselves *are* humility and essential love and unity and freedom."[19] Here, we begin to catch a glimpse of the open, wild, free space that Ruusbroec associates with the "God-seeing life." But it is costly to enter and inhabit this space. Humble forsakenness, as well as the profound relinquishment that lies at the heart of it, is a kind of death. "We are we are annihilated in humility," says Ruusbroec. And yet, paradoxically, through this "this renunciation of ourselves ... [this] inward hidden going-down, without mode ... we become free and one with the freedom of God."[20] Nothing of the old life remains.

It should not come as a surprise, given the ever-deepening movement into humility, forsakenness, annihilation, and the "inward, hidden going down" that characterize the "active life" and "inward yearning life," that the fundamental character of the "God-seeing life" turns out to be a descent into darkness, the abyss, the desert. Or that loss should stand at the center of this experience. Still, the intensity and extent of this descent into loss is extraordinary. And the sense of destabilization and displacement is so radical and unrelenting that even the extreme language used to describe and evoke it hardly seems sufficient to help us understand into what kind of space the journeying soul has traveled. The itinerary seems to collapse under its own weight; all that is left is an ecstatic absence.

Yes, absence becomes a kind of ecstasy, an overflowing into an immensity that cannot be held or known, that leaves one bewildered and lost. In the *Espousals*, Ruusbroec describes it this way: "And the abyss of God calls the abyss inward; that is, all who are united with the Spirit of God in enjoyable love. The inward call is an overflowing of essential brightness. And this essential brightness, in an embrace of a fathomless love, causes us to lose ourselves and to stream away (from ourselves) into the wild darkness of the Godhead."[21] God's essential indwelling in the simplicity of our spirit, says Ruusbroec, draws us inward and "makes us wander away from ourselves into the abysmal, unknown darkness. There we lose ourselves in the waste void."[22] Elsewhere, he notes: "With respect to being lost in the darkness of the desert nothing is left over . . . . In it, God and all those united (to God) are sunken away and lost, and they can never find themselves again.[23]

Here one encounters the bewildering reversal that so often surfaces in mystical literature and is a defining feature of Ruusbroec's mystical vision: to be found in God is to become utterly lost. Yes, there is deep unity, enjoyable love, and essential brightness. But the experience is too immense, too volatile, too dynamic and unpredictable to allow for any sense of security or permanence. "God and all those united to [God]," says Ruusbroec, are "sunken away and lost. . . . [We] wander away from ourselves into the abysmal, unknown darkness."[24]

There is something so daunting, so forbidding in this vision of lostness. Yes, there is the suggestion of a unity with God beyond ideas or concepts; the promise of an experience of reintegration with the deepest ground of your own life. But what is it to be "sunken away and lost in an abysmal, unknown darkness?" To feel that everything has been taken away: every form of security, every semblance of sure knowledge? Here, it seems, even God is sunken away and lost. And yet there is also an embrace of fathomless love, and it is this love that carries one into the abysmal, unknown darkness.

There is no effort here to soften the starkness of this loss or to suggest that the way into this darkness entails anything less than a complete undoing of the self, the very fabric of reality. But, in an historical moment when exile and loss have become etched so deeply into human experience, and the very question of God's existence or presence in our lives has become so troubled for so many, Ruusbroec's mystical vision of loss resonates in unexpected ways. His radical characterization of absence and loss, including the loss of God, and his sense of darkness as the necessary ground of love, can help us, I think, reimagine what it means to enter and dwell within the immensity of loss for the sake of love.

I think again of Michel de Certeau's important reminder of the social context and meaning of lostness in the mystical tradition. And the significance of solidarity and accompaniment in responding to it. In reflecting on the widespread social fragmentation in the sixteenth and seventeenth centuries, the acute sense of dislocation and loss that arose from it, and the unexpected emergence of mystic thought and practice in response to it, Certeau invites us to consider the connection among and between these realities. Mystics, he says, "do not reject the ruins around them. They remain in them; they go to them . . . their *solidarity* with the collective, historically based suffering— which was demanded by circumstances but also desired and sought after as a test of truth—indicates the place of mystic 'agony,' a 'wound' inseparable from the social ill."[25]

Certeau has in mind here the witness of Teresa of Avila and Ignatius of Loyola, both of whom enacted in their own lives a profound descent into the ruins. But it is not difficult to sense something comparable at work in the world of Ruusbroec and his contemporaries for whom the "social ill" that emerged in the wake of the Black Death was so devastating. And for whom lostness described not an isolated mystical experience but a widely shared social reality. This was also true for Ruusbroec's predecessor in the Flemish mystical tradition, Hadewijch, from whom he learned so much. "I wander in darkness without clarity / Without liberating consolation, and in strange fear," writes Hadewijch in one of her stanzaic poems.[26] And elsewhere: "I am astray inside myself as no one else is."[27] Such expressions of utter displacement resound throughout Hadewijch's work and anticipate the radical lostness that will appear also in Ruusbroec's writings. And while it is not always possible to assign a distinct or specific meaning to these expressions of lostness, or to know whether the one who wanders in such darkness can expect to find any relief from it, they offer sobering reminders of the high cost of embarking upon such a path.

* * *

I have been traveling now for three days across the *puna* in the high Andes of Argentina, with my good friend Rubén Martinez and with two biologists, Ricardo and Patricia, who have invited Rubén and me to join them on this trip. It is an open, often desolate place. Also beautiful and endlessly varied. Huge salt flats shimmering in the late autumn sun; still-active volcanoes dusted with early snow rising on the distant horizon; sudden outcroppings of jet-black basalt; and short grasses, tinted with red and gold and perfectly adapted to this harsh climate, carpeting the hills: *rica rica, coyron, tolar grande*. Occasionally we catch sight of *vicuñas*, shy, tawny-colored deer-like creatures, so graceful in their loping movements across the landscape. Also llamas. And once or twice, we glimpse *Puna Rheas*, the ostriches of the altiplano, whose speed and agility astonish us as they race far into the distance. We keep a close watch for those rare sources of water, *ojos de aguas*, seasonal arroyos, vegas and lagunas, which is where birds are often found. We spot palomas, swallows, Andean teals, gaviotas, and Andean coots, among others. Also flamingos. Or as they are known here: *los flamencos. Los flamencos del altiplano*. This is one of the main reasons we are here: to search them out and monitor their well-being, especially the recently hatched chicks. They will be leaving the altiplano soon, and Patricia and Ricardo, who have been studying them for many years, and who are participating in an international conservation effort on their behalf, need to assess the health of the community, which is under growing threat from increased lithium mining.

The health of the human community is also being threatened. The places through which we travel in our journey south across the altiplano—Tolar Grande, Antofogasta, and some places so tiny and remote that we never learn their names—are being simultaneously buoyed and damaged by the explosion of lithium mining. The world's insatiable thirst for lithium, not least for our smartphones and the burgeoning electric car industry, is putting immense pressure on this fragile ecosystem. And even though some places in the altiplano are experiencing economic benefits, much of the labor comes from outside the area, and the longtime inhabitants of these remote settlements are often left as poor and marginalized as ever.

So too is the water supply here under continuous threat: upward of 65% of the total water supply in this arid region is needed to process the mineral. There is also growing evidence to suggest that lithium extraction harms the soil and causes air contamination. In nearby Salar de Hombre Muerto, locals claim that lithium operations have contaminated streams used by humans and livestock, and which are also necessary for crop irrigation. Across the border in Chile, there have been clashes between mining companies and local communities, who say that lithium mining is leaving the landscape disfigured by mountains of discarded salt and canals filled with contaminated water with an ugly, unnatural blue hue. Tensions over lithium mining are palpable across the altiplano. The landscape is under siege, more and more creating what Ariel Dorfman calls a "wounded desert . . . pockmarked, assaulted, hollowed out."[28]

We arrive at Laguna Grande by late morning after several hours of hard driving through remote country. As we crest the final hill, we see them for the first time: thousands of *flamencos* fanned out across the laguna. From this distance, they are tiny dots. But with our field glasses, we can see them more clearly: luminous, graceful creatures, at home in this hidden corner of the altiplano. No one speaks. After a while, we drive closer to the laguna so that Patricia and Ricardo can get down to work. Counting the hatchlings is particularly important today. In a few weeks, they hope to return and, with the help of friends, ring the young birds for observation and study. Today is devoted to careful observation and preparation for that crucial work. Ruben and I each go our own way, wandering along the shore to observe the birds.

I cannot recall too many thoughts from that day; they came and went like the clouds drifting overhead. Yes, I wondered about the life of these beautiful birds; I tried to learn what I could from Patricia and Ricardo about their life in this place, their habits, their needs, how secure they are from threats to their existence. These threats are many and varied, not least from the increased mining in this part of the altiplano and persistent egg poaching. But mostly, I gave myself over to watching these magnificent animals. What I remember: their stillness, their sudden movement into flight, their reflection as they glide just above the surface of the water, their fierce attention to the hatchlings—silvery gray and downy—in the crèche at the center of the laguna. Also the sudden gusts of wind that ruffle their feathers, the vicuñas grazing on the far shore, the snow-covered peaks in the distance. All of it part of a vibrant, mysterious whole: utterly beyond my capacity to grasp.

Later, we rejoin Patricia and Ricardo for a simple lunch of bread, cheese, mortadella, and fruit on a precipice high above the laguna. We inquire about the progress of their work. They share their excitement about the condition of the birds and their nervousness about the ringing work to come. It will be their first time attempting such work with this particular colony and they will have only one chance at it this season. They need to prepare carefully and get it right. They are hopeful about what this work will contribute to our understanding of the life of these birds, and to their health and well-being.

It is humbling to be in the presence of people whose knowledge of both particular animals and the landscape through which we are moving is so intricate and deep. Sometimes we feel a little sheepish asking them our simple, elementary questions. But we try not to let that get in the way of our learning.

"What do they do at night?" we ask. "Well, they stay right here," says Ricardo, laughing. "What else?" Still, they acknowledge that, even after many years of studying these birds, they have only a rudimentary understanding of their nocturnal habits, of how they spend those long, cold hours, or how they or their hatchlings endure the bitter cold that descends on these high Andean lagunas. It is not easy to say. "And what about their migration patterns?" we ask. "Where to they go from here?" There is a long pause. "We don't really know," says Patricia. "We still don't know that much about it."

An astonishing admission. After eighteen long years of close observation, she answers with a confession of uncertainty. After a few moments she elaborates, telling us what they do know about the migration habits of the birds—at least on some occasions and in relation to certain places. But she admits that there are huge holes in their knowledge of the life of these creatures, that their movements and habits remain mysterious and to a great extent unknown. Will this change? It is clear from listening to them that they hope that their research will deepen their understanding over time. And that this growing understanding will help them work more effectively on behalf of the *flamencos* in their shared conservation work in the high Andes.

There is something else I notice that day talking with Patricia and Ricardo that has stayed with me in the years since: their great respect for mystery, their capacity to accept and even embrace the vastness and unknowability of the world within which these birds live and move. They are scientists of course, and they are always seeking to push back against the unknown and to grasp ever more fully the subtle beauty and intricacy of these animals and the ecosystem they inhabit. But there is also, in their posture toward their work, a fundamental respect for all that cannot be known, for the immensity of the lifeworld of these beings. And there is a deep and abiding sense of humility in relation to the lives of these magnificent creatures. Their commitment to live and work out of that posture of humility and to cultivate a habit of wonder and regard for the vastness of the world within which these birds live and move is so evident and so moving.

I think again of the words of the Acoma poet Simon Ortiz: "We are measured / by vastness beyond ourselves."[29] A reminder of the call to attend, honestly and deeply, to the immensity through which we find ourselves moving. To open ourselves to it, and allow our deepest values to be shaped by it. Sometimes we respond to this call. Still, it seems increasingly clear that there is something in us that shrinks from doing so, that insists on reducing the world to something entirely knowable, something we can control and manipulate. Out on the edges of our consciousness, we sense the presence of what Ortiz calls "the vastness we do not enter." Here on this high desert plateau, the cost of this refusal is becoming ever clearer. But on this day, in the company of Ricardo and Patricia, I begin to sense that it may still be possible to recover a reverence for these *flamencos* and *salares* and *lagunas* of the high Andes. A sense of respect for the mystery of this place. And a renewed feeling for the healing power of emptiness.

"There must be places," says Philippe Diolé, "that join pressing weight with emptiness. Their density and immobility lend themselves at the same time to penetration and to reflection. Thought merges with stones, with water, with light."[30] Places where the most elemental dimension of our existence reveals itself, where we are invited to fall silent and open ourselves again to mystery.

* * *

Here at Laguna Grande, we are only a few miles from the Chilean border. But looking west from where we stand, the border that separates these two nations seem hardly to exist. There is only an open, endless space in which

animals, people, weather systems, and thought move back and forth continuously, following their own mysterious rhythms. So too with other
borders: between the present and the past, between the living and the dead.
These liminal spaces are palpable here in this desert landscape.

"We are not far from Calama, and Chacabuco," says Ricardo, invoking
those notorious places in the Atacama Desert where untold numbers of
human beings were imprisoned, killed, and disappeared during the Pinochet
dictatorship. Most of this story remains untold, untellable. The desert has
swallowed up almost every trace of those who were lost there, and what the
desert has not taken, the military has made sure to erase. History made its
own mark upon this vast landscape, but, in the present moment, it is almost
completely unreadable.[31] Nor is memory stable or reliable. The effort to remember and tell the stories of the disappeared is undermined by the lost
bodies. Still, there are some who remain committed to entering this space of
absence; who continue searching for traces of the disappeared; who bear the
weight of this emptiness.

How to respond to this erasure? What to say or do? We fall silent considering these unanswerable questions. After a few moments, Ricardo asks
us whether we have seen Patricio Guzmán's film, *Nostalgia de la luz?*[32] Yes.
It turns out we have all seen it. And for the next few minutes we fall into
an animated conversation about the film, and our shared feeling of admira-
tion for the steadiness and courage of Guzmán's gaze—into Chile's wounded
past, into the vast silence of the Atacama, and into the farthest reaches of
space. Also for the way the giant telescopes of the Atacama are revealed as
instruments that invite a careful consideration of what it means to exca-
vate the past—the deep past of the universe, but also the more recent past of
Chile's fractured history. We consider together, with the help of Guzman's remarkable film, the question of what it means to see, how to gaze into the past
with all the attention and moral force we can summon, how this contemplative work can serve the ethical-spiritual practice of remembering.

Here in this place, not far from where many thousands of human beings
were abducted, tortured, and disappeared, the moral force of this question
reaches us with renewed intensity, inviting us to consider our own relationship to this place and its troubled history. Rubén and I find ourselves
thinking also about our relationship with the wounded places in our own
country, especially in the deserts of the American Southwest that have become so important to us. Rubén recalls the work he been engaged in for
many years accompanying those who risk crossing the Mexico-US border

into the Sonoran Desert, the terrible cost so many have paid in doing so, and the witness of those who have risked entering those desolate places without water, food, clothing, or legal advocacy. I think of the long history of nuclear testing in the Nevada, Utah, and New Mexico deserts, the enduring impact of fallout on victims throughout that region, and those radical Franciscans who have stood for so many years near the nuclear testing grounds in Nevada in silent protest against the profound violence of this practice. And I recall also the enduring wound of Manzanar, the internment camp on the edge of the Mojave Desert, where thousands of Japanese Americans were imprisoned during World War II, which has now become a site of memory.[33] These places of loss have become unexpectedly present to us here in the stillness of this high Andean desert, enfolded into a constellation of memories whose meaning we are only beginning to consider in this moment.

It helps so much to feel the honesty and depth of Guzman's gaze upon the Atacama Desert and on the mostly invisible traces of history that mark it so profoundly. This is especially true of the care and attention with which he attends to the lives of the women of Calama who have spent most of their lives searching for any faint traces of those lost to them long ago in this vastness. Their search has proven mostly fruitless, but these women have remained tenacious in their commitment to scour these empty, arid places, struggling continuously against the temptation to despair or give up, carried forward on a current of stubborn hope. The acuity of their gaze is its own emblem of hope.

Embedded in their gaze is an undeniable element of nostalgia, a sense of "return pain" that comes from searching out the places of wounding. We see it in the faces of these women, and we hear it in their voices. The pain of loss. The pain of returning again and again to the place of loss, which it turns out is no place. Guzmán is so respectful toward the experience of these women and creates a space at once intimate and expansive where they can give voice to their longing, their grief, their still-pulsing hope. At the same time, he is attentive to certain larger questions about memory and history that emerge from this close focus on the loss of these women. "In *Nostalgia*," he says, "there is, of course, an element of philosophical reflection on the relationship between human life and the life of the cosmos, on human memory and the memory of the stars, of infinity. It's a film about the past, a demonstration that the most important thing in life is the past, because the whole territory of the past is fundamental for people and the future."[34] The deep past of the universe is a constant presence in the film and the gaze of those giant telescopes in the Atacama serve as a continuous reminder of the relative brevity of our own human past. Still, meditating on that deep past, especially in this place, inevitably raises questions about the more recent past and about whether we possess the capacity or will to bear it in mind. Also about the meaning and significance of memory. When this past has been erased, or threatened with erasure, as it has been here, the work of memory takes on a profound nobility and moral value—even if memory itself cannot be fully recovered and the past remains mostly hidden or lost.

There are echoes here of how Colombian writer Juan Gabriel Vásquez speaks of the work of memory as a way of practicing *awareness*. In his novel *The Informers,* a writer named Gabriel Santoro is conducting interviews with a family friend, a Jewish Colombian woman named Sara, who emigrated from Germany in the 1930s and whose story, part of a complex history of the relationship between Colombians and Germans in World War II, he hopes to tell. During one of the interviews, Sara asks him why Santoro wants to write about her life. "I could have said that there were things I needed to come to understand," he says. "That certain areas of my experience . . . had escaped me, generally because my attention was taken up with other more banal ones, and I wanted to keep that from continuing to happen." Santoro seems to only half believe this. But as he continues describing his motivation to her, he eventually gives voice to an idea that he is only now beginning to realize may be at the root of this work: "To become aware: that was my intention, at once simple and pretentious; and to think about the past, oblige someone to re- member it, was one way of doing it, arm wrestling against entropy, an attempt to make the disorder of the world, whose only destiny was a more intense disorder, stop, be put in shackles, for once defeated."[35] An intention at once simple and pretentious: the narrator seems to recognize that giving such weight to the work of becoming aware and thinking about the past and imag- ining that such work can actually change things could be considered naive. And he hesitates to own it fully. When, after all, has anything ever changed through awareness and memory? Still, one can feel in his words a longing to believe it might be true, a hope that the work of remembering will help to create new historical possibilities, forge a different and more just future.

So it is in Guzmán's film. "I am convinced that memory has a gravitational force," says Gaspar Galaz, an astronomer who appears toward the end of Guzmán's film. "It is constantly attracting us. Those who have a memory are able to live in the fragile present moment. Those who have none don't live anywhere."

The fragile present moment. This is where the women of Calama live. And it is their own fierce commitment to remember that allows them to live there. Their voices and their faces give particular, embodied expression to the wounds of loss—in *Nostalgia* and in other testimonials. And even glimpses of hope. "This is what I ask of his murderers," says Monica, one of the women whose husband was disappeared, "to reveal where his remains are . . . I think they could be buried in the desert. The desert is so immense here [*Aquí el desierto es tan inmenso*]. Maybe they left some pieces behind." One of her companions, Juana, has, after many long years of searching, at last recovered traces of her husband Manuel's remains from the desert: "two fragments of vertebrae and a fragment of the spine—three small pieces of Manuel. I waited thirty-eight years to have something of him. I stared at the pieces, and I remembered him. My daughter took my hand and together we touched his remains. There are no words to express what I felt. I was moved to the deepest part of my soul [*Me conmovió hasta lo más profundo de mi alma*]."[36]

Pieces. Fragments of a life that is no longer. But made present again through touch, through memory, through feeling. This is no small consolation. But do these discoveries bring healing? Reconciliation? Peace? None of the women mention these things. Not explicitly. Too much remains unresolved, obscured, broken. And there is also their clear need to focus on the "fragile present moment." The compelling need to look as carefully as possible at what remains, to touch, to remember. "There are no words."

The recovery of these "pieces" from the immensity of the desert seems for some only to have sharpened of the pain of their loss. Vicky, another of the women of Calama who has spent most of her adult life searching the desert, notes: "After thirty-eight years, I continue to maintain the hope that someday, roaming in the desert, I will find the rest of Jose's mutilated body and the other men too. I will be able to mourn those beloved bones and give them a proper burial. I have spent more than half my life trying to understand the reasons for such cruelty—and why they continue to hide the truth, denying the men the chance to rest in peace and condemning us to be eternal desert walkers [*las eternas caminantes del desierto*]."[37] It is not easy to listen to the voices of these women, to feel the depth and extent of their lostness, or to know how to respond. Still, I am grateful for their presence here in this high desert place and for their courageous witness. There is such power in their refusal to cease gazing into the immensity, in their capacity to inhabit their own lostness, in the depth of love that grounds their work, and in their invitation to others to accompany them in this work.

* * *

Can the commitment to love be purified and deepened in such places of emptiness and unknowing? The journey into the high desert of the Andes has given this question new weight and meaning for me. I think of the stillness and depth of Ricardo's and Patricia's regard for those *flamencos*. The commitment of the women from Calama to wander endlessly in the desert in search of traces of their lost beloveds. And back in Córdoba, the challenge of slowing down and paying attention to the lives of those with whom we share this place; and to my own life. And to my own life. Learning to accept and even embrace the depth of unknowing that grounds every aspect of our lives and opening ourselves to what is revealed in that dark silence.

It is precisely here, I begin to see, that so much of the enduring value of the late medieval Flemish mystical tradition is to be found. This is especially true of its profound honesty, its refusal to say with any certainty what happens to us when we are plunged into the depths, or what loss and absence *mean*, or if *any* meaning can be assigned to them. The extreme negations at the heart of this mystical traditions serve as a caution against placing too much confidence in our assertions about experience. Still, it would be misleading to suggest that no meaning whatsoever can be found in these places of emptiness. Or that nothing can come of becoming lost inside such immensity. There is always the hope, often faint, other times more proximate, of finding what Ruusbroec calls "the kernel of love which is hidden from us in darkness, in fathomless unknowing."[38]

The desert and the experience of becoming lost in the desert is, for Ruusbroec, critical to this hope. Nor is he alone among late medieval mystics in employing the imagery of the desert to explore the question of how the soul comes to know God; Hadewijch, Meister Eckhart, Mechtild of Magdeburg, and others also used this imagery to probe the furthest reaches of the soul's experience of God.[39] But Ruusbroec offers us a particularly clear-eyed and compelling vision of the desert as a locus of love. And in doing so, he helps to show how the experience of loss and emptiness can unexpectedly nourish and open up the space of love. In *The Spiritual Espousals*, Ruusbroec describes the Godhead itself as "a dark stillness and a wild desert."[40] Elsewhere he envisions "our created essence" as "a wild, waste desert, wherein God lives," a reminder of the profound unity between God and the human person, a shared essence or being. A shared desert.[41] In Ruusbroec's mystical vision, the human person is endlessly expansive, open, wild. As Paul Mommaers describes it: "The innermost depths [of the person] are in no sense a secluded, compact essence. Rather, by its very nature the ground of the human is groundless. It is always and in each individual sheer openness to the most all-encompassing reality—God. . . . By nature, we *are* a ceaseless relationship with God."[42] Which also means, by extension, that we are a ceaseless relationship with one another. Still, this relationship can only be realized or fulfilled by allowing ourselves to become "lost in the darkness of the desert" and there becoming "one with God in the fathomless abyss of God's love."[43] In that desert, Ruusbroec insists, "we must wander modelessly and without manner. For we cannot come out of our essential being into our super essential being otherwise than with love."[44]

The idea of the desert as a space in which the human person realizes an expansive and encompassing experience of love is one of the critical insights of Ruusbroec's work. But its importance lay not only in what it says about the capacity of individual persons to become more open to the reality of love but also in what it suggests about our capacity for realizing love in community. To become lost in the desert requires, on the most fundamental level, becoming freed from illusory ideas of self-sufficiency and the narrow bounds of ego-identity that make it impossible to live in openness to love. "We lose ourselves in the waste void," says Ruusbroec. "We become empty within . . . unwrought from ourselves . . . lost to ourselves."[45] It is this relinquishment of the narrowly bounded self, this radical loss of ground, that allows us to become open to a "naked love in emptiness . . . immersed in love."[46] There is profound *enjoyment* in this experience, says Ruusbroec, like standing before a "becalmed, glowing, motionless fire" wherein "all things [are] burnt away." *All things.* Including the self or the small, constrained thing we have for so long considered the self to be. Naked love in emptiness is, he suggests, utterly unbounded: "wild and waste as wandering, for there is no mode, no trail, no path, no abode, no measure, no end, no beginning, or anything one might be able to put into words."[47] Love comes to fruition in an endless, ineffable, expansive desert.

What does this mean in practice? And what does it mean to share this desert space with others? For Ruusbroec, it means above all, to "follow love and go out of ourselves."[48] Into the "common life"—the very ground of our existence in God as a shared, communal reality. "Union with God is particular to each one who receives God in love," he says, "and it is common to all those who love, for there we all come together in one."[49] The common life, rooted in love, allows for no separation between or among us. Nor does it allow us to remain aloof from the life and needs of the other. "The greater and nobler a person is [in love], the more he is common to all who have need of him, corporally and spiritually, says Ruusbroec."[50] The common life flourishes in the desert. "In this wild, wide oneness / The Poor in spirit live united," says Hadewijch.[51] Here the experience of unity with God in love becomes the ground within which a deeper, wider unity in love with all can be realized and practiced.

The work of translating these ideas into our own idiom is not always easy. Still, it can make such a difference. Little by little, these ideas have become woven into my understanding and experience of my life here in Córdoba. Especially the challenge of learning to inhabit an open, empty space where I can attend to the lives of others. Letting go of constraining assumptions about who I am or what I am doing here. Often this means simply allowing myself to receive the kindness and hospitality that are so generously offered to me here, that remind me again and again that I am not only an *extranjero*, estranged from this place and this culture, but at home, part of an emerging community. And it means learning to be present to others, listening carefully and deeply to their stories, opening myself to the beauty, complexity, and pain of their lives. Including the incomprehensible loss of the disappeared. Learning to pay attention. Making space, leaving room for silence and emptiness. Entering the desert--within the rhythms of our daily life, but also in deeper solitude and silence.

* * *

Sometimes the longing to enter this silence, this place of unknowing, is itself incomprehensible. Nor is the meaning of what happens to you there always legible. Even if it feels absolutely necessary.

This is how it seemed to Portuguese writer Fernando Pessoa, for whom the longed-for immensity was not a vast desert but simply the night sky above his beloved Lisbon: "Oh, night, in which the stars masquerade as light, oh night, equal only to the Universe in magnitude, make me, body and soul, part of your body, and let me lose myself in mere darkness, make me night too, with no dreams to be as stars to me, nor longed-for sun to light the future."[52] *Make me night too.* What a strange, haunting plea: to dream of becoming lost in darkness, without a sun to light the future. A difficult, even bleak image. And yet, there is also something beautiful and mysterious here, something close to that radical identification with immensity that J. M. G. Le Clézio suggests can sometimes arise without warning for those who enter the desert: "Perhaps," Le Clézio writes, of one of the nomadic figures in his novel *Desert*, "he was no longer waiting for anything, no longer knew anything, and now resembled the desert—silence, stillness, absence."[53] The borders between self and immensity become unexpectedly porous, and subjectivity itself becomes open, endless, expansive. I think also of the deep bewilderment that Clarice Lispector suggests often arises in the struggle to locate yourself within your own life and within a world that seems to withhold its meaning: "Everything is so fragile. I feel so lost. I live off a secret that glows in luminous rays that would darken me if I didn't cover them with a heavy cloak of false certainties. May the God help me: I am without a guide and it is dark once again."[54]

These expressions of the self as open, boundless, and fragile, recognizable only against an endless horizon or in the depth of night, hint at a complex, varied, and widely shared preoccupation among certain modern and contemporary writers to rethink identity in terms that take seriously the particular losses, both personal and collective, of our historical moment. This is often a deeply ambiguous experience—the exhilarating sense of living in a way that is less constrained and constraining, where the boundaries are not so sharply defined, the horizon not so close, existing in close proximity to something that feels like a kind of death, a descent into the darkness and emptiness so utter and complete that you yourself *become* the night, become lost in the inexhaustible space of the desert. And there are sometimes uncanny echoes here of those older expressions of loss found among the mystics—the sense of wandering in a "waste void," becoming "empty within . . . unwrought from ourselves . . . lost to ourselves."

But what if you cannot get lost? What if you cannot access the deep freedom to which Ruusbroec and other mystics allude when they speak of getting lost in the desert or the deep silence of the night? What if the harsh facts of contemporary historical existence make such an experience impossible? The Chilean writer Alejandro Zambra speaks to just this kind of experience in his spare and haunting novel *Ways of Going Home*. Here we encounter a sustained reflection on what it means for members of the author's generation—the children of those who were kidnapped, tortured, exiled, and killed by members of the Augusto Pinochet regime—to try to live within their own history, something that many find difficult or impossible to do. There are too many blank spots on the map too many places where the spectral presence of the wounded or killed or disappeared or complicit obscure the vista—whether of the past or the future. The simple experience of wandering through a landscape unmarred by historical trauma is no longer possible. Nor, it seems, is it possible any longer to become lost.

Last night I walked for hours. It was as if I wanted to get lost down some unknown street. To get absolutely and happily lost. But there are moments when we can't, when we don't know how to lose our way. Even if we always go in the wrong direction. Even if we lose all our points of reference. Even if it begins to grow late and we feel the weight of morning as we advance. There are times when no matter how we try to find out what we don't know, we can't lose our way. And perhaps we long for the time when we could be lost. The time when all the streets were new.[55]

The utter lostness of not being able to get lost anymore. When the traumas, physical, psychic, and social are too deep and the way out into the unknown has been blocked.

It is not easy to respond to such testimony or to know whether language or stories can speak to it in any meaningful way. This, it seems, is part of what apophatic spiritual practice means in this historical moment: acknowledging the depth of our loss and relinquishing any sense that its meaning or significance can ever be fully articulated or grasped. Still, the challenge and the call to attend carefully to the particularity of loss—the way it becomes incarnated in actual bodies, in history—remains. Paying attention. Becoming aware. Not looking away. Not allowing ourselves to be persuaded that the losses do not matter. Naming, documenting, and engaging all that has been lost. Recovering the gravitational force of memory.

Still, what if the history we seek to remember contains only gaps or scars where those bodies once resided, scars that can never fully be healed? How do we learn to live in relation to those scars, acknowledging and honoring them, even as we struggle to inhabit the absence they have created? How can we make visible all that has been rendered invisible? How can we learn, again, to see?

Gregory of Nyssa long ago described the ground of apophatic spiritual practice as a "seeing which consists in not seeing," a reminder that the mystery we seek to behold "transcends all knowledge, cut off on all sides by incomprehensibility, as by a kind of darkness."[56] A cautionary word, born of respect, against trusting too much in the mind's capacity to grasp what is ultimately unknowable (at least in conventional terms). But also part of an exhortation to gaze more deeply, more honestly at those dimensions of our own experience that remain shrouded in darkness. A reminder of the need for a different kind of seeing, unconstrained by categories of thought that limit or distort the truth of what we behold.

Czeslaw Milosz argues for something similar to this in his 1980 Nobel lecture, reimagining the ancient contemplative task in terms that allow for a deeper engagement with our complex and troubled historical experience:

"To see" means not only to have before one's eyes. It may mean also to preserve in memory. "To see and describe" may also mean to reconstruct in imagination. A distance achieved thanks to the mystery of time must not change events, landscapes, human figures into a tangle of shadows growing paler and paler. On the contrary, it can show them in full light, so that every event, every date becomes expressive and persists as an eternal reminder of human depravity and human greatness. Those who are alive receive a mandate from those who are silent forever. They can fulfill their duties only by trying to reconstruct precisely things as they were by wrestling the past from fictions and legends.[57]

These words emerged from the ashes of World War II, and their power and meaning derive in no small part from the particularity of the suffering that marked that historical moment. Still, there is something deeply resonant in the moral challenge expressed here, a call to consider what it will mean for us to reconstruct the "events, landscapes, human figures" of our own time that are already at risk of disappearing forever into the shadows of the past. This commitment to see, even (or especially) if what one longs to see remains opaque and obscure and painful, is now increasingly part of what it means for us to practice spiritual honesty.

Living in Argentina brought this home to me in a new way. The proximity of La Perla, the ongoing witness of Las Madres de la Plaza de Mayo, and the intense preoccupation with the fate of *los desaparecidos* among many persons I came to know during my time there challenged me to reconsider my relationship to this acute and seemingly unrepairable loss and absence. What would it mean for me to turn my gaze toward this reality and not look away, even if it meant entering and inhabiting the darkness myself? What would it mean for me and for those who share this space with me to make such seeing the ground of our effort to practice accompaniment, of our own commitment to respond to the mandate we have been given from those "who are silent forever?"

Such questions create their own space of unknowing, and a recognition that any response will be inadequate. Still, living in Argentina and feeling the increasingly strong purchase of these questions on my soul led me to listen more carefully than I had before to certain voices—especially among contemporary Latin American poets and writers—whose conscience has been formed under the long shadow of dictatorial repression (a shadow that continues to this day to impact the life of the community), and who seemed to me to have something important to contribute to an emerging "mysticism of absence."[58]

Increasingly I have come to see the work of such writers as critical to the larger moral-spiritual task of engaging loss, whether on a personal or collective level. And critical to the work of thinking about what it means to inhabit absence and grapple with the palpable loss of meaning—including meaning we associate with the mystery of God—that so often arises from such experience. To name this loss and absence and to inquire into its impact on our shared life can become its own spiritual practice—born of the ethical imperative to listen to and stand with those whose voices have been ignored or silenced.[59] This brings such work into unexpected alignment with one of the ideas that Michel de Certeau has suggested is crucial to thinking about and responding to mystical literature: the need to pay attention to the gaps, silences, and places of suffering. The insistent attention to humility, affliction, and lostness that one encounters in the work of figures like Marguerite Porete, Hadewijch, and Ruusbroec is part of a larger pattern one sees repeated endlessly in mystical literature: the abyss as a privileged place of encounter with the sacred, and the sacred conceived of and experienced as a site of loss. So it often is with contemporary literary accounts arising in the aftermath of loss: gaps, silences, and suffering opening up a space for considering new questions about the meaning of absence in our lives.

* * *

Sometime during 2013, not long after I arrived to live in Córdoba, I happened upon Patricio Pron's beautiful, raw, and honest reflection on loss—*My Fathers' Ghost Is Climbing in the Rain*. My experience at La Perla was still fresh and I was struggling to situate the reality of *los desaparecidos* into some kind of framework of meaning, wondering whether it was even worth trying to do so. Pron's novel, shaped by its own careful attention to the gaps and silences in Argentine life following the period of the dictatorship, helped me begin to sense the extreme difficulty of trying to locate oneself within this traumatic reality. It helped me to slow down and pay more careful attention to all that could not be said or known but whose presence was felt everywhere. The book became a touchstone for me, and I found myself returning to it again and again during the time I lived in in Argentina.[60]

Pron is a member of the generation of Argentinos who grew up after the period of *la dictadura*, whose parents struggled and suffered through the violence and fear and displacement during that time (some of whom were themselves disappeared, never to return). He, along with so many others of his generation, is concerned with asking what it means to live in the aftermath, and whether it is possible to construct a life made up of absence and scars. The novel's protagonist has been living away from Argentina, distancing himself from such questions; not surprisingly, he suffers from an acute sense of psychological fragmentation whose precise sources he cannot easily locate. Returning home to Argentina, he finds himself drawn into his father's belated efforts to engage his own past, long-obscured by the violence and terror of *la dictadura*.

The story emerges in fragments: a man his father had known who had been thrown into the bottom of a well and left to die; a young woman who had sought his father's help in a moment of crisis but had been left to fend for herself and who eventually disappeared; the pain his father lives with still, born of a sense of having lived through a moment that could have and perhaps should have unfolded differently, and his remorse, his desire to make reparation for what he did and failed to do. This is not the son's story, nor is it his responsibility. Not directly. But in thinking about his father's story, he is brought to a new awareness of how much he and his mother and so many of their contemporaries suffered during this time. How much they lost. And he begins to see and feel more deeply than he has done before the utterly bleak climate of his own childhood, something that haunts him still.

The powerlessness in the face of everything that was happening and the fear, which as a child I'd thought my parents didn't feel and yet they felt much more than I'd thought: they lived with it and fought against it and held us in it like one holds up a newborn in a hospital room so that the baby becomes one with the air that surrounds him and will surround him and therefore lives; and the lack of an organization, which in those years meant a lack of boundaries and of direction and of binding ties, and friends who couldn't be seen again because of the risk that such meetings would be interpreted as a return to the struggle, and the loneliness and the cold.[61]

The simple effort to recall the powerlessness and fear that marked his parents' lives and that eventually seeped into his own brings with it a renewed sense of dread. Also feelings of acute vulnerability that arise from recalling and feeling anew the "lack of boundaries and of direction and of binding ties," the "struggle, and the loneliness and the cold." Here, surfacing again in the process of recollection, is the harsh climate of insecurity where his sense of the world was formed.

Or perhaps it would be more accurate to say unformed or deformed: "Something had happened to my parents and to me and to my siblings," he says, "that prevented me from ever knowing what a home was or even what a family was, though everything seemed to indicate I had both."[62] A bewildering sense of displacement, the inability to recover a past or imagine a future even in the midst of apparent normalcy and stability. A feeling of homelessness. Appearances are deceptive. The veneer of normalcy and stability is undermined continuously by the force of the buried but not forgotten past. It destabilizes every effort to find a secure place to stand. This, Pron's narrator observes, is "the fate of the disappeared, of their family members and of their attempts to repair something that couldn't be repaired."[63]

There is an awful finality to that idea, a sense of utter bleakness and hopelessness. Still, it captures something real and undeniable that must find its place in an emerging grammar of loss: the sense of what it is to live with brokenness. Such a grammar must somehow be both particular and expansive, able to encompass experience that is utterly personal but also widely shared and situated within a social and political context that is still unfolding, still unfinished.

No one who has witnessed or participated in the marches on *El Día de la Memoria por la Verdad y la Justicia* can doubt the deep commitment among Argentinos to seek justice and reparation for the crimes committed during the period of *la dictadura*. Those efforts continue even now and have yielded important legal settlements against the perpetrators. They have also led to the discovery and return of many children born during that period, whose parents were killed by the state, and who were adopted by military families. Only now, many years later, are these children learning their true identities and returning to their families of origin. These efforts at reparation and healing matter. And they are ongoing. Still, as Pron's work makes clear, living in the aftermath of this historical trauma brings with it a painful awareness that what has been broken can never be completely repaired or healed. There is no escape from the sense of loss and absence and dread that has been left in the wake of these events. It retains a formidable and enduring power. And it must somehow be incorporated into the lives of persons and communities.

The question of how to face and respond to the debilitating power of this trauma haunts Pron's novel. Perhaps, he suggests, it can only be faced indirectly and on a small scale. At least initially. "My father," the protagonist notes, "had started to search for his lost friend and I, without meaning to, had also started shortly afterward to search for my father. This was our lot as Argentines. And I wondered whether this could also be a political task, one of the few with relevance for my own generation"[64] It is difficult to miss the note of betrayal and disillusionment in these words, born of the recognition of how little the often-corrupt political system has done to create the conditions for true healing and reconciliation. But there is also something else: an expression of stubborn hope in the possibility of a different kind of politics born of personal regard and moral responsibility toward the other.

There are echoes here of Emmanuel Levinas's insistence that all politics, all ethics is rooted in the fundamental obligation to always keep the *face* of the other before you: "the face speaks to me and thereby invites me to a relation," says Levinas.[65] By virtue of the deepening sense of relationship and intimacy with the other kindled by this practice, there also arises a renewed commitment to practice accompaniment and work for the transformation of unjust structures. Accompaniment in this sense is more than a set of values; it is an embodied spiritual practice through which you seek to stand with and respond to the life of the other. Even if, or perhaps especially if, the other has somehow become lost to you. As, in this case, where father has become lost to son and son to father. A personal, particular loss that opens out onto something immeasurably larger and deeper, a loss that has also befallen so many others. Searching for the lost other as part of a "political task" means always and in every case attending to its personal character—seeking out the face of the one *you* have lost—but also recognizing this search as fundamentally communal. "A loss that might seem utterly personal, private, isolating," suggests Judith Butler, "furnishes an unexpected concept of political community, even a premonition of a sort of nonviolence."[66]

Such work requires tremendous risk. It means entering empty places and dark silences that may in the end remain unknowable, impossible to navigate. Working to understand how attention to this emptiness, silence, and darkness can be lived into, can become incorporated into a practice of solidarity. A contemplative practice that, to paraphrase Certeau, can become part of a tactic of resistance.[67]

Pron's protagonist gives eloquent testimony to the power of renewal that may yet be realized through such sustained attention to darkness and loss. Memory has a crucial role to play in this renewal, even if the memories themselves are incomplete and fragmentary and can never be fitted together again into a coherent story: "I . . . knew that this story had to be told in a different way, in fragments, in whispers and with laughter and with tears, and I knew that I would be able to write it only once it became part of the memories I'd decided to recover, for me and for them and for those who would follow."[68] A personal story, told in fragments and whispers. It does not feel like much. And in a way it isn't. But the modesty of the effort takes on a different meaning when understood as a response to the "mandate from those who are silent forever"; to "see and describe"; to "reconstruct precisely things as they were by wrestling the past from fictions and legends." The work of bearing witness, however fragmentary and partial that witness is, has its own inherent power and dignity. "To see and describe." There is a contemplative character to this witness, born of a desire to gaze into the abyss of suffering and loss and not turn away. To listen carefully and closely enough to the stories of loss that you can begin to feel them as your own.

Can such contemplative witness contribute to the work of reparation? Given the depth and extent of the loss, it is difficult to see how. But the narrator, who has been grappling for so long with the harsh logic of his own painful losses, slowly arrives at a different way of formulating the question. The fragments and whispers, he begins to see, possess their own unexpected spiritual power.

> As I thought all this, standing beside the telephone, I noticed it had started to rain again, and I told myself I would write that story because what my parents and their comrades had done didn't deserve to be forgotten, and because I was the product of what they had done, and because what they'd done was worthy of being told because their ghost—not the right or wrong decisions my parents and their comrades had made but their spirit itself— was going to keep climbing in the rain until it took the heavens by storm.[69]

There is such deep humility in this orientation: a willingness to inhabit a space of uncertainty and doubt, to reckon honestly with loss, to feel the pain of that loss. Also a simple, halting, effort to bear witness from the place of loss. And love—for his parents and their comrades especially. But the power of this love does not stop there. It opens out and out into frayed but still beautiful fabric of the larger community. It is the audacity of this vision of love that moved me most deeply about Pron's narrative when I first read it while living in Argentina. And it moves me still.

The fundamental question posed by the novel—how to locate ourselves amid all the losses that haunt our lives and how to reimagine community in light of these losses—is, it seems to me, one of the essential questions of this moment. It is also close to the question that so preoccupied late medieval Christian mystics like Ruusbroec and Hadewijch about whether it is possible discover within the abyss of darkness a shared ground of love. They testified to the paradoxical power of loss to generate a renewed sense of community, and believed that the "common life" can only take hold in an abyss of dark silence.

* * *

I am standing near the *quincho* behind our house tending to a fire. This evening we are hosting an *asado* for friends, colleagues, students, and members of the community, and it has fallen to me to prepare the coals for the meal. My friend Diego Fonti, a philosopher who teaches for us in the *Casa* program, joins me, offering a few tips about the art of the *asado*. He asks me how I am doing, how *we* are doing—Jennifer, the children, the students, all of us. He knows we have been in Argentina barely two months and are still finding our footing here; that we are still feeling a little lost. His kindness touches something in me, and I begin describing how things are unfolding for us, what it feels like for us to be here, how difficult it has been finding our way, or even understanding what we are doing here. So much of our competence, our confidence, our identity, has been stripped away and this has been at times an utterly bewildering experience.

I turn back to the fire and prod the leñas—the coals are starting to glow. Standing there with Diego, I am also conscious of something else: the extraordinary feeling of being embraced by the community here in Córdoba, an intimate and joyful experience. I have not yet tried to articulate any of this, and I still have little understanding of how our deep sense of loneliness and dislocation can coexist with a burgeoning experience of being welcomed into this community. But this rich, dense experience is slowly beginning to surface in language. And Diego is a good and sympathetic listener. He nods and smiles as if he understands. I think he *does* understand. An unexpected touch of kinship.

More guests are arriving for the *asado*, and soon I will need to begin cooking. But we continue our conversation by the fire a little bit longer. He asks me about my experience at La Perla earlier that day. I hesitate, unsure of whether to say anything, or whether I have anything to say. But his generosity in opening up this space moves me to try. And I find myself describing to him, haltingly and with such acute awareness of the limits of language, some of what has stayed with me. The abysmal silence of the black door. The fragmentary stories of *los desaparecidos*. And the presence of others, keeping vigil together in that dark silence.

I also share with him questions that were just beginning to form in my mind: what will it mean for me to summon the courage to avoid becoming a mere bystander in relation to what has transpired there? To acknowledge the culpability of my own country for the events leading up to the disappearance and death of thousands in Argentina? Also my own responsibility (however indirect) for all those acts of violence perpetrated by my country—here and elsewhere—for which there has never been any recourse or restitution? The whole immense reality of it all. Diego listens carefully as I struggle to give voice to my anguish. He pauses a long time before responding: "Look, my friend," he says, "when it comes to this kind of thing, my dead are your dead. And your dead are my dead. We share this world. We share this experience."

That moment of kindness, the gift of my friend's invitation to stand with him in our shared anguish, has remained with me. So much about this experience remains unknowable, incommensurable. But there is also our capacity for sharing experience, including the experience of loss and dislocation, what Ruusbroec describes as "compassion and a common shared suffering with all." Sometimes we are able to do this through language and storytelling. But often the immensity of experience reduces us to silence. We feel again the weight of emptiness. The heaviness of existence, the seeming impossibility of ever being able to climb out from under it. But sometimes there is an unexpected gift of coming to behold our own loss and estrangement as a place of encounter, in "the dark silence in which all the loving are lost." A place of darkness and silence that emerges as the ground of solidarity and community.[70] In such moments, we realize that we are already wandering in the dark, deep in the lostness, together.

5

On the Dark Path

Poland, 2016

They hasten, those who have glimpsed that truth, on the dark path.
Untraced, unmarked, all inner.

—Hadewijch of Antwerp[1]

We have to look closely to see it: her name, preserved on microfiche, emerging from the shadows, preserved on microfiche. Sabina Landsberger-Zerkowski. Deported to Westerbork. Then to Sobibór—10.3.43. These words are hand-written on a small card, an artifact of the Nazis' fanatical commitment to re-cord and document their efforts to exterminate all Jews from Europe. A small card. A few words only. But they contain information crucial to the quest that has brought us to this place. We now know where she was sent. We now know where she died. It is a terrible moment of discovery.

I am standing in a cramped room in the Jewish Historical Museum in Amsterdam with my old friend Ralph Black. He has come here in the hopes of pulling back the veil that has long obscured his understanding of what became of his great-grandmother Sabina. And I am accompanying him. Now we know: the words on the card leave no doubt. She was taken from her home in Amsterdam, held for a time in the Dutch Theatre, then sent first to a concentration camp at Westerbork, two hours northeast of Amsterdam, and from there transported by train to the far eastern edge of Poland. To Sobibór. There she was murdered by the Nazis, together with at least 167,000 others from Poland, France, Germany, the Netherlands, Slovakia, and France who were all brought to that place to die. Suffocated in gas chambers fed by the exhaust of a large gas engine. Then dropped into holes in the frozen earth.[2]

We stand for several long moments looking at that card. No one speaks. Not Ralph, me, or the museum curator who has unearthed the card. It is too much to take in. There is nothing to say. Eventually, after a few moments, we

The Insurmountable Darkness of Love. Douglas E. Christie, Oxford University Press. © Oxford University Press 2022.
DOI: 10.1093/oso/9780190885168.003.0006

thank the curator and make our way out of the building into the chill of this autumn afternoon. Ralph asks if he can have some time alone, and we agree to meet back at the hotel in a few hours. Later that evening, over dinner, we begin the painful process of trying to bring to language what we discovered earlier that day: a halting, back-and-forth conversation, marked by hesitation and long silences. Our thoughts and conversation drift here and there, leading us eventually to the question of what kind of response we can make. At least in this moment. It soon becomes clear: we will go to Sobibór.

This moment contains an entire universe, but it is haunted by an absence. And a huge silence. Later, I read Edmond Jabés's emphatic declaration in *The Book of Margins*: "God's triumph: All Absence means presence to nothingness, means awakening to the void."[3] And I think back to that moment in Amsterdam. Those hastily scrawled words on a small card. Then: a perfunctory but potent notation, recording and ensuring Sabina's imminent deportation and death. But now? I am not sure. A sign of something, perhaps, but what exactly? Those few words: her death sentence, and clear evidence of where she died. But also a haunting sign that she once lived, was alive when those words were written. Something rather than nothing. Enough in that moment to set us moving together toward eastern Poland. Still. Absence remains. As for "presence to nothingness" or "awakening to the void," I cannot easily say what these ideas mean, or might mean, for me or for my friend. But I so appreciate the uncompromising honesty of Jabés's words and the silence toward which they seem to gesture. A caution against saying or trying to say too much. These words also help clarify what was being asked of me in that moment, in a sense the only thing that is being asked of me: loving my friend and brother, accompanying him to a place of incomprehensible darkness.

Several months earlier, we had made the initial decision to set out on this journey together, to meet in Amsterdam, and learn what we could about Sabina's fate. But it was neither simple nor easy. We were sitting under a weeping willow tree on a beautiful summer evening talking, when Ralph began describing to me his visit to the Dutch Theatre in Amsterdam earlier that year and the astonishing discovery he had made: his great-grandmother Sabina's name was listed on a wall memorializing the Dutch Jews who had been held prisoner there by the Nazis, then deported and killed. An utterly unnerving discovery that he had been thinking about ever since. Was there more to discover? He wasn't sure. And he was hesitent to probe further. How much more did he really want to know? I recall that moment so clearly: the stillness of the evening, Ralph's carefully measured words, his uncertainty about what if anything he should do next. Whether he should pick up this thread. Or perhaps leave it. My dear friend, suddenly facing this terrible abyss.

Later that evening, I found him alone in the kitchen. What if we went together?, I asked. To Amsterdam. To see what we could discover. He looked up at me. Can I think about it? Of course. A few weeks later he called and asked me if I was still willing to go. And that is how we found ourselves standing together that day gazing at Sabina's deportation card. And slowly coming to the realization that we would follow the path that took her to her death.

I have only the faintest sense of what this will mean for my old friend, and no words we exchange in this moment or in the days ahead will change that. Nor can I say what it will mean for me. This is one of the things our time together slowly reveals—something I understood abstractly at the time but had little experiential knowledge of—the impossibility of knowing where we are going, or even why. The utter ineffability of the space we are entering into together. Such ideas had long been known to me from my reading of the mystics: the radical limits of what can be said about the encounter with God in the abyss; the necessary relinquishment of control. Still, I had somehow managed to keep them at a relatively safe distance and minimize my own risk. No longer. Already the immensity was opening up before us. Soon we would begin walking out into it.

The Flemish Beguine and mystic Hadewijch of Antwerp says: "They hasten, those who have glimpsed that truth, on the dark path, Untraced, unmarked, all inner." This is an old and recurring idea among mystics—the recognition that the search for truth entails abandoning the sure knowledge that has always guided you for the sake of something more capacious and mysterious and unknowable. The awareness that only by risking yourself completely, losing yourself within this immensity or, as Jabés says, making yourself "present to nothingness" can you hope to find your way. An unresolvable but unavoidable paradox. For reasons that are not easy for me to understand or explain, even now, Hadewijch and her vision of the dark path became part of the journey I undertook with my friend Ralph to look for traces of his lost family. Part of it is Hadewijch's sensitivity to the realities of absence, exile, and despair, and her willingness to face and enter what she and many of her contemporaries referred to simply as "the abyss." Especially what she calls "the deep, insurmountable darkness of love."[4]

Not an answer to anything certainly, but an open space where it becomes possible to consider what it means to confront and respond to unimaginable absence and loss, all that is unknown, unknowable, sunk in darkness.

Perhaps also a space for rethinking the meaning of faith in light of all that has been lost to us. Tadeusz Rósiewicz writes:

> Faith in what exists
> Is knowledge not faith
> But faith in what does not exist
> Is true faith.[5]

What does not exist, for me: any certitude about how to respond to the naked, brutal facts of Sabina's arrest, disappearance, and murder. Or about its possible meaning or the meaning of anything arising in its aftermath. I have no access to these things. They remain hidden, unknown, perhaps unknowable. But to say these things do not exist does not mean they can never exist or that they can never be known. It is simply to acknowledge the importance of learning to enter and inhabit the gaps that now occupy the space where the solid edifice of sure faith once stood. And to do so out of respect for the radical incommensurability of all loss.

* * *

We sit in silence as the train pulls out of Amsterdam Centraal. Soon, we are moving through the German countryside. Overcast sky. Deep green fields. Red tiled roofs. Burnt orange leaves on the trees. Little garden plots. Occasional egrets and hawks. The world spinning by. Or, rather, we are racing through it, heading east. Yes, east, following the route that the Dutch Jews took leaving Westerbork. We travel in comfort of course. And this is the new Germany. Still. It is difficult not to feel the power of this particular itinerary. Sabina Landsberger-Zerkowski traveled this route many years ago in circumstances I cannot begin to imagine. She was eighty-two years old when she was taken from her home, imprisoned, and sent east with many thousands of other human beings to die. According to the records, she was killed the day after her arrival at the camp in Sobibór. She is our ghostly companion along this journey.

I look at Ralph sitting across from me. He shakes his head, then turns again to gaze out the window. We continue moving together in silence through a haunted landscape.

Looking out the train window, I become aware of the presence of others who are accompanying me on this journey—my teachers in darkness especially. It is like pulling on a spool of thread that begins unraveling in my memory. I write down some of the names: Elie Wiesel, whose Joban cry of loss in *Night* I first encountered while studying with Elliot Aronson as an undergraduate at the University of California, Santa Cruz; it shocked my still-untested young mind awake. I recall also Claude Lanzman's *Shoah*, which I watched in its entirety on successive nights in 1985 in an old theater in Berkeley; the face and voice of Simon Srebnik upon his return to Chelmno— "this is the place . . . it was terrible . . . no one can describe it"—never left me. Around the same time, I fell under the spell of the great Italian writer Primo Levi, finding his deep humanity in the face of the horrors of Auschwitz an expression of a spiritual capacity that I could neither name nor comprehend but which I received as a gift and a challenge; his suicide in 1987 left me, along with so many others, with a sense of unutterable loss.

We continue moving steadily east, through Osnabrück, Hanover, Wolfsburg. I think of others who are with me on this journey, whose work has shaped my thinking, especially about the meaning of spiritual practice in the face of unknowing. Simone Weil, the twentieth-century French Jewish philosopher and writer whose unwavering focus on the reality of affliction— especially that of her compatriots suffering under German occupation—and on the fundamental moral task of standing with one another in affliction helped me see a new and powerful vision of solidarity. And Etty Hillesum, the Dutch Jewish writer who was killed in Auschwitz but left behind a diary from her time in Westerbork that reveals such extraordinary courage and spiritual honesty. "Such words as 'God' and 'Death' and 'Suffering' and 'Eternity' are best forgotten," she said in response to all that had befallen her and her companions in the camps. "We have to become as simple and as wordless as the growing corn or the falling rain. We must just be."[6]

I recall also Anne Michaels, whose *Fugitive Pieces* opened up for me something new and terrible in the landscape of absence and loss: "I will speak a dark language with the music of a harp," she says, paraphrasing one of the ancient Psalms (49:4), offering her own brave response to Theodor Adorno's assertion regarding the impossibility of poetry in a post-Holocaust world.[7] And W. G. Sebald, in whose works I found the journey into post-Holocaust emptiness and loss traced with such delicacy and psychological honesty that it became impossible for me to feel removed or distant from it. Also Edmond Jabès, whose work I began reading in Argentina during a time when I needed, without quite knowing why, the stark emptiness and honesty of thinking marked deeply by a long and difficult journey into desert;

and whose obsession with the desert not only helped me understand the radical moral task created by absence and loss, but also created an unexpected bridge with the spiritual traditions of early Christian monasticism that had for so long occupied my thinking. Here, I sensed, was a shared sense of the importance of a blasted-out silence where nothing false can live. "There is no possible return if you have gone deep into the desert," says Jabès.[8]

How, I wonder even now, have these different figures come to inhabit such a prominent place in my thinking? Why am I so drawn to them? And how have they come to occupy so much of the same mental terrain as that of the ancient Christian mystics of darkness and the desert? It is not easy to answer to these questions. But I am beginning to understand how significantly all of them together have contributed to my moral-spiritual education. And how, for all their differences, there is also something they share: a radical, uncompromising honesty; a reticence to claim knowledge or understanding of things that can never be understood or explained; and a commitment to search out the truth of things in darkness and silence.

The words of Etty Hillesum come back to me in this moment: *As simple and wordless as the growing corn or the falling rain.* She wrote these words close to the end of her life when almost any hope she had of surviving had disappeared. A moment when words that once meant something, or seemed to, had lost their capacity to signify. It is time to become simple and wordless, she says, because the new reality unfolding before her cannot be encompassed by any kind of language. Relinquishment into a wordless silence is all that is left.

These and other voices are present to me as we move deeper into Germany. So too is the silence out of which their voices arise and to which they inevitably return. The question of how to speak or whether to speak at all, to which they give such assiduous and honest attention, begins to become my own.

* * *

When and under what circumstances is it ethical to speak of a given experience—your own or another's, in particular the experience of profound suffering or loss? What are the limits of language in being able to represent and evoke such experience? What happens to language under the pressure of such experience, when conventional ideas, words, and grammar can no longer bear the weight they are asked to carry. Must some other form of expression, or perhaps a kind of "textual silence," take their place?[9] These and other questions continue to surface in my mind as we make our way east on this gray November afternoon. And they remain with me long afterward.

I return here to Adorno's statement: "To write poetry after Auschwitz is barbaric." His assertion has long been cited as a comment on the radical limits of language or thought in a post-Holocaust world and on the profound moral challenges underlying attempts to say anything in response.[10] His observation has had a long afterlife, provoking a range of responses regarding the limits and capacity of speech after the Holocaust. It is, at its root, a question about the incommensurability between language and experience, especially the experience of unfathomable suffering. And it provides a useful analog for thinking about the limits (and possibilities) of speech in response to mystical experience, especially mystical experience in which the subject finds herself or himself—as so often happens—utterly bewildered, lost, forsaken. Michel de Certeau describes the challenge and possibility of "mystic speech" (and its underlying silence) this way: "An ab-solute (unbound), in the mode of pain, pleasure, and a 'letting-be' attitude (Meister Eckhart's *gelazenheit*), inhabits the torture, ecstasy, or sacri-fice of a language that can *say* that absolute, endlessly, only by erasing itself."[11] What emerges when one is moved to speak of an experience of immensity but is left uncertain whether language still signifies, whether the words have any meaning or purchase on reality? Is erasure and the emptiness it leaves behind finally the only meaningful way to conceive of such speech?

I have noted Adorno's revision of his initial statement in which he wrote, some years later: "perennial suffering has as much right to expression as the tortured man has to scream"—an acknowledgment of the inevitable and necessary, if also limited, expressions arising from suffering. And a recognition of the paradox of speech that carries within it the force and feeling of the suffering subject without necessarily conveying any particular meaning. Certainly not a meaning that points to a resolution to that suffering. Adorno notes the immense difficulty of saying anything in response, asking what it means for anyone who has escaped—purely by accident—the fate of Auschwitz, to go on living.[12] This is an impossibly difficult and painful question, not only for those (most of the living) who somehow escaped the camps, but also for survivors of the Holocaust, some of whom—Paul Celan and Primo Levi among them—found it impossible to "go on living." Still, for these writers as for so many others, the need to speak, to bear witness, to resist falling into the abyss of silence has proven both irresistible and necessary. Even if speaking yields only broken shards and does little or nothing to push back the curtain of darkness. Even though the abyss remains. Why then speak at all? And how?

For me, Primo Levi's response to this question in the preface to his memoir *Survival in Auschwitz* is among the most compelling and meaningful:

> As an account of atrocities . . . this book of mine adds nothing to what is already known to readers throughout the world on the disturbing question of the death camps. It has not been written in order to formulate new accusations; it should be able, rather, to furnish documentation for a quiet study of certain aspects of the human mind. Many people—many nations—can find themselves holding, more or less wittingly, that "every stranger is an enemy." For the most part this conviction lies deep down like some latent infection; it betrays itself only in random, disconnected acts, and does not lie at the base of a system of reason. But when this does come about, when the unspoken dogma becomes the major premise in a syllogism, then, at the end of the chain, there is the Lager. Here is the product of a conception of the world carried rigorously to its logical conclusion; so long as the conception subsists, the conclusion remains to threaten us.[13]

Why speak? For Levi it is not to offer yet another account of the atrocities. Or to formulate new accusations. No, it is, he says, to "furnish documentation for a quiet study of certain aspects of the human mind."

Readers of Levi's work may well question whether the harrowing account he gives of his experience is really consistent with this dispassionate, seemingly irenic statement of intent. Atrocities abound in this work. Still, his observations here reveal something critical about his own relationship with these events and what he is seeking to understand for himself. He gives particular attention to what he calls "certain aspects of the human mind"—especially the enduring and pernicious idea that "every stranger is the enemy." The recognition that this conviction becomes first an "unspoken dogma," then "the major premise of a syllogism," and, finally, "at the end of the chain . . . the Lager" occupies the moral center of Levi's great work and is its primary focus—the terrible question of how and why we return again and again to thinking that leads to "the Lager." That is, how do we allow ourselves to become seduced, continuously it seems, by the dogma that "every stranger is the enemy." This is not part of a "system of reason," Levi says, something to be engaged with rational arguments. It is more like an "infection," a spiritual sickness that requires both a clear-eyed diagnosis and a radical intervention.

Levi offers one other important comment about why he has chosen to speak. Or, rather, why he has felt compelled to speak. "Its origins," he says "go back, not indeed in practice, but as an idea, an intention, to the days in the Lager. The need to tell our story to 'the rest,' to make 'the rest' participate in it, had taken on for us, before our liberation and after, the character of an immediate and violent impulse, to the point of competing with our other elementary needs. The book has been written to satisfy this need: first and foremost, therefore, as an interior liberation."[14] The formation of this idea, this intention, he says, had already taken hold of him when he was in the Lager, but during a time when he was effectively mute, unable to speak at all. Hence the "immediate and violent impulse" to speak—not only in his own voice but also as part of a collective expression. He speaks of the "need to tell *our* story." And of the desire to include others in that story. The impulse to speak, while deeply personal, was aimed at making "the rest" "participate in" the story. The "immediate and violent impulse" to speak, Levi's words suggest, was born of a desperate need to overcome the deadly silence and isolation of the Lager, the desire to be knitted back into the lives of "the rest." And yes, to *make* "the rest" somehow share with those who had endured this horror, not only the horror itself but also its long aftermath.

He does not say why this collective dimension of speaking is so important to him. At least not explicitly. But if one reads his words here in light of his earlier observations about the persistence of the "infection" that "every stranger is the enemy," one possible meaning becomes clear. Telling the story, as well as making "the rest" participate in it, effectively undermines the pattern of silencing and evasion that feeds the infection and allows it to continue afflicting the larger community. Speech, Levi wagers, has the potential to heal, liberate. It is telling that he concludes his comments here with a note about the hope of "interior liberation"; this hope is at the very heart of this impulse to speak, to "tell our story."

Still, the question remains: *How* to speak? What forms of speech are possible, necessary, in response to the compelling desire to "tell" what happened, while also respecting the need to refrain from saying or attempting to say what cannot finally be expressed? Speech that honors the silence out of which these words arise? It is here, I think, that Edmond Jabès's work is so important. Part of this has to do with Jabès's sustained commitment to probe the horror of the Holocaust in light of what he called "the book of our silence, the desert"—for him the only place empty and wild and silent enough to enact this work. His experience of exile from

Egypt marked him deeply and informed his years-long struggle to respond to the larger and deeper losses of the twentieth century. Like many of his contemporaries, he wondered whether it was possible to continue speaking at all. Or whether silence is the most appropriate and respectful, perhaps the only, possible response.

Jabès himself did not remain silent. But his dense, fragmentary, gnomic ruminations reflect a profound respect for the silence that grounds and gives meaning to speech. "We are," he says, "bound by silence . . . by the greater silence of lovers, of martyrs, of the dead."[15] To listen carefully and deeply to this silence, he suggests, is a fundamental ethical-spiritual task. Often the silence remains opaque, empty, a void. But sometimes, from within that silence, important questions emerge, including whether writing has any meaning or purpose. Especially in the absence of hope. He asks: "Does continual writing signify hope even where hope is written off?" And offers this tentative response: "You no longer expect anything, but you still write."[16] An honest admission of the difficulty of knowing whether language can still signify in the aftermath of the Shoah. But elsewhere, addressing Adorno's challenge more directly, Jabès offers this important gloss on his own ambivalence about language: "Adorno once said that after Auschwitz we can no longer write poetry. I say that after Auschwitz we *must* write poetry but with wounded words."[17] Such wounded words, he suggests, are necessary. Sometimes, in their raw force, meaningful. Even if there is also and always the deep silence of desert, the void, the night, all born of the experience of loss and exile. What Jabès calls "the dried blood of the wound."[18]

I think here also of Paul Celan's important witness, above all in his poetry, but also in his 1958 Bremen Prize speech, where he addressed the question of loss and its relation to language directly: "Reachable, near and not lost, there remained in the midst of the losses this one thing: language." A hopeful-sounding statement about the enduring possibilities of language to speak and conjure meaning. But this is only part of the story. Celan asserts that language has been altered forever by its descent into darkness.

> It, the language, remained, not lost, yes in spite of everything. But it had to pass through its own answerlessness, pass through frightful muting, pass through the thousand darknesses of deathbringing speech. It passed through and gave back no words for that which happened, yet it passed through this happening. Passed through and could come to light again "enriched" by all this.[19]

Not lost, in spite of everything. An astonishing affirmation of what remains possible, of the enduring vitality of language, even in the midst of unspeakable loss. But Celan's statement is also marked by such severe negations—answerlessness, frightful muting, the thousand darknesses of deathbringing speech—that it is difficult to understand what language can still mean. Or if it can mean anything. Especially given his conviction that it "passed through and gave back no words for what happened." Even so, there is his clear sense that language *did* pass through, "enriched" somehow by this passage.

Celan's poetry reveals how he himself navigated this passage. But the Bremen speech is noteworthy for his honest effort to locate himself in relation to these questions, to say something about what was at stake for him in trying to find a way of speaking that could address both the immensity of loss and a still-emerging reality that has yet to be imagined or lived into: "In this language," he says, "I have sought, during those years and the years since then, to write poems: so as to speak, to orient myself, to find out where I was and where I was meant to go, to sketch out reality for myself ... it was an attempt to gain direction." And there was also the search to understand whether language could still accomplish that profound task of addressing another. Poems, he notes, are "underway ... making towards something ... standing open, occupiable, perhaps towards an addressable Thou, towards an addressable reality."[20]

There is something so moving and generous and hopeful in Celan's response to the question of whether it remains possible to speak and address one another amid profound loss. The sense of movement toward something, someone: an addressable Thou. Even so, this open, occupiable space so often remains hemmed in by silence, by its own kind of answerlessness.

I am also trying to sketch out reality for myself. Holding close the loss that has brought Ralph and me here and taking care not to move too quickly to give it a meaning. Seeking out my own direction in language and in silence. And considering carefully all that my friend is carrying. This is not easy to do.

Still, I am not sure I really have a choice. So, I turn my attention to the horizon opening up before me. And I listen. To the silence, yes. But also to my friend as he works to articulate his own sense of what walking this unfolding path means and who he is becoming along the way. Ralph is a poet, and I have come to appreciate his sensitivity to the music of language, his awareness of the silence that is always woven into that music, and his recognition of the limits of what language can say. Especially in this moment.

I am also listening to and thinking with other writers whose reflections on language and silence open a space in which I may inhabit more fully my emerging understanding of what it means to enter and keep silence. And what it means to speak. I find myself thinking especially about Anne Michaels's *Fugitive Pieces*, a novel I first read several years ago and which I am returning to now with new questions and more feeling. She addresses herself with such fierce honesty to the experience of bewilderment and pain that so often pulses through the experience of facing immense silence. And of speaking with wounded words.

The narrator of the novel, Jakob Beer, is struggling to understand his experience as a Holocaust survivor and as a writer. As a seven-year-old Jewish child in Poland, he was concealed behind a wall when the Germans came for his family. His parents were killed, and his sister Bella was taken away, disappearing from his life forever. Jakob escaped and hid in the nearby forest and bogs where he was eventually found by a Greek archeologist, Athos, who smuggled him to Greece and kept him hidden there until the end of the war. Later he emigrated to Canada. It is there that Jakob begins opening himself to the long, painful work of facing what has happened to him, his parents, his sister; also facing what it will mean for him to become a writer, to speak of this absence, if he can speak of it at all.

"I stepped into the night." A simple act undertaken after dinner with his old friend Athos, but filled with unexpected weight and portent. He walks alone into the night, on the streets of Toronto and, it turns out, into his own broken past:

> I took in the cold beauty of Lakeshore Cement, with its small gardens someone thought to plant at the foot of each massive silo. Or the delicate metal staircases, a lace ribbon, swirling around the girth of the oil reservoirs. At night, a few lights marked port and starboard of these gargantuan industrial forms, and I filled them with loneliness. I listened to these dark shapes as if they were black spaces in music, a musician learning the silences of a piece. I felt this was my truth. That my life could not be stored in any language but only in silence. . . . But I did not know how to seek by way of silence. So I lived a breath apart, a touch-typist who holds his hands above the keys slightly in the wrong place, the words coming out meaningless, garbled. Bella and I inches apart, the wall between us. I thought of writing poems this way, in code, every letter askew, so that loss would wreck the language, become the language.[21]

Loss has already wrecked the language. This is part of what it means for him to live in the aftermath. Jakob himself has become unlanguaged. Which is one of the reasons silence presents itself so insistently to him. As a question, a challenge, maybe a last resort. A space beyond or without language that he can perhaps learn to inhabit, survive inside of. Or disappear into. We "fall silent in turn," says Jabès, "with the hope of dissolving into it."[22]

Dissolution. A strange, difficult idea whose very sense and meaning feels ephemeral, ungraspable. There are echoes here of death. Or a release into a trackless space beyond language or understanding. Still, this release so often eludes us. Instead, there is only the jarring, ragged sense of being caught somewhere in between.

Reading Jakob's account, I struggle to imagine what it is to inhabit a life that can be "stored . . . only in silence." Its necessity is so clear. But there is no comfort here; Jakob does not know how "to seek by way of silence." He is fated, like so many others, to live a breath apart from the very thing (the very one) he seeks. His only recourse is to return to language, where every letter is askew, where words are inadequate, "meaningless, garbled." Loss has wrecked the language, *become* the language.

* * *

I shift in my seat and gaze out the window of the train. The landscape is receding into darkness. So are my thoughts. I look over at my friend and wonder what if anything I can say to him, or to myself, about the concerns that have brought us here. And whether it matters. We seem to speak less and less about it the deeper we descend into Germany. Perhaps there is simply nothing to say. I am slowly coming to accept this, even as I feel myself yearning to say something, if only to create a bridge between us, find a way to share more deeply in this experience. But I wonder whether language can do this, whether it is even possible.

Clarice Lispector says: "I must speak because speaking saves. But I have no word to say."[23] It feels strange and more than a little disconcerting to find myself moving into a space of such radical silence. But it is helpful to know this sense of being caught between the necessity and impossibility of speaking is known to others. Increasingly, it seems to me that accepting this paradox and refusing the temptation to soften or circumvent it is the only honest response I can make to the knowledge that has come to me on this journey. Still, I feel with Jabès the immense challenge of inhabiting this space:

It is very hard to live with silence. The real silence is death and this is terrible. To approach this silence, it is necessary to journey into the desert. You do not go to the desert to find identity, but to lose it, to lose your personality, to become anonymous. You make yourself void. You *become* silence. You must become more silent than the silence around you. And then something extraordinary happens: you hear silence speak.[24]

What silence is this? What speech? Jabès does not say. Not directly. Instead he proposes an itinerary, a practice: enter the desert, lose yourself, make yourself void, become silence. A practice of radical relinquishment that will, if taken seriously, undo every preconception and idea you have of yourself, existence, everything. A more withering ascetic practice it would be difficult to imagine. At the heart of this practice is the void, an empty space that nourishes what cannot be thought or said. Also a haunting image of the unmoored self, perhaps the only way to think about or imagine the self in light of endless loss. And a silence that is a kind of death. You may indeed hear "silence speak," says Jabès. But only after you have acknowledged the depth of your loss, your nothingness.

This desert is a terrifying immensity, an emptiness that we rightly fear to enter, but without which we cannot truly engage existence. It is, as an imaginative, metaphorical, existential space, open, unfinished. It has no particular "meaning." There is no "ultimate meaning" to be found there. No "God" at the end or center of it. At least no God that can be known or named. Only the void. "Not to think anymore. To be the thought of the universe. To drown in it, O void, O nothingness!" Jabès exclaims in *The Book of Resemblances*.[25] There is such pathos in this cry, such honesty and worthiness in these wounded words. They are utterly personal in character and reflect Jabès's sense of what kind of response to incomprehensible loss is possible and necessary. But they also raise questions for the rest of us about the place of silence in our responses to suffering and loss. For Jabès, this is the great ethical concern that must guide everything we do. It is also, at least for him, a theological concern:

God, as the absolute Other of others: as if we must first become familiar and share responsibility with other faces before we can approach through them the absolute Other without face. As if on all drowned faces there glowed the loss of His. As if His face had paid the loss of all of ours.

Here is distress, the despair of love within love, infinite pain within pain, delirium blazing within delirium. Here is passivity rent in its deep sovereignty. Here, like a bottomless cliff, like the dark of all nights.

How far does our responsibility go? The void is forged by our hands.[26]

"How far does our responsibility go?" This, I think, is the key question. And it is critical to the work that has drawn me to this particular place, and this moment, with my friend. How far does *my* responsibility go?

Jabés's strange, beautiful words defy any simple attempt at explication. But they invite a deep, honest engagement. And they point to something that I think can only be learned in the emptiness of the desert or in the deepest recesses of the night: only by relinquishing everything, our sense of self, our ideas about God, everything, can we hope to discover within ourselves the capacity for fulfilling our fundamental obligation toward the Other, especially "those drowned faces," our only access to the face of God. We must ourselves become empty, open, lost: "All absence," says Jabés, "means presence to nothingness, means awakening to the void."[27]

* * *

It is evening when the train pulls into Berlin Hauptbahnhof. We find a taxi and make our way to the hotel. Faint traces of pink streak the sky; leaves scattering in the breeze; frost on the ground. There are few signs of Berlin's wartime past, at least few that we can easily read. We have arrived in a vibrant, modern city. Gleaming new architecture, jazz pulsing from underground clubs. The faces and dress of many of those we pass on the streets reflect what I have read about the new Germany: immigrants from Turkey, refugees from Syria, North Africa, and elsewhere. There is also a resurgent Jewish population.

Still, it is not difficult to feel Berlin's haunted past. The transport trains from Westerbork, I realize, must have come through here on their way east. A terrible thought. And this evening, we pass close to the very places—synagogues on Levetzow Street and Heidereuter Alley and the Jewish cemetery on Gross Hamburger Street and Rosen Street—where members of Berlin's Jewish community were held and then deported to ghettos (Theresienstadt) and killing centers (Auschwitz-Birkenau) in eastern Europe. These ordinary Berlin neighborhoods are marked forever by the immensity of that erasure. My proximity to these places in this moment is unnerving, and it only deepens the questions that have pursued me for this entire trip: How can I situate my-self in relation to these places, to the stark absence that remains? What will it mean for me to respond to the enduring presence of what W. G. Sebald describes as "The marks of pain which . . . trace countless fine lines through history."[28] I do not know.

The next day, before pushing on to Warsaw, we decide to visit the Berlin Jewish Museum. I knew little about the museum before arriving in Berlin. But as we slowly descend into an underground labyrinth of echoing, cav-ernous "void spaces" (this, I learn later, is what the architect Daniel Libeskind chose to call them), I feel a sense of uneasiness taking hold of me, the strain of this emptiness pushing down on my consciousness. A strange feeling of disorientation, the empty spaces depriving me of any sure footing or sense of location. I become aware of my breath shortening, my pulse racing. I begin looking for an escape route. Later I wonder: Agoraphobia? Or some version of *horror vacui*? I am grasping now, I realize, after a conceptual structure to help me understand what happened to me inside these spaces, trying to the-orize something that cannot be encompassed in language or thought. Still, in that moment, my feelings were too dense for thought. I felt like I was falling into, through these spaces, becoming lost to myself.

Is this something like what Heidegger calls "falling into the uncanny?" Perhaps. This at least comes closer to evoking the sense of estrangement and dislocation that was so palpable on this day. But in truth I do not know how to describe this experience or what to call it.

On this day, this space—open and expansive and dark and impenetrable enough to hold, without explanation, all the pain and loss of a great erasure—also holds me. Not in a way that enables me to take possession of it or grasp its meaning. But by allowing me simply to inhabit it, become unmoored by it. A difficult and not altogether welcome feeling. But I sense that, in relation to the questions that have brought me here, it is no longer possible to main-tain a safe distance or to inhabit the more carefully demarcated, constrained space that has long shaped my identity. Later, emerging into the late after-noon sun, these "void spaces" remain with me, continue working on me, opening me up.

What to make of this? What can *I* make of this? These questions haunt me as I consider the concerns that have brought me here: struggling to under-stand what it will mean to accompany my friend into a place of utter lostness; asking what it will mean for me to *share* this loss with him, with others (*can it be shared?*); learning to respect the limits of language and thought, accepting the fractured, wounded character of anything that can be said, even as I work to formulate my own response to this loss and come to terms with a necessary silence. You need to "make yourself void" says Jabés. I have almost no idea what this means. But here in this place, I feel myself drawing closer. What these "void spaces" make clear is the near impossibility of representing absence and loss. I should know this already. But I resist the idea that this vast space or silence is itself the ground, that finally there is nothing to say. That absence is everything. And that anything I might say will be drawn inevitably back into that void space that I must learn to become present to nothingness.

The space inside this museum, contrived to express and embody this vast, unspeakable absence, an absence that continues to make its presence felt after more than sixty years, offers a place to begin. Still, what kind of space is this? And what is it asking of those of us who enter and become lost within it? Is it, I begin to wonder, a kind of contemplative space? A space that decenters and disorients and opens up a space for thought beyond thought? The contemplative life, says Thomas Merton, is "a confrontation with poverty and the void, a renunciation of the empirical self, in the presence of death, and nothingness, in order to overcome the ignorance and error that spring from the fear of 'being nothing.' "[29] There is nothing serene or consoling about this space or about the contemplative practice that unfolds here. On the contrary, it is designed to discomfort us, to provoke us into a stark recognition of the severe limitations of every effort to say where or who we are in this moment. To remind us, invite us into a more profound reckoning with the extent of our loss. An aching, bottomless, loss with no beginning or end, embedded in history and in our bodies, but also impossible to locate or encompass with language or thought. Always exceeding our grasp.

I pause from time to time to look up into these void spaces and begin to feel more and more the impossibility of locating myself here. Also the need to abandon any pretense that I can do so. I realize too that this deepening feeling of dislocation has already begun to alter my sense of myself as a thinking subject. Emptiness and absence dominate the field. My thoughts about myself, my personality, my identity, begin to dissolve. They do not matter. There is only this emptiness.

And yet I have not dissolved. Nor have I fallen out of time. I am leaning against the cold, steel surface of this building here in Berlin on a November day in 2016. I am gazing upward into this immensity of this space, pausing for a moment to consider what has brought me here and what lay ahead as I make my way toward an as-yet-unknown destination somewhere in eastern Poland. The blunt force of history has determined the shape of everything about this moment—Sabina's abduction, disappearance, and death, the journey I am embarked on with my friend, this bleak, empty space, the questions forming within me (and just as quickly dissipating). But now to engage all of this, how to inhabit this space and these questions? How to think about them? I am already carrying within me the weight of a particular loss whose potency, obscurity, and intractability make thought difficult, at times impossible. Not thought then, but something else: a strange sense of being carried into an emptiness and absence too raw and vast to comprehend: that I do not wish to comprehend it. All that is left to me in this space is the need to relinquish thought and let the emptiness gather.

These are of course personal concerns. But here in this place, the larger, more encompassing significance of these concerns surface with renewed force. The "void is forged by our hands," says Jabés. It does not exist without us, without our participation in and response to it. We are the only ones who can forge the void that we must also inhabit. I do not pretend to know what this means. But new questions are forming within me. What will it mean to recognize the void and take it seriously? What will it mean to summon the courage to relinquish myself to it, disappear into it? Not only as a personal gesture but as a part of a collective response to all that has been lost? I look around and see all these other souls moving through the space with me. I have little knowledge what has brought them here. Few words are exchanged among and between us. It is mostly silent, but not empty of feeling. There is a sense of intimacy in moving through the space together—an improvised ritual of shared attention to loss and absence.

I recall other improvised rituals of attention that have shaped and formed me: especially the long hours spent sitting in silence in the open, empty space of Redwoods Monastery chapel; then standing and silently, slowly circumambulating that empty space. One foot, then another. Pausing, breathing in and out. Not going anywhere. Just walking. Sharing this wordless experience with others. Touching deeply personal and often-hidden experiences of grief and loss; also losses that are more widely shared that permeate this space of prayer and which we hold and struggle with together in the silence. Sometimes finding consolation, sometimes encountering only more difficult questions and deeper pain. Never knowing with any certainty what this practice means. But continuing day after day to sit, to walk, to wander together in the silence and emptiness. Learning to trust the space, the practice of entering and inhabiting the silence together.

Prayer. The mysterious work of opening ourselves, again and again, to the presence of the One we seek in silence—beyond all thought and understanding. Or to an absence that also transcends language and thought: "You ask me how to pray to someone who is not," writes Czeslaw Milosz.[30] Less a denial of the very possibility of prayer than a recognition of impossibility of ever saying with certainty what it means or whether any assurance about its ground can ever be known. "Profound prayer is a meditation upon the nothing," says Clarice Lispector.[31]

Is this vast, open, labyrinthine void beneath the streets of Berlin perhaps a space where meditation upon the nothing becomes not only possible but necessary? I do not want to push too hard on this idea or make of this emptiness something that it is not. Still, I cannot escape the sense that this space corresponds somehow to other empty, silent spaces of prayer that have for so long touched and formed me.

At Redwoods in a particular way, yes. But also at the great ninth-century mosque of Ibn Tulun in Cairo, where I once spent the better part of a day walking and dreaming my way through its mathematically precise porticos, losing myself little by little within those elegant lines and vistas and silences. And in the cloister at Senanque, which I entered in the depth of night many years ago to celebrate the Easter vigil, the darkness pierced suddenly by a dry lavender bush bursting into flame, our prayers arising from the silence and resounding deeply against the ancient stone walls, then returning again to silence. I felt this too at the nuclear test site in the Nevada desert, where I gathered in silence with others in a gesture of resistance against our continued dependence on these weapons of mass destruction and the political policies that make their future use seem inevitable. And on the streets of San Salvador, on the anniversary of the martyrs, where I joined with others to create *alfombras*—carpets constructed of colored sand—to remember the lives of those who risked so much to stand with the most marginalized.

These are not all the same kinds of spaces. Nor do they function in the same way imaginatively or in practice. Still, in their stark emptiness, the sense of that comes from entering them and getting lost in their immensity, as well as the difficult moral questions that arise from reckoning with that lostness, they have become joined in my imagination and experience. Can these spaces perhaps be understood in terms of what Michel de Foucault has described as "heterotopias"--spaces of otherness that make possible certain kinds of imaginative, spiritual, and political work?[32] Ritual spaces where the constrained and limiting identities that are too often foisted upon us by structures of power can be resisted and more open, expansive identities can be constructed and perhaps shared with others? Spaces of emptiness and silence where thought and imagination are, for a time, suspended, and openness to painful or ineffable elements of experience can be considered and engaged? In solitude. Or, as here in this space, in the presence of others.

This is how contemplative spaces have often functioned. So too with sites of memory. Moving through Libeskind's museum, I find myself so grateful for its empty, open, ineffable character. And for the invitation to confront and struggle with an absence that has long troubled me and that surfaced again only a few days earlier during that terrible moment of discovery in Amsterdam. Also for the gift of being able to share this wordless space with my friend and with all these nameless others who have been drawn here on this November day. And for the opportunity to suspend thought and drift for a time in this emptiness.

Later, reading Anthony Vidler's perceptive essay on Libeskind's museum, "Building in Empty Spaces," I find myself drawn to consider this experience in light of his assertion that we are increasingly inhabiting a kind of "no-space" or "void" (one of the unexpected consequences of cyberspace's dominance in our lives); or, as in the case of the Berlin Jewish Museum, a kind of "exhausted space." In such spaces, Vidler notes, we find ourselves in a "phenomenological world . . . upset by unstable axes, walls and skins torn, ripped and dangerously slashed, rooms empty of content with no exits and entrances." It is perhaps too simple to say that Libeskind's museum emulates or embodies spatially a world that so many human beings in the late twentieth and early twenty-first centuries increasingly sense to be part of their own psychological, emotional, and spiritual experience. But the sense of bewilderment you feel wandering through this space does feel strangely familiar, an echo of experiences for which we often lack language or narrative. Here you encounter and move through a space that reflects the loss of perspective, the collapse of depth, and the labyrinthine character of so much of our experience of modernity—something Vidler attributes at least in part to what he describes as Libeskind's "implied architectural rereading" of Walter Benjamin's work. Here is a space that reveals the necessity, even inevitability, of wandering, of absentmindedness, of becoming lost.

This particular reading of the museum leads Vidler to make an astonishing claim for the power of such immense, disorienting spaces to shape and reshape our imagination, to help us feel in a new way our connection to one another, our shared past, and all that has been lost:

If there can be no "logic" on earth that explains each subject's experience of light and dark, form and space, vertical and horizontal . . . then we might at least leap straight up to the so-called "mystical" experience that, as Benjamin understood so well, could be no more nor less than collective tradition, the collective memory of the past, that weighs so strongly on the present and controls in ways unknown our imagination of the future. In such a world, Libeskind's ellipses, his wandering paths and warped spaces without perspective and ending blindly, can only be seen as so many tests of our own abilities to endure the vertigo experience of the labyrinths that make up our modernity.

Reading these words, I feel a sense of recognition regarding my own experience of moving through Libeskind's museum that day: a piercing sense of loss and absence; an inability to locate myself or form thoughts that have any reliable ground or meaning. Grief. Heaviness. Emptiness. But also an unexpected feeling of intimacy: sharing this space with my friend Ralph, and with others, feeling myself drawn into a common experience. Being invited to consider again whether this loss, this absence is also mine.

Is this part of what Vidler means by invoking the "mystical"? The sense that the distance we so often feel between us and these experiences of immensity is not in fact real? That we are immersed in, *held* in these spaces of loss and collective tradition, together with others? I am not sure. I do know that entering this void space and moving through it silently with my friend has provoked me to relinquish my inclination simply to think *about* the space and instead allow myself to be drawn down into it. To move through the space. To allow myself to become disoriented, lost, open. To listen.

Still, I do not know what it will mean for me to enter the void space and listen. Or to carry this space within me and live out of this emptiness. But moving through this space, I begin to feel the power of these questions differently. I think again of Jabès's stark claim: "All absence means presence to nothingness, means awakening to the void." I sense in a new way the need to relinquish any sense of being able to name or determine the meaning of what is calling to me here. To open myself to absence.

We emerge into the late afternoon light, blinking and amazed, still held by the immensity of that space. We talk about it on the way back to our hotel, or try to; but our conversation is fragmentary, filled with stops and starts and silences. We begin to sense the absurdity of trying to say anything about it. Still, there is a real longing to connect with each other about what happened to us in that space. There is also, I think, a profound uneasiness at the prospect of allowing absence and silence to eclipse language and meaning: it cannot simply be nothingness, can it? And so we struggle to wrest even the tiniest scrap of meaning or presence from that emptiness, even as we recognize the futility of trying to do so. The void spaces, in their radical emptiness, evoke the lost presence of all those victims of the Holocaust, each one utterly singular and each one now silent forever. The impulse to refrain from speaking is, perhaps, one of the only meaningful ways of honoring that silence.

Wounded words, yes, but also silence. It is this tension that Elie Wiesel addresses himself to in responding to all those whose voices will never again be heard: "Tell them that silence, more than language, remains the substance and the seal of what was once their universe, and that, like language, it demands to be recognized and transmitted."[33] Here is the fundamental, perhaps irresolvable tension: the moral obligation to respect silence, and at the same time to recognize and somehow "transmit" the unsayable. Silence, absence, nothingness: elements of a grammar of loss.

* * *

Is it meaningful to speak of faith in this space of silence, absence and nothingness? Of God? Or Love? These are not new questions—either for me or for so many who have found themselves compelled to rethink the meaning of faith in light of devastating loss. But here in this place, I feel them surfacing with increasing urgency. And I feel the need to take them more seriously than I have done before. It is becoming clear to me that absence and loss must be part of the language of faith, must inform and deepen it. And that love, if it is to mean anything, must confront and respond to the abyss. As for God, this remains among the most difficult questions imaginable, nor can anyone answer it for anyone else. Still, in this moment, I am facing them for myself and asking what it will mean for me to walk through this space of unknowing with courage and openness. And share this space with my friend.

"To believe," says Christian Wiman, "is to believe you have been torn from the abyss, / yet stand waveringly on its rim."[34] Hardly an easy or comfortable place to stand. And far from my childhood faith where the language of prayer bound me fast to the unshakable reality of God. But this is where I find myself now, standing uneasily on the edge of something vast and unknowable. Drawn toward this abyss but unsure of what it will mean to face and respond to it. "Deep calls to deep," says the psalmist (Ps. 42:7). But what is this depth?

Is it navigable, knowable? Or, as so often seems to be true, inscrutable and empty and bewildering? "He has walled up my way, so that I cannot pass, and he has set darkness upon my path," says Job (Job 19:8). Sometimes, the abyss can seem to swallow up everything, not only faith, but the very idea of God. And the world itself: "God has grown old ... His mind is getting weaker and it is full of holes. The Word has become gibberish. So has the world, which arose from the Mind and the Word. The sky is cracking like desiccated wood, the earth has decayed in places and now falls apart under the feet of animals and people. The edges of the world are fraying and turning to dust."[35] What can it possibly mean, in light of such utter disintegration, to maintain a sense of faith? Is despair the only possible response? Or perhaps a humility born of the recognition that the way ahead is shrouded in darkness?

These troubling questions seem to be more and more with us, a necessary part of what it means to engage experience that is often utterly illegible, incomprehensible, unsayable, what Jabés describes as "unconditional presence, absence. Everywhere, always the same emptiness."[36] An emptiness that sometimes threatens to cancel out the very possibility of faith or creates the conditions for faith to be deepened and purified, making room for unknowing and despair and even the absence of faith. Where emptiness becomes a place of encounter, in or beyond faith, with the most bewildering experiences of absence and loss.

I suspect it is these questions more than anything else that have drawn me in this moment to engage the work of the thirteenth-century Flemish mystic Hadewijch of Antwerp—in particular her sense of the critical importance of darkness, absence, wandering, exile, and despair to the experience of faith. And her openness to what she calls "unfaith," the radical undoing of faith for the sake of a more honest encounter with God in the abyss. I am searching for my own "wounded words," for a way of expressing the dismal sense of abandonment that so dominates this landscape of loss through which I am moving, and which has increasingly shaped my own sense of faith. I find myself in this moment drawn especially the question of what it means, as Hadewijch counsels, to "always fall back into the abyss of humility?"[37]

Wandering, homelessness, and exile figure significantly in Hadewijch's thought and reflect her sense of how deeply precarious, unstable, and uncertain faith could be. The terms journey or road (weghen) and wander or stray (dolen) recur continuously in her work, often evoking experiences that are intensely difficult and painful: "I wander in the land of aliens," she says in one of her stanzaic poems.[38] In another, she declares: "On dark roads of misery / Love indeed lets us wander / In many an assault, without safety, / Where she seems to us cruel and hostile."[39] And elsewhere: "Often I cry for help like one in despair. / And suddenly I am unhorsed, on foot. / —What use is it, alas, to recount my misery?"[40] These are potent images that make it clear how deeply uncertainty and insecurity shaped her experience of self and her search for God. Still, we should not imagine these images as being so far removed from the actual experience of the wandering Beguines during this time who, by virtue of the life they had chosen, often found themselves displaced and moving through difficult and uncertain landscapes: "Here," notes Tanis Guest, "it is not the difficulties of the spiritual journey which are imposed on the roads, but the condition of the roads which is aptly compared to the inward struggle."[41] This struggle became central to the ethos that for Hadewijch defined how the journeying soul should think of herself: "Prefer wandering in continual exile far from the Beloved," she says, "to coming out (after the enjoyment of much happiness) somewhere below him."[42] Two ideas of distance seem to compete with one another here. Still, wandering and exile are lifted up as valuable and important precisely because the thought of coming out "somewhere below" the Beloved is too painful to bear. Because the precarity born of wandering is more honest, more vulnerable. It closes the distance between God and the soul. Better to wander then. Better to hasten, join "those who have glimpsed that truth, on the dark path. Untraced, unmarked, all inner."[43]

Toward the end of *The Mystic Fable,* Michel de Certeau cites Hadewijch as an exemplary figure in the long tradition of wanderers who became "consecrated to the total loss in the totality of the immense." It is displacement, uncertainty, precarity that marks the life of the wanderer and ultimately defines the mystic: "He or she is mystic who cannot stop walking and, with the certainty of what is lacking, knows of every place and object that it is *not that*; one cannot stay *there* nor be content with *that*. Desire creates an excess. Places are exceeded, passed, lost behind it. It makes one go further, elsewhere. It lives nowhere."[44]

This sense of being "nowhere," moved and dislocated by desire, always moving between here and there, describes not only a way of life but also a condition of the soul, something that Hadewijch's often-mournful poems make so clear:

> Now light, then again heavy,
> Now dark, then again clear.

> In freeing comfort, in restrained fear,
> In taking and in giving,
> Those disposed to
> The quest of love
> Forever have to live here.[45]

The "here" that she describes is, in truth, no place that can be grasped or known. It is in between, on the way to somewhere else. And often it is marked by the pain of absence.

> Ah! I speak from the anguish of my heart,
> My adversity is all too great,
> And lacking love is death to me,
> For I am denied fruition of her.[46]

Anguish, adversity, darkness, heaviness, despair: these are the fundamental elements of her spiritual landscape. "I am astray inside myself as no one else is," she says.[47]

Uncertainty and instability and insecurity remain critical elements of her deepening awareness of the darkness of faith, and of love. It is only by becoming open to lostness and unknowing and insecurity, she claims, that one can hope to know oneself, and God. But this knowledge is fleeting, paradoxical, and painful, for what it elicits in us is not only a palpable sense of God's nearness and intimacy but also a feeling of great distance and absence. A sense of standing waveringly on the rim of the abyss. And of being drawn close to the Beloved.

This dramatic, dynamic process—the continuous movement back and forth between intimate beholding and painful absence—is for Hadewijch nothing less than the manifestation of *minne*, or love, the very heart of mystical awareness. To become a lover, she claims, is to find oneself caught in this endlessly fruitful and endlessly painful movement: "Now light, then again heavy, / Now dark, then again clear." For those drawn to enter the abyss of love, there is no security or stability; rather, there is only the experience of wandering through a country of storms, madness, suffering, forsakenness, and absence.

There is something undeniably difficult and troubling in this vision of love. And in the attitudes and sensibilities that seem to arise from it. It can sound at times almost pathological, born of experience so fraught and painful and mournful that it is almost impossible to imagine how one can survive it. Still, for Hadewijch these tumultuous dimensions of spiritual experience are real. And they are part of what it is to find herself drawn into the depths of love. The experience of love, she suggests, is a kind of madness, far beyond our capacity to control or even understand: deep, insurmountable, and dark. And utterly necessary.

This is how she describes one of her most important and consequential encounters with this darkness:

> I was in a very depressed frame of mind one Christmas night, when I was taken up in the Spirit. There I saw a very deep whirlpool, wide and exceedingly dark; in this abyss all beings were included, crowded together, and compressed. The darkness illuminated and penetrated everything. The unfathomable depth of the abyss was so high that no one could reach it. I will not attempt now to describe how it was formed, for there is no time now to speak of it; and I cannot put it in words, since it is unspeakable.[48]

In the dense and paradoxical language that characterizes so much of Hadewijch's work, she evokes an ecstatic, visionary experience in which she is brought into the presence of a dark, deep, wide whirlpool. An abyss. Yet she is not alone. "All beings were included here," she says, suggesting the encompassing, inclusive, communal character of this space. The darkness illuminates and penetrates everything (one can hear echoes here of Dionysius's "bright darkness"). But there is no getting to the end or bottom or top of it. Sheer endlessness. Nor can it be described in words, "since it is unspeakable." Here is an image that verges on collapsing under its own weight and almost seems to disappear. Only silence remains. Even so, Hadewijch circles back and, appearing to contradict herself, identifies this mysterious abyss as "the entire omnipotence of our Beloved."

This formal theological expression belies the formidable and destabilizing power of the soul's encounter with the alternating presence and absence of the beloved, something Hadewijch evokes with a bewildering range of images. "Love," Hadewijch says, "is terrible and implacable, devouring and burning without regard for anything." Elsewhere she likens it to a torrent: "The soul," she says, "is contained in one little rivulet; her depth is quickly filled up; her dikes quickly burst."[49] Or, when reflecting on the painful absence of *minne*, she likens the experience to entering a wild, desolate landscape: "It is a wonder not understood that has taken my heart captive in this way and causes [me] to wander in a desert wilderness. Such a cruel desert was never created as that which love can create in her landscape."[50] Here we begin to sense the strange power and wildness of love in Hadewijch's experience and to understand better why she insists that it can never be contained or fully grasped or known.

This is what it means to descend into what she calls, along with many other mystics of this period, "the abyss of love."[51] And to be confronted by its essential unknowability. Hadewijch describes this matter-of-factly but also with a real sense of loss: "Love's nature is to me unknown / For her being and her depths / Are hidden from me."[52] But what does it mean to encounter and experience this abyss? Hadewijch describes it this way:

> [The lover] so far falls down into nothing
> That what [s]he then sees and hears
> And understands in the nature of Love
> Seems to [her] remote and unreachable.[53]

What kind of love it is that remains unknown, hidden, remote, unreachable? In which loss and absence define the terms of the relationship? And yet which, impossibly it seems, is never far away? "To lose one's way in her is to touch her close at hand," says Hadewijch.[54] She nowhere attempts to explain or account for this paradox. But she stands fast in her insistence that "Love's deepest abyss is her most beautiful form."[55]

Hadewijch knew so well what it meant to inhabit the darkness and what it could mean for our efforts to learn how to love. The precarity and the pain of loving are always bound up, for her, as it was for her near contemporary John Ruusbroec, with the question of how love can be manifested in what she calls "the common life," that is the embodied expression of love in community. This, according to Hadewijch, is what love wants to create within us: a deepened capacity to stand with others, especially the lost and forsaken, in a simple, compassionate embrace. But to realize this capacity within ourselves, we must be willing to relinquish everything:

> To be wholly devoured and engulfed
> In her unfathomable essence,
> To founder unceasingly in heat and cold,
> In the deep, insurmountable darkness of Love.

There is something forbidding, even awful, in this evocation of love's work in the soul, and of the experience of the vulnerable soul in the presence of love. To be devoured and engulfed in the "unfathomable essence" of love. To "founder unceasingly in [the] heat and cold" of love's abyss. To endure its emptiness, darkness, absence. Even to the point of entering hell:

> [The one] who knows Love and her comings and goings
> Has experienced and can understand
> Why it is truly appropriate
> That Hell should be the highest form of Love.[56]

Hadewijch was not the only figure from this period who thought of love as requiring such radical self-emptying.[57] But she took as seriously as anyone the question of what it means, for the sake of love, to risk everything, "to be wholly devoured and engulfed" by love. And what it could mean to live with a sense of shared vulnerability, refusing to stand aloof from the loss, absence and pain running through our lives. Allowing "the insurmountable darkness of love" to overtake us, call us back toward one another, open up a horizon where we can begin to envision again the common life.

* * *

We approach Sobibór circuitously. From Berlin, we travel through Warsaw and then into the depths of the Bialowieza Forest, where we pause overnight to catch up with ourselves amid the silence of those great trees. Then we turn south, through a landscape once alive with Jewish communities, now marked by a terrible absence. We struggle to find the place. It is hidden by trees, something we later learn was by design: when the Nazis abandoned the site, they first bulldozed the buildings, then planted trees in an attempt to obscure the horror they had perpetrated there. Nor can we find anyone who can or will tell us the where to find it. We wander for hours, eventually stumbling on the camp almost by accident. We climb from our car and scan the site, uncertain about what to expect now that we have finally arrived. It is bitter cold. The wind is blowing. No one else is around. We hesitate, but then set off down a rough path, and on to a wide avenue between trees. It is the same path, we learn later, along which prisoners walked to their death—named by the Nazis the "Road to Heaven."

We emerge in a clearing and find ourselves in the company of a small group of people, bundled up against the cold, picking their way slowly across the frozen ground. Little flags have been planted in different places in the ground among the tree stumps. We notice what appear to be excavations. It is mostly silent. We stand there for a long time taking in this scene. What is happening here? What is this work? After a while, one of the workers spots us standing at the edge of the clearing and walks over to greet us. We learn from him that we are indeed witnessing an excavation. After more than sixty years, a small coalition of groups from four different countries has formed to search for the remains of those who died here in Sobibór. And for any evidence they can piece together about what happened here. This is their work.

There are no dramatic discoveries for Ralph and me that day. No trace of his great-grandmother Sabina. Still, simply moving together though the place where she died, feeling the frozen earth under our feet, gazing up into the immense gray sky above is a gift. And a terrible weight; I can feel the immense sadness my friend is carrying. But there is also the unexpected presence of these men and women working their way painstakingly across every inch of ground, searching for traces of the lives of those who were brought here and murdered by the Nazis. Their presence and their work in this place are deeply moving to us both. A courageous form of witness, of resistance to the narrative of horror that has for so long defined this place. An impossibly heavy but also necessary work: seeing or trying to see what has been rendered invisible.

This is the challenge of cultivating what Georges Didi-Huberman calls an "archaeological point of view"—a way of seeing deeply into the past that has particular importance in places where systematic erasure has left almost no trace of those who lived and died there. Reflecting on his own experience of struggling to comprehend the site at Auschwitz-Birkenau, where his grandparents died, and of trying to see the place in spite of the depth of erasure there, he asks: "Is this to say that there's nothing to imagine because there's nothing—or so little—to see?" A painfully difficult question, and one that surfaces with particular force for us that day at Sobibór. Didi-Huberman offers this unequivocal response: "Certainly not. To look at things from an archeological point of view is to compare what we see in the present, which has survived, with what we know to have disappeared. . . . We can therefore never say, 'There's nothing to see, there's no more to see.' . . . we must know how, how to see in spite of everything. Despite the destruction, the erasure, of all things."[58] It takes courage to see this way: a willingness to open yourself to what you would rather not see. A willingness to face and even enter the abyss.

"Keep your mind in hell and despair not." That was the counsel of the nineteenth-century Russian monk Staretz Silouan to those seeking to understand how they could meet the deepest suffering of their lives and in the lives of others and not lose hope. A strange, forbidding and difficult exhortation, the spirit of which seems to be this: enter the abyss. Or recognize the abyss you already inhabit. Allow yourself to see and feel, as Hadewijch observed, that "in this abyss all beings [are] included, crowded together, and compressed." Do this for your own sake but also for the sake of all those other beings.

Later that day, Ralph and I sit for an hour or so with Wojciech Mazurek in a small, shabby trailer perched at the edge of a nearby field. He is one of the chief archaeologists on the site, and this is his office. A humbler space it would be difficult to imagine. Nor are the resources that have been committed to the project great. The entire effort is threadbare and precarious. But sitting and talking with him, we begin to sense the simple dignity and integrity that guides this work. When the opportunity to work at Sobibór came to him, he did not hesitate; he left his career in classical archeology to give himself over to this work in this forgotten corner of eastern Poland. Along with his son and many others who have also felt called to do this work: Polish Catholics and Jews from Israel and Europe and other parts of the world. All of them committed to the slow, painstaking work of paying attention. Of trying to see in spite of everything.

The work at Sobibór continues and will do so for the foreseeable future. It is humble, hidden work, not widely known or celebrated but filled with such power and meaning, something I have come to think of as a work of love. This is what has remained etched into my soul from that day. I was drawn to this place by love, by a desire to stand with my friend in his pain and loss. Still, such gestures of love cannot help but feel a little foolish. After all, what good do they do? What do they achieve? The loss remains and can never be undone. And yet here we were—Ralph and I—entering the void and bearing witness to the eternal importance of a single life. And here were our companions, poring over the frozen earth as part of their own effort to do the same. All of us, together, on the dark path.

6

An Intimate Immensity

California, 2016

In our minds, there is awareness of perfection . . . .
This awareness . . .
makes all the difference in what we do.

—Agnes Martin[1]

Late April 2016. My father is in a hospital near Seattle undergoing intensive
radiation treatment for lung cancer. I am in Los Angeles, attending to my life,
as I must. My sister lives near the treatment center and is caring for him. I
know he is in good hands. But I feel the ache of distance from him. An acute
awareness of how little time is left, and the immensity of what he is facing.
And I along with him. The past few months have brought us closer: I have
been traveling to stay with him in his home in Idaho, cooking for him, sitting together looking out onto the Sawtooth Mountains, catching up. I am
getting to know him again and can sense a growing acceptance and tenderness between us; little by little we are learning to let go of the old grievances.
Still, I feel regret over all the time that has been lost to us. And I am uneasy
at the prospect of accompanying him as he draws close to the end of his life,
uncertain about whether I will be able to remain open and responsive to him,
fearful that I will somehow shrink back and fail at the only thing that matters
to me now: loving him. I am also, I begin to realize, hungry for a sign of his
love for me and afraid it may not come. Old questions, surfacing again with
renewed force, here at the end.

One morning, at home in Los Angeles, I open the paper and read about
an exhibition on the work of Agnes Martin that has recently opened at the
Los Angeles County Museum of Art. Christopher Knight, the often-unfor-
giving art critic for the *Los Angeles Times* writes: "In stripped-down canvases,

The Insurmountable Darkness of Love. Douglas E. Christie, Oxford University Press. © Oxford University Press 2022.
DOI: 10.1093/oso/9780190885168.003.0007

Martin created an entirely distinct, largely unprecedented artistic vocabulary for spiritual consciousness." An astonishing, unequivocal expression of appreciation that draws me in immediately. But who is Agnes Martin? Have I ever seen her work? I cannot recall. Still, I am more than a little intrigued, drawn in by Knight's unguarded response to her work. "Once you've nestled into her seemingly simple, initially inscrutable, finally profound vision of art," he says, "it's like enveloping your mind's eye in a soft, methodical, determined but exalted radiance."[2] I pause and think about those strange, beautiful words: *a soft, methodical, determined but exalted radiance*. This is enough for me. I put the paper down, check my schedule for the week and quickly rearrange things. The next day I go to see the show.[3]

It is not easy for me to say how much the prospect of my father's worsening condition affected me as I entered those bright, airy rooms where Agnes Martin's canvases hung. But I know I felt the weight of it. I wanted, perhaps without being fully aware of it, to be enveloped in that exalted radiance, to feel something that would return me to my own ground and perhaps help me orient myself differently to all that that lay ahead. That is not what happened. At least not initially.

Gazing intently at her simple grids, drawn in pencil on six-foot-square canvases and washed in a thin oil paint, I notice subtle variations in color and tone and geometrical form. And a sense of stillness, spaciousness. But always, insistently, the grid. I move slowly from one canvas to another, standing, looking intently at each one, feeling increasingly perplexed. No, not perplexed exactly. That would suggest a greater degree of engagement than I am feeling. I am becoming bored. How disappointing. Surely, I am not looking closely or carefully enough. Or appreciating the skill and patience it took to create these works. Still, I remain unmoved. "Initially inscrutable" was how Knight described Martin's paintings. Maybe I need to give them a little more time.

I circle back to the first room and begin again, moving more slowly this time. Mixing up the order in which I look at the paintings. Stepping in close, noticing the hand-drawn, slightly imperfect pencil lines, then drifting back, sensing how the grids became gradually softer, more opaque, more . . . cloudlike. There is something undeniably serene about these works. And I feel this. But they also seem to me impenetrable, resistant to the kind of affective response that has for so long been such an important part of my experience of visual art. I feel like I am working too hard. Seeing and feeling too little.

Nothing I saw that day really moved me. But her images stayed with me. And I returned to the show twice more. The first time a month or so later with two friends, one of whom, my geometry-obsessed friend David Albertson, helped me see and appreciate the logic and aesthetic subtlety of the grids more fully than I had before. And then again, in the fall, by myself. That third visit was the most satisfying. Martin's paintings were slowly becoming more familiar to me, and I found myself looking forward to being in their presence. I also felt more relaxed than I had on my initial visit and less concerned about the need to understand or engage them in a particular way. I was *enjoying* them more, allowing myself to get lost in them. Also lost somewhere in myself, thoughts drifting this way and that, or no thought at all. Just emptiness. Returning again and again to the simplicity of the grid, and to the warm, pastel stripes of her later work. I felt myself dropping into their purposeless depth. Held within an unexpected stillness. Feeling things.

Not the hoped-for "exalted radiance" of that first visit perhaps. But something important and moving. My father was still alive, but the end of his life was drawing near; also the end of something in me. I was attending to him, along with my brothers and sister, as well as I could but also struggling to face the great sense of loss opening up within me. Returning again and again to spend time with these canvases, absorbing their repeating geometrical patterns, their delicate, imperfect graphite lines, their openness, their deep feeling, helped me. I was slowly being drawn, without quite knowing how or why, to enter a space of emptiness. Until it became part of me.

My father died in December that year. The end came quickly and with a raw force for which I was completely unprepared. Nor was I was prepared (what could have prepared me?) for the silence and absence that followed. Or for the sudden awareness that I was now inhabiting a world utterly unknown to me, bewildering and painful in its stark emptiness. I could not have articulated this at the time. And even now it is not easy to say what happened to me in that moment, or what it has meant to live in the aftermath. But I have continued thinking about it ever since. Or perhaps I should say thinking *with* it. Meditating upon it. Considering what it is to live within this emptiness.

I have also been thinking also about the continued presence of Martin's paintings within my consciousness and noticing how important that presence has become to me—in some ways more so now than when I first encountered them. Wondering also about how these abstract forms—that I have gradually come to think of as "forms of emptiness"—have come to inhabit and shape my consciousness so deeply, both provoking thought and inviting a relinquishment of thought. Becoming increasingly aware of how they have continued to open up an imaginative space within me that invites an honest confrontation with some of the most difficult, painful questions in my life. And noticing how, paradoxically, they help create the conditions for recovering lost traces of innocence, freedom, and joy.

Thinking about these two experiences together has also led me to think more deeply than I had before about the way certain forms or images, that are themselves evocations of formlessness, can mediate and make present what Gaston Bachelard calls "intimate immensity."[4] Night, desert, abyss, void—key images in the apophatic mystical tradition—are themselves emblems of formlessness: images that point to and make present the ineffable, the incommensurable, the unknowable, that create the possibility for experiencing an expansive, formless kind of knowing. Also an unexpected intimacy.

Entering such a space can facilitate an exhilarating, even ecstatic sense of expansion—of identity—something Karl Ove Knausgaard describes as "a feeling of inexhaustibility."[5] But it can also bring about a dissolution of the self, an erasure of boundaries, an experience of disorientation and bewilderment so profound that all sense of place and home and belonging disappears completely. Still, there is also a consistent testimony on the part of those mystics who have relinquished themselves to this space that this radical loss can give birth to an unexpected openness and innocence, a deep freedom that Meister Eckhart calls "living without a why." A feeling of intimate, joyous relationship with others and with God. A sense of being plunged into an intimate immensity.

Speaking of her experience as an artist, Martin once noted: "What we make, is what we feel. The making of something is not just construction. It's all about feeling . . . everything, everything is about feeling . . . feeling and recognition!"[6] During those final few months with my father, I struggled to locate myself within my own feelings about the immensity of his approaching death—to accept my own helplessness and uncertainty and to embrace the simple work of being present to him. Encountering those simple, beautiful grids of Agnes Martin offered me a new idiom and imaginative structure for engaging and responding to this immensity and helped me begin to feel and recognize it within myself.

* * *

In her 1973 "Statement about Her Work," Martin writes: "Although help-lessness is the most important state of mind, the holiday state of mind is the most efficacious for artists: 'Free and easy wandering' it is called by the Chinese sage Chuang Tzu."[7] This observation is suggestive of the artist's long and painstaking effort to understand the role of the mind in the creative process, and the kind of spiritual experience that is sometimes facilitated by both the production and reception of art. What Martin calls "the holiday state of mind"—open, free, unencumbered—stands in uneasy tension with "help-lessness," a state of mind the artist associates with blindness, darkness, and even a sense of "complete panic," but which she contends is indispensable to the artistic process. Nor is there any sense that these two states of mind can be easily reconciled with each other. Nevertheless, they both seem to be elements of an awareness arising from a relinquishment of ego, something that also enables artistic work of honesty and depth to emerge and take form.

In Holland Cotter's review of a 1989 exhibition of some of Martin's gray paintings, he describes sensing, in the ineluctable evidence of the artist's hand, "a signature without an ego." And he contends: "It is hard to think of any other painting today that makes self-identity and self-abnegation so nearly one thing."[8] These observations draw us close to the vocabulary one often finds among mystics and contemplatives—detachment, self-abnega-tion, the relinquishment of identity that creates the conditions for something new and more expansive to emerge. Martin often spoke in such terms about her art, although never systematically; many critics have done so also. This correspondence between the mystical and the aesthetic is, I believe, mean-ingful and helpful for understanding her work. And it helps to situate her work as part of an emerging dialogue between contemporary artistic produc-tion and contemplative or mystical thought. Often this dialogue is implicit, the associations between these two forms of expression impressionistic and intuitive, but sometimes it is more explicit. It is just this kind of association to which Arden Reed calls attention in his book *Slow Art*, which theorizes the contemplative in relation to "the slow" and asks whether the production and reception of "slow art" in the contemporary period can be understood as akin to religious practices during earlier ages of faith. And whether we can reimagine the meaning of "aesthetic practices that create social spaces for contemplative engagement."[9]

More broadly, the question arises about how best to understand and speak about the sense of depth, transcendence, bewilderment, and wonder that so often characterizes our subjective experience of visual art, and when it is meaningful, even in a post-religious age, to invoke the language of spirituality, contemplation, or mysticism to interpret such experience.[10] The work of particular artists—such as Agnes Martin, Eric Orr, Hilma af Klint, and James Turrell—that engages space and light and darkness and geometry in ways that so often seem to evoke a feeling of a radical immersion within a nameless, open, ungraspable immensity, offer valuable insight into this powerful but often-implicit sense of spiritual depth.[11] Something that Martin herself describes as an "awareness of perfection." Still, even if we trace the aesthetic and spiritual influences behind Martin's work, as Nancy Princenthal and others have done, the contemplative character of her work eludes any simple categorization.[12] This is part of what is so moving about beholding her paintings: how open and expansive they are, how insistently they move toward the ineffable. It is not that there is nothing to say about them. Rather it is that Martin's paintings, with their soft, intricate geometrical patterns draw you in and hold you fast, and do not so much invite you to *think about* relinquishment and self-abnegation as to *experience it.*

That at least was what happened to me. I was, without fully realizing it, searching for a way to release myself into the boundless immensity that was in that moment opening up within and around me. This is part of the reason, I think, that I felt hesitant to speak about Martin's work or try to say what it meant to me. I found that I wanted simply to be present to it, to be inside the space it opened up within and around me. To feel myself moving through that immensity. Even if I could not say why. Later, I discovered Martin's reflections on the pleasure of disappearing into formless, expansive spaces and began to understand better my own response to her work:

> When people go to the ocean they like to see it all day. They don't expect to see, to find all that response in painting. . . . There's nobody living who couldn't stand all afternoon in front of a waterfall. It's a simple experience, you become lighter and lighter in weight, you wouldn't want anything else. Anyone who can sit on a stone in a field awhile can see my painting. Nature is like parting a curtain, you go into it. I want to draw a certain response like this . . . that quality of response from people when they leave themselves behind. My paintings . . . [are] about merging, about formlessness. . . . A world without objects, without interruption.[13]

Encountering her work for the first time in the spring of 2016, I did not feel anything like this sense of merging or formlessness. I was, I suspect, too preoccupied with my own thoughts and concerns. Or too impatient: I wanted the work to yield itself to me more easily, to mean something. But it refused to cooperate with my particular ideas of what it should be or mean and I realized that the question of meaning or significance would have to wait. Still, something kept drawing me back to her work. And I found myself gradually learning to respond to it on its own terms. Enjoying its empty, open, unencumbered character. Learning to see both the particular character of what was emerging before me—its shape, texture, and form—and something less easily describable opening up out beyond it. Also within me. Learning to sit on a stone in a field. It "is not what is seen," Martin once noted. "It is what is known forever in the mind."[14]

How did she arrive at this way of knowing? And how did she discover and develop the artistic forms that allowed her to express it? Her own life provides hints. Born on a farm in rural Saskatchewan, Canada, she immigrated to the United States in 1932 at the age of twenty in the hopes of becoming a teacher. After earning a degree in art education, she moved to the desert plains of Taos, New Mexico, where she made abstract paintings with organic forms, which attracted the attention of renowned New York gallerist Betty Parsons. In 1957, Parsons persuaded Martin to join her roster of artists and move to New York. There, she lived and worked in an old sailmaker's loft on Coenties Slip in lower Manhattan, part of a community of artists—including Ellsworth Kelly, Robert Rauschenberg, Jack Youngerman, and Barnett Newman—in whose company she began to find her own artistic vocabulary and identity.

Martin's focused pursuit of an aesthetic form that would enable her to give expression to what mattered most to her resulted in the creation of a series of delicate graphite grids. She charted a new artistic terrain that lay outside both the broad gestural vocabulary of abstract expressionism and the systematic repetitions of minimalism. Her practice drew upon Taoist, Zen Buddhist, and American Transcendentalist ideas, ideas that were also important to Ad Reinhardt (and his long-time friend Thomas Merton), John Cage, and others whom she encountered in New York during this period.[15] Her notion of painting reflects the sense of openness, simplicity, and freedom that she came to, at least in part, with the help of these vibrant systems of spiritual thought and practice. She was becoming increasingly sensitive to the importance of stripping away the extraneous and evoking "a world without objects, without interruption . . . or obstacle." Her emerging aesthetic-spiritual vision required her, and those who engaged her work, "to accept the necessity of . . . going into a field of vision as you would cross an empty beach to look at the ocean."[16]

Her work gained increasing acclaim and was featured in a series of exhibitions in New York during this period. But in 1967, at the height of her career, Martin experienced a crisis. Her close friend Ad Reinhardt died. And she faced the prospect of losing her home and studio to developers. Also, she was struggling with the growing strain of mental illness—what one of her friends called "an extremity of distress." Martin would later describe this period of her life as a time when she had been "penetrated by the night . . . overtaken . . . in the outer darkness." The official diagnosis was schizophrenia. She had already been hospitalized on many occasions. But things had now reached point where she felt she could no longer stay in New York. Martin bought a truck with a camper and spent the next year and a half wandering across the United States and Canada. "I was there alone," she relates. "I had this problem, you see, and I had to have my mind to myself."[17]

We know relatively little about this period of solitary wandering. But it is difficult not to sense the pathos, even desperation, of this gesture. And its utter necessity for her: she had to learn to face herself in solitude. Eventually she returned to the Southwest and began building an adobe house on a remote mesa near Cuba, New Mexico. She stopped painting entirely during this time, instead pursuing writing and meditation in isolation. Then, in 1974, with the help of architect Bill Katz, Martin built a log cabin that she used as her studio and gradually resumed painting. But her return to painting was marked by a subtle shift in style: no longer defined by the delicate graphite grids of her earlier work, her new paintings displayed bolder geometric schemes, evoking the warm palette of the arid desert landscape where she remained for the rest of her life.

During the years when had stopped painting, Martin wrote, and her reflections on the artistic process offer important insight into the spiritual commitments underlying her work. The language she often employed to describe the experience of painting or of standing before a painting—merging; formlessness; the sense of being drawn into a world without objects, without interruption; a simple experience; an experience so potent and compelling that "you wouldn't want anything else"—reflects her efforts to find language for what she had long sought to express, wordlessly, in her canvases. These writings, which can be read as a kind of sustained Midrashic commentary on her work, evoke again and again the sense of open, formless thought and deep feeling that many came to associate with her work. And which often led critics and commentors to draw upon the language of spiritual and mystical thought in interpreting and responding to it.

Reflecting on Martin's inclusion in MOMA's 1965 exhibition, "The Responsive Eye," William Seitz employs a category he calls "invisible painting" to describe the particular power of her work. "It is easy to associate these large paintings with religious and mystical states," he says. "The contemplation of nothingness, which they invite while retaining their identity, quickly goes beyond purely visual sensation." He also notes "the particular quality of visual attention they require, demanding that the eyes accommodate to them 'as they do to a dimly lit room.'"[18] Similarly, Hilton Kramer, reviewing two exhibitions of Martin's paintings in New York in 1976, describes her work as evoking "a kind of mystical pictorial architecture." It is, he says, "an art of private spiritual avowals . . . [that] has the quality of a religious utterance, almost a form of prayer."[19] And Rosalind Krauss comments appreciatively on the profound silence of Martin's work, something she attributes to the way the grid creates a barricade to speech. "This silence," Krauss suggest, "[is] due . . . to the protectiveness of its mesh against all intrusion from outside. No echoes of footsteps in empty rooms . . . no rush of distant water—for the grid has collapsed the spatiality of nature. . . . With proscription of nature as well as of speech the result is still more silence."[20] Martin herself was sensitive to the limits of language and images for mediating experience and valued silence. "My interest is in experience that is wordless and silent," she notes, "and in the fact that this experience can be expressed for me in art work which is also wordless and silent."[21]

I felt something of this myself as I stood before her paintings. My initial desire to engage and respond to her work by talking about it or by conceiving of it in a certain way gradually gave way to a recognition of the limited value of anything I might say about her work or my experience of it. On the day I saw the exhibit with my friend David, we spoke together about some of things we observed or felt. Because of his own long study of the geometry of spiritual experience, he was particularly sensitive to the special rhythms and intricacies of these canvases and moved by what they evoked for him. Also intrigued to think about how Martin's canvases might be situated within a long and still-unfolding tradition of reflection on the power of images to open up imageless spaces in the mind.[22] Still, we gradually left off talking, preferring a more solitary, silent encounter with these beautiful, elegant paintings. Descending into stillness, thought without form.

Gradually, I came to see that it was more complicated, and that this formless thought was arising in response to the particular, formal character of Martin's work—those hand-drawn pencil lines, for example, repeating, intersecting, disappearing into a limitless horizon. Their simple, deeply personal, eloquence touched me. A signature without an ego perhaps. But a signature nevertheless. Traces of the artist's hand with their own intimate texture and shape. They drew me in and held me, even as they left me at times lost, drifting, daydreaming. Feeling things. I gradually became aware that these delicate, precise forms—bounded but expansive—were opening up a space within me for encountering, even inhabiting, a nameless, formless emptiness, something I wanted and needed, even if could not say why. Others have also noticed this aspect of her work. "Grids can be inclusive or exclusive things, lines prescriptive or liberating," notes Charles Darwent. "What happens after they stop matters as much in Agnes Martin's paintings as their progress across the canvas."[23] This is not only a comment about the formal, spatial character of her work. It is also an observation about what can happen to the one who experiences them. About the feeling of merging, formlessness . . . Inhabiting a world without objects, without interruption— an intimate immensity.

* * *

This is the expression Gaston Bachelard uses in the *Poetics of Space* to evoke what it feels like to encounter, enter, and move through vastness, within and without. Rereading Bachelard's beautiful, challenging work in this moment, I felt moved by the idea of intimate immensity in a way I had not been before. It seemed to gesture toward something I had long been aware of from my reading of the mystical tradition—the sense of a vast, trackless space within, and the possibility of inhabiting or even sharing this space with another— and which had now begun to take on new meaning for me as I accompanied my father during the final months of his life. It was no longer an abstract idea or something to think about, but an urgent, imminent reality: the vastness of death especially, and all that lay beyond death, unknown and unknowable. Facing the end with my father, I noticed my usually restless thoughts becoming gradually stilled, open, simple. I noticed also that I was becoming less impatient with him, less anxious about how we spent our time together, less concerned with what we talked about. Also less guarded. I was slowly recovering a capacity, long lost to me, for being present to him without falling prey to the power of the old stories. It was an unexpected gift.

I cannot say with any certainty how much my encounter with Martin's work that spring and summer contributed to this. But somehow I think it did. And reading Bachelard, I found myself thinking about the experience in a new way, thinking especially about what makes immensity intimate. And how the intimacy I share with my father—something so ordinary, so personal, so close at hand—can also be so endlessly expansive, a space utterly unencompassable by the imagination, yet so much like home. So it is with Martin's paintings, so intimate but also silent, empty, open. I pondered especially Bachelard's account of what calls a "phenomenology of the immense."

"Since immense is not an object," he says, "a phenomenology of the immense would refer us directly to our imagining consciousness. In analyzing images of immensity, we should realize within ourselves the pure being of pure imagination. It then becomes clear that works of art are the *by-products* of this existentialism of the imagining being. In this direction of daydreams of immensity, the real *product* is consciousness of enlargement."[24] But I wonder: Is it even possible to engage the "product"—what Bachelard calls here the "consciousness of enlargement"? Do we ever have any sure access to this? Or is it, in its quicksilver character, always eluding us, always drifting away from us? In moments of immediate encounter—before a work of art or within the space of prayer—I rarely think about such questions. I am too immersed in the space, lost to myself. It may well be that I am experiencing in such moments what Bachelard calls "a consciousness of enlargement." But like the "awareness of perfection" to which Martin refers, it is fleeting and insubstantial. I feel things in the presence of her canvases. But it is not easy to translate these feelings into thought or language. There is a sense of intimacy here, especially when I move close and feel the presence of those imperfect, hand-drawn pencil lines, traced waveringly along the texture of the canvas by the artist. But there is also something else that becomes more apparent when I move further from her work—a compelling form whose simple, radiant emptiness seems to open out onto an expansive, purposeless immensity. "You can drop through her paintings into the memory of sensation" says Kasha Linville.[25] Yes, I feel this. Especially in this moment.

Is this part of what Bachelard means by "consciousness of enlargement"? Something we become aware of in the presence of certain works of art or images of formlessness found in mystical texts—that are themselves "by-products" of that more fundamental "product" of enlarged consciousness?

And do these images and metaphors create this space of immensity? Or do the fundamental and recurring images of immensity—night, abyss, desert, void, grid—arise in the imagination in response to our experience of immensity? Are they expressions, however limited and provisional and imprecise, of the soul moving through that endlessness?

These questions leave me a little dizzy. And I sense the difficulty, perhaps impossibility, of arriving at anything like a certain response to them. Nor does Bachelard offer much help in addressing these particular questions. Instead, he simply affirms that "immensity is within ourselves. It is attached to a sort of expansion of being that life curbs and caution arrests, but which starts again when we are alone. As soon as we become motionless, we are elsewhere."[26] I find myself wanting to follow him into this solitude, this elsewhere, and ask what means to enter and inhabit this space. To consider what it means, experientially, to risk opening myself to what Martin calls "merging . . . formlessness."

In this moment, I am thinking only of my father. He is dying. And I am struggling to locate myself within the immensity shaped by this inevitable fact. I am already in it, already traveling with him. But I am aware also of my resistance to go too deeply into this silence and darkness. I do not want to follow him too closely. I hesitate to open myself to what I know is coming. I am not ready to let him go and am doing everything I can to shield myself from this yawning space.

I consider this as I stand over the stove making dinner for my father. It is early evening. I have come to be with him in his home in Idaho. The light has mostly faded from the winter sky. Only a faint purple glow reflecting off the Sawtooth Mountains in the distance. The snow is deep. The trees still and quiet. Darkness is descending.

I walk outside to check the grill: the pork chops are done. Inside, potatoes are simmering. Now a salad. My father was never much of a cook, even less so now in his illness. This is something simple I can do for him. He still has his appetite. And there is pleasure in cooking for him, and sharing a meal. We sit together, just the two of us, eating, mostly in silence. He expresses his appreciation for the food. Still, I can tell he is a little surprised by my cooking. He wonders where I got it from (how little he knows me even now). It doesn't matter. We savor this moment together. But we do not talk about what is coming.

Ten years before, when my mother was dying, I so wanted to talk with her about what she was thinking, what she was feeling, what she was going through. I thought it would help—both of us. But she did not want to talk. She had nothing to say. She was already traveling far into another country. And I could not reach her there. So we sat together in silence. That was how we spent the last couple of weeks before she died. It was not easy for me to accept this. There were things I needed to say, things I needed, wanted to hear from her. But I could not reach her, not in words. This was frustrating and painful. Gradually I came to see the impossibility of what I was asking of her, and began to accept the necessity of entering together into a space of silence. I am trying not to make the same mistake with my father, trying not to resist or fight against what Martin calls "experience that is wordless and silent."

I think again of Simon Ortiz's words: "We are measured by vastness beyond ourselves."[27] Also his sobering reminder of "the vastness we do not enter." That we fear to enter, preferring (for obvious reasons) something smaller in scope and reach. Less overwhelming. That knife's edge. Do I really want to enter this vastness? Do I have a choice? Perhaps I have already begun slipping into it without realizing it.

* * *

In one of the oldest accounts of such experience in the Christian mystical tradition, Pseudo-Dionysius's *The Mystical Theology*, there is the suggestion that entering the vast space of darkness is less about something you will or intend and more like something you "slip into" or "plunge into"— and not always with a clear understanding of how you got there. The phrase "slipping into the darkness" shows up several times in the *Mystical Theology*, where it evokes not only the profound character of the experience but also, its often-mysterious and untraceable origin.[28] The verb *eisduno/eisduo* means "get into" something, "put it on," but also perhaps haphazardly "to slip into it." There is a sense here of edging or falling into a penumbral or liminal space, where old markers of identity that once felt secure begin to dissolve: "Here, being neither oneself nor someone else, one is supremely united to the completely unknown by an inactivity of all knowledge, and knows beyond the mind by knowing nothing."[29] There is in this space a sense of something close to helplessness: "Now as we [slip] into that darkness which is beyond intellect, we shall find ourselves not simply running short of words but actually speechless and unknowing."[30] The greatest darknesses, Dionysius seems to suggest, are often slipped into, stumbled into, as if backward, even unwittingly.

This dense, elliptical language reflects the immense challenge (perhaps impossibility) of speaking of such experience at all. Or of assigning it any intelligible meaning. Who is acting here? Who is being acted upon? How much, finally, can be known? These questions, necessary and important as they are, rarely offer access to a satisfying or meaningful response. Which is why language itself often feels like it is succumbing to darkness or silence. Still, this evocation of the ineffability of such experience and the sense of helplessness in finding yourself drawn (perhaps unwittingly) into a darkness far beyond your capacity to describe or understand captures something important about the utterly mysterious character of our encounters with immensity. And the need for humility and respect in responding to them.

I felt these questions pressing down on me with ever greater force during that last summer with my father. And I found myself becoming sensitive in ways I had not been before to the need for silent attention—to my father but also to my own felt experience. Still, to enter such silence did not necessarily mean relinquishing language and thought altogether. At least it did not mean this for me. I found myself working toward a different and more complex relationship to language, navigating the borderlands between silence and speech, saying what I could, but also allowing silence to gather and do its own work. And listening carefully to the testimony of others who knew something of this liminal space, who helped me locate myself within my own. Thinking about what happens to you when you find yourself slipping into darkness, becoming speechless, sunk in unknowing. Noticing how such darkness can sometimes leave you with a sense of utter loss and abandonment; other times with a feeling of relief at being able to move for a time in a place beyond all images, words, concepts. Thinking also about how this empty, imageless space can sometimes yield an awareness of unbidden exhilaration and joy, a sense of "living without a why."

This strange, beautiful idea, which appears in the work of Meister Eckhart, Marguerite Porete, and other late medieval mystics, is at the heart of what it meant for them to relinquish narrow, constraining forms of knowledge—of God, self, world—for the sake of acquiring a deeper, more boundless way of knowing, and for the sake of a more encompassing awareness of love.[31] Such ideas can feel distant and abstract, until they suddenly become critical and necessary—when, for example, you realize your deep attachment to an idea of yourself that leaves you anxious and uncertain and fearful and unable to escape the constricting space of your fear. In such moments, the call to let go of everything in darkness can come as a relief—even if the cost of such relinquishment seems far beyond anything you are willing or able to pay. But the ache to live without fear has its own power and can, unexpectedly, open you to the possibility of risking everything for the sake of a new, more capacious way of being in the world. Meister Eckhart and Marguerite Porete saw this clearly. And reading their work, I found myself increasingly drawn to think about what it might mean to inhabit this space myself.

Eckhart is startlingly direct about how difficult this relinquishment of our narrow, confining idea of the self can be and why we resist it so fiercely. But he is also alert to its significance and what it can mean to let go of this resistance and slip into darkness. In one of his German sermons, he reflects on the story of the twelve-year-old Jesus leaving the crowd with which he was traveling and, without his parents' knowledge, returning to Jerusalem to teach the elders in the temple. It is this departure that Eckhart highlights in his sermon and it becomes for him an emblem of what it means to leave all for the sake of a more expansive sense of self and God. "You must leave the crowd," he says, "and return to the source and ground whence you came." This means "all your activity must cease . . . your knowledge cannot subsist and is of no avail . . . your knowing must become pure unknowing."[32] Like Dionysius, who advocates for "an *inactivity* of all knowledge" that makes possible a knowledge "beyond the mind" and an experience of unity with "the completely unknown," Eckhart invites a cessation of "activity" (all the strategies we employ to situate experience within particular categories of meaning) and a recognition that conventional knowledge is "of no avail." Only in "inactivity" it seems can one hope to arrive at a "pure unknowing" and return to the "source and ground."

These observations about the need to let go of all activity reveal something important about Eckhart's understanding of the need for utter spiritual honesty. Still, why is "activity" so problematic? What exactly does "inactivity" look like and mean? And why does knowing (at least a certain kind of knowing) prevent the soul from returning to the source and ground? Eckhart address these questions principally through his analysis of the "praxis of detachment" (*abegescheidenheit*), an idea that cuts to the very heart of his understanding of what it means to practice radical spiritual honesty.[33] In another German sermon, a meditation on the story of Jesus casting the money changers out of the temple (Mt. 21:12), Eckhart calls into question the logic of mercantilism especially as it pertains to spiritual practice. "Merchants," he says, "do good works for the glory of God, such as fasts, vigils, prayers and the rest, all kinds of good works, but they do them in order that our Lord may give them something in return, or that God may do something they wish for . . . they want to give one thing in exchange for another."[34] In a similar vein, he critiques those who "want to love God as they love a cow. You love a cow for her milk and her cheese and her own profit," he says. "This is what all those . . . do who love God for outward wealth or inward consolation."[35] To "be receptive to the highest truth," says Eckhart, you must refuse the inclination to create an identity born of works or virtues or to think of spiritual practice according to the logic of quid pro quo. You must become "empty and free."[36] Detachment means letting go of every claim to virtue or knowledge, every partial and provisional identity. Falling into "nothingness." Becoming "nothing."[37]

Eckhart's contemporary, the French Beguine and mystic Marguerite Porete (1250–1310) also grappled with the question of how to break free from the tyranny of constructing an identity from virtues or works and how to let go of everything preventing the soul from opening itself to love. She took this question to its very limit in her articulation of what she called "the annihilated life."[38] At the heart of her vision, she describes a soul who has become "so small" in her annihilation that "one cannot find her," so "transparent in understanding that she sees herself to be nothing in God and God nothing in her."[39] Souls this transparent are incapable of saying anything about their experience or locating themselves within it: "Such creatures know no longer how to speak of God, for they know not how to say where God is any more than how to say who God is."[40] They become, as she says, "exiled, annihilated and forgotten."[41]

The utterly uncompromising character of this language reflects both the immensity of the space into which the mystic finds herself drawn and the difficulty of accepting the depth of relinquishment necessary for becoming this vulnerable, this open. Porete's interlocutor, speaking on behalf of "reason," asks: "Is she not out of her mind, the soul who speaks thus?"[42] So it seemed at the time to many of those who read Porete and Eckhart. But the extremity of language and thought that led them both to be condemned by church authorities is also part of what made them so compelling to so many of their readers. It still does. The language of loss, exile, and darkness opens up a vast horizon, where the soul sees, perhaps for the first time, what it might mean to become "nothing" for the sake of God. How to leave behind the evasions of the marketplace for the terrible freedom of the abyss. Still, is it really possible to let go this completely?

Eckhart's readers (or listeners) clearly felt the challenge of this question, and he includes them and their questions in his own reflections. In response to his teaching: "You must leave the crowd . . . your knowing must become pure unknowing," one of his interlocutors poses a question: "Am I supposed to be in total darkness?" To which Eckhart responds, without hesitation: "Certainly. You cannot do better than to place yourself in darkness and unknowing."[43] *Place yourself in darkness and unknowing*: this is a more active, self-aware, and intentional gesture, perhaps, than Pseudo-Dionysius's ambiguous and elusive notion of "slipping into" darkness. But the language is somewhat deceptive, for Eckhart does not imagine this as something that one achieves or accomplishes. To the contrary: waiting and openness and receptivity are critical. Even so, learning to live this way brings with it a sense of risk and vulnerability, something that helps to account for the reaction of dismay that sometimes arose among Eckhart's listeners: "Oh sir, must everything go then, and is there no turning back?" Eckhart's response is devastating in its simplicity and directness: "No indeed, by rights there is no returning."

Reading Eckhart and Porete in this moment, I feel uncertain about my own capacity for practicing such radical detachment, for relinquishing old and narrow markers of identity. But their words speak to a desire I have felt growing in me for some time now—to overcome my long-standing inclination to protect myself, to keep a safe distance from the kind of vulnerability and risk that might help me inhabit my own life more deeply. I have hidden myself for too long. From my father certainly. And no doubt from myself. Can I risk opening myself to him? Can I resist the impulse to "return" to a safe, familiar place where I can keep my distance? I find myself slipping into darkness in spite of myself. Still, I identify with Eckhart's interlocutor, who asks, incredulous and fearful: "Must everything go then, and is there no turning back?"

Eckhart's teaching does not seem to allow for hesitation or doubt or compromise. But how many of his readers, I wonder, felt themselves perched somewhere on the edge of their own fearfulness and doubt, hesitating before the prospect of such a profound relinquishment? Feeling aghast at the abyss opening up before them? His uncompromising vision seems not to take this into account at all. Still, he consistently gives voice to his readers' doubts and uncertainties, and thinks with them about their questions, especially questions about the challenge of letting go. A kind of conversation emerges in which the unspeakable, unknowable character of this experience emerges, even if briefly, into language.

"But what *is* this darkness?" asks an unnamed interlocutor. "What do you call it? What is its name?" It is tempting to read these questions as theoretical or abstract or evasive. As attempts to seek refuge in the world of definitions, explanations, things that can be grasped more easily by the mind than the yawning space of darkness opened up by Eckhart's teaching. No wonder. If we try to describe for ourselves what it feels like to be *inside* this immensity, we find ourselves running up against the very limits of language; feeling the inadequacy of all comparisons, perhaps feeling the terror of looking out over an endless abyss. Seen from this perspective, these questions take on a different meaning. Nor, I think, should they be seen as evasive. "What *is* this darkness?" I take this to be an honest question, haunted perhaps by apprehension, but also filled with longing: What is this darkness I am being invited into, that is already drawing me in, overtaking me? Where *am* I? These questions are, I begin to realize, familiar to me. The questioner wants to know (and I along with him) not what the darkness is *like* (the weakness of simile) but what it *is*. And what it is to be lost inside it.

There is a moment in Krzysztof Kieślowski's film *Dekalog* when a father and son are seen sitting together in an apartment somewhere in a Warsaw drinking tea. It is winter. Out of the shared silence comes a question: "What is death?" the boy asks his father. Earlier that day, on his way home from school, he had encountered a dog frozen to death in the snow. The experience left him shaken and struggling to work out the meaning of what he had seen. Now he was looking to his father for help. The boy listens as his father patiently explains how the heart stops beating and how eventually blood no longer reaches the brain. And death comes. This is how it happens. But the boy seems to be after something else. "No," he says, addressing his father once again: "I mean what *is* death?" The father looks intently at his son, struggling to take in the weight of this question. But he says nothing in response. He does not know what to say. Not in that moment anyway. Together father and son descend into the silence opened up by this presence of this sudden, unexpected immensity.[44]

It is impossible to know how much silence gathered around the conversations between Eckhart and his students. But one can sense in the exchanges between them traces of the silence Eckhart describes throughout his sermons as the very ground out of which the "secret word" (of God) is spoken in the soul. The ground of everything. The question posed here—"What *is* this darkness?" is grave and deep. And, like the question the son asks the father in *Dekalog*, it bears elements of something unknowable within it. Perhaps it is not surprising then that the response that Eckhart does eventually give reverberates with the depth of this silent ground. "The only name [darkness] has," he says, is " 'potential receptivity . . . the *potential* of receptivity in which you will be perfected.'" He makes no attempt to *define* darkness. Or to give his listener a secure place to stand. He points rather to the quality of attention and openness required of anyone who hopes to enter this mysterious space.

Receptivity. Not a skill or a virtue. More like a disposition. Still, it would be misleading to suggest that Eckhart's teaching about what it means to enter darkness ends here. It does not. His invitation to practice simple receptivity opens the way to a further deepening of awareness of who you are in this place of "pure unknowing." A deepening that is realized and made possible by *practicing* the very emptiness you seek: "Keep yourself empty and bare," he says, "just following and tracking this darkness and unknowing without turning back . . . [become] a desert . . . [enter] a state of pure nothingness." A series of exhortations, reminders of what it means to practice responding to your own potential receptivity. Refrain from seeking explanations for your experience that prevent you from facing and responding honestly to your life. Resist categories of thought and self-understanding that distance you from yourself and your silent ground. Do not flee from what is emerging within you. "Absolute stillness for as long as possible is best of all for you," says Eckhart. "Stand still and do not waver from your emptiness."[45]

Potential receptivity: it is not easy to say precisely what this means or what it might mean to practice it. It is not passivity. But neither is it an act of the will or something one *does*. How then to think about it? Simone Weil once noted: "We do not obtain the most precious gifts by going in search of them, but by waiting for them."[46] Waiting, listening, remaining poor, empty, and bare. This is not a virtue or a work; nor is it anything for which we can claim ownership. It is nothing except openness and receptivity. A space where it becomes possible to notice that, as Eckhart asserts: "God lies in wait for us with nothing so much as with love."[47]

I consider this in light of my hesitation before the darkness unfolding before me, and my uncertainty about how I will meet it or enter or respond to it. Whether I am willing to wait in darkness for love. Whether I am willing to risk getting lost in this immensity. Like Mary Magdalen in the desert. Porete says: "When she was in the desert, Love overtook her, which annihilated her, and . . . because of this Love worked in her for her sake, without her . . . and she had no why since Love had overtaken her."[48] Reading Porete's words, I consider again what it might mean for me in this moment to stand in simple openness to all that is emerging in my life. To allow myself to be overtaken by love.

* * *

Is there something about immensity itself that helps open us to intimacy? Perhaps it is the need to let go (*gellasenheit,* or "releasement," was one of Eckhart's favorite terms for it) that upends our long-held notions of agency and control, of who is acting on whom. That makes it possible to be at once intentional and unselfconscious. That helps you to pay attention with every fiber of your being to what you are seeking, while acknowledging that it must arise in its own time and in its own way. That makes you susceptible to being overtaken. As happened to me one summer afternoon along the coast of Southern California.

I was traveling from Los Angeles to Chula Vista with my family, and we had stopped in La Jolla for something to eat. After lunch, on our way back to the car, I noticed a sign on the sidewalk: "Phenomenal: California Light, Space, Surface."[49] We were standing in front of the Museum of Contemporary Art San Diego. Should we have a look at the exhibition? Skeptical glances from the kids made this seem unlikely. But we checked the time and discussed the possibility of looking for ice cream afterward. Eventually, it was decided that we would indeed "have a look." We would not stay long.

Inside the museum, we followed the signs leading to one of the exhibits: "Eric Orr: Zero Mass." Past the sign, there was a narrow passageway leading toward a dark opening. That was all. We looked at one another and at the uncertain path ahead. No one moved. Maybe not, I thought. That old feeling of fear of the dark. We paused to talk about it. Eventually, we arrived at a compromise: we would go as far as we could and, if it got too weird, we would turn back.

We moved slowly together down a curving pathway that became steadily darker. Then, after a few minutes, we lost sight of one another completely. I could hear their voices. But I did not know where they were. I reached out my hand, feeling for anything that would help me locate myself. There was a barrier of some kind enclosing the space. Not a wall, but softer. It gave a little against the pressure of my hand. Some kind of fabric perhaps. I kept my hand there as I moved slowly forward. This will guide me I thought. I felt a tug on my sleeve: it was one of the boys. We were straggling along together into the darkness attached to one another as if by a climber's rope. I became aware of a little twinge of anxiety. Was this okay? Is everyone else okay? None of us could see anything; it was impossible to know where we were going. I wondered whether we should just turn around and go back. But then I recalled what the guide at the entrance said to us: just keep moving. Give it time. Yes, we were supposed to keep moving until we got farther inside. Then we could stop. Was it time to stop?

I stopped. The path had opened up into a kind of chamber. I stood in the dark breathing slowly. I could see nothing. I could not see any *thing*. No, not even—yes this is exactly the right expression—the hand in front of my face. I waved it around in front of me. I could feel a slight disturbance in the air, a little whoosh, whoosh. But that was all. I was sightless and disoriented. But bewilderment gradually gave way to amusement, and then something like wonder. What was this place? Where were we? Where were we going? Questions came and went quickly. I stood there for a long time looking out into what exactly? I realize that I said "looking out into" mostly from habit. But I was not looking out into anything really. I was not looking at all. So what then? I could not say.

Gradually, I began to relax. There was a stillness inside this space, a kind of warmth even. I knew the children were nearby. And Jennifer. A tug on the sleeve. A soft whisper: Are you there? Yes, I am here. That was the only evidence we had of one another's presence: a soft touch, a familiar voice. Perhaps it is not so different from the voice on the other end of a phone call. You are there. I know that. But I have to conjure your presence through your voice. It is not difficult to do. I know that voice so well. It is like that here. Somewhere, not too far away, you are standing. I cannot see you. But I hear you breathing. I feel you near me in the darkness. Exhilarating.

I am not sure how long we remained there, moving through the darkness together. The uneasiness I felt at first entering the space began to dissipate. For the others also. We slowly settled in, accepting the darkness for what it was, or at least what it seemed to be. Then something strange and unexpected happened: faint outlines of figures began emerging from the darkness. Ghostly apparitions. Gradually they took form: embodied presences. I counted: five, six, seven, eight other persons moving around with me in this little space. My wife, our children. Two or three others not known to me. Amazing. I discerned the faint image on someone's T-shirt. The curved walls enclosing the space became visible. I still could not make out any faces. But the darkness was beginning to lift. How? And why? Nothing about the space itself had changed. No one had introduced any light. Somehow our capacity to see in that space was shifting, opening up. It had to be us. Something *in us* was opening up. It was difficult not to smile at the strange wonder of it.

What kind of darkness was this? Was it really darkness at all? And how did we move from blindness to seeing? In that moment none of us could say. Nor did we try. But something unusual and unexpected had happened to us: we found ourselves, even if only for a few minutes, displaced and unable to find any visual cues to guide us, immersed in an unexpected perceptual void. Then, slowly emerging from this mysterious space, regaining a purchase on the world, but somehow altered.

Later, I read Eric Orr's account of what happens to the person who embarks on this journey (written in 1973 at the time of the first public exhibition of this work):

You walk into a space. The space is dark. Someone is in it. You hear disembodied voices. The space seems to grow lighter. You are using rod vision and your pupils are expanding. First you begin to see shadows, then forms, but never faces. There is no way to visibly tell the floor from the wall or the wall from the ceiling. You are in an undifferentiated space, a space without definition. Someone walks away and disappears into a granule visual field. There is nothing in the space but light, the light bleeds through the wall.[50]

The simple clarity of this account reflects with uncanny accuracy so much of my own experience of *Zero Mass*. And it offers an explanation of sorts for how and why the space works the way it does: for the many long minutes it takes for your eyes (your rod vision) to catch up or adjust, you are indeed moving around in darkness. Until you are not. It also suggests something about what can happen, physiologically and perceptually, to those who enter and inhabit this space: a kind of Ganzfelt effect. And it reveals something important about the artist's own vision for the work, the ideas and questions that preoccupied him in its creation.

Still, this explanation of how the space works does not wholly account for how it actually feels to descend into that undifferentiated darkness or for the kinds of questions it provokes: "Either the Darkness alters — / Or something in the sight / Adjusts itself to Midnight," says Emily Dickinson.[51] Not an explanation of anything, but a meditation on the mystery of how it feels to inhabit and perceive things in the night. Reflecting on my experience of entering this space, I recall especially the disorienting force of losing my capacity to see, of not being able to say where I was, where I was going. Perhaps, even who I was. Dawna Schuld's observations about the destabilizing effect of entering *Zero Mass* reflect my own experience: "The apparent emptiness in which we find ourselves," she says, "undermines the stable sense of self that carries on unquestioned outside it." This, I begin to see, is part of Orr's genius: he creates spaces that evoke what Schuld calls the "'primordial minimal,' a sense of oneness that exists prior to language, intellection and differentiation."[52] These spaces are contrived, of course, part of a sustained effort to reimagine conventional boundaries of perception. But it does not matter. On this afternoon, I delight at being able drift through the dark, empty space of *Zero Mass*, and welcome the sense of the hard edges of my self giving way to something less secure, more diffuse, and undifferentiated. Enthralling.

But there is also something else: an unexpected intimacy with the others who are moving through this space with me begins to take hold. A sense of simple presence. Joy. Perhaps also a momentary sense of freedom that comes from knowing myself as both more (and less) than who my carefully cultivated identity says I am. A sense of myself as open, encompassing, fluid. Not separate from others but united with them in the empty, silent space. In this moment, I find myself unencumbered by my need to account for or explain or determine the meaning of things. I let the darkness take hold of me, carry me.

Eventually we emerge from this space, laughing, squinting, a little relieved to be back in the familiar light of day. Everything so sharp and luminous. Is this how it always is—this etched-glass clarity? Or is this another part of the contrast effect of the work? Yes, no doubt it is. Still, part of me is already nostalgic for that darkness, the sense of drifting, touching, and being touched in that beautiful, purposeless obscurity.

This was many years ago. I recall that moment now as I think about whether I can somehow enter and share the darkness that is now descending upon my father. Or at least be present to him in that space. I am not sure. I am still hesitant to let go of the words and explanations I am counting on the help me grasp what is happening. "I must still / grow in the dark like a root."[53] Yes, I need to grow in the dark, learn to open myself to all I cannot see or know. Learn to let go. Especially now.

* * *

December 2016. My father is now in northern California, where we moved him to be close to my brother. But his health is failing rapidly, there are no further medical interventions possible or advisable, and he has now entered hospice. I have come to join my siblings in accompanying him. To say goodbye.

It is late. I am walking down the hall with my two brothers to see how he his doing. We hear him even before we arrive at his room: he is moaning, crying out. The nurses are helping to reposition him in his bed, and this seems to be causing him pain. Or is it something else? I do not know. It is hard to see him this way. He is so utterly helpless. Does he have any sense of what is happening to him? I cannot really tell. He seems very far away. And alone. Yes, we are here with him. And we have been with him almost continuously these past several months. But he is now descending into a solitary place known only to him.

After a few minutes, he grows quiet. His breathing slows. The pain appears to have subsided. We gather around his bed. No one speaks. But we can sense we are close to the end. *We.* Yes, that is the thought that surfaces in that moment. It is my father's life that is drawing to a close. But we are all coming to the end of something.

Touch. That is what comes to me first. I do not know what to say. But I can hold him, touch him. I reach out my hand and lay it on top of his chest. His breath is ragged, labored. In and out, rising and falling. All of my awareness is concentrated in my hand on his chest. I feel his breath passing into my body. His embodied presence.

His eyes are closed. He begins moaning softly again. Over and over. It is pitiful to hear him make this sound. My father. "What is it?" my brother asks him. No answer. Is he in pain? My brothers and I exchange glances. After a few minutes, I go to consult with the hospice nurse. I discover that she has already given him a small dose of morphine to help with the pain. We consider the possibility that it might need to be increased. But for the moment, we decide to wait and see.

It is now past midnight. We have already been here for several hours. I check in with my brothers about what we should do. We decide to take turns staying with my father during the night. It is agreed that my brother Mike, who lives nearby and who has done more than any of us to care for my father these past months, should go home to get some much-needed rest. My other brother, Tim, will also get some sleep and return around 4:00 a.m. I take the first watch.

The door closes and I find myself alone with my father.

"I have had a good run," he said to me the last time I went to see him. It is true. He is fond of repeating this phrase or others like it. "I really can't complain," he says, smiling. But I could see in his eyes how much he was struggling. The chemotherapy and radiation treatments had helped slow the spread of the cancer. But they had also diminished him, making it difficult for him to breathe or walk or, at times, think clearly. We had all wondered at one time or another during the last year: Is the treatment worse than the disease? It was the path he had chosen, and we accepted it and supported him in it. But now it had finally begun to catch up with him. And in this moment, sitting here with him in the darkness, it had also caught up with me.

I do not know what to do with myself. I sit on the bed next to him and wait. For what? I do not know. I do not want to say: wait for him to die. That is too brutal, too awful. I do not want him to die. I am afraid of him dying. Waiting for what then? Maybe it is more like: I will wait with you as you make this passage. Even though I have no idea what that means. Even though it is his passage alone to make.

I look at him lying there in bed. His eyes are closed, his mouth is open. He is breathing. But where is he? I do not know. Nor can I reach him where he is. I sense this. I hope he is aware of my presence, I hope he is aware of that. I say this out of my helplessness because there is nothing else I can offer. Earlier that evening, my brother Mike reminded him that we were all there. He opened his eyes for a moment, but he did not seem to register anything. It was impossible to know.

Loss. I am trying to prepare myself for losing him. But then I think: this is foolishness. You cannot prepare yourself for what has not yet happened. Not really. Even so, I can feel my trepidation, my fear, my sadness building. The pressure is growing. It is ok I tell myself. It is ok. Breathe. My dear father.

Loss bleeds into loss. Sitting there in the dark, I find myself thinking about other losses. Personal losses, losses endured by others, *loss*.

My thoughts are racing. I remember the young child who drowned in a pool in our neighborhood when I was young; the incomprehensible grief of his parents. I remember my uncle (my namesake) dead from alcohol poisoning at age forty-two and my mother's wretched sadness at the loss of her little brother. I remember the phone call with the news that my cousin David had died of AIDS. The end of my marriage, my grief and remorse at my inability to find my way back. And my mother, gone for more than ten years now after a long struggle with cancer. Personal losses, ordinary yet profound, each one leaving its own mark on my soul.

There are other, collective losses, too large for my mind to encompass, but which have pierced me deeply, some of which I have alluded to elsewhere in this book. How much of this loss have I absorbed into my consciousness? How much can I hope to absorb? I do not know. Nor can I say clearly what difference it has made to my life, to how I live, and my ethical commitments to have encountered these losses and struggled with them. I only know that sitting there with my father that night, many of these images rush into my mind unbidden. They were there already. But they are calling for my attention again. And somehow they are becoming stitched together as part of a haunted fabric of loss, which now includes my father.

It feels so strange to travel this way in my mind. I wonder: Is this one of the gifts my father is giving me here at the end of his life? Reminding me by his presence, his life, and the life he has given to me, and now by his fragility, of the utter preciousness of existence? And of the need to open my soul more fully to this gift? I know this already. Or I think I do. But I can feel myself being called deeper into awareness of this truth by his impending death.

Memento mori: "always keep before you the day of your death and then there will be no fault in your soul." Evagrius and other ancient Christian contemplatives offered this simple counsel as a way of encouraging us to overcome our habitual tendency to become inattentive to what is before us: our own life, the lives of others, the life of the world. "No fault in your soul": another way of describing an open heart, a clear conscience, an expansive awareness. A simple exercise, but so difficult to realize moment by moment.

Or *mono-no-aware*, a beautiful and ancient way of understanding how our capacity for attention and awareness can be opened up and deepened and made more sensitive in the face of loss; how careful, disciplined practice of attention to the ephemeral existence of persons and things can heighten our feeling for their preciousness and beauty, for existence itself. In Japanese Buddhist philosophy and aesthetics, *aware* refers to the way emotions are touched or elicited by engagement with the senses. But it is more than this, for it also suggests what Sam Hamill describes as a "particular quality of elegant sadness, a poignant awareness of temporality."[54] The gift of becoming aware of the simple, astonishing beauty of anything, even as we recognize that it, and we along with it, will one day be no more. This moment of awareness holds everything.

I recall this haiku by Issa:

> Last time, I think,
> I'll brush the flies
> from my father's face.[55]

Looking at my own father's face that evening, I think: not long now, not long. And the tears begin flowing again.

I try to imagine him placing his hand on my mother's womb while I was still moving around in the darkness inside her. How he reached out to steady me as took my first halting steps. Or held me when I fell. I want to remember these things. Or feel them at least, even if I cannot remember them.

I reach out again and place my hand on his chest. I feel it rising and falling with his breath. I fall into rhythm with him. We breathe in and out, in and out, together.

Looking at him now, I recall how deeply we struggled as we worked out how to be together in the world. He held all the authority—moral and psychological—and I looked up to him, trusted that he knew what he was doing. And maybe he did. But his exercise of authority sometimes felt harsh to me, and created a sense of distance between us. And later a sense of resentment and hurt over who he could not be for me. He was, I suspect, doing the best he could, trying to teach me about respect and discipline. Perhaps sometimes he acted out of his own frustration and weariness. Maybe he was not as sure of himself as he seemed to me to be at the time. Perhaps he wondered sometimes whether he was being a good father to his son. I do not know. I never asked him about it. And now it is no longer possible. Still, I know I need to consider these questions again before laying them to rest. Before saying goodbye to him.

I recall also his kindness and goodness to me, especially in moments of crisis: the time he bailed me out of jail; the time he took me to the hospital after I wrecked the family car in high school and waited patiently while the doctor sewed stitches into my face; his understanding and compassion toward me when he found out my marriage was ending. So many things.

I lie down on the couch in the next room and adjust the pillow under my head. But I do not sleep. I lie there, thoughts drifting. Feeling so much. Then the door opens. My brother Tim has come to take his place beside my father. We exchange a few words and embrace. I walk in to look at my father again. His withered body. His pained face. He is working so hard just to breathe. It is terrible to behold. I lean down and place my hand on his chest. I close my eyes and stand there holding him for I do not know how long. Then I lean down and kiss him. I look at him once more to fix the image of him in my mind. After a few minutes, I turn and walk out into the night, making my way slowly back to my brother's house to get some sleep. Will I see him again, alive? I wonder.

A few hours later, my brother Mike shakes me awake: he is gone. I rise and dress and we walk together down the path to where my father's body lies, my brother Tim with him, awaiting our return.

"Say goodbye to everything. With a wave of your hand, say goodbye to all you / have known."[56] These words return to me now, but with new meaning. As a commentary on the kind of attitude required to pray honestly and deeply, they remain compelling. But in this moment, the imperative voice feels too strong, too unyielding. I am not ready to say goodbye. And I wonder if I will ever be ready. Still, I know I cannot escape or evade the truth toward which these words point: my father is gone. And I cannot cling to him or the world in which he was once alive. Some other world is opening up before me. But I do not yet know what it will be to inhabit that world or make my home there. I do not feel ready for this. Not yet.

The summer after my father died, I gathered with my family in the Wood River Valley in Idaho to mourn his passing and celebrate his life. Late one afternoon, we traveled up to a remote spot along the Wood River to scatter his ashes in this place he loved so much. One by one, we walked to the edge of the river, took a handful of his ashes and cast them out over the water, watching as they drifted lazily in the mist, slowly dropped into the rushing current, and then disappeared. Such a complicated, beautiful, painful moment. A sense of communion as he became joined to the river, the trees, birdsong, and all of us gathered along the riverbank. But also a deep and sudden absence.

Later I read David Ferry's beautiful words and thought again of my father:

> Where did you go to, when you went away?
> It is as if you step by step were going
> Someplace elsewhere into some other range
> Of speaking, that I had no gift for speaking . . .
> Elsewhere somewhere in the house beyond my seeking.[57]

Elsewhere. Somewhere. Or nowhere. Speaking a language inaccessible to me. Wandering through an immensity whose range and depth I will never grasp.

And yes, in this moment, beyond my seeking. Still, I stand looking out into that immensity full of longing. Is he really lost to me? I am still learning to inhabit this space and live within the "purity of unknowing" that is its fundamental climate. Learning to let go of the illusion that I can communicate freely and easily across the gulf that separates us from each another. I try to imagine another mode of communication—wordless and imageless—a way of being present to him, in love, within this intimate immensity.

"Love was always love, anytime and anyplace, but it was more solid the closer it came to death."[58] It is hardly a surprise that my own awareness of this reality became so strong during the last year of my father's life. The person whose love I had been yearning for all my life was about to leave this world. So: more solid, yes. Even as it became more elusive and uncertain. Even as I found myself increasingly called to let go of the impulse to define and control the meaning of our relationship and allow myself to feel the power and beauty of his presence in my life. His love.

"I am nothing except Love," says Marguerite Porete.[59] An astonishing claim, uttered with unselfconscious confidence. Love had overtaken her in the immensity of the desert. Beyond any claims she might make for herself. In simple, transparent openness to what had always been present to her in that emptiness. A kind of innocence.

* * *

So it is with those paintings that so captured me during the spring of 2016, and that helped me navigate that difficult final passage with my father. They are helping me still. For reasons I cannot completely understand, Agnes Martin's work has come to inhabit a space within me in which my father also moves. An empty space. But filled with tracings akin to those gentle graphite markings. Circumscribed by his death. But opening out onto an endless horizon. Shorn of particular thoughts. But full of feeling: helplessness in the face of this great loss, and longing for an innocence I once knew in his presence.

Martin's turning point as an artist came in the 1960s, with her radical embrace of the grid as the defining element of her art, expressed simply and beautifully in her work *The Tree* (1964). She wrote later: "When I first made a grid I happened to be thinking of the innocence of trees and then this grid came into my mind and I thought it represented innocence, and I still do, so I painted it and then I was satisfied. I thought, this is my vision."

Innocence. Freedom. Happiness. Perfection. These were the things Martin found herself preoccupied with most of all. And her paintings reflected her efforts to *represent* them. Make them present. Even so, she also knew what it meant to descend into helplessness, and it is difficult to behold those delicate trembling graphite lines and not feel this too. Her fragility. Her uncertainty. Her suffering. Still, there was always her insistent attention to the immense space opening up before her.

These days, I think often of my father and of my own innocence. It is mostly lost now, surfacing in unexpected moments when I recall who I once was in his presence: a child filled with wonder. Open, alive, curious. Perhaps it is not completely lost after all. "In our minds, there is awareness of perfection," claims Martin. "It's a simple experience, you become lighter and lighter in weight, you wouldn't want anything else."

I cherish those painting and their evocation of innocence. Also the innocence that endures within me, in spite of everything. I think of those moments in the spring and summer of 2016 when I allowed myself, little by little, to risk getting lost in the intimate immensity of Martin's work, its stillness and silence, its disturbing intensity. Beginning to feel in a new way my own helplessness; and gradually, without knowing it, preparing to say goodbye to my father. Also recovering something long lost to me but now reemerging at the at the edges of my awareness: that elusive and beautiful holiday state of mind.

7

The Common Life

Argentina, 2015

> We must, without sparing, lose all for all.
>
> —Hadewijch of Antwerp[1]

We enter the silence together. Nine students and myself. It is 9:00 p.m., Tuesday evening: an hour set aside for sitting in stillness, our regular weekly practice. We meet in the *quincho*, a small outdoor space set apart from the main house. A few thin pillows are scattered in a circle on the linoleum floor. Candles burning. Some initial instructions are given about sitting and breathing and on the value of a "prayer word" or mantra for helping still the mind. Nothing too strict or formal (some spend the time lying on their backs on the floor, eyes closed, others curled up on their sides in a corner of the room). No words are spoken. No thoughts or feelings revealed. Whatever "happens" is hidden from view, held in the silence. Sometimes we listen to music. Sometimes we spend time writing. Everything arising out of silence and returning to silence. Always at the end we walk together, slowly, around the room: one step, then another, and another. The darkness of the room. The candles burning. Ten figures moving slowly together, bare feet scuffing along, faint breathing, in and out, in and out. Going nowhere. Then *abrazos*, *besos*, smiles and little whispers of affection. After a while, we depart the *quincho*, one by one, wandering out into the night.

The shared silence. The intimacy. The sense of relief that we can let go, at least for a little while, of every inclination to explain or account for what is happening to us. We cannot explain it anyway. Sometimes we can hardly say a word. This life we are living: ineffable. Better to acknowledge this and relinquish the illusion that somehow, somewhere, there are words sufficient to encompass our experience.

The Insurmountable Darkness of Love. Douglas E. Christie, Oxford University Press. © Oxford University Press 2022.
DOI: 10.1093/oso/9780190885168.003.0008

We are far from home, living together in Córdoba, Argentina: *extranjeros,* drawn together out a shared desire for community and a longing to lose ourselves for a time in the life of this rich, vibrant culture. Most of us, I suspect, had only the faintest understanding of what it would mean to leave home and come here to live. Or how it would feel to participate in the immersive experiment in shared living rooted in the Jesuit ideal of "education for solidarity" that brought us here.[2] Or how much we would be changed by opening ourselves to the life of this place.

Slowly this has begun to change—not least because of the extraordinary generosity with which our Argentine friends have invited us into their lives. The invitation to spend a long, lazy afternoon and evening at a family *asado,* or to join in an impromptu pickup game of *fútbol* in the park, or to share a *mate* with friends by the river. There is such warmth and affection, so little ceremony or formality, in these invitations to enter the lives of our friends. Hospitality is at the heart of everything here. Still, sometimes sharing in the lives of others is challenging and difficult. I feel this especially in the deepening relationship with particular communities here in Córdoba who struggle daily under the punishing force of inequities rooted in differences of social class, race, or immigration status. Communities that, to my amazement, have invited us into their lives and to share their work. At Nuestro Hogar III, a community comprising mostly immigrants from Bolivia and Peru, whose small, makeshift homes are built on top of an old landfill out on the edge of the city; at La Luciernaga, a community of mutual support and work for young men and women from the streets in *el centro*; and at Barrio Argüello, at an after-school *apoyo* for children run by *las hermanas Salesianas,* in a long-neglected and dangerous part of the city.

The invitation to enter and share in the life of these communities is deeply humbling. Not least because of the clear sense that they are entrusting us with something precious: the texture of their lives in all its complexity, pain, and beauty. This includes their struggle to respond to all they have been given to carry; their dignity and courage in the face of it; the joy that surfaces continually in our exchanges with them; but also the sense of precarity and fragility that is part of the fabric of their lives. They are opening themselves to us, making themselves vulnerable, and inviting us to do the same. It is an amazing gift. Still, it is not easy work. Sometimes the gaps in language, culture, social position, and experience simply feel too wide to bridge. Other times we come up against the limits of our empathy, courage, and imagination, our hesitation to open ourselves to become part of things. Difficult questions surface: Can we learn to open ourselves to complicated, challenging gift of our life in this place? Can we become worthy of the trust our friends are placing in us?

It is not easy to face these questions. Doing so means examining, critically and honestly, our motivations for being here in this place. Considering the significance of our respective subject positions, our relative privilege, born of class, race, and citizenship. It means examining our capacity and willingness to risk ourselves, asking whether we are prepared to relinquish hardwon aspects of our own identities and open ourselves fully to our life in this place. It also means asking ourselves whether we are capable of paying attention. Whether we are capable in this moment and in this place of giving and receiving love.

I say we. Many of the experiences and questions I am describing here were shared with others. Still, I am trying to give voice to them in the way they surfaced and took hold of me. And I know that not all of us experienced these things in the same way. There are, it seems, many ways to navigate the experience of being an *extranjero*. Often, in talking with my students, my colleagues, my own family members, I was struck by their flexibility and openness, their resilience, qualities that I did not always find easy to access in myself. Still, they often experienced their own struggles—with homesickness, loneliness, and the frustration at being unable to inhabit their lives here as fully and deeply as they wanted to. And almost every day, questions arose about what it would mean to open themselves more fully to the work of accompanying and being accompanied by those with whom they lived and worked. We talked about these things often, on the bus, in class, and during shared meals. And I noticed how, over time, we became more sensitive to the incommensurability of certain experiences and the importance of listening carefully and deeply to one another.

This is part of why entering the space of shared silence became such an important part of our intentional practice. This became a space set apart to become still and quiet and attune ourselves to the deeper currents moving through us; where we could think about what we were experiencing and attend to what we were feeling; where we could learn let go of our preconceived ideas of what our experience meant or might mean and simply be present to all that was unfolding within and around us. A simple practice that we made room for on a regular basis, even if we could not always say why it mattered to do so. A practice that helped us learn to slow down and pay attention.

Entering the silence this evening, I feel a sense of gratitude gather and deepen, not least because of the presence of others moving through the silence with me. Their weariness and fragility are palpable, but so is their openness and vulnerability. I feel gratitude also for the presence of others in the community who have invited us into their lives: Ale, Chicha, Diego, Ariel, Martin, and many others. Their kindness, generosity, and openness to us is moving and humbling. So too is their continuous invitation and challenge to us to let go of our expectations, to open ourselves to the life of this place. Their gentle reminder to us that all we are being asked to do in this moment is take the time to notice, with appreciation, the gift of all that is being offered to us. And to respond in kind.

Still, there are other, more difficult thoughts and sensations—arising from assaults against human dignity that are so much a part of everyday life here—that are harder to absorb, harder to make room for or respond to in this silence. The steady pressure of inflation that often makes it difficult to keep food staples on the table; power outages that randomly but regularly plunge the city into darkness and uncertainty; the devastation caused by torrential rains and hail in communities with few means to protect themselves from it; and the sense of moral injury that comes from being continually rendered invisible. Many of these harsh realities arise from chronic structural inequities for which meaningful social, economic, or political resolution remains frustratingly remote—something that contributes to the feelings of anger, exhaustion, and helplessness that so often arise in conversations with our friends who bear the weight of these inequities in their own bodies. But we also witness their extraordinary resiliency and grace and a sense that the only meaningful response to these pressures is to be found in community.

Still, it is not easy to understand our own place in all that is unfolding around us. Are we actually part of things here? Can we really share in the lives of our friends and neighbors? Or does our own social reality, our position as *extranjeros* who will sojourn here for a while and eventually depart for home, undermine any real effort on our part to enter in and participate? What does accompaniment even mean in this situation?

Such questions often weigh heavily on us –amidst the work we undertake every day, and in those moments when we pause and consider what this work means and what we are doing here. Like the moments we spend together in silence and darkness. This space of silence has become for us a kind of improvised cloister where we withdraw for a time to locate ourselves again in the life of this place. To slow down and notice and feel the gift of all that is given to us. And to hold and struggle with the immensity of what we are encountering in our lives, to face those things we would rather not face. To pay careful attention to this reality that has now become part of our lives.

And to consider how the practice of attention can help us enter more fully into the life we have been invited to share with others in this place.

I consider again those words of Ruusbroec: "this is the dark silence in which all the loving are lost." An intuition of how it feels to open yourself to loving and being loved by others, sharing in what Thomas Merton calls "the hidden ground of love."[3] A space where all the lost are held and loved, together. The common life.[4]

To speak of the common life is also to call to mind another beautiful idea arising from the ancient Christian tradition: *apocatastasis panton*, the hope of a renewal (restoration) of all things in God—often in spite of all evidence to the contrary. This ancient expression of eschatological hope, articulated by Origen of Alexandria, Gregory of Nyssa, John Scotus Eriugena, among others, reflects a conviction that the bonds that unite us in love are, ultimately, indissoluble.[5] That we belong to one another, now and forever. It is a quixotic idea, hardly credible in some ways, certainly not provable. Still, this conviction—the refusal to accept that a single soul will be lost—retains a tenacious hold on the Christian imagination. And it suggests something important about the expansive meaning of community within Christian spiritual thought and practice, and the profound sense of unity that binds us one to another. It transcends space and time and is unconstrained by death. It lives even when the hope of life seems to have been utterly extinguished.

These are old questions. About what, if anything, endures. Also about how and in what sense everything and everyone belongs, fits together into a mysterious whole. "What one of us lives through, each must, so that this, of which we are / part, will know itself," says Carolyn Forché.[6] A way of understanding prayer as part of a deeply felt perception of mystical unity, something that knits life together, that makes it possible to see and feel and respond wholeheartedly to our shared life.

Can such unity be given embodied expression? Help us respond to the most profound experiences of dissolution and loss? I recall a moment many years ago when this idea began to take hold of me more viscerally and concretely than it ever hadbefore, when I felt its truth and power manifested in a beautiful expression of lived faith. It was a moment that awakened in me a new sense of shared life amid darkness and loss and that became critical to my decision, some years later, to move to Argentina.

* * *

I am kneeling on the ground, picking up a small handful of salt. It is coarse, dark, red. I open my fingers and let it drift to the ground. Again and again I do this, marveling as I see these words slowly form before me: *juntos somos libres*. "Together we are free." Then: *Unidad. Esperanza. Paz. Amor. Fe.* Words full of feeling and hope that are also prayers. It is November 2010, the anniversary of the martyrs of the University of Central America (UCA) in San Salvador. Here on a narrow street running through the campus, hundreds of people have gathered to honor the martyrs and are now bent over the ground creating, from colored salt, *alfombras*, or carpets. There are dozens of these *alfombras* stretching out before me into the distance. They are filled with the images and words of the martyrs, with crosses and churches, birds, and trees—expressions of hope for a future different from the one that has led to the violent deaths of these women and men and of so many others.[7]

A solemn occasion, marked by great seriousness of purpose, but also by laughter and a sense of play. The creation of the *alfombras* is a social, sometimes familial practice, a shared work that, in the midst of immense pain and loss, binds and heals. We are creating something beautiful to express our feeling for these witnesses and what they meant, and still mean, for our lives. There is unexpected joy in this work.

Later that evening, hundreds more people, Salvadoreños, but also many who have come here from around the world to join in the anniversary memorial, walk together in a procession along this *camino*, the *alfombras* marking the way toward a large field where we join in a communal mass in memory of the martyrs. The ritual gathering continues long into the night, with music, sharing of food, conversation, and storytelling. Also long moments of silence and stillness: necessary for holding close those who have died, for feeling the pain of their absence, for summoning the courage and faith to believe in their ongoing presence.

There is such an evident longing to draw close to the martyrs among those gathered here on this day—a longing to feel their presence, and in so doing to rekindle a sense of hope within the community. The presence of the martyrs is indeed palpable. But this is due in no small measure to the actions and gestures of all those who have come here to bear witness to their own faith, to call forth by their own embodied presence a vision of hope for the future. The need to remember, to touch and be touched by the memory (and presence) of the martyrs, is strong. So too is the longing to give it concrete form—through the creation of *alfombras*, the commitment to walk together through the streets of San Salvador with images of the martyrs held aloft, the making of rich, beautiful music, the willingness to enter into a deep silence where the painful memory of the pierced bodies of the martyrs (and all of those lost in the violence of the civil war) and the power and beauty of their lives can penetrate the soul. These gestures, at once communal and personal, are the means through which so many of the hidden longings and hopes of those gathered here on this day come to expression.

On this day, the work of paying attention is undertaken in the practical work of constructing these simple, beautiful works of art. Even so, there is a hidden dimension to this work that cannot easily be discerned: the shared effort to attend to the lives of all those who have died, many of whom disappeared never to be seen or heard from again. It is for their sake that we are gathered, to cherish their memory and imagine the possibility of enacting a different future. That is why we are down on our hands and knees shaping and reshaping the colored sand. Taking our time. Working carefully. Making something beautiful. Enjoying the simple companionship that seems to spread and grow along with the emerging carpets.

I pause from time to time to look up and see how the work is proceeding elsewhere. Everyone around me is utterly absorbed in constructing their *alfombras*. Much of this work is shared: the gathering of sand, the decisions on where and how the colors should be arranged, the improvised choices that alter the design along the way, the occasional shouts of delight at some problem that has been solved. Friends, families, but also strangers working side by side to bring these beautiful creations into being. I also notice some people working alone, often on a particular corner of an *alfombra*—pouring all their concentrated attention into the intricate creation of a face or symbol or abstract design. Solitary work, undertaken in the company of others, but possessed of its own deep inwardness. There are also the daydreamers: pausing to admire the work of others or looking up at the passing clouds overhead or breathing in the fragrance of the flowers—drifting for a moment through thoughts or feelings known only to them. Considering, perhaps the loss woven into all this beauty. Then entering back in again to the common work.

There is such beautiful simultaneity in this work: everyone and everything moving together as part of a seamless whole. The loss and suffering and fragmentation wrought by the civil war are ever present: in the images and the words, but also in the silences. The *alfombras*—fragile, delicate, ephemeral—embody this. Soon they will be swept away by wind, sun, rain. Still, there is also a surprising and tenacious mixture of defiance and hope among those gathered in this space: joining together, creating these carpets, remembering those who have borne witness with their lives, grieving all that has been lost. Sharing all of this with one another. Prayer—the contemplative work of attending carefully to reality as it unfolds before us—as common work.

This is a particular kind of prayer to be sure, rooted in the distinctive cultural, political reality of this place and oriented toward keeping alive the witness of the martyrs and the historical and ecclesial narrative in which they played such a crucial role. And it expresses something old and deep in the Christian spiritual imagination, the awareness of how embodied, communal practice can mediate the expression and experience of a profound and intimate sense of divine presence. A sense of presence that is at once deeply personal and shared with others and that comes to expression in language, images, and gestures, as well as in the stillness and silence and emptiness that ground them. And that also makes room for and is responsive to the reality of absence. On this night, prayer comes to expression in and through the gritty, complex, contentious history of this place, especially the widely shared sense of loss. And it becomes a means for articulating—in form and movement and images, but also in emptiness and silence—an emerging but still-fragile hope for the future.

Love's "deepest abyss is her most beautiful form," says Hadewijch.[8] This strange and beautiful idea comes from one of the Flemish mystic's *Mengeldichten* (*Poems in Couplets*) and expresses an intuition that recurs in different ways throughout the Christian mystical tradition, namely, love and the possibility of love must always pass through the deepest and most incomprehensible places in our experience. Often the most painful places. Love is born not in the absence of loss, this tradition suggests, but somewhere in the depths where the old categories of meaning have dissolved, where loss itself can be recognized as the ground of love.

The abyss where love is born. Community created out of shared darkness. These ideas, so important in the Christian mystical tradition, also touch on questions increasingly urgent in the present historical moment, in particular the question of how or whether to pray in the midst of such unutterable loss. And whether the work of prayer—especially silent, hidden, wordless prayer—can contribute in a meaningful way to the healing of the body. The social body, yes, but also the shared body of the living and the dead. The body of Christ.

That day on the streets of San Salvador, I felt the power of these questions in a new way. Participating in the communal creation of *alfombras* became a kind of sacrament, an embodied prayer. But what did our gestures, our silence, our singing mean? And did they help us know anything of the bewildering and painful loss of others, or live differently as a result of that knowledge? Did the effort to open ourselves to that loss and stand with others in that dark silence have any meaning? It was impossible to know.

Still, as the days unfolded and I was drawn deeper into the life of this place, I began to notice how prayer seemed to run like a strong current through every aspect of life here. And how often prayer seemed to exist for its own sake without a particular end or purpose guiding or shaping it. In simple expressions of gratitude or joy. In attention to the presence of another. In the practice of hospitality. I noticed also how difficult it was to tell where prayer ended and other aspects of shared life here began, the boundaries between one thing and another becoming nearly invisible. Prayer was expansive, open, inclusive of everything. And almost always bound to the practice of *solidaridad* arising from an awareness of one's own life as knitted to the lives of others in God.

This open, inclusive, expansive sense of prayer was so strong on the day of the anniversary memorial in San Salvador. Every external form—the *alfombras*, the songs that pierced the night air, the procession through the streets of San Salvador, the blood-stained garments of the martyrs hanging in the small museum nearby, the palm leaves on which images of those who have given their lives were held aloft, the reading of the scriptures, the sharing of food—gave embodied expression to a deep interior reality, a sense of community whose bounds cannot be measured. All of this and more held in the deepening silence of the night.

* * *

"Our life and death is with our neighbor," says Abba Antony.[9] The truth and ethical force of this ancient monastic teaching, and the centrality of love to the practice of prayer in the desert, seems self-evident. Yet how difficult it is to live with this loving awareness. The effort to cultivate a meaningful sense of community rooted in a fundamental regard for the other inevitably runs up against the force of our prejudices and fears, making it sometimes feel almost impossible to sustain this awareness. Which is one of the reasons why the ancient traditions of spiritual practice arising from the desert took so seriously the need to face oneself in silence and solitude. And why they came to understand the very possibility of community to depend on this exacting work of solitary struggle.

It is not easy to reconcile this teaching of regard for the neighbor with the image of the monk hidden away in the solitude and darkness of the cave. Nor can one ignore the potency of this impulse to withdraw in solitude for the subsequent Christian spiritual tradition: the Irish monks in their *dochans*, or beehive cells, at Skellig Michael; Marguerite Porete in her lonely abyss; Hadewijch in her wandering exile; Julian of Norwich in her anchorhold; John of the Cross in his prison cell; Ignatius of Loyola in this cave at Manresa; Seraphim of Sarov in his small cabin in the Russian forest. How and where does "the neighbor" fit into this solitary, contemplative work? Is it really possible for those drawn into the depths of the desert to hold before them the reality and concerns of the other? Can community be nourished in solitude and stillness? Or, to reframe the question slightly differently: Is community possible without a deep feeling for the unity that binds us to one another?

These questions occupy a fundamental and enduring place within the Christian contemplative tradition. They were also evident, both directly and indirectly, during that memorial gathering in San Salvador. And they became increasingly important to me during the time I lived in Córdoba. The challenge of understanding how to open ourselves to a world mostly unknown to us, how to be present to those with whom we lived and worked, and how to share their lives made this inevitable and necessary. This meant, among other things, searching out the deep sources of our commitments, honestly examining our own identities and agendas, and learning to face the fears and anxieties that sometimes prevented us from opening ourselves fully and deeply to the work of accompaniment. The space of silence I described at the beginning of this chapter was emblematic of this work—not a monastery or a hermit's cell, but a space set apart to enter together stillness and struggle with all that was unfolding within and around us. But we also came to understand this space as part of a more sustained practice of attention that included, and should somehow inform, our daily life and work. Our regard for our neighbors. A space that helped provide a ground for inhabiting and responding to our life and work in this place more fully and deeply.

It seems so simple: being present and aware in every moment of your life, and present to those who share your life. But it is immensely challenging and difficult. Which is why we found ourselves returning again and again to that shared space of silence. And committing ourselves to "thinking with" silence and darkness, developing our own way of understanding how to integrate contemplative thought and practice into the fabric of everyday life and how to feel the texture of everyday life as informing and giving meaning to contemplative practice. Especially helpful to us was distinctive spiritual ethos of the early Jesuits, memorably formulated by Jerome Nadal, S.J., in the idea of *simul in actione contemplivus*, or "contemplative likewise in action."[10] What would it mean, those early followers of Ignatius of Loyola wanted to know, to become a "contemplative in action?" The first Jesuits never thought of the work of contemplation as separate from ordinary life or from the commitment to love and serve those who they found themselves called to accompany. Nor did they live a cloistered life. They lived "in the world," and understood contemplation as standing at the heart of all meaningful action in the world.

Simul in actione contemplivus: there is a beautiful wholeness in this idea, suggestive of an entire way of living: always, and in every small gesture, living out of the depths, with an awareness of the divine presence moving in and through everything. Becoming open, as the Ignatian tradition describes it, to "finding God in all things." Things of beauty, certainly, but also aspects of existence marked by suffering and struggle and death. Reality in all its complexity and ambiguity. Contemplation understood in terms of what the Jesuit writer Walter Burghardt has described as a "long loving look at the real."[11] An open, inclusive vision of contemplative thought and practice rooted in the conviction that it is impossible to engage anyone or anything except in and through an awareness of your shared life in God, and that there can be no separation at all between the awareness of God that is the ground and heart of your ownself-awareness and the loving response to others arising from that awareness. Ignatius articulated this awareness in terms of something he called *acatamiento* or "affectionate awe"—an orientation toward life and prayer that helps create a space for a tender and enduring regard for the other, and that becomes the ground of life in community.[12]

This Ignatian ideal draws upon a much older tradition of reflection on this question that stretches back to the earliest moments of the Christian spiritual.[13] At the heart of this tradition is the question of how the work of cultivating a profound awareness of God in stillness and silence (*contemplatio*) can contribute to a meaningful ethic of care for others (*actio*); but also how the simple practice of attention to and care for others can deepen one's awareness of the presence of God in and through everything. How the practice of contemplation *in* action or action infused with contemplative awareness can help to reknit community.

These ideas became important to me, as well as to the little community of which I was a part in Córdoba, as we struggled to open ourselves to the complex and often-challenging reality within which we were now living. Especially significant was the challenge of learning to pay attention, without judgment or prejudice, to the life of the place and to those with whom we were sharing our lives. Attending carefully to the real differences in language, culture, and social class that so profoundly shaped our lives. But also attending to our own complex, shifting identities, learning to take responsibility for who we were becoming in this place. Sometimes this reflective work unfolded intuitively and unselfconsciously—during days spent working alongside our Argentine friends in their communities; on long solitary bus rides into *el centro*; in preparing and sharing meals. This was the simple work of learning to keep our eyes open, to observe and take in the world and consider our place in it. Other times this reflective work was more disciplined and focused—on those nights devoted to entering silence; on our visits to La Perla; and in the work of thinking critically, with the help of ancient and contemporary interlocutors, about the challenge of becoming—in this moment and in this place—*simul in actione contemplivus*.

In the beginning, it was surprising to find ourselves engaging the work of mystical writers whose lives and thinking seemed so distant from our own. But, in time, as we gradually learned to read them "in place" and in response to questions arising from our own lives, their work became more meaningful to us—especially in their insistence on the importance of learning to inhabit silence and darkness and their recognition that such contemplative relinquishment was critical to the work of learning to behold one another in love. Which is why we found ourselves so often thinking about our lives in the company of those mystics who had inhabited these spaces, who knew what it was to empty themselves for the sake of participating in a larger whole. And considering with them how our own descent into silence and darkness might help us open ourselves more fully and honestly to the lives of others, learn to *participate* in their lives.

It does not seem like this should have been so difficult. And often it was not, the sharing of life and experience with others sometimes arising easily, effortlessly. Yet, when you are not sure of your own place, or you are struggling to communicate in a language not your own, or you find yourself unable to read and interpret subtle social cues or even to laugh at jokes, it can be difficult to enter in and participate. I felt these things often. And I struggled to resist the impulse to shrink back, close myself off, refuse the invitation to make myself vulnerable and enter in by way of my own helplessness. To note how common such experience is does not make it any less painful or difficult. And it raises the question of how, amid such struggles, it remains possible to open yourself to others, to participate in their lives. Sometimes, I began to see, it simply takes practice. An exercise of courage. But sheer will-power is not always enough. Often it requires something stronger and deeper than this— reflecting on the sources of your fear and insecurity, examining the things that keep you from opening yourself to others and recognizing your unity with them. This is a work that unfolds daily in the midst of your shared life with others, but which sometimes must be undertaken in silence and darkness.

Evagrius of Pontus, one of the most creative and powerful thinkers to emerge from the fourth-century Egyptian desert, considered this work fundamental to the question monastic identity. We were not living as monks. But thinking about our lives in relation to these ancient questions about monastic identity proved surprisingly fruitful for our efforts to understand how the work of attention to the self in silence and solitude could deepen life in community. "A monk," says Evagrius, "is one who is separated from all and united with all."[14] The koan-like simplicity of this statement is deceptive. What does it mean to be "separated from all?" And why is it necessary? Also, what is it about such separation that makes it possible to realize "unity with all?" These questions reflect a struggle that preoccupied not only early Christian monks but also subsequent generations of Christian mystics who often felt called to withdraw into silence and darkness for the sake of renewing their commitment to love. And who struggled to understand what happened to them when they entered these depths, and what this descent into the abyss and the unraveling of the "old self" that so often took place there meant for their relationship with the larger community.

The tensions here, between separation and unity, withdrawal and return, are complex and not easy to navigate. Imaginatively, they seem to occupy very different places and do different things, perhaps even point to a fundamental and irresolvable contradiction. Or is it perhaps more of a creative, dialectical tension, marked by a profound sense of synchronicity and reciprocity? Not first one, then the other, but something more subtle and powerful: a dance in which separation and unity move together within the mystery of a whole life. Solitude, yes. But solitude undertaken for the sake of the other. Holding the other close in the depths of a shared solitude.

Such a conception of community requires a suspension of many of our assumptions about it means to share life with another. It also raises questions about what it means to be joined to others in silence, solitude, and darkness. And how a separation born of solitude can deepen the sense of a life shared with others. It also asks us to take seriously the idea of prayer as a sharing of spirit not constrained by the boundaries of time and space and to consider the kind of risk we undertake in opening ourselves to the vast, trackless space solitude opens up within and beyond us.

Contemplative practice, in the sense I am considering it here, refers to a wordless apprehension of God in and through all that exists. An encounter with a nameless ground whose depth and breadth invites a radical relinquishment of the self into a great immensity. It is both deeply personal and communal, inclusive of the whole of reality. It moves simultaneously inward, into the depths of human consciousness, and outward, toward a fuller engagement with one's fellow human beings and the wider world. This double movement requires everything a person can give of himself or herself—because the movement within almost always involves a harrowing confrontation with the unhealed parts of one's soul in a space of radical unknowing, and because the movement outward calls forth an ever-deeper sacrifice of oneself, a willingness to live beyond oneself, on behalf of others. This fundamental tension—often articulated in the tradition in terms of the relationship between contemplation and action—points to the reality of *struggle* in the life of prayer, especially the struggle to stand in the midst of and hold in a compassionate embrace the reality of a broken world. To reckon honestly with oneself and with God in silence and darkness means learning to live in God *and* in and for the world at the deepest possible level.

The ancient Christian monastic movement—born of sustained contact with silence and darkness—provides a useful lens for understanding how contemplative practice came to be seen as contributing to the reknitting of community. This desert monastic movement was itself formed at a historical moment of intense and widespread loss, in which the social and cultural fabric that had long bound life together in the ancient Mediterranean world had begun to fray to the breaking point. The impulse to withdraw into the solitude and silence of the desert was in part a response to this loss and represented a sustained effort to face it with courage and honesty on behalf of the wider community. It was a healing work that began in the depths of one's own soul but opened out to include everyone and everything, in the conviction that paradise—a world whole and untarnished—might yet be rediscovered and made manifest through the practice of sustained openness and attention.

In his treatise *On Thoughts*, Evagrius of Pontus gives expression to this vision of paradise as part of his account of "the place of prayer." "When the mind has put off the old self and shall put on the one born of grace," says Evagrius, "then it will see its own state in the time of prayer resembling sapphire or the color of heaven; this state scripture calls the place of God that was seen by the elders on Mount Sinai."[15] The blue sapphire of the mind of which Evagrius speaks—that condition of serene and encompassing awareness of being immersed in the life of the divine—did not arise spontaneously in the life of the monk in a kind of blissful ignorance of suffering and loss around him; rather, it emerged through long struggle and a sustained attention to the sources of the alienation and fragmentation that afflicted the monks and their society. Contemplative practice in this sense meant opening oneself to the long, difficult process of relinquishing one's attachment to the ego's isolating and alienating power and realizing in oneself a more open and encompassing relationship with the whole of reality.

It is tempting to see this contemplative work as having a mostly personal character. But the sayings and stories that emerge from the deserts of Egypt, Syria, and Asia Minor consistently bear witness to the complexity and importance of the social reality underlying these early monastic experiments—the spiritual work of the monk almost always arising in one way or another in response to difficulties rooted in interpersonal or social tensions.[16] To "seek salvation" or wholeness meant, necessarily, inquiring into the deeper sources of one's alienation or estrangement from one's brothers or sisters and about the possibilities of seeking reconciliation with them. It also meant learning to attend carefully to the pain, fear, and anxiety of others, resisting the inclination to distance yourself from or judge them, and considering what it would mean for you to give them your deepest attention and regard. Contemplative practice, so deeply rooted in silence and solitude, also had a significant social meaning and became a source of healing within the community. So much so that these solitary travelers became known to at least some of their contemporaries in Late Antiquity as: "T[hose] by whom the world is kept in being."[17]

* * *

Solitude and community. Opening yourself to the fragmentation and alienation that haunts existence, allowing yourself to become vulnerable to the suffering of others. The healing power of holding deep within yourself their needs and concerns. These are among the most important and valuable elements of the early Christian monastic experiment. And the questions raised by this ancient contemplative tradition continue to reverberate. How can the simple practice of paying attention impact the life of the larger community? How does work undertaken in solitude and silence contribute to reconciliation and healing? What difference does it make to the life of the community to cultivate and live with an awareness of a shared ground of love?

I have spoken earlier of the witness of St. Antony of Egypt—of the power and enduring influence of the story of his descent into the abyss, his struggle and radical relinquishment of self in solitude, and his re-emergence into the community as a healing, reconciling presence. The *Vita Antonii* has a mythic character that evokes with naked honesty what it is to face oneself in the depths, and how such work can open up a space for a more compassionate regard for the other. And it reveals the near impossibility of praying apart from an awareness of the deep spiritual and ethical relations uniting your own life to the lives of others. So it is with the evocation of the descent into the depths found in the work of Marguerite Porete, Hadewijch, Ruusbroec, and others, that suggests why a sustained relinquishment of the self into "pure unknowing" is necessary for discovering what it means to live within the "abyss of love" and to hold close all those who share those depths with you.

The desert tradition has its own way of articulating what it is to inhabit the open, expansive space of prayer and how the work of prayer helps kindle love for others. Yet it can seem at times that the work of prayer has very little to do with others. Evagrius's famous definition of prayer—"the ascent of the mind towards God"—is both simple and clear, but it offers little sense of the social or interpersonal meaning of prayer.[18] Nor does his insistence that true prayer is imageless—an experience that arises beyond any idea or concept we may form in our minds—clarify how the one seeking God in prayer beyond thought and images is brought to a more open-hearted relationship with others.[19] Similarly, when John Cassian speaks of the importance of "that ineffable prayer which rises above all human consciousness, with no voice sounding, no tongue moving, no words uttered . . . prayer that centers on no contemplation of some image or other," it is not clear how we are to understand the relationship of such experience to the life of the larger community.[20]

These astringent, almost abstract ideas about prayer, which foreshadow the rich tradition of apophatic thought to come, do however offer hints about why it matters so much to seek out and cultivate an awareness of oneself and God free from images, ideas, or concepts. And about how such simple, open awareness can create the conditions where love can grow and flourish.

The space of prayer, says Evagrius, is empty, open, and still. It is here that it becomes possible to see yourself honestly and deeply and to begin working out who you are in relation to others. Slowly, imperceptibly, you learn to face and examine the sources of old resentments—often rooted in anger, jealousy, or pride—that cloud the mind and make it difficult or impossible to regard others with love. It is the continuous, sustained examination of these impulses in solitary reflection that allows prayer to effect its healing power. Which is one of the reasons memory figures so significantly in his writings on prayer. "When you are praying," he says, "guard your memory vigorously . . . the memory brings before you either fantasies of objects from the past, or recent concerns, or the face of the one who has caused you hurt."[21] Memory, in the way Evagrius is describing it here, is dense, ambiguous, and often troubling. Here, especially if one is inattentive or unaware, one can find oneself contending with a huge reservoir of grievances, unhealed wounds, and unresolved anxieties; and struggling with the powerful, obsessive images that they often produce, images that that catch and hold the mind and turn it away from the "place of prayer." Still, these images could also sometimes prompt a more honest reckoning with your relationship to others: suddenly catching sight (in your memory) of "the face of the one who has caused you hurt" is also an opportunity to go deeper, to repair what has been broken between you. Prayer becomes a space of potential healing.

Evagrius is uncompromising in his insistence that prayer—that sense of deep communion with God that is inclusive of everyone and everything—cannot thrive in a climate of anger or resentment. "When you are praying as you should," he notes, "such things will come over you that you may think it utterly just to resort to anger, but there is absolutely no such thing as a just anger against your neighbor."[22] Elsewhere he counsels: "Everything you do to avenge yourself against a brother [or sister] who has wronged you, will become a stumbling block for you at the time of prayer."[23] And: "If you desire to practice prayer as you should, cause hurt to no soul, or else you run in vain" (Phil. 2:16).[24]

The disarming simplicity of these teachings belies the difficulty of trying to put them into practice. Going deeper in prayer meant not only dealing with distractions, or wandering thoughts, but also facing something much more troubling—the sense that you might never be free of the obsessive, corrosive concerns that weigh you down and keep you from opening yourself to others in love. The practice of prayer, for so many who entered the desert, meant acknowledging and grappling with the deeper sources of their discontent, especially those rooted in resentment or anger toward others. Entering the darkness and silence of the desert—which was conceived of as place of intense vulnerability where the debilitating power of the demons so often surfaced and insinuated themselves into the mind of the praying monk—meant struggling to avoid being swallowed alive by anger, fear and anxiety. But it also meant seeking and sometimes finding release, a place beyond the reach of the demons' tormenting power—a place of peace and deep equanimity that Evagrius called *apatheia*, or impassability: the very "health of the soul."[25] Here, it became possible to begin praying with what John Cassian calls an "unstirring calm of mind."[26]

Prayer, in the sense that Evagrius, Cassian, and other early monastic writers understood it, ushers in a deep freedom—from obsessions, resentments, old wounds—and makes it possible to cultivate a simple, loving regard for the other. Such freedom, the early monks believed, could emerge in no other way but in the solitary and often lonely struggle to face yourself in silence: "Sit in your cell and your cell will teach you everything." I return to the image of the monk hidden away in the cave, utterly vulnerable to the force of the demons, reduced little by little to a condition of transparency, humility, and openness—to God and others. It is not long before we see this same figure accompanying others in their struggle; helping carry the weight of what they themselves cannot carry; refusing to render judgment; practicing simple kindness. Coming to know *apatheia*, or impassibility, a clarity and openness of mind that makes it possible to live with one's heart open toward the other. It is no surprise that Evagrius, in a kind of summation of the entire contemplative project, should declare: "Love is the offspring of impassibility."[27]

This way of understanding prayer and the way prayer can nourish the ground of love also helps to illuminate the relationship between solitude and community in the ancient monastic tradition. "A monk is one who is separated from all and united with all," says Evagrius. How to become "united with all," enter deeply into a shared life with others? Only, it seems by becoming "separated from all," learning to face yourself in solitude and silence, seeking there a deep freedom beyond the grip of judgment and recrimination, a freedom that makes it possible to behold the other in love.

Separation (or creating space, which is another way of understanding this teaching) makes it possible to see yourself more clearly, more "dispassionately." Not simple or easy, but critical to any hope of learning to live in community with others.

"It is not possible to love all . . . equally," Evagrius acknowledges. "But it is possible to conduct our relationships with all without passion and free from resentment and hatred."[28] This is the work of the cell: learning to let go of limiting ideas about your identity that cloud your vision and cause you to see yourself as separate or distant from others, or somehow pitted against them. Coming to see yourself *in* others. "A monk," says Evagrius, "is one who esteems himself as one with all people because he ever believes he sees himself in each person."[29] This simple but astonishing teaching reflects the heart of the ancient monastic ethos, the necessary separation required by solitude and silence always opening out onto a sense of unity with others that is and must be the ground of all human relations.

But the question of how much one can ever truly identify with another person is challenging and difficult. There are real dangers here, especially the danger of assuming you know what it means to identify with or feel for another, that separate identities can somehow become fused. Difference matters and must always be respected. And the practice of empathy, that mysterious capacity to feel something close to what another person feels, must always be rooted in humility, an awareness of the limits of what you can know and feel. This apophatic principle guides so much of ancient monastic practice. And we catch echoes of this principle in our own efforts to understand what it means to practice empathy. It "requires knowing you know nothing," suggests Leslie Jamieson. It "means acknowledging a horizon of context that extends perpetually beyond what you can see . . . realizing no trauma has discrete edges."[30] This too is part of what it means to seek unity with the other: resting in darkness, acknowledging all you cannot see or know or understand. Still, there is something profound and moving in the idea, cherished by the ancient monks and given such powerful expression in their sayings and stories, that it is possible to learn, however partially and imperfectly, to see yourself *in* another. To set your own interests aside and look out onto the world through the eyes of the other. Difference, yes. But also unity born of openness, vulnerability, and love. The common life.

It is not easy to respond to the growing recognition that you are "no longer at ease here, in the old dispensation," to summon the courage to break with the world you have always known, to relinquish your hard-won identity for something as yet unknown.[31] To fall into the depths. Still, there is something compelling and irresistible in the idea that it might be possible to leave behind those limiting ideas and images of ourselves, God and one another that keep us trapped and fearful and alone. Which is why the work of relinquishment, especially when it is undertaken in the company of others, and for the sake of others, can be so liberating and healing. And why prayer, understood as a practice that helps create a simple, open space of love, becomes so critical to the work of accompaniment.[32]

* * *

The call comes to us late one afternoon. A friend of ours and one of the professors in the Casa program, Juan Carlos, needs help. Mendiolaza, the small town north of Córdoba where he lives, has been hard hit by flooding. They have lost power and the streets are clogged with mud and debris. Juan Carlos is wondering whether we can come up to help with the cleanup. Or join in in whatever way we are able. The students are just arriving home and are tired from a long day at their praxis sites. I can see it in their faces. Still, we talk it over, and after a few minutes everyone agrees to go. We hire a *transporte* and, fighting late afternoon traffic, slowly make our way north.

It is dark when we arrive at the main plaza. We soon find Juan Carlos standing talking with some of his neighbors and a group of friends from different parts of Córdoba who have arrived to help out. Everyone seems to be talking at once and there is lots of laughter. *Mate* appears and is passed around. Little *chistes* and teasing. The warmth of old friends and neighbors gathering together. There is work to do. But first *abrazos y besos*. Conversation. Touching in.

There is a generator, and temporary lights are strung up in an old, unused storefront. On the table inside sits a large pile of chicken carcasses, along with onions, carrots, potatoes, and bunches of herbs, all waiting to be cut up and cooked. Just outside, a makeshift gas stove is being assembled. A van pulls up and several large pots are unloaded. Also plastic plates, cups, and utensils. And several cases of bottled water. The houses surrounding the plaza are dark; no one will be cooking at home tonight. But here there will be a feast.

This account, I realize, perhaps gives the impression of more organization and clarity of purpose than really existed that night. It is a completely improvised affair, with no clear sense of how best to match needs and tasks with particular persons. No one is in charge. By now I have grown accustomed to this: the well-known Argentine flair for creating something delightful and unexpected from the most meager elements and often without any plan. Abandoning all pretense of following a map and simply throwing yourself headlong into the work and revising as needed. So it is this evening. One practical effect of this approach in a group is that seldom is anyone certain about where to go or what, if anything, to do. We are there to help. But how and in what way? The only solution: make yourself available to help with whatever task presents itself. Or, if nothing presents itself, wait. Enjoy the company and the conversation. And so we do.

Eventually, under the expert guidance of some highly skilled women from the neighborhood, a few members our group find themselves plunging into the work of cutting apart the whole chickens, chopping carrots and onions and potatoes and herbs. Others, because knives are in short supply, mill around the makeshift kitchen and join in the rolling, raucous conversation.

Another small group forms and departs to help with flood cleanup in another part of the town. We make our way slowly along a dark, narrow road that leads toward the river. A couple of flashlights help show the way. Soon we find ourselves in a *placita* surrounded by a cluster of small, mud-caked houses. All around us are up-ended trees and other detritus that has poured downstream in the flood. There is a rank smell. We stand looking at this pile of tangled branches and garbage, uncertain about how or where to begin. Soon, shovels and brooms appear and are handed around, and we set to work clearing the mud from inside the houses and dragging the trash and debris into a huge pile. It is slow going and not at all pleasant. But the company is good. Our hosts are patient with us as we struggle to work our way through the mess. Soon we are sharing stories and jokes, moving awkwardly between two different languages and cultures. Our sometimes-halting Spanish is, it seems, both amusing and appalling to them. Many of the jokes are at our expense. But they are mostly gentle, filled with affection. We do not make much progress with the cleanup. But we keep at it, working side by side into the night.

After some time, one of the neighborhood children arrives and announces that they are ready for us back at *la cocina*. We put down our tools and make our way back, mud soaked and stinking, to rejoin the others. It is almost midnight. Sitting atop the gas stove is a huge pot of chicken stew—a variation of *Cazuela Gaucho*—a dish brought to Argentina, we are told, by Russian Jews in the nineteenth century. The aroma is intoxicating. Someone has brought loaves of bread and fruit. Plates are passed around. We sit huddled in small groups, eating and drinking, mostly in silence. The night is growing colder. But no one wants to leave.

A strange, beautiful evening.

The experience of that night touched something in me and remains with me even now, drawing me deeper into thinking about what it means to practice the common life. A reminder of how awareness of oneself as part of a larger whole grows and deepens. The simplicity of the experience is part of what made it so memorable and impactful. We arrived in response to a felt need, but also with a recognition that none of us possessed any particular skills that might be put to use in this work. All we could do was show up and follow the lead of our hosts, stumbling at times over relative incompetence and helplessness. We were received graciously by our Argentine friends, who neither judged us nor worried about our lack of efficiency or skill. All of which helped us gradually to let go of our self-consciousness and our need to contribute and simply join the shared work. And to be overtaken with a sense of awe and gratitude at having been invited into this circle. Sharing life with others.

There is nothing extraordinary or unusual in this. Still, it captures something about the shape and texture of our life in Córdoba that only became more pronounced as time unfolded: the sense of deep reciprocity and sharing that characterized almost all aspects of everyday life. This was symbolized most simply and powerfully by the sharing of *mate*, the Argentine national drink that appears everywhere and is always, always, an expression of a deep communal reality. Drinking *mate* with family, friends, or strangers—following an informal but long-practiced process of pouring yerba mate into a small gourd, adding water and sometimes a pinch of sugar, then sipping on the *bombilla*, passing it around, from one person to another, refilling the hot water as needed, laughing, talking—often goes on for hours. The sharing of *mate*, which is woven so deeply into the fabric of Argentine life, beautifully embodies the contemplative, communal sensibility that lay at the heart of this culture. Never rushed, utterly "low-tech," and drawing upon a tradition more than five hundred years old, it never fails to create a warm, convivial, open space. A space with no other purpose than the sharing of life with friends.

It was not always easy for those of us coming from North America to participate in this ritual. Part of this, I think, has to do with its utter purposelessness. Also, the sheer amount of time given over to it. There is no such thing as "sharing a quick *mate*." Often, it takes up an entire afternoon or evening. Concern with time fades almost completely. For some of us, this was challenging. Our own cultural prejudices regarding the preciousness (and commodification) of time were hard to shake. It was not easy to let go of the sense that there was something else we ought to be doing. Even if this was not true. But what was there to do that could not wait a little longer? Or be attended to afterwards? Or forgotten altogether? Coming to this awareness took time. And repetition. And, although few of us realized it in the moment it was happening, it soon became clear that we were being initiated into a new, less purpose-driven and utilitarian way of being in the world. A way of being not unlike what Meister Eckhart and Marguerite Porete evoke in speaking of the importance of learning to "live without a why"—itself a response to purpose-driven commodification of spiritual practice in their own time. Here in this simple practice we discovered something similar: an invitation to give ourselves over to the simple, purposeless enjoyment of time with friends.

Learning to drink *mate*—with friends or neighbors or with strangers—taught us more about letting go of the ideas and pretentions we had in coming to Argentina than almost anything else we did. It became emblematic of the work of relinquishment that we eventually came to see as so central to our life in that place. Especially letting go of the idea that we were there to help, or to make a difference. Or that our ideas of what should happen at any given moment or our inclination to control and manage the outcome of things should be given any particular value. All of us from North America carried these cultural predispositions within us to one degree or another. But almost nothing frustrated or undermined our life and work in Argentina more than giving into them. What, after all, did we really have to contribute? We were visitors here and knew relatively little about this place or its culture. How misguided, foolish, arrogant even, to imagine that we had something important to contribute.

But if we were not contributing, why were we there? There was no good answer we could give to this question. It was often frustrating, even bewildering not to be able to say what we were doing or why. But this loss of ground also made it possible, eventually, to begin seeing our life here differently, with a greater sense of humility and openness. And this helped to alter and deepen the character of our relationships with others. It served as a reminder, again and again, of the fundamental invitation before us: to enter more simply and fully into the life of the place and to accept the gift of friendship and trust that was being offered to us. That was enough.

The practice of accompaniment: the simple work of being present to one another in whatever situation or moment arises, and to do so without putting yourself at the center. In fact, learning to forget yourself a little. Letting go of your own sense of self-importance. Allowing yourself to enter in and become part of a reality that is both deeply communal and utterly reciprocal. Learning to stand with others in the midst of a shared life. This idea was at the heart of our work in Argentina: learning to be present to others, without expectation, without judgment, without agenda. So simple. But not always easy to practice. This was especially for those of us arriving here from North America with our often-compulsive attitudes toward work, and our inclination to always want to make the most efficient use of time. It was deeply humbling to find ourselves called to question these basic cultural values and to open ourselves to a way of being, and being with others, that was more open, free, and unencumbered. And to discover that our worth was determined less by what we accomplished or contributed than it was by the quality of our presence.

But there was also the challenge of learning to open ourselves to the unknown and uncertain. Coming to feel and accept the depth of our own displacement and becoming more aware of and sensitive to the displacement of others. Allowing ourselves to be continuously decentered, cracked open, stripped of our old identities. And becoming less preoccupied by the need to define experience in terms of its meaning for us and more attentive to the reality and experience of others. Especially the reality of loss.

* * *

The question of how to think about and respond to loss has become one of the most pressing concerns of this historical moment. So too the question of whether it is possible to situate loss in any meaningful way within traditions of spiritual thought and practice, and whether those traditions can help us address and respond to the utterly particular, fathomless, and often-incomprehensible reality of loss. I have noted already the way currents of loss, exile, and annihilation course through traditions of mystical discourse. And how often the sense of fragmentation and abandonment expressed in these texts corresponds to and even offers a response to the profound social, political, and cultural loss of the historical moment in which they were written. How the sense of God as hidden, obscure, lost in darkness, and unknowing, often reflects this wider, deeper loss. And often gives rise to a longing to become utterly lost within this unknown immensity: "Leave aside this everywhere and everything, in exchange for this nowhere and nothing," says the anonymous author of the *Cloud of Unknowing*. Such longing often arises from and comes to expression in a hunger for direct, unmediated experience. Especially the experience of giving and receiving love.

In an address given in October 2000 at Santa Clara University on "The Service of Faith and the Promotion of Justice in American Jesuit Higher Education", Peter-Hans Kolvenbach, S.J., acknowledged the importance of learning to respond to this hunger: "When the heart is touched by direct experience," he said, "the mind may be challenged to change. Personal involvement with innocent suffering, with the injustice others suffer, is the catalyst for solidarity which then gives rise to intellectual inquiry and moral reflection."[33] I had read these words before coming to live in Argentina and knew they were part of an important critical conversation in Jesuit higher education about how to deepen the commitment to justice in university education—what Fr. Kolvenbach called a "well-educated solidarity."

These ideas had already begun to impact the way I understood my work with students in Los Angeles as the boundaries between classroom and community gradually became more porous and open. Still, they took on a new and powerful meaning in Córdoba, where "direct experience" came to inform and challenge our "intellectual inquiry and moral reflection" in significant and unexpected ways. So too the idea of a "well-educated solidarity" gradually became less abstract and more vital and meaningful than it had been before. Especially because of the way it challenged the ideal of "service"—important but also limited—that has become so prevalent in Jesuit higher education. "Service placements," where I serve you and you receive my service, are often reflective of an imbalance of power and of a sensibility that rarely challenges our own social locations or spiritual identities. Solidarity and accompaniment speak of a very different attitude and orientation: open, receptive, less invested in how I can contribute, and more focused on how I can participate with others in a shared work. Questions of identity and purpose begin to take on different, more complex meanings. So too with questions of what it means to participate in community.

These questions have a way of shifting as experience deepens. At first, the question might be: Who am I in this place? Or: What is my identity, my role here? But then you begin to wonder: Does this really matter? Perhaps not in the way you originally thought it did. Gradually, you come to realize that you are being invited to take your place alongside others, to wait, to listen, to humbly enter a social reality that is not your own and that already possesses its own inherent integrity. Who you are or what your role is turns out to be not the primary concern (if it ever was) at all. It is instead about learning to be present, asking what it will mean to open yourself to the lives of others, learning to see. This is the contemplative heart of this work: learning to see, without prejudice or fear. Learning to behold the whole.

In one of his *Duino Elegies*, Rainer Maria Rilke articulates this inclusive, encompassing idea of contemplative practice so beautifully. We are invited, he says, to

> See ourselves
> and ourselves *in* everything.
>   healed and whole
>   forever.[34]

This luminous vision of wholeness is both alluring and almost impossible to hold in the mind. It has the character of a dream or an intuition: ephemeral but leaving its own potent trace, providing a thread that can help guide us into a nameless, pulsing immensity. Learning to imagine this immensity, and asking what it will mean to inhabit it and be inhabited by it is, it seems to me, a critical task in this moment. And it is here that both the mystic and poet make such important and necessary contributions. I think, for example, of Tracy K. Smith's powerful evocation of this immensity, which she says, is "Like a wide wake, rippling / Infinitely into the distance, everything / That ever was still is, somewhere / Floating near the surface, nursing / Its hunger for you and me."[35] This is not a distant or abstract idea, but a living reality, pulsing reality, an ebbing and flowing tide, drawing us out into the depths. And there is Hadewijch's strange, powerful vision of the dark abyss: "A very deep whirlpool, wide and exceedingly dark; in this abyss all beings [are] included, crowded together, and compressed."[36] Another kind of whole, another vision of unity, shrouded in darkness. As it is with Ruusbroec, who describes his own idea of mystical unity as a "dark silence in which all the loving are lost"—an intimation of a mysterious whole shared by all the loving, all the lost.

Here in this place, I feel myself beginning to touch and be touched by this whole, even as I struggle to respond to the fragmentation and brokenness and loss that that is so much in evidence here. This whole, I begin to sense, is utterly personal but also encompasses a reality far beyond me. I feel myself hovering on the edge of some new thing I cannot easily name. But what is it? What is it asking of me? Can I "surrender to the expectant silence that follows a question without an answer?"[37]

This expectant silence deepens and grows the longer I am here in Córdoba. I have been plunged into the complex, unpredictable, and vibrant current of life here, and it is carrying me along into some unknown place. The silence that grounds my life here pulses with so many questions I cannot easily answer. But I begin to see that these questions, about the history, culture, and social reality of this place, constitute the very ground of my contemplative practice. And that this practice is part of the work of social, political, and spiritual renewal and transformation.

Ignacio Ellacuría, S.J., a Spanish Salvadoran priest, philosopher, and theologian, who was murdered on the night of November 16, 1989, in San Salvador, offers important insight into how contemplative thought and practice fit into this work, especially through his insistence that all spiritual practice is and must be "historicized."[38] Ellacuría reconsiders the meaning of contemplation found in *The Spiritual Exercises of St. Ignatius* and articulates a spirituality capable of addressing and responding to the historical reality of trauma and loss that has become such a pervasive part of contemporary experience. This means, at the outset, resisting the idea that contemplation belongs to some kind of rarefied (and dehistoricized) realm. "It is confused prejudice," he says, "to judge the degree of contemplation by whether the object of contemplation appears more or less sacred, more or less internal, more or less spiritual. That would mean assuming that God is more present, more readily heard or contemplated in the internal silence of idleness than in committed action."[39] To believe this and to act in accordance with such belief is, Ellacuría asserts, to risk missing the call to encounter God in the midst of history. In contrast, he offers an understanding of contemplative practice that is rooted in and responsive to history and that opens the way toward an ethic of accompaniment.

Such spiritual practice requires a willingness to reflect on where you stand and on how your capacity to behold the other is affected by your own social position and commitments. "Contemplation should be undertaken from the most appropriate place," says Ellacuría. "The 'where' from which one seeks to see decisively determines what one is able to see; [it is] fundamental to what one sees and how one sees it." Ellacuría insists that in this historical moment the "appropriate place" is with the "poor of the earth." For this reason, he says: "contemplation depends on a spirituality of poverty . . . identifying with the cause of the poor."[40] These are difficult, challenging words. But they express something hopeful and important: that the practice of attention can awaken in us a profound sense of our relationship with and responsibility for others. *Simul in actione contemplivus.* Becoming aware of what it means to live with and for others from the depths of one's being. Relinquishing the security of the known and established and participating in the darkness and insecurity shared by all. Here is a vision of contemplative practice that depends on silence and stillness and solitude but is also deeply communal and oriented toward practical love. Close to what the Gospels and the subsequent Christian contemplative tradition refers to simply as "the one thing necessary" (Lk. 10:42).

This approach to contemplation, especially for those whose social class, race, or privilege protect them from the harshest expressions of structural injustice, invites a searching consideration of what it means to stand in "the appropriate place" and to behold and respond to the lives of those facing the most acute vulnerability and precarity. I return here to that distinctive, encompassing way of seeing (and living) that the German theologian Johan Baptist Metz calls a "mysticism of open eyes." Metz, like Ellacuría, asks what it will mean to open up and deepen and resituate mystical thought and practice in response to suffering and loss arising from systemic injustice. This moment, he says, calls for a "a God-mysticism with an increased readiness for perceiving, a mysticism of open eyes, which sees more and not less. It is a mysticism that especially makes visible all invisible and inconvenient suffering, and—convenient or not—pays attention to it and takes responsibility for it."[41]

It is difficult to imagine a more profound and ethically forceful vision of spiritual practice than this. In its call to "make visible," that which is invisible—especially "invisible and inconvenient suffering"—it recasts the ancient contemplative ideal of seeing to consider in a new way what it will mean to open our eyes to the most painful and bewildering realities. The question of what it means to "*see* God" and whether it is meaningful to speak of God or the experience of God apart from an honest reckoning with the reality of invisible suffering has, in the late twentieth and early twenty-first centuries, become urgent and inescapable. A political mysticism of "open eyes" offers a way to recover the deep seeing of the Christian mystical tradition, while recentering the ineffable reality of suffering and loss. It also promises to deepen and strengthen the sense of mystical unity among and between all living beings that is at the heart of the common life. Whatever contemplative practice means in the present moment, it will have to take seriously the commitment to practice a mysticism of open eyes. It will mean learning to become, as *Laudato Si'* expresses it, "painfully aware, to dare to turn what is happening to the world into our own personal suffering and thus to discover what each of us can do about it."[42] This holistic and critical vision of contemplative practice invites a descent into the abyss—part of an expression of solidarity and love and a commitment to reimagine the meaning of community.

* * *

"Attention in search of prayer will find prayer," says Evagrius, "for if anything else follows attention it is prayer."[43] Prayer in the contemplative tradition is fundamentally relational and contributes so importantly to the reknitting of community. Still, as this saying of Evagrius makes clear, *prosoche*, or attention, occupied a central place in this ancient understanding of prayer. But attention to what? And to whom? And what exactly does attention do? For Evagrius, and for the ancient monastic tradition as a whole, attention is at the very root of any effort to see—oneself, God, and one's neighbor. To see and take responsibility for everything and everyone altogether. The monks were acutely aware of how easily thoughts become scattered, attention lost. And how the distracted and preoccupied mind, clouded by anxiety, anger, and fear, becomes unable to behold anyone or anything with openness and compassion. How easy it is to become lost to oneself. And to lose the capacity to feel and respond to the presence of others. "Attention in search of prayer" is a search for connection, relationship, love. Darkness and silence—in which attention is strengthened and distilled—become part of a deep ethical-spiritual practice that helps us clarify our commitments to others.

The twentieth-century French writer Simone Weil offers an important commentary on this ancient idea, sharpening and deepening Evagrius's teaching in significant ways. "Prayer *consists* of attention," she says. "It is the orientation of all the attention of which the soul is capable toward God says Weil. The quality of attention counts for much in the quality of the prayer."[44] There is no prayer without attention, Weil suggests. Here, as with Evagrius, the question of how to pray is simplified, distilled down to its essential element. Attention here means allowing the mind to become still, quiet, open. It is at once a quality of awareness and an ethical commitment. Still, the prospect of opening oneself to the intensity of sustained attention is, Weil contends, something we can hardly bear to face. "Something in our soul has a far more violent repugnance for true attention than the flesh has for bodily fatigue." But attention, as she understands it, has undeniable power, especially in helping us face and begin to heal those parts of ourselves where love has not yet taken hold of us. "Every time that we really concentrate our attention," Weil says, "we destroy the evil in ourselves." And we allow more room for the presence of God, for love, to suffuse our souls. Still, if the practice of attention has a profound inward orientation, it also leads inexorably outward, toward the other, toward a deeper engagement with the world. Nowhere is this more apparent than in our orientation toward those caught in intense suffering. Here Weil expresses the full, indeed miraculous, effect of learning to pay attention in prayer:

> Not only does the love of God have attention for its substance; the love of our neighbor, which we know to be the same love, is made of this same substance. Those who are unhappy have no need for anything in the world but people capable of giving them their attention. The capacity to give one's attention to a sufferer is a very rare and difficult thing; it is almost a miracle; it *is* a miracle. Nearly all those who think they have this capacity do not possess it. Warmth of heart, impulsiveness, pity are not enough.[45]

Weil herself struggled deeply to embody this kind of attention in her life, often at great cost; her refusal to eat anything more than her suffering compatriots in occupied France had available to them during World War II likely precipitated her early death. This was for her a way of paying attention to the plight of others, of accompanying them, sharing in their suffering: it was a way of practicing prayer.

These observations invite a serious consideration of what it means to give our full attention to anyone or anything. To pay attention, Weil insists, is to practice love. Nowhere is this more difficult or necessary than in the presence of affliction (*malheur*). Or, as Weil describes it: "To contemplate what cannot be contemplated (the affliction of another) without running away."[46] At the heart of this work is the invitation to let go of one's self-preoccupation and to learn to see others "as they are related to themselves and not to me."[47] Or, to return to John Ruusbroec's remarkable and demanding teaching, it means learning to let go of all partial and provisional supports and opening youreself to "the dark silence where all the loving are lost." Accepting and living in shared darkness and loss as the very ground of the common life.

* * *

I have described earlier Ruusbroec's profound understanding of loss, as the very ground of the spiritual itinerary that leads the soul to God. I want to return to his work here, in the context of community, and ask how loss—the experience of falling into an immensity of darkness—can inform and make possible a deep and enduring encounter with the very source of love. And how loss, especially when it is shared with others, nourishes and helps sustain what Ruusbroec calls the common life. How it creates the conditions for a kind of homecoming in which no one is any longer a stranger to the other, and in which individual or personal identity gives way to something more capacious and encompassing: a boundless sharing of life in God.

For Ruusbroec, as for so many other Christian mystics, the sense of loss, especially the loss of security, of every partial or provisional identity marker, and the dissolving of the self into an unknowable abyss, is inextricably bound to the question of what it means to open oneself in love (*minne*). At the deepest or highest level of the mystical journey there is, he says, only dark-ness; a radical relinquishment of identity that defies every attempt to say where one is or who one is. Ruusbroec offers a bewildering cascade of images to describe or evoke this abyssal place—evoking with a beautiful simulta-neity both the God who exists beyond all language and images and compre-hension and the deconstructed, transparent self, radically open to God and others. We come to inhabit, he says, a "[dark] unfathomable modelessness"; an "abyss of namelessness"; an "engulfment flowing away into essential bare-ness"; a "fathomless whirlpool of simplicity"; a "totally uncomprehended ground"; and, finally, "a dark silence."[48] At its very heart, he says, this is an experience of "unfathomable love."[49]

What does it mean to enter and become lost in this "abyss of nameless-ness?" What does it do to us, and for the larger community? Ruusbroec's response to these questions is startlingly direct and hinges on what he understands to be the renewing power of relinquishment and loss: "With respect to being lost in the darkness of the desert," he says, "nothing is left over, for there is no giving or taking there, but a simple, one-fold essence. In it, God and all those united (to God) are sunken away and lost, and they can never find themselves again in this modeless essence."[50] Elsewhere, he observes of this experience, that there is only "darkness, bareness, and nothingness . . . [in which one] is enveloped and falls into modelessness as one who wanders about lost."[51] We become, he says, "lost to ourselves . . . [and] sink away from ourselves forever, without return."[52] The experience of radical loss, says Ruusbroec, is "wild and waste as wandering, for there is no mode, no trail, no path, no abode, no measure, no end, no beginning."[53]

Loss, as well as the radical relinquishment that loss enables, breaks down the hardened categories of identity that keep us from knowing and loving one another. Here, in the dark silence, we begin to know ourselves not as discrete beings separate from other beings, but as persons borne along by love, sharing in a reality that is common to all. "Such Souls are alone in all things and common in all things," says Porete.[54] They experience a "rich outflowing . . . to love in commonness," notes Ruusbroec.[55] "You must be glad of the life in common," says Hadewijch, "through which you now have guidance toward Love."[56] Here, in the "abyss of namelessness," we learn to inhabit, become lost in, and transformed by the "common life."[57]

"We must, without sparing, lose all for all," says Hadewijch.[58] Everything must go. Your idea of yourself. Your conception of God. Everything. Only radical openness remains. Prayer becomes a space of utter vulnerability, loss the ground of love, accompaniment, communion.

* * *

How does the possibility of living this way arise in the soul? How does it eventually come to seem not only viable but necessary? Is it possible to choose it? Or does it emerge mostly in response to the experience of loss, brokenness and vulnerability, and the realization that the old, isolating ideal of self-sufficiency can no longer be sustained? How can loss open the way to a deeper apprehension of the meaning of love?

These questions have long preoccupied me. But living in Argentina brought them into sharper relief. Not least because of how bewildered I often felt as I struggled to navigate my way, uncertainly, through a language and culture and social reality so different from my own. But also because of the unexpected sense of intimacy that arose within what I gradually came to see as a space of shared lostness: everyone moving around inside the darkness together, bound to one another, touching and being touched within a space of shared vulnerability.

The embodied experience of entering in and making a life here was much, much more difficult than I had imagined it would be. Nor was I as adaptable or flexible or creative as I thought I was. My competence for accomplishing the most basic tasks of living—driving, shopping for food, participating in an intelligible conversation with my neighbors—seemed often to elude me completely. It was humbling and exhausting and regularly left me questioning my capacity to do or contribute anything. I began to notice also that my very idea of myself, my sense of my status and identity, which had been so clear and secure (if also relatively unexamined) in my own country, was slowly giving way to something more opaque, unstable, and ill-defined. I was a stranger in this place. No one knew anything about what I had accomplished in my life or who I had been before coming here. Nor was it easy to relinquish my old identity, to accept my status as a kind of child, a beginner with little understanding about how to proceed. Often I felt utterly lost.

In time, I came to see this as gift, something that helped me become more aware of and honest about my own vulnerability and need, and more sensitive to the vulnerability and need of others. My encounter with community members in Nuestro Hogar III, La Luciérnaga, and Barrio Argüello, for example, whose lives are marked by a depth of precarity, insecurity, and unpredictability far beyond anything I have experienced or can comprehend, brought this home to me with particular force. But sharing their lives also allowed me to experience their uncommon resilience and courage and to feel myself touched and carried by their kindness and generosity. The simple, daily encounters, punctuated by the warmth of *besos* and *abrazos* and so often characterized by an unguarded delight at the prospect of our being able to hang out together, often left me abashed and humbled; and they filled me with a desire to respond in kind. I found myself wondering: Could I open myself to these new friends and neighbors as they were so honestly and deeply opening themselves to me? Could I resist the temptation to stand aloof from them or imagine my own life as somehow separate from theirs? Could I truly enter in and become part of things here?

These were among the most important questions I found myself facing whenever I entered the silence and paused to reflect on my experience. The capacity to reckon with my insecurity and helplessness and to open myself to my vulnerability, I began to see, was critical to any hope I had of becoming part of the life of this place, of learning to open myself in love to others, of sharing in their lives. But could I summon the courage to go deeper? Could I learn to let go of my fear of losing control and open myself to those whose lives I was being invited to share? I knew that learning to live in this place with integrity and love depended on my being able to address these questions honestly. Still, I needed help.

I found this help in the presence of the community that I discovered and became part of in Córdoba—students, community leaders, taxi drivers, cooks, professors, my wife, our children, and so many others. I found it also in the company of those contemplatives and mystics who had long struggled with these questions and whose articulation of those struggles helped me give voice to my own. Especially those who asked themselves again and again what it means to become lost in the abyss of love.

Accompaniment takes so many different forms and expressions: to let go and experience a profound sharing of life that allows each to be present to the other; to suspend your own narrow prerogatives for the sake of participating in a more capacious and inclusive whole; to feel and be pierced by and respond to the unconsoled sorrow of others; to practice openness, friendship, solidarity. In our life here in Córdoba, this came to mean many things: listening and absorbing the stories of others; helping neighbors clean up after a storm; joining in vigils in memory of *los desaparecidos*; preparing an *asado* for the community; and, always, sharing *mate*. Spending time freely, profligately. "If I happen to waste a day, I am grateful for it," said Abba Sisoes—that ancient desert ideal touching and revealing something essential and necessary about our shared life in this place.

Somehow silence, darkness, and emptiness are part of this, indispensable to the work of recognizing and responding to the aching longing we feel to be joined to one another in love. Necessary to the cultivation of an awareness that makes real attention to and regard for one another possible. The very ground that enables us to notice and cherish the simple moments of touch, laughter, and intimacy that nourish and sustain us and bind us to one another. The dark silence where all the loving lose themselves.

I recall a day spent with the community at Nuestro Hogar III toward the end of our first year in Argentina when I began to sense this so deeply. By then we had become aware of the serious challenges facing the community and, to the extent that we could, responded to the invitation to share in their lives, witnessing for ourselves the courage, dignity, and resourcefulness with which they met these challenges. But there was also a continuous unfolding of joy. One day a call came to our house: It was our friend Ale inviting us to join them for the upcoming celebration of Día del Niño. The whole neighborhood would be there. Could we come? Of course. A few days later, we arrived, making our way slowly down the narrow dirt road toward the school. Hundreds of people were gathered outside, greeting one another, beginning to prepare for the day. Inside it was the same. In every classroom, we encountered groups of children, playing games, making musical instruments or little crowns, painting faces; the hallways were also packed with children and parents, on the move, seeking the next adventure, the next game, the next delight, everyone lost inside the joy of the day, utterly lost, without care. At least for that moment. And those of us who had gathered to accompany them also lost ourselves, drawn into the swirling, exuberant, pulsing life of this moment. And yet there was stillness here too. A sense of time slowing down. Especially in that moment when your eyes met the eyes of another (Sofia!), or when the recognition of how to make a drum, or how to fold an origami crane, or how to construct and cook empanadas began to dawn in your consciousness. I remember thinking: everything that matters is here in this moment. A sense of *kairos*, the fullness of time, and *koinonia*, the beloved community. In that moment of abandon, of freedom from care, I began to sense in a new way what it feels like to move within and be carried by a great immensity.

Later that night, we return to our circle in the *quincho*, opening ourselves again to the simple but necessary work of entering the silence together. Slowing down. Breathing. Listening. Walking. Paying attention. Opening ourselves to all those we have been given to know and love. Allowing joy to gather. Also facing those things we would rather not face, struggling to open ourselves to the persistent reality of loss—in ourselves and in the lives of others. Soon we will emerge from this place and walk out again into our lives, opening ourselves to the invitation to be present and share our lives with one another. But for the moment, we are moving together through this dark silence, holding one another close, learning little by little to inhabit the common life.

Notes

Introduction

1. Han Kang, *The White Book*, trans. Deborah Smith (London: Portabello Books, 2017), 7.
2. John Ruusbroec, *The Complete Ruusbroec*, English translation with the original Middle Dutch text, edited with an introduction by Guido de Baere and Thom Mertens, vol. 1 (Turnhout, Belgium: Brepols, 2014), 325. For a comment on the translation of this text, see Chapter 4, note 4.
3. "[God] is known through knowledge and through unknowing." Pseudo-Dionysius, *The Complete Works*, trans. Colm Liubheid (New York and Mahwah, NJ: Paulist Press, 1987), 108–109; see also Daniel Jugrin, "*Agnosia*: The Apophatic Experience of God in Dionysius the Areopagite," *Teologia* 67, no. 2 (2016): 102–115.
4. Simon Ortiz, "Culture and the Universe," in *Out There Somewhere* (Tucson: University of Arizona Press, 2002), 104–105.
5. John Wortley, trans., *The Book of the Elders: Sayings of the Desert Fathers: The Systematic Collection* (Collegeville, MN: Liturgical Press, 2012), 211.
6. Meister Eckhart, *The Complete Mystical Works of Meister Eckhart,* trans. and ed. Maurice O'C. Walshe (New York: Crossroad, 2009), 56.
7. The invocation of the term "mystical theology" here will perhaps call to mind for some an old and even antiquated approach to theological reflection. In the Christian tradition, this idea traces its roots back to the work of Pseudo-Dionysius's *The Mystical Theology,* and others who understood the work of theological reflection to be deeply rooted in an awareness of the ineffable mystery of God, often encountered only in darkness. See Bernard McGinn, *The Foundations of Mysticism: Origins to the Fifth Century* (New York: Crossroad, 2004) for a critical evaluation of the birth and unfolding of this tradition of theological thought and practice within Christianity. Subsequent volumes of this work trace the shifting approaches to mystical theology in the later tradition. In the twentieth century, the idea of mystical theology was given important expression in the work of the Russian theologian Vladimir Lossky, *The Mystical Theology of the Eastern Church* (Cambridge: James Clark, 1957), although it remained somewhat on the margins of much contemporary theological reflection. More recently, it has been subject of a sustained critical reassessment. See, e.g., Mark McIntosh, *Mystical Theology: The Integration of Spirituality and Theology* (Malden, MA: Blackwell, 1998); Sarah Coakley, *Powers and Submissions: Spirituality, Philosophy and Gender* (Oxford: Blackwell, 2002); Beverly J. Lanzetta, *Radical Wisdom: A Feminist Mystical Theology* (Minneapolis: Augsburg Fortress, 2005); Paul Rorem, *The Dionysian Mystical Theology* (Minneapolis: Fortress, 2015); Bernard

McGinn, ed., *The Renewal of Mystical* Theology (New York: Crossroad, 2017); Mark A. McIntosh and Edward Howells, eds. *The Oxford Handbook of Mystical Theology* (Oxford: Oxford University Press, 2020).

8. Albert Camus expressed something similar more than seventy years ago, describing how the plague "swallowed up everything and everyone. No longer were there individual destinies; only a collective destiny, made of plague and the emotions shared by all. Strongest of these emotions was the sense of exile and of deprivation, with all the crosscurrents of revolt and fear set up by these." Albert Camus, *The Plague,* trans. Stuart Gilbert (New York: Vintage, 1991), 167.

9. Catherine Keller, *Cloud of the Impossible: Negative Theology and Planetary Entanglement* (New York: Columbia University Press, 2014); Steven Chase, *Nature as Spiritual Practice* (Grand Rapids: Eerdmans, 2011); Timothy Morton, *Dark Ecology: For a Logic of Future Co-Existence* (New York: Columbia University Press, 2016); Rob Nixon's *Slow Violence and the Environmentalism of the Poor* (Cambridge, MA: Harvard University Press, 2011), should also be included here for its incisive examination of the social-political meaning of seeing and not seeing, and for his careful explication of how differences in power so often determine who is seen and who is rendered invisible.

10. Josef Sorett, *Spirit in the Dark: A Religious History of Racial Aesthetics* (New York: Oxford University Press, 2016). For an important critique of the language of darkness in mystical theology in light of black theology, see Andrew Prevot, "Divine Opacity: Mystical Theology, Black Theology and the Problem of Light-Dark Aesthetics," *Spiritus: A Journal of Christian Spirituality* 16, no. 2 (2016): 166–188.

11. Judith Schalansky, *An Inventory of Losses*, trans. Jackie Smith (New York: New Directions, 2018).

12. Fanny Howe, *The Wedding Dress: Meditations on Word and Life* (Berkeley: University of California Press, 2003), 15. Bewilderment is, in Howe's understanding, not only a personal experience of dislocation. It also has a powerful potential political significance: "The politics of bewilderment belongs only to those who have little or no access to an audience or a government. It involves circling the facts, seeing the problem from varying directions, showing the weaknesses from the bottom up, the conspiracies, the lies, the plans, the false rhetoric; the politics of bewilderment runs against myth, or fixing, finding, and defending. It's a politics devoted to the little and the weak; it is grassroots in that it imitates the way grass bends and springs back when it is stepped on. It won't go away but will continue asking irritating questions to which it knows all the answers" (23).

13. Morton, *Dark Ecology*, 78–79.

14. Constance Fitzgerald, "Impasse and Dark Night," in *Women's Spirituality: Resources for Christian Development*, 2nd ed., ed. Joann Conn (New York: Paulist Press, 1996), 410–435; Constance Fitzgerald, "From Impasse to Prophetic Hope: Crisis of Memory," *CTSA Proceedings* 64 (2009): 21–42.

15. Barbara Holmes, *Joy Unspeakable: Contemplative Practices of the Black Church*, 2nd ed. (Minneapolis: Augsburg Fortress, 2017). "The word *contemplation*," argues Holmes, "must press beyond the constraints of religious expectations to reach the

potential for spiritual centering in the midst of danger. Centering moments accessed in safety are an expected luxury in our era. During slavery, however, crisis contemplation became a refuge, a wellspring of discernment in a suddenly disordered life space, and a geo-spiritual anvil for forging a new identity" (46).

16. Barbara Brown Taylor, *Learning to Walk in the Dark* (New York: HarperOne, 2008); Rebecca Solnit, *Hope in the Dark: Untold Histories, Wild Possibilities* (Chicago: Haymarket, 2016). Solnit's book is more about hope than darkness. But she sees them as bound together. She cites with appreciation Virginia Woolf's journal entry from 2015: "The future is dark, which is on the whole, the best thing the future can be, I think." And adds this gloss: "Dark, she seems to say, as in inscrutable, not as in terrible." Solnit sees the future's unknowability as carrying with it an important truth—that we are not living in a closed system but may yet bring into being something that has not been before. That darkness can become a ground for hope (1).

17. W. G. Sebald, *The Rings of Saturn*, trans. Michael Hulse (New York: New Directions, 1998), 173.

18. Alejandra Pizarnik, *The Galloping Hour: French Poems*, trans. Patricio Ferrari and Forrest Grander (New York: New Directions, 1998), 27.

19. John of the Cross's "dark night" is perhaps the best-known expression of this idea in the Christian mystical tradition, but his work must be situated within a much deeper tradition of reflection on the night as a space of mystical encounter with God. John of the Cross, *The Collected Works*, rev. ed., trans. Kieran Kavanaugh and Otilio Rodriguez (Washington, DC: ICS, 2010), 353–460. See also Sam Hole, *John of the Cross: Desire, Transformation, and Selfhood* (Oxford: Oxford University Press, 2020), esp. 132–162.

20. Robert Faggen, ed., *Striving Towards Being: The Letters of Thomas Merton and Czeslaw Milosz* (New York: Farrar, Strauss, Giroux, 1997), 120, 122.

21. Edmond Jabès, *The Book of Margins*, trans. Rosemarie Waldrop (Chicago: University of Chicago Press, 1993), 129.

22. Fernando Pessoa, *The Book of Disquiet*, ed. Jerónimo Pizzaro, trans. Margaret Jull Costa (New York: New Directions, 2017), 297. A phenomenology of emptiness needs also, I think, to account for its *weight* and *density* and how difficult it can be to carry it. See Jeanette Winterson, *Weight: The Myth of Atlas and Heracles* (New York: Cannongate, 2005), esp. 97–100.

23. Hadewijch, *The Complete Works*, trans. Mother Columba Hart (New York and Mahwah, NJ: Paulist Press, 1980). "Despair in darkness": 321: "Noble Unfaith": 65; "Affliction": 49. The twentieth-century French mystic Simone Weil also took up the question of affliction (*malheur*) in her writing, where it became for her a way of grappling, simultaneously, with the acute suffering of those living through war and the abysmal conditions of contemporary factory life; with the loss and abandonment necessary for approaching God; and with the meaning of shared suffering in work accompaniment and solidarity. *Gravity and Grace*, trans. Emma Crawford and Marion van der Ruhr (London: Routledge, 2002), 80–84. See also Anne Carson, *Decreation: Poetry, Essays, Opera* (New York: Vintage, 2006), 157–183 for a creative, critical examination of the idea spiritual emptiness in the work of Sappho, Marguerite Porete, and Simone Weil. For a thoughtful account of the experience of abandonment

in the early Eastern Christian tradition, see Elizabeth Anderson, "The Experience of Abandonment by God in Syriac Christian Ascetical Theology," *Spiritus* 20, no. 1 (Spring 2020): 79–104.

24. On the idea of *practicing* emptiness in the Christian mystical tradition, see Charlotte C. Radler, "Living from the Divine Ground: Meister Eckhart's Praxis of Detachment," *Spiritus* 6, no. 1 (2006): 25–47; Donald F. Duclow, "The Hungers of Hadewijch and Eckhart," *Journal of Religion* 80, no. 3 (July 2000): 421–441; Holly Hillgardner, *Longing and Letting Go: Christian and Hindu Practices of Passionate Non-Attachment* (New York: Oxford University Press, 2016); Pyong-Gwan Pak, "The Vernacular, Mystical Theology of Jan van Ruusbroec: Exploring Sources, Contexts and Theological Practices," Ph.D. diss., Boston College. August, 2008. Especially "How to Cultivate an Authentic Emptiness," 409–416. Two recent works highlighting the shifting, ambiguous meanings of emptiness in contemporary thought and practice: Gay Watson, *A Philosophy of* Emptiness (London: Reaktion, 2014); John Corrigan, *Emptiness: Feeling Christian in America* (Chicago: University of Chicago Press, 2015). On the practice of "staying with," see Donna Haraway, *Staying with the Trouble: Making Kin in the Chthulucene* (Durham, NC: Duke University Press, 2016).

25. Eckhart, *The Complete Mystical Works*, 59; Marguerite Porete, *The Mirror of Simple Souls*, trans. Ellen. L. Babinsky (New York: Paulist Press, 1993, 215; John Ruusbroec, *The Spiritual Espousals and Other Works*, trans. James Wiseman (New York: Paulist Press, 1985), 168.

26. Wortley, *The Book of the Elders*, 205.

27. Luca Di Santo, "Kenosis of the Subject and the Advent of Being in Mystic Experience," *Qui Parle* 17, no. 1 (Fall/Winter 2008): 147–173: "It is only when the self is outside of itself—no longer actively constructing the world around it, but rather attuned to it in a purely passive-receptive manner—that it truly is itself" (149).

28. Hadewijch, *The Complete Works*, 344.

29. Hadewijch, *The Complete Works*, 239.

30. Andrew Graham-Dixon, *Caravaggio: A Life Sacred and Profane* (New York: W. W. Norton, 2010), 310: "The Madonna had been made to look dirty and indecorous. She had been made to look real." See also Teju Cole's beautiful meditation on Caravaggio's work and his compelling case for why its raw honesty and vulnerability resonates so deeply amid the trauma of our own historical moment: "In Dark Times, I Sought out the Turmoil of Caravaggio's Paintings," *New York Time Magazine*, September 23, 2020.

31. Hadewijch, *The Complete Works*, 356.

Chapter 1

1. Fanny Howe, "The Passion," in *Gone* (Berkeley: University of California Press, 2003), 55.

2. Karl Rahner, "Understanding Christmas," in *Theological Investigations*, vol. 23 (New York: Crossroad, 1992), 140–148.

3. John Ruusbroec, *The Complete Ruusbroec*, English translation with the original Middle Dutch text, edited and with an introduction by Guido de Baere and Thom Mertens, vol. 1 (Turnhout, Belgium: Brepols, 2014), 220.

4. Edmond Jabès, *The Book of Resemblances 2: Intimations: The Desert*, trans. Rosemary Waldrop (Hanover, NH: Wesleyan University Press, 1991), 52.

5. The increasing attention given to apophatic thought within philosophy, theology, literary criticism, and art history in recent years has been astonishing and impressive. I note here some of the main works I have consulted to suggest something of the context within which my thinking about these matters has grown and developed. Michael A. Sells, *Mystical Languages of Unsaying* (Chicago: University of Chicago Press, 1994); Denys Turner, *The Darkness of God: Negativity in Christian Mysticism* (Cambridge: Cambridge University Press, 1995); William Franke, *A Philosophy of the Unsayable* (Notre Dame: University of Notre Dame Press, 2014); William Franke, *On the Universality of What Is Not: The Apophatic Turn in Critical Thinking* (Notre Dame: University of Notre Dame Press, 2020); Jean-Luc Marion, *Negative Certainties*, trans. Stephen E. Lewis (Chicago: University of Chicago Press, 2015); Sarah Coakley, *Power and Submissions: Spirituality, Philosophy and Gender* (Oxford: Wiley-Blackwell, 2002); Kevin Hart, *The Dark Gaze: Maurice Blanchot and the Sacred* (Chicago: University of Chicago Press, 2004); Ray L. Hart, *God Being Nothing: Toward a Theogony* (Chicago: University of Chicago Press, 2016); Bruce Millem, "Four Theories of Negative Theology," *Heythrop Journal* 48 (2007): 187–204; Diane Enns, *Love in the Dark: Philosophy by Another Name* (New York: Columbia University Press, 2016); Barbara Maria Stafford, *Ribbon of Darkness: Inferencing from the Shadowy Arts and Sciences* (Chicago: University of Chicago Press, 2019).

Studies of darkness, dusk, and the night, in art, culture and society, also have a place in the contemporary discussion of what it means to engage and respond to the apophatic in the present moment. Nina Edwards, *Darkness: A Cultural History* (London: Reaktion, 2018); Peter Davidson, *The Last of the Light: About Twilight* (London: Reaktion, 2015); Hélène Valance, *Nocturne: Night in American Art 1890–1917*, trans. Jane Marie Todd (New Haven: Yale University Press, 2018); Geoff Dyer, *The Ongoing Moment* (New York: Vintage, 2007).

6. Emily Dickinson, *The Complete Poems*, ed. Thomas H. Johnson (Boston: Little Brown, 1960), 200.

7. Richard R. Niebuhr, "The Strife of Interpreting: The Moral Burden of Imagination," *Parabola* 10, no. 2 (1985): 40.

8. These terms have distinct meanings in the history of Christian monasticism and should not be thought of as identical to one another. Still, I use them here to refer, broadly speaking, to prayer that takes place in darkness or the night. See R. F. Taft, *The Liturgy of the Hours in East and West: The Origins of the Divine Office and Its Meaning for Today* (Collegeville: Liturgical Press, 1986); Mary W. Helms, "Before the Dawn: Monks and the Night in Late Antiquity and Early Medieval Europe," *Anthropos* 99 (2004): 177–191.

9. Simon Ortiz, "Culture and the Universe," in *Out There Somewhere* (Tucson: University of Arizona Press, 2002), 104–105.

10. Henri Cole, "Middle Earth," in *Middle Earth* (New York: Farrar, Straus and Giroux, 2003), 14.

11. Thomas Merton, *The Hidden Ground of Love*, ed. William H. Shannon (New York: Farrar, Straus, Giroux, 1985), 115.

12. Kobayashi Issa, *The Spring of My Life and Selected Haiku*, trans. Sam Hamill (Boston: Shambala, 1997), xii–xiv.

13. Robin Coste Lewis, "Plantation," in *Voyage of the Sable Venus and Other Poems* (New York: Knopf, 2015), 4.

14. Vicente Aleixandre, "Lightless," in *A Longing for the Light: Selected Poems of Vicente Aleixandre*, ed. Lewis Hyde (Port Townsend, WA: Copper Canyon Press, 2007), 63.

15. Jaime Saenz, *The Night*, trans. Forrest Grander and Kent Johnson (Princeton: Princeton University Press, 2007), 33.

16. Aracelis Girmay, "On Living," in *Kingdom Animalia* (Rochester, NY: BOA Editions, 2011), 30.

17. Floyd Skloot, *In the Shadow of Memory* (Lincoln: University of Nebraska Press, 2003), 176.

18. Forrest Gander, "What It Sounds Like," in *Be With* (New York: New Directions, 2018), 27.

19. Czeslaw Milosz, "On Prayer," in *The Collected Poems, 1931–1987* (New York: Ecco Press, 1988), 434.

20. Carolyn Forché, "Prayer," in *Blue Hour* (New York: Harper Collins, 2003), 21.

21. R. S. Thomas, "Via Negativa," in *Collected Poems: 1945–1990* (London: Phoenix, 1995), 220.

22. William Franke, *On What Cannot Be Said: Apophatic Discourses in Philosophy, Religion, Literature and the Arts*, vol. 1: *Classic Formulations* (Notre Dame: University of Notre Dame Press, 2007) is an excellent comparative sourcebook for apophatic work in the West, from the Bible to the Middle Ages. See also Ayudogan Kars, *Unsaying God: Negative Theology in Medieval Islam* (New York: Oxford University Press, 2019); and Michael Fagenblat, *Negative Theology as Jewish Modernity* (Bloomington: Indiana University Press, 2017).

23. Theodore Roethke, "In a Dark Time," in *Selected Poems* (New York: Library of America, 2005), 116.

24. Gregory of Nyssa, *The Life of Moses*, trans. Abraham J. Malherbe and Everett Ferguson (New York: Paulist Press, 1978), 95.

25. Pseudo-Dionysius, *The Complete Works*, trans. Colm Luibheid (New York: Paulist Press, 1987), 135, 138.

26. Ruusbroec, *The Complete Ruusbroec*, 125.

27. Christian Wiman, "One Time," in *Hammer is the Prayer: Selected Poems* (New York: Farrar, Straus and Giroux, 2016), 100.

28. Soren Kierkegaard, "Truth Is Subjectivity," in *Concluding Unscientific Postscript*, ed. and trans. Howard V. Hong and Edna H. Hong (Princeton: Princeton University Press, 1992), 169ff.

29. Bernard McGinn, "The God beyond God: Theology and Mysticism in the Thought of Meister Eckhart," *The Journal of Religion* 61, no. 1 (January 1981): 1–19.

30. *The Cloud of Unknowing*, trans. James Walsh (New York: Paulist Press, 1981), 121.

31. Antoine de Saint-Exupéry, *Flight to Arras,* trans. Lewis Galantière (New York: Harcourt, 1986), 10.

32. Benedicta Ward, trans., *The Sayings of the Desert Fathers: The Alphabetical Collection*, rev. ed. (Collegeville: Liturgical Press, 1984), 139.

33. Ward, *The Sayings of the Desert Fathers*, 3.

34. Ruusbroec, *The Complete Ruusbroec*, 136.

35. Marguerite Porete, *The Mirror of Simple Souls*, trans. Ellen Babinsky (New York and Mahwah, NJ: Paulist Press, 1993), 85: "And this Soul, who has become nothing, thus possesses everything, and so possesses nothing; she wills everything and she wills nothing; she knows all and she knows nothing."

36. John of the Cross, *The Collected Works,* rev. ed., trans. Kieran Kavanaugh and Otilio Rodriguez (Washington, DC: ICS, 2010), 50–52.

37. Hadewijch, *The Complete Works*, trans. Mother Columba Hart (New York: Paulist Press, 1980), 344.

38. Ruusbroec, *The Complete Ruusbroec*, 235.

39. Porete, *The Mirror of Simple Souls*, 102.

40. Hadewijch, *The Complete Works*, 356–367.

41. Raymond Carver, *Where I Am Calling From: Selected Stories* (New York: Atlantic Monthly Press, 1998), 138–150.

42. Hadewijch, *The Complete Works*, 356. On the significance of the abyss in medieval mysticism, see Bernard McGinn, "The Abyss of Love," in *The Joy of Learning and the Love of God: Studies in Honor of Jean Leclercq*, ed. Rozanne Elder (Kalamazoo: Cistercian, 1995), 95–120; and Bernard McGinn, "Lost in the Abyss: The Function of Abyss Language in Medieval Mysticism," *Franciscan Studies* 72 (2014): 433–442.

43. Michel de Certeau, *The Mystic Fable.* vol. 1, trans. Michael B. Smith (Chicago: University of Chicago Press, 1992), 81.

44. Porete, *The Mirror of Simple Souls*, 91.

45. Hart, *The Dark Gaze*; Fernando Pessoa, *The Book of Disquiet,* ed. Maria José de Lancastre, trans. Margaret Jull Costa (London: Serpent's Tail, 1991); Simone Weil, *Gravity and Grace,* trans. Emma Crawford and Mario von der Ruhr (London: Routledge, 2004), especially "To Accept the Void," 10–11; Jabès, *The Book of Resemblances*, vol. 2.

46. Pessoa, *The Book of Disquiet*, 312.

47. W. G. Sebald, *Austerlitz*, trans. Anthea Bell (New York: Random House, 2001), 14, 20–27.

48. Tracy K. Smith, "Annunciation," in *Wade in the Water* (Minneapolis: Greywolf, 2018), 72.

49. Theodor W. Adorno, "Cultural Criticism and Society," in *Prisms*, trans. Shierry Weber Nicholsen (Cambridge, MA: MIT Press: 1983), 34.

50. Theodor Adorno, *Negative Dialectics,* trans. E. B. Ashton (New York: Continuum, 1973), 361–363.

51. Edmond Jabès, *The Book of Margins*, trans. Rosemarie Waldrop (Chicago: University of Chicago Press, 1993), ix, x.

52. Joanna Moorhead, "Javier Sicilia: I have no more poetry in me," *The Guardian*, October 28, 2011. https://www.theguardian.com/lifeandstyle/2011/oct/29/javier-sici lia-mexican-poet-son. I am grateful to my friend and colleague Rubén Martínez for introducing me to the work and witness of Javier Sicilia and for giving me the opportunity to meet and speak with him when he visited Loyola Marymount University in April 2012. I am grateful also for the witness of LMU students, faculty, and staff who joined Sicilia in a silent vigil on campus as an expression of their solidarity with the victims of the ongoing violence in Mexico.

53. An important counterpoint or complement to Sicilia's position can be seen in the work of Cristina Rivera Garza, *Grieving: Dispatches from a Wounded Country*, trans. Sarah Booker (New York: Feminist Press, 2020), especially "The End of Women's Silence," 151–154.

54. Louise Gluck, "Midnight," in *Faithful and Virtuous Night* (New York: Farrar, Straus and Giroux, 2014), 34.

55. Henri Cole, "The Constant Leaf," in *Nothing to Declare* (New York: Farrar, Straus & Giroux, 2015), 63.

56. Thomas Merton, *Witness to Freedom: Letters in Times of Crisis*, ed. William H. Shannon (New York: Farrar, Straus, Giroux, 1994), 261.

57. Agnes Martin, "Statement about Her Work," in *Agnes Martin: Her Life and Art*, ed. Nancy Princenthal (London: Thames and Hudson, 2015), 131–132.

58. Patricio Guzmán, *Nostalgia de la luz* [Nostalgia for the light], Icarus Films, 2011.

59. Linda A. Mercadante, *Belief without Borders: Inside the Minds of the Spiritual but Not Religious* (New York: Oxford University Press, 2014); Elizabeth Drescher, *Choosing Our Religion: The Spiritual Lives of America's Nones* (New York: Oxford University Press, 2016).

60. Robert Fuller, *Spiritual but Not Religious: Understanding Unchurched America* (New York: Oxford University Press, 2001); Leigh Eric Schmidt, *Restless Souls: The Making of American Spirituality* (San Francisco: HarperSanFrancisco, 2005). See also the 2017 Pew Research Center survey results: "More Americans Now Say They're Spiritual but Not Religious," Washington, DC: Pew Research Center, 2017, https://www.pewresearch.org/fact-tank/2017/09/06/more-americans-now-say-theyre-spiritual-but-not-religious/.

61. Sandra M. Schneiders, "Religion vs. Spirituality: A Contemporary Conundrum," *Spiritus: A Journal of Christian Spirituality* 3, no. 2 (2003): 163–185.

62. David D. Hall, ed., *Lived Religion in America: Toward a History of Practice* (Princeton: Princeton University Press, 1997); Nancy T. Ammerman, ed., *Everyday Religion: Observing Modern Religious Lives* (New York: Oxford University Press, 2007); Meredith B. McGuire, *Lived Religion: Faith and Practice in Everyday Life* (New York: Oxford University Press, 2008); Ruth Frankenburg, *Living Spirit, Living Practice: Poetics, Politics, Epistemology* (Durham: Duke University Press, 2004).

Recent research suggests the growing significance of eclectic spiritual practice among communities that cannot be easily located on traditional maps of religious belonging or identity: Courtney Bender, *The New Metaphysicals: Spirituality and the American Religious Imagination* (Chicago: University of Chicago Press, 2010);

Kelly Besecke, *You Can't Put God in a Box: Thoughtful Spirituality in a Rational Age* (New York: Oxford, 2014); Ariel Glucklich, *Everyday Mysticism: A Contemplative Community at Work in the Desert* (New Haven: Yale, 2017).

63. Charles Taylor, *A Secular Age* (Cambridge, MA: Harvard University Press, 2007).

64. See Michael Warner, Jonathan Van Antwerpen, and Craig Calhoun, eds., *Varieties of Secularism in a Secular Age* (Cambridge, MA: Harvard University Press 2010); especially Simon During, "Completing Secularism: The Mundane in the Neoliberal Era," 105–125, who offers an insightful reading of the "mundane" that is neither religious nor secular; and William Connolly "Belief, Spirituality, and Time," 126–144, who argues that the alternative to transcendence is not only an exclusive humanism, as Taylor suggests, but also what he describes as an "immanent naturalism" or "mundane transcendence"—expressions that avoid the reductions of a closed understanding of immanence and leave open possibilities for engaging a non-religious or trans-religious transcendence. Thomas Carlson, *With the World at Heart: Studies in the Secular Today* (Chicago: University of Chicago Press, 2019), argues persuasively for an understanding of secularity "that should be counted also fundamentally religious" (209).

65. David Tracy, *Fragments: The Existential Situation of Our Time* (Chicago: University of Chicago Press, 2020), 1–33.

66. There is growing evidence in recent scholarship for the possibility of a critical, creative, and engaged response to historical expressions of mystical-spiritual thought and practice. See, e.g., Pierre Hadot's brilliant recovery of the arts of "spiritual practice" in ancient Greek philosophy and early Christian life and thought, *The Philosophy of Everyday Life*, ed. Arnold Davidson, trans. Michael Chase (Malden, MA: Blackwell, 1995); Bernard McGinn's multivolume history of Western Christian mysticism, *The Presence of God: A History of Western Mysticism*, 7 vols. (New York: Crossroad, 1991–2020); David Marno's subtle and original study of John Donne's devotional poetry that gives us new access to the spiritual practice of attention in the early modern period, *Death Be Not Proud: The Art of Holy Attention* (Chicago: University of Chicago Press, 2017); Moshe Sluhovsky's creative retrieval and reimagining of the role that certain penitential and meditation practices, and the belief systems that gave them meaning, played in the early modern project of "self-transformation," *Becoming a New Self: Practices of Belief in Early Modern Catholicism* (Chicago: University of Chicago Press, 2017); Noreen Khawaja's beautiful, probing account of what she calls "the religion of existence," rooted in her perceptive analysis of the work of Kierkegaard, Heidegger, and Sartre and her articulation of something she describes as "new form of asceticism," *The Religion of Existence: Asceticism in Philosophy from Kierkegaard to Sartre* (Chicago: University of Chicago Press, 2016); and the work of Michel de Certeau, which occupies a central place here, not least for his capacity to reimagine *mystic* as a fundamental, if also unruly, category of religious thought and practice and for his deep sensitivity to the social-cultural dislocations that so often give it meaning, *The Mystic Fable*, vol. 1. and *The Mystic Fable*, vol. 2, trans. Luce Giard and Michael B. Smith (Chicago: University of Chicago Press, 2015).

67. Thomas Merton's *Contemplative Prayer*, published posthumously in 1969, remains an important early example of this approach, drawing on ancient Christian monastic

thought and practice to ask about the possibility of contemplative prayer amid the social and political upheavals of mid-twentieth century America. *Contemplative Prayer* (New York: Herder and Herder, 1969). This work of Merton's benefits from being read in relation to his other, more explicitly politically engaged work where contemplative practice and social engagement are always set in dialectical relationship with each other; as well as his work engaging other religious traditions, where contemplative practice becomes the ground of an open and profoundly dialogic exploration of shared experience. See, e.g., Thomas Merton, *Seeds of Destruction* (New York: Farrar, Straus, Giroux, 1981).

Martin Laird's fine trilogy of "guides to the Christian practice of contemplation" have extended and deepened Merton's work in important ways and attend with particular care to experiences of affliction, depression, failure, and other struggles that manifest so often within the contemporary experience of prayer. Martin Laird, *Into the Silent Land: A Guide to the Christian Practice of Contemplation* (New York: Oxford, 2006); *A Sunlit Absence: Silence, Awareness, and Contemplation* (New York: Oxford, 2011); *An Ocean of Light: Contemplation, Transformation, and Liberation* (New York: Oxford, 2019).

68. Gustavo Gutierrez, *We Drink from Our Own Wells: The Spiritual Journey of a People*, trans. Matthew J. O'Connell (Maryknoll, NY: Orbis, 1984); Segundo Galilea, *The Future of Our Past: The Spanish Mystics Speak to Contemporary Spirituality* (Notre Dame: Ave Maria Press, 1985); Barbara Holmes, *Joy Unspeakable: Contemplative Practices of the Black Church* (Minneapolis: Augsburg Fortress, 2004); Maria Clara Bingemer, "Seeking the Pathos of God in a Secular Age: Reflections on Mystical Experience in the Twentieth Century," *Modern Theology* 29, no. 3 (July 2013): 248–278.

69. The work of Byung-Chul Han on the "art of lingering" serves as an important reminder of how the contemplative dimension of contemporary philosophy can be brought to bear on the question of what it means to cultivate a more spacious relationship to time. Byung-Chul Han, *The Scent of Time. A Philosophical Essay on the Art of Lingering*, trans. Daniel Steuer (Medford, MA: Polity, 2017). And Christian Wiman's beautiful literary-spiritual reflection on darkness and loss reveals how the "black holes in our lives" that undo us utterly can also become "part of the works of sacred art that we in fact are." Christian Wiman, *My Bright Abyss: Meditation of a Modern Believer* (New York: Farrar, Strauss and Giroux, 2013).

70. Andrew Prevot, *Thinking Prayer: Theology and Spirituality Amid the Crisis of Modernity* (Notre Dame: University of Notre Dame Press, 2015) offers a compelling model of this kind of "thinking with" as it relates to prayer—a particular kind of critical, theological thought that draws on and is nourished by that which cannot be said.

71. Ellen Bryant Voigt, "Autumn in the Yard We Planted," in *Shadow of Heaven* (New York: Norton, 2002), 76.

72. Ray L. Hart, *God Being Nothing: Toward a Theogony* (Chicago: University of Chicago, 2016), 41.

73. Porete, *The Mirror of Simple Souls*, 185.

74. Reginald Gibbons, "On Apophatic Poetics (I & II)," in *How Poems Think* (Chicago: University of Chicago Press, 2015), 87–122.

75. Jeff Sharlett, *This Brilliant Darkness: A Book of Strangers* (New York: W.W. Norton, 2020), 313.

76. Pope Francis, *Laudato Si': On Care for Our Common Home* (Mahwah, NJ: Paulist Press, 2015), §19.

77. Certeau, *The Mystic Fable*, vol. 1.

78. Roque Dalton, "Como tú," in *Poetry Like Bread*, ed. Martín Espada (Willimantic, CT: Curbstone Press, 2000), 128–129.

79. Rainer Maria Rilke, Letter to Clara Rilke, Jan. 1, 1907, *Letters of Rainer Maria Rilke, 1892–1910*, trans. Jane Bannard Greene and M. D. Herter Norton (New York: W.W. Norton, 1969), 253.

Chapter 2

1. J. M. G. Le Clézio, *Desert*, trans. C. Dickson (Boston: Verba Mundi, 2009), 5.

2. Helen Waddell, trans. *The Desert Fathers* (London: Constable, 1936), 63.

3. Waddell, *The Desert Fathers*, 34.

4. Elizabeth S. Boman, ed., *Monastic Visions: Wall Paintings in the Monastery of St. Antony at the Red Sea* (New Haven: Yale University Press, 2002); William Lyster, ed., *The Cave Church of Paul the Hermit at the Monastery of St. Paul, Egypt* (New Haven: Yale University Press, 2008).

5. Micheline Aharonian Marcom, *The Daydreaming Boy* (New York: Riverhead, 2004), 61–62.

6. Renée Daumal, *Mount Analogue*, trans. Carol Cosman (Woodstock, NY: Overlook, 2004), 109, 56.

7. John Wortley, *The Book of the Elders: Sayings of the Desert Fathers. The Systematic Collection* (Collegeville, MN: Liturgical Press, 2012), 25.

8. Benedicta Ward, trans., *The Sayings of the Desert Fathers: The Alphabetical Collection* (Collegeville, MN: Liturgical Press, 1984), 64.

9. Carolyn Forché, "Blue Hour," in *Blue Hour* (New York: HarperCollins, 2003), 7.

10. Susan Brind Morrow, *The Names of Things: A Passage in the Egyptian Desert* (New York: Riverhead, 1997), 35.

11. Edmond Jabès, *The Book of Margins*, trans. Rosemarie Waldrop (Chicago and London: University of Chicago Press, 1993), xvi.

12. John Cassian, *Conferences*, trans. Colm Luibheid (New York: Paulist Press, 1985), 101.

13. Evagrius of Pontus, *The Greek Ascetic Corpus*, trans. Robert E. Sinkewicz (Oxford and New York: Oxford University Press, 2003), 209.

14. Pierre Hadot, *Philosophy as a Way of Life*, ed. Arnold Davidson, trans. Michael Chase (Oxford: Blackwell, 1995), 81–144.

15. Evagrius, *The Greek Ascetic Corpus*, 206.

16. Simone Weil, *Waiting for God*, trans. Emma Craufurd (New York: Putnams, 1952), 57.

17. Wortley, *The Book of the Elders*, 22.

18. Deborah Digges, "Love Letters Mostly," in *The Wind Blows Through the Doors of My Heart* (New York: Knopf, 2010), 15.

19. John Climacus, *The Ladder of Divine Ascent*, trans. Colm Luibheid and Norman Russell (New York: Paulist Press, 1982), 268–269.

20. On the complex relationship between solitude and community in ancient Christian monasticism, see Graham Gould, *The Desert Fathers on Monastic Community* (Oxford: Clarendon, 1993).

 The question of the place and meaning of solitude within the lives of persons and communities continues to reverberate with real force in much contemporary discourse. See Sue Halpern, *Migrations to Solitude* (New York: Pantheon, 1992); Anthony Storr, *Solitude: A Return to the Self* (New York: Ballantine, 1998); Sylvain Tesson, *The Consolations of the Forest: Alone in a Cabin on the Siberian Taiga,* trans. Linda Coverdale (New York: Rizzoli, 2013); David Vincent, *A History of Solitude* (Cambridge: Polity, 2020); Stephen Batchelor, *The Art of Solitude* (New Haven: Yale University Press, 2020).

 Fay Bound Alberti, *A Biography of Loneliness: The History of an Emotion* (New York: Oxford, 2019), examines with great insight and care the difficult and often-painful sense of loneliness that sometimes makes its presence felt for those who find themselves drawn into solitude. And Thomas Dumm, *Loneliness as a Way of Life* (Cambridge: Harvard, 2008) offers an astute reading of the political meanings and implications of solitude, loneliness, and silence: "The inclination of modern life, with its distractions and shallowness, obscures the deeper fact of our separation from each other. So we need to establish a certain distance from our distractions in order to think more clearly about what it is we are seeking from each other. It is in the silence that we may come to recognize the fact of our ghostly existence, our fatal separation from one another, and from our better selves. And yet it is this separation that we must preserve so as to come to understand the dangers of our ongoing attempts to overcome it" (23).

21. Isabel Colegate's *A Pelican in the Wilderness: Hermits, Solitaries and Recluses* (New York: Counterpoint, 2002) describes the wide, deep, and variable allure of silence, stillness, and solitude both within and beyond religious traditions, and how profoundly it has shaped the life and thought not only of monks and hermits but also artists, poets, dissidents, political prisoners, and others.

22. Meister Eckhart, *The Complete Mystical Works of Meister Eckhart*, trans. and ed. Maurice O'C. Walshe (New York: Crossroad, 2009), 490. See also Sermon 69: "A man may go out into the fields and say his prayers and know God, or he may go to church and know God: but if he is more aware of God because he is in a quiet place, as is usual, that comes from his imperfection and not from God: for God is equally in all things and all places, and is equally ready to give Himself as far as in Him lies: and he knows God rightly who knows God equally in all things" (353).

23. Ariel Glucklich uses this term to evoke the challenge and possibility of cultivating deep spiritual awareness within everyday life in the intentional, contemplative community of Neot Smadar in the Negev: *Everyday Mysticism: A Contemplative Community at Work in the Desert* (New Haven: Yale University Press, 2017).

24. Evagrius, *The Greek Ascetic Corpus*, 98.

25. Columba Stewart, "Evagrius and the 'Eight Generic *Logisimoi*,'" in Richard Neuhauser, ed., *In the Garden of Evil: The Vices and Culture in the Middle Ages* (Toronto: PIMS, 2005), 3–34; Douglas Burton-Christie, "Evagrius on Sadness," *Cistercian Studies Quarterly* 44, no. 4 (2009): 395–409.

26. Thomas Merton, *Woods, Shore, Desert: A Notebook, May 1968* (Santa Fe: Museum of New Mexico Press, 1982), 16.

27. Athanasius, *The Life of Antony and the Letter to Marcellinus*, trans. Robert C. Gregg (New York: Paulist Press, 1980). For an excellent account of the theological, political, and ecclesial context of *The Life of Antony*, see David Brakke, *Athanasius and the Politics of Asceticism* (Oxford: Clarendon, 1995), esp. 201–272.

    James Goehring rightly notes that the solitary character of Antony's struggle deep in the heart of the Egyptian desert is in some respects a literary creation on the part of Athanasius. This is not to say that solitude did not figure importantly into the experience of the early Christian monks. It did. But Antony's story, which became paradigmatic for subsequent generations of monks and came to stand for the early Christian monastic story, must be placed alongside other, often very different stories, in which Christian monastic practice was less radically solitary and more communal than it has often been depicted to be. See James E. Goehring, "The Encroaching Desert: Literary Production and Ascetic Space in Early Christian Egypt," *Journal of Early Christian Studies* 1 (1993): 281–296.

28. Peter Brown, *The Making of Late Antiquity* (Cambridge, MA: Harvard University Press, 1978), 89–90.

29. Ward, *The Sayings of the Desert Fathers*, 176.

30. On Athanasius's theological and ecclesial motives in the writing of the *Vita Antonii*, see the classic study Robert C. Gregg and Dennis Groh, *Early Arianism: A View of Salvation* (Philadelphia: Fortress, 1981).

31. Henry David Thoreau, *Walden*, ed. J. Lyndon Shanley (Princeton: Princeton University Press, 1971), 111: "I love a broad margin to my life. Sometimes, in a summer morning, having taken my accustomed bath, I sat in my sunny doorway from sunrise till noon, rapt in a revery, amid the pines and hickories and sumachs, in undisturbed solitude and stillness, while the birds sang around or flitted noiseless through the house, until by the sun falling in at my west window, or the noise of some traveller's wagon on the distant highway, I was reminded of the lapse of time."

32. See, e.g., Andrée Hayum, *The Isenheim Altarpiece: God's Medicine and the Painter's Vision* (Princeton: Princeton University Press, 1990).

33. Gustavo Gutierrez, *We Drink from Our Own Wells: The Spiritual Journey of a People* (Maryknoll, NY: Orbis, 1984). Gutierrez cites his debt to Bernard of Clairvaux, one of the most influential early Cistercian writers, for this idea: "This is what Bernard of Clairvaux put so beautifully when he said that when it comes to spirituality all people must know how to 'drink from their own well'" (5).

34. Wortley, *The Book of the Elders*, 15.

35. *The Temptation of Saint Anthony*, created, designed, and directed by Robert Wilson; music and libretto by Bernice Johnson Reagon, based on the book by Gustave

Flaubert, *The Temptation of Saint Anthony*, trans. Lafcadio Hearn (New York: Modern Library, 2002), world premiere June 20, 2003, Ruhr Triennale Geblasehalle Duisburg; see also Felicia R. Lee, "Translating Flaubert, in the Gospel Tradition," *New York Times*, October 20, 2004.

36. Flaubert, *The Temptation of Saint Anthony*, 18.

37. Christian Wiman, "Darkness Starts," in *Hammer Is the Prayer* (New York: Farrar, Straus and Giroux, 2016), 23.

38. Barbara Holmes, *Joy Unspeakable. Contemplative Practices of the Black Churches*, 2nd ed. (Minneapolis: Fortress Press, 2017), 46–59.

39. Maria Clara Bingemer, "Seeking the Pathos of God in a Secular Age," *Modern Theology* 29, no. 3 (July 2013): 248–278.

40. Johann Baptist Metz, *The End of Time? The Provocation of Talking about God*, trans. J. Matthew Ashley (Mahwah, NJ: Paulist Press, 2004), 40. Matthew T. Eggemeier, "A Mysticism of Open Eyes: Compassion for a Suffering World and the Askesis of Contemplative Prayer," *Spiritus: A Journal of Christian Spirituality* 12, no. 1 (Spring 2012): 43–62.

41. Eula Biss, *Notes from No Man's Land: American Essays* (Minneapolis: Greywolf, 2009), 43.

42. Sara Uribe, *Antígona González*, trans. John Plueker (Los Angeles: Les Figues Press, 2016), 80–81. This is one of the critical questions in this extraordinary work, which recasts the ancient story of Antigone to confront and respond to the gaps and absences that the unrelenting violence in contemporary Mexico has created.

43. See, e.g., *Gregory of Nyssa, the Letters,* intro. trans. and commentary, Anna M. Silvas (Leiden, Boston: Brill, 2007), 115–122. Still, scholarship on early Christian pilgrimage demonstrates how complex the phenomenon was and how varied the responses to it were. Vasiliki M. Limberis, *Architects of Piety: The Cappadocian Fathers and the Cult of the Martyrs* (New York: Oxford University Press, 2011); Georgia Frank, *The Memory of the Eyes: Pilgrims to Living Saints in Christian Late Antiquity* (Berkeley: University of California Press, 2000); Bruria Bitton-Ashkelony, *Encountering the Sacred: The Debate on Christian Pilgrimage in Late Antiquity* (Berkeley: University of California Press, 2005).

44. Bernard McGinn, "Ocean and Desert as Symbols of Mystical Absorption in the Christian Tradition," *Journal of Religion* 74, no. 2 (April 1994): 155–181.

45. Hadewijch, *The Complete Works*, trans. Mother Columba Hart (Mahwah, NJ: Paulist Press, 1980), 187.

46. John Ruusbroec, *The Complete Ruusbroec*, vol. 1., English translation with the original Middle Dutch text. Edited and with an introduction by Guido de Baere and Thom Mertens (Turnhout, Belgium: Brepols, 2014), 194,124.

47. Eckhart, *The Complete Mystical Works of Meister Eckhart*, 338.

48. Paul Bowles, "Baptism of Solitude," in *Their Heads Are Green and Their Eyes Are Blue* (New York: Harper Perennial, 2006), 133–134.

49. Thomas Merton, *Learning to Love: Exploring Solitude and Freedom: The Journals of Thomas Merton*, vol. 6: *1966-1967*, ed. Christine M. Bochen (San Francisco: HarperSanFrancisco, 1997), 322.

50. Columba Stewart, "The Desert Fathers on Radical Self-Honesty," *Vox Benedictina: A Journal of Translations from Monastic Sources* 8, no. 1 (1991): 7–54.

51. Hans Georg Gadamer, *Philosophical Hermeneutics*, trans. David Linge (Berkeley: University of California Press, 2008), 9: "The historicity of our existence," Gadamer suggests, "entails that prejudices, in the literal sense of the word, constitute the initial directedness of our whole ability to experience. Prejudices are the biases of our openness to the world. They are simply conditions whereby we experience something, whereby what we encounter what something says to us."

52. Morrow, *The Names of Things*, 127–128.

53. Athanasius, *The Life of Antony*, 75, 73, 94. Such statements are also, of course, reflections of the hagiographical tradition that sought to portray the saint as an "*alter Christus*" and, in this particular case, advance Athanasius's theological ideas. Even so, there is evidence throughout the early monastic literature that solitude and silence were understood to be indispensable to the work of cultivating humility and compassion and to sustaining the life of the community.

54. Musō Soseki, *Sun at Midnight*, trans. W. S. Merwin and Soiku Shigematsu (San Francisco: North Point Press, 1989), 57.

55. Derek Walcott, "Love after Love," in *Collected Poems: 1948–1984* (New York: Farrar, Straus and Giroux, 1986), 328.

56. *The Book of the Elders*, 211.

Chapter 3

1. Hadewijch, *Mengeldichten*, 26, in *A Companion to John of Ruusbroec*, ed. John Arblaster and Rob Faesen (Leiden: Brill, 2014), 371.

2. Edith Cobb, *The Ecology of Imagination in Childhood* (New York: Columbia University Press, 1977), 28.

3. Gary Snyder, *The Practice of the Wild* (San Francisco: North Point Press, 1990).

4. I am thinking here especially of the influence on my thinking of certain biologists I came to know during this time, two in particular: Rob Burton and Howard Towner. On trips with Rob and his band of brothers from UC Santa Cruz into the eastern Mojave Desert, I learned to slow down and look at the landscape and the flora and fauna in a way that was completely new to me: the texture and patterns and life of the place brought vividly to live through slow, patient observation. And with Howard, my colleague at Loyola Marymount University, I traveled to the mountains of Baja California to help map the migration patterns of the Green-tailed Towhee, something that entailed long hours of sitting and listening for the song of this elusive bird. Both men possessed a capacity to see and feel the living world far beyond anything I was then capable of, but they invited me into their work, with generosity and grace. And, with their help, I slowly began to see and feel more than I had before and open myself to this work in a new way.

5. Benjamin Madley, *An American Genocide: The United States and the California Indian Catastrophe, 1846–1873* (New Haven: Yale University Press, 2016), 210–211.

Madley's argument for describing the assault against Indigenous communities in California as genocide is utterly persuasive and calls for a radical rethinking of the history of California, as well as the ethical implications for those of us inhabiting the state today. His inclusion of Sally Bell's account of the massacre helps contextualize what happened here within the larger pattern of genocide that can be seen throughout California history:

> My grandfather and all my family—my mother, my father, and me—we were around the house and not hurting anyone. Soon, about ten o'clock in the morning, some white men came. They killed my grandfather and my mother and my father. I saw them do it. I was a big girl at the time. Then they killed my baby sister and cut her heart out and threw it in the brush where I ran and hid. My little sister was a baby, just crawling around. I didn't know what to do. I was so scared that I guess I just hid there a long time with my sister's heart in my hands. I felt so bad and was so scared that I just couldn't do anything else. Then I ran into the woods and hid there for a long time. I lived there a long time with a few other people who had got away. We lived on berries and roots and didn't dare build a fire because the white men might come back after us. So we ate anything we could. We didn't have clothes after awhile, and we had to sleep under logs and in hollow trees because we didn't have anything to cover ourselves with, and it was cold then—in the spring. After a long time, maybe two, three months, I don't know just how long, but some time in the summer, my brother found me and took me to some white folks who kept me until I was grown and married.

6. Darren Frederick Speece, "Seeds of Rebellion: Sally Bell Grove and the Origins of the Redwoods Wars," *California History* 94, no. 2 (2017): 4–21; and Darren Frederick Speece, *Defending Giants: The Redwood Wars and the Transformation of American Environmental Politics* (Seattle: University of Washington Press, 2016), 181–190. Speece makes a compelling case for understanding the renaming of this grove in honor of Sally Bell as hugely significant in the efforts to save this place from the threat of clear-cutting by Georgia-Pacific.

7. Aldo Leopold, *A Sand County Almanac: And Sketches Here and There* (New York: Oxford, 1949), 210, 214.

8. Lauret Savoy, *Trace: Memory, History, Race, and the American Landscape* (Berkeley: Counterpoint, 2015), 33–34.

9. See also: Alison Hawthorn Deming and Lauret Savoy, eds., *The Colors of Nature: Culture, Identity and the Natural World*, 2nd ed. (Minneapolis: Milkweed, 2011); Carolyn Finney, *Black Places, White Spaces: Reimagining the Relationship of African Americans to the Great Outdoors* (Chapel Hill: University of North Carolina Press, 2014); J. Drew Lanham, *The Home Place: Memoirs of a Colored Man's Love Affair with Nature* (Minneapolis: Milkweed, 2016).

10. Savoy, *Trace*, 43.

11. Rob Nixon, *Slow Violence and the Environmentalism of the Poor* (Cambridge, MA: Harvard University Press, 2011).

12. Pope Francis, *Laudato Si': On Care for our Common Home* (Mahwah, NJ: Paulist Press, 2015), §139.

13. Savoy, *Trace*, 47.

14. Luis Cernuda, *Written on Water*, trans. Stephen Kessler (San Francisco: City Lights Books, 1994); "Return to Darkness," 93–94 and "Solitude," 82, both in *Written on Water*.

15. Robert Hass, "Iowa City, Early April," in *Sun Under Wood* (New York: Ecco, 1996), 35.

16. Freeman House, *Totem Salmon: Life Lessons from Another Species* (Boston: Beacon, 1999), 202.

17. Marguerite Porete, *The Mirror of Simple Souls*, trans. Ellen L. Babinksy (New York and Mahwah, NJ: Paulist Press, 1993), 102.

18. I have addressed these questions at greater length in *The Blue Sapphire of the Mind: Notes for a Contemplative Ecology* (New York: Oxford, 2013). It is helpful to note that while spirituality can and often does refer to ideas and practices arising out of particular religious traditions, it also refers to the often-implicit and inchoate sense of what William James has called "the more"; or what poet Czeslaw Milosz calls simply "the real." Such language—often willfully indeterminate in relation to any particular commitment to theism—captures something important about the way many contemporary persons approach the question of spirituality. In particular, it reflects a growing feeling that the language of spirituality needs to be continuously translated and reinterpreted if we are to find a meaningful way to express our own relationship with the sacred. In relation to the natural world, the efforts to name this new and still-emerging sensibility are striking in their range and diversity.

    Allan Hodder, for example, calls attention to an attitude he describes as a "mindful naturalism," a sense of the self as so deeply immersed within the rhythms of the natural world that any notion of human identity separate from that larger, more encompassing reality becomes almost impossible to conceive. Fiona Ellis speaks of an "expansive naturalism," a sense of nature as capable of revealing and making present to us a great immensity. Timothy Morton notes the importance of an ecological-spiritual sensibility that can help us rediscover "the liminal space between things" where the depth and power of the relationship between and among diverse living beings can be seen and felt. And Cathy Rigby considers whether this particular historical moment, with its acute challenges related to climate change, might make it possible to respond to the challenge of "rematerializing religion and spirituality." See Allan Hodder, *Thoreau's Ecstatic Witness* (New Haven: Yale University Press, 2001), 66; Fiona Ellis, *God, Value and Nature* (Oxford: Oxford University Press, 2014); Timothy Morton, "The Liminal Space between Things: Epiphany and the Physical," in *Material Ecocriticsm*, ed. Iovino Serenella and Serpil Oppermann (Bloomington: Indiana University Press, 2014), 269–282; Kate Rigby, "Spirits That Matter: Pathways toward a Rematerialization of Religion and Spirituality," in *Material Ecocriticsm*, 283–290.

19. *Laudato Si'*, §233.

20. *Laudato Si'*, §233.

21. More than fifty years ago, in his important article "The Historical Roots of our Environmental Crisis," *Science* 155, no. 3767 (March 1967), 1203–1207, Lynn White Jr. cited St. Francis as an almost singular exception to what he viewed as Christianity's deeply anthropocentric attitude toward the natural world. White's view of St.

Francis as an exemplary and exceptional figure within Christianity turned out to be overstated. Still, the fundamental truth of his insight—that Christianity had long neglected its obligation to care for the natural world—helped provoke a deep and widespread rethinking of Christianity's ethical and spiritual relationship with nature. *Laudato Si'* has now brought this conversation about Christianity's capacity and commitment to revere the natural world and the place of saints and mystics in helping articulate a more holistic and ethical vision into the present moment.

22. Roger D. Sorrell, *St. Francis of Assisi and Nature: Tradition and Innovation in Western Christian Attitudes towards the Environment* (New York: Oxford University Press, 1988).

23. Recent scholarship on Francis that has been especially helpful to me: Augustine Thompson, O.P. *Francis of Assisi: A New Biography* (Ithaca: Cornell University Press, 2012); André Vauchez, *Francis of Assisi: The Life and Afterlife of a Medieval Saint,* trans. Michael F. Cusato (New Haven and London: Yale University Press, 2012); Joann Acocella, "Rich Man, Poor Man: The Radical Visions of St. Francis," *The New Yorker,* January 14, 2013, 72–77; see also Robert Glenn Davis, *The Weight of Love: Affect, Ecstasy and Union in the Theology of Bonaventure* (New York: Fordham University Press, 2017) for a beautifully insightful analysis of Bonaventure's theological-mystical "reading" of the life of Francis.

24. *Laudato Si'* describes this deepening awareness as an "ecological conversion" something that entails coming to "a loving awareness that we are not disconnected from the rest of creatures, but joined in a splendid universal communion," *Laudato Si'*, §220.

25. *Laudato Si'*, §19.

26. Jane Bennett, *Vibrant Matter: A Political Ecology of Things* (Durham, NC: Duke University Press, 2010). Stacy Alaimo, *Bodily Natures: Science, Environment and the Material Self* (Bloomington: Indiana University Press, 2010) describes something close to this in proposing what she calls "trans-corporeality" as a more inclusive and integral way of thinking about how the embodied self responds to, interacts with, and constructs meaning in relation to other embodied lives—a theoretical rejoinder to the corrosive dualisms that continue to undermine our capacity for living in the world with care and respect.

27. Hadewijch, *The Complete Works,* trans. Mother Columba Hart (New York: Paulist Press, 1980), 284; Patricia Dailey, "Children of Promise: The Bodies of Hadewijch of Brabant," *Journal of Medieval and Early Modern Studies* 41, no. 2 (Spring 2011), 317–343.

28. Pierre Hadot, *The Philosophy of Everyday Life,* ed. Arnold Davidson, trans. Michael Chase (Malden, MA: Blackwell, 1995), 261.

29. *Laudato Si'*, § 239.

30. Thomas Merton, *Woods, Shore, Desert* (Santa Fe: Museum of New Mexico Press, 1982). A more complete account of Merton's time in California can be found in Thomas Merton, *The Other Side of the Mountain: The End of the Journey,* ed. Patrick Hart (San Francisco: Harper, 1998), 89–114, 169–202.

31. Merton, *Woods, Shore, Desert,* 48.

32. Thomas Merton, "Rain and the Rhinoceros," in *Raids on the Unspeakable* (New York: New Directions, 1966), 9–26; "Day of a Stranger," *The Hudson Review* 20,

no. 2 (Summer 1967), 211–218; "A Life Free from Care," *Cistercian Studies Quarterly* 5, no. 3 (1970): 207–227 (transcript of a taped conference on the occasion of Merton's retirement to the hermitage, August 20, 1965).

33. Merton, *Woods, Shore, Desert*, 24.

34. Merton, *Woods, Shore, Desert*, 16.

35. David Steindl-Rast, "Man of Prayer," in *Thomas Merton Monk: A Monastic Tribute*, ed. Brother Patrick Hart (Kalamazoo: Cistercian, 1983), 79–89. Quotations are taken from 79–81.

36. The growing interest in these questions in the contemporary moment is striking and bears at least a distant relationship to the way such concerns have long been addressed within contemplative and mystical traditions. See David Orr, "Slow Knowledge," in *The Nature of Design: Ecology, Culture and Human Intention* (New York: Oxford, 2002), 35–42; Douglas E. Christie, "The Eternal Present: Slow Knowledge and the Renewal of Time," *Buddhist Christian Studies* 33 (2013): 13–21; Mark C. Taylor, *Speed Limits: Where Time Went and Why We Have So Little Left* (New Haven: Yale University Press, 2014); Jonathan Crary, *24/7: Late Capitalism and the Ends of Sleep* (London: Verso, 2014).

37. Benedicta Ward, trans. *The Sayings of the Desert Fathers: The Alphabetical Collection*, rev. ed. (Collegeville, MN: Liturgical Press, 1984), 222.

38. Thomas Merton, *Zen and the Birds of Appetite* (New York: New Directions, 1968), 50.

39. Thomas Merton, *The Hidden Ground of Love*, ed. William H. Shannon (New York: Farrar, Straus and Giroux, 1985), 569.

40. Merton, "Day of a Stranger," 211–218.

41. Merton, "Day of a Stranger," 213–214.

42. Merton, "Day of a Stranger," 215.

43. Merton, *The Hidden Ground of Love*, 73.

44. Merton, *The Hidden Ground of Love*, 371.

45. Meister Eckhart, *The Complete Mystical Works of Meister Eckhart*, trans. and ed. Maurice O'C. Walshe (New York: Crossroad, 2009), 57.

46. Porete, *The Mirror of Simple Souls*, 108.

47. Hadewijch, *Mengeldichten*, 26, 371.

48. Merton, *The Other Side of the Mountain*, 102.

49. Merton, *Woods, Shore, Desert*, 28.

50. John Ruusbroec, *The Complete Ruusbroec*, vol. 1, English translation with the original Middle Dutch text, edited and with an introduction by Guido de Baere and Thom Mertens (Turnhout, Belgium: Brepols, 2014), 232.

51. Branka Arsić, *Bird Relics: Grief and Vitalism in Thoreau* (Cambridge, MA: Harvard University Press, 2016), 129–130.

52. Arsić, *Bird Relics*, 21–22.

53. See, e.g., David M. Robinson, *Natural Life: Thoreau's Worldly Transcendentalism* (Ithaca: Cornell University Press, 2004), 48–76; H. Daniel Peck, *Thoreau's Morning Work: Memory and Perception in* A Week on the Concord and Merrimack Rivers, the Journal, and Walden (New Haven: Yale University Press, 1990), 3–36.

54. Arsić, *Bird Relics*, 30–31.

55. Arsić, *Bird Relics*, 254.

56. Cora Diamond, "The Difficulty of Reality and the Difficulty of Philosophy," *Partial Answers: Journal of Literature and the History of Ideas* 1, no. 2 (June 2003), 2.

57. Arsić, *Bird Relics*, 255.

58. Arsić, *Bird Relics*, 256.

59. Henry David Thoreau, *Walden*, ed. J. Lyndon Shanley (Princeton: Princeton University Press, 1971), 97–8.

60. Arsić, *Bird Relics*, 257.

61. Arsić, *Bird Relics*, 270, 274.

62. Sharon Cameron, *The Bond of the Furthest Apart: Essays on Tolstoy, Dostoevsky, Bresson and Kafka* (Chicago: University of Chicago Press, 2017), 11.

63. Henry David Thoreau, *A Week on the Concord and Merrimack Rivers* (New York: Penguin, 1998), 235–236.

64. Thoreau, *A Week*, 284.

65. Thoreau, *A Week*, 304, 307.

66. Freeman House, *Totem Salmon*, 202.

67. Wendell Berry, "How to Be a Poet (to remind myself)," *Poetry*, January 2001, 270.

68. Speece, "Seeds of Rebellion" and *Defending Giants*. Today, the InterTribal Sinkyone Wilderness Council plays a critical role in preserving the cultural, spiritual, and ecological heritage of this land.

69. I am grateful to my friend Sharon Duggan for sharing her personal recollections of this critical work. She played an important role during the early 1980s (and beyond)—together with many others—in mounting the legal defense against Georgia-Pacific's rapacious logging practices in the forests in and around the Lost Coast.

Chapter 4

1. Philippe Diolé, *The Most Beautiful Desert of All*, trans. Katherine Woods (London: Jonathan Cape, 1959), 165.

2. I am immensely grateful to Alicia Partnoy, a survivor of the Argentine military's campaign of terror and my colleague for many years at Loyola Marymount University in Los Angeles, for sharing her experience with me. In conversations and later reading her beautiful, courageous book *The Little School*, I was confronted by the depths of her experience of loss, and it compelled me to think more carefully about it. Her book became a strong and consistent presence in our work with students in Córdoba and helped us rethink what it means to pay attention, to bear witness, especially in moments of acute social crisis. Alicia Partnoy, *The Little School*, trans. Alicia Partnoy with Lois Athey and Sandra Braunstein (San Francisco: Midnight Editions, 1998). See especially her thoughtful, honest reflection on the question of "religion" (61–63).

3. James P. Brennan, *Missing Bones: Revisiting the History of the Dirty War* (Berkeley: University of California Press, 2018) offers a painstaking analysis of Argentina's so-called dirty war, with particular attention to La Perla. See especially chapter 4: "Death Camp: La Perla," 36–50.

4. This translation is adapted from that of C. A. Wynschenk Dom's version in light of the recent Brepols edition. In *The Adornment of the Spiritual Marriage; the Sparkling Stone; the Book of Supreme Truth*, trans. C. A. Wynschenk Dom (Westminster, MD: Christian Classics, 1974), 178, the English translation reads: "This is the dark *silence* in which all the loving lose themselves." In the recent critical edition (*The Complete Ruusbroec*, English translation with the original Middle Dutch text, edited and with an introduction by Guido de Baere and Thom Mertens, vol. 1 [Turnhout, Belgium: Brepols, 2014]), 325), the English translation reads: "This is the dark *stillness* in which all the loving are lost." The Middle Dutch word "*Stille*" can be rendered as "stillness" but also as "silence." In English, both words evoke the depth and mystery that for Ruusbroec is at the heart of this experience. And in the Christian contemplative tradition, both "silence" and "stillness" express significant, if often very different, elements of spiritual experience. In the context of the present work, the word "silence" carries greater weight and meaning, in part because of its capacity to convey the ineffability and bewilderment of experience and the inadequacy of language to plumb the depths of it. Also because of its capacity to evoke unspeakable loss, especially the loss of ground and identity in the search for God. So too it opens up a space for considering the possible relationship of mystical silence to other kinds of silence, including the silence that figures so importantly in accounts of repression and genocide. Marguerite Feitlowitz's analysis of the way members of the Argentine military junta employed silence and darkness to control and terrorize prisoners is especially pertinent here. Marguerite Feitlowitz, *A Lexicon of Terror: Argentina and the Legacies of Terror* (New York: Oxford University Press, 1998).

5. Clarice Lispector, *Água Viva*, trans. Stefan Tobler (New York: New Directions, 1973), 7.

6. Michel de Certeau, *The Mystic Fable*, vol. 1, trans. Michael B. Smith. (Chicago: University of Chicago Press, 1992), 81.

7. Ole J. Benedictow, *The Black Death, 1346–1353: The Complete History* (Woodbridge, Suffolk: Boydel, 2004), 110–118.

8. Michel de Certeau, "Mystic Speech," in *The Michel de Certeau Reader*, ed. Graham Ward (Oxford, Wiley-Blackwell, 2000), 201–202.

9. Ruusbroec, *The Complete Ruusbroec*, vol. 1, 127.

10. Ruusbroec, *The Complete Ruusbroec*, vol. 1, 590.

11. Ruusbroec, *The Complete Ruusbroec*, vol. 1, 235.

12. Ruusbroec, *The Complete Ruusbroec*, vol. 1, 152–153.

13. Ruusbroec, *The Complete Ruusbroec*, vol. 1, 154–155.

14. Ruusbroec, *The Complete Ruusbroec*, vol. 1, 160.

15. Ruusbroec, *The Complete Ruusbroec*, vol. 1, 179–180.

16. Ruusbroec, *The Complete Ruusbroec*, vol. 1, 186–187.

17. Hadewijch, *The Complete Works*, trans. Mother Columba Hart (New York and Mahwah, NJ: Paulist Press, 1981), 356.

18. Archbishop Sophrony, *St. Silouan the Athonite* (Younkers, NY: St. Vladimir's Seminary Press, 1999), 210.

19. Ruusbroec, *The Complete Ruusbroec*, vol. 1, 316.

20. Ruusbroec, *The Complete Ruusbroec*, vol. 1, 319–320.

21. Ruusbroec, *The Complete Ruusbroec*, vol. 1, 220.

22. Ruusbroec, *The Complete Ruusbroec*, vol. 1, 342.

23. Ruusbroec, *The Complete Ruusbroec*, vol. 1, 136.

24. Ruusbroec, *The Complete Ruusbroec*, vol. 1, 136, 342.

25. Certeau, "Mystic Speech," 86.

26. Hadewijch, *The Complete Works*, 229.

27. *Poetry of Hadewijch*, trans. Mariecke J. E. H. T. Van Best (Leuven: Peeters, 1998), 43.

28. Ariel Dorfman, *Desert Memories: Journeys through the Chilean Desert* (Washington, DC: National Geographic, 2004), 95–96.

29. Simon Ortiz, "Culture and the Universe," in *Out There Somewhere* (Tucson: University of Arizona Press, 2002), 104.

30. Diolé, *The Most Beautiful Desert of All*, 165.

31. This is one of the central questions raised in Raúl Zurita's *Inri*: how to imagine and reclaim a past that has been erased, rendered invisible, made illegible. Raul Zurita, *Inri*, trans. William Rowe (Grosse Pointe Farms, MI: Marick Press, 2009).

32. Patricio Guzman, *Nostalgia de la Luz* (Brooklyn, NY: Icarus Films, 2011). DVD.

33. Rubén Martínez, *Crossing Over: A Mexican Family on the Migrant Trail* (New York: Metropolitan Books, 2001); *Desert America: Boom and Bust in the New Old West* (New York: Metropolitan Books, 2012). Both books have had a significant impact on my thinking about the desert.

   My invitation to participate in nonviolent resistance at the Nevada National Security Site (formerly the Nevada Test Site) arose from friendships with Franciscans in Oakland, California (in particular Louis Vitale, OFM, the former provincial of the Santa Barbara Province of Franciscans) and with those who were inspired by the Catholic Worker Movement (in particular Anne and Terry Symens-Bucher) who helped create the "Nevada Desert Experience"—an organization committed to gathering at the edge of the Security Site for vigils, religious services, and nonviolent civil disobedience (http://nevadadesertexperience.org/). The impact on those who have lived in proximity to or downwind from these testing sites is still being documented. See also Andrew Kirk, *Doom Towns: The People and Landscapes of Atomic Testing* (New York: Oxford University Press, 2017); Emmett Gowin, *The Nevada Test Site* (Princeton: Princeton University Press, 2019).

   My experience and thinking about Manzanar has been deeply impacted by my participation in the historically Japanese American West Los Angeles United Methodist Church. A number of the older members of the community were incarcerated at Manzanar and continue to bear witness to the meaning of that experience for the larger community. The annual pilgrimage to the Manzanar National Historical Site, sponsored by the Manzanar Committee, has become a significant force for spiritual, cultural, and political renewal during the past fifty years (https://manzanarco mmittee.org/who-we-are/).

34. Chris Darke, "Desert of the Disappeared: Patricio Guzmán on Nostalgia for the Light," *Sight & Sound*. 22, no. 8 (August 2012). Extended Web interview: *Sight & Sound*, February 19, 2015. https://www2.bfi.org.uk/news-opinion/sight-sound-magazine/interviews/desert-disappeared-patricio-guzman-nostalgia-light.

35. Juan Gabriel Vasquez, *The Informers*, trans. Anne McClean (New York: Riverhead, 2009), 24.

36. Paula Allen, *Flowers in the Desert: The Search for Chile's Disappeared*, 2nd ed. (Gainesville: University Press of Florida, 2013), 102–103.

37. Allen, *Flowers in the Desert*, 114–115.

38. Ruusbroec, *The Complete Ruusbroec*, vol. 1, 591.

39. Bernard McGinn, ed., *Meister Eckhart and the Beguine Mystics: Hadewijch of Brabant, Mechthild of Magdeburg, and Marguerite Porete* (New York: Continuum, 1994), especially the chapter by Paul A. Dietrich, "The Wilderness of God in Hadewicjh II and Meister Eckhart and His Circle," 31–43.

40. Ruusbroec, *The Complete Ruusbroec*, vol. 1, 194.

41. Ruusbroec, *The Complete Ruusbroec*, vol. 1, 194, 591.

42. Paul Mommaers, *Jan Van Ruusbroec: Mystical Union with God* (Leuven: Peeters, 2009), 66–68, offers a helpful corrective to the way "essence" (*wesen*) has often been understood in relation to Ruusbroec's thought. Mommaers notes that: "the Thomistic notion of *essential* was often read into Ruusbroec's *wesen*, but . . . the Middle Dutch word must rather be understood here as 'being' or 'existence' . . . ."

43. Ruusbroec, *The Complete Ruusbroec*, vol. 1, 136.

44. Ruusbroec, *The Complete Ruusbroec*, vol. 1, 591; Satoshi Kikuchi, *From Eckhart to Ruusbroec: A Critical Inheritance of Mystical Themes in the Fourteenth Century* (Leuven: Leuven University Press, 2015), 247–248.

45. Ruusbroec, *The Complete Ruusbroec*, vol. 1, 342, 337, 250.

46. Ruusbroec, *The Complete Ruusbroec*, vol. 1, 246, 251.

47. Ruusbroec, *The Complete Ruusbroec*, vol. 1, 534.

48. Ruusbroec, *The Complete Ruusbroec*, vol. 1, 254.

49. Ruusbroec, *The Complete Ruusbroec*, vol. 1, 506.

50. Ruusbroec, *The Complete Ruusbroec*, vol. 1, 136.

51. Hadewijch, *Mengeldichten*, 26, in *A Companion to John of Ruusbroec*, ed. John Arblaster and Rob Faesen (Leiden: Brill, 2014), 371.

52. Fernando Pessoa, *The Book of Disquiet*, ed. Maria José de Lancastre, trans. Margaret Jull Costa (London: Serpent's Tail, 1991), 36–37.

53. J. M. G. Le Clézio, *Desert.*, trans. C. Dickson (Boston: Verba Mundi, 2009), 18.

54. Lispector, *Água Viva*, 38.

55. Alejandro Zambra, *Ways of Going Home*, trans. Megan McDowell (New York: Farrar, Straus and Giroux, 2013), 49.

56. Gregory of Nyssa, *The Life of Moses*, trans. Abraham Malherbe and Everett Ferguson (New York: Paulist Press, 1978), 95; Ann Conway-Jones, "Exegetical Puzzles and the Mystical Theologies of Gregory of Nyssa and Dionysius the Areopagite," *Vigiliae Christianae* 75, no. 1 (2020): 1–21.

57. Czeslaw Milosz, *Beginning with My Streets: Essays and Recollections* (New York: Farrar, Strauss and Giroux, 1991), 280–281.

58. See An Yountae, *The Decolonial Abyss: Mysticism and Cosmopolitics from the Ruins* (New York: Fordham University Press, 2017), esp. "The Mystical Abyss: Via Negativa," 25–46. Literary works from Argentina and Chile that have shaped my thinking about these questions include Carolina de Robertis, *Perla* (New York: Vintage, 2013); Samanta Schweblin, *Fever Dream*, trans. Megan McDowell (New York: Riverhead, 2017); Andrés Neuman, *Talking to Ourselves*, trans. Nick Caistor and Lorenza Garcia

(New York: Farrar, Straus and Giroux, 2015); and *Fracture,* trans. Nick Caistor and Lorenza Garcia (New York: Farrar, Strauss and Giroux, 2020); and Mariana Enríquez, *Things We Lost in the Fire,* trans. Megan McDowell (New York: Hogarth, 2017).

59. I am grateful to my friend and colleague Diego Fonti for sharing with me his unpublished essay, "*Desapariciones*: A Meditation on Piety Due to Victims of Violence." See also Maria Clara Bingemer, "Seeking the Pathos of God in a Secular Age: Theological Reflections on Mystical Experience in the Twentieth Century," *Modern Theology* 29, no. 3 (July 2013): 248–278.

60. Patricio Pron, *My Fathers' Ghost Is Climbing in the Rain,* trans. Mara Feye Lethem (New York: Knopf, 2013), 192. Originally published as *El espíritu de mis padres sigue subiendo en la lluvia* (New York: Literatura Random House, 2011); see Geoffrey McGuire, *The Politics of Memory: Violence and Victimhood in Contemporary Argentine Culture* (Cham Switzerland: Palgrave McMillan, 2017), 55–72.

61. Pron, *My Fathers' Ghost,* 188.

62. Pron, *My Fathers' Ghost,* 192.

63. Pron, *My Fathers' Ghost,* 196.

64. Pron, *My Fathers' Ghost,* 197.

65. Emmanuel Levinas, *Totality and Infinity: An Essay on Exteriority,* trans. Alphonso Lingis (Pittsburgh: Duquesne, 1969), 198.

66. Judith Butler, "On Grief and Rage," *Pen America* 18 (May 8, 2015): 16–20.

67. Michel de Certeau, *The Practice of Everyday Life,* 3rd ed., trans. Steven Rendell (Berkeley: University of California Press, 2011). This question is not of course unique to Argentina. In the United States one can note the work of Japanese Americans who sought and won reparations for their unjust internment during World War II. Naomi Hirahara and Heather Lundquist, *Life after Manzanar* (Berkeley: Heyday, 2018). And there is also a growing call for reparations for the immense losses endured by African Americans during the time of slavery. See Ta-Nehisi Coates, "The Case for Reparations," *Atlantic,* June 2014. At the root of such work is a commitment to pay attention, to gaze into the absence left behind by violence, not to turn away and create a new politics, a new sense of community in its wake.

68. Pron, *My Fathers' Ghost,* 198.

69. Pron, *My Fathers' Ghost,* 198.

70. For a compelling argument on the importance of silence as the ground of witness, see Michael Jackson, "The Prose of Suffering and the Practice of Silence," *Spiritus* 4 (2004): 44–59.

Chapter 5

1. Hadewijch d'Anvers, *Écrits mystiques des Béguines,* trans. Jean-Baptiste Porion (Paris: Éditions du Seuil, 1954), 134. Cited in Michel de Certeau, *The Mystic Fable,* vol. 1: *The Sixteenth and Seventeenth Centuries,* trans. Michael B. Smith (Chicago: University of Chicago Press, 1992), 299.

2. Jules Schelvis, *Sobibor: A History of a Nazi Death Camp*, trans. Karin Dixon (Oxford: Berg, 2007). See also Chris Webb, *The Sobibor Death Camp: History, Biographies, Remembrance* (New York: Columbia University Press, 2017); Yizhak Arad, *The Operation Einhard Death Camps: Belzec, Sobibor, Treblinka*, rev. and exp. ed. (Bloomington: Indiana University Press, 2018).

3. Edmond Jabés, *The Book of Margins*, trans. Rosemarie Waldrop (Chicago: University of Chicago Press, 1993), 129.

4. Hadewijch, *The Complete Works*, trans. Mother Columba Hart (New York and Mahwah, NJ: Paulist Press, 1980), 356; Paul Mommaers, *Hadewijch: Writer, Beguine, Love Mystic* (Leuven: Peeters, 2004); Giles Milhaven, *Hadewijch and Her Sisters: Other Ways of Loving and Knowing* (Albany: State University of New York Press, 1983); Mommaers (in *Hadewijch: The Complete Works*, xii) describes Hadewijch as "the most important exponent of love mysticism and one of the loftiest figures in Western mysticism."

5. Tadeusz Rósiewicz, "The Gates of Death," in *New Poems*, trans. Bill Johnston (Brooklyn, NY: Archipelago Books, 2007), 252.

6. Etty Hillesum, *An Interrupted Life*, trans. Arno Pomerans (New York: Pantheon, 1983), 145.

7. Anne Michaels, *Fugitive Pieces* (New York: Random House, 1996), 157.

8. Edmond Jabés, *Book of Resemblances 2: Intimations: The Desert*, trans. Rosemarie Waldrop (Hanover, NH: Wesleyan University Press, 1978), 103.

9. These are difficult, contentious, and much debated questions, especially in the late twentieth and early twenty-first centuries. Jessica Lang, *Textual Silence: Unreadability and the Holocaust* (New Brunswick: Rutgers University Press, 2017), offers a helpful way of thinking about how silence functions in memoirs, novels, poems, and diaries arising from the Holocaust and why the presence of such silence is so important for understanding the ethical demands of reading, including the need to engage seriously with inaccessibility, blankness, and illegibility.

10. Theodor W. Adorno, "Cultural Criticism and Society," in *Prisms* (Cambridge, MA: MIT Press: 1983), 34.

11. Michel de Certeau, "Mystic Speech," in *The Michel de Certeau Reader*, ed. Graham Ward (Oxford: Blackwell, 2000), 189.

12. Theodor Adorno, *Negative Dialectics* (New York: Continuum, 1973), 361–363.

13. Primo Levi, *Survival in Auschwitz: The Nazi Assault on Humanity*, trans. Stuart Woolf (New York: Simon and Schuster, 1996), 9.

14. Levi, *Survival in Auschwitz*, 9.

15. Jabés, *The Book of Margins*, 80–81.

16. Jabés, *The Book of Margins*, 97.

17. Jabés, *The Book of Margins*, ix, x. See also Susan Gubar, *Poetry after Auschwitz: Remembering What One Never Knew* (Bloomington: Indiana University Press, 2003).

18. Jabés, *The Book of Margins*, 67.

19. Paul Celan, "Speech on the Occasion of Receiving the Literature Prize of the Free Hanseatic City of Bremen," in *Selected Prose and Poems of Paul Celan*, trans. John Felstiner (New York: W.W. Norton, 2001), 393. On the Bremen Prize speech, see also John Felstiner, *Poet, Survivor, Jew* (New Haven: Yale University Press, 2001), 395.

20. Celan, "Speech," 396.

21. Michaels, *Fugitive Pieces*, 111.

22. Jabés, *The Book of Margins*, xv.

23. Clarice Lispector, *Água Viva*, trans. Stefan Tobler (New York: New Directions, 2012), 77.

24. Jabès, *The Book of Margins*, xvi.

25. Jabès, *The Book of Resemblances*, 89.

26. Jabés, *The Book of Margins*, 165.

27. Jabés, *The Book of Margins*, 129.

28. W. G. Sebald, *Austerlitz* (New York: Random House, 2001), 14.

29. Thomas Merton, "Rain and the Rhinoceros," in *Raids on the Unspeakable* (New York: New Directions, 1966), 17–18.

30. Czeslaw Milosz, "On Prayer," in *The Collected Poems 1931–1987* (New York: Ecco, 1988), 424.

31. Lispector, *Água Viva*, 24.

32. Michel Foucault, "Of Other Spaces," *Diacritics* 16 (Spring 1986): 22–27.

33. Elie Wiesel, *One Generation After*, trans. Lily Edelman and Elie Wiesel (New York: Schocken, 2011), 198.

34. Christian Wiman, *Hammer Is the Prayer: Selected Poems* (New York: Farrar, Straus and Giroux, 2016), 100.

35. Olga Tokarczuk, *Primeval and Other Times*, trans. Antonia Lloyd-Jones (Prague: Twisted Spoon Press, 2010), 242.

36. Jabés, *The Book of Margins*, 75.

37. Hadewijch, *The Complete Works*, 60.

38. Hadewijch, *Poetry of Hadewijch*, trans. Marieke J. E. H. T. van Baest (Leuven: Peeters, 1998), 213.

39. Hadewijch, *Poetry of Hadewijch*, 247.

40. Hadewijch, *The Complete Works*, 153. On the question of loss, displacement, and exile, see Ray Wakefield, "Homeless Mystics: Exiled from God," in *Weltanschauliche Orientierungsversuche im Exil / New Orientations of World View in Exile*, ed. Evelyn M. Meyer, Greg Divers, and Reinhard Andress (Leiden: Brill, 2010), 37–43.

41. Tanis M. Guest, *Some Aspects of Hadewijch's Poetic Form in the "Strofische Gedichten"* (The Hague: Martinus Nijhoff, 1975), 192–193.

42. Hadewijch, *The Complete Works*, 59.

43. Hadewijch d'anvers, *Écrits mystiques des Béguines*, 134. Cited in Certeau, *The Mystic Fable*, vol. 1, 299.

44. Certeau, *The Mystic Fable*, vol. 1, 299. On this concluding section of *The Mystic Fable*, see Amy Hollywood, "Love Speaks Here: Michel de Certeau's *Mystic Fable*," *Spiritus* 12, no. 2 (Fall 2012): 198–206.

45. Hadewijch, *Poetry of Hadewijch*, 67.

46. Hadewijch, *Poetry of Hadewijch*, 70–71.

47. Hadewijch, *Poetry of Hadewijch*, 43.

48. Hadewijch, *The Complete Works*, 289. Columba Hart's English translation of this passage presents certain difficulties, in part because of the phrase "very depressed," which suggests a meaning in English that does easily align with the Dutch. In contemporary

English usage, "depressed" has come to be closely associated with a specific clinical diagnosis, one whose meaning is often highly contentious. The Dutch says simply, "*Ic lach op enen kerstnacht tenen male ende wart op ghenomen inden gheeste*," which does not contain any adjective that means anything like "depressed." Van Mierlo, the critical editor, notes that "*ic lach*" probably means "bedridden" but with the combination of "*tenen male*" it probably means "dejected." After "*enen kerstnacht*," "*tenen male*" does suggest "completely," so Van Mierlo says that she was probably feeling "down." Most of the modern translators offer some form of this "dejection" or "depression"; Willaert has "saddened" and Mommaers has "dismayed." According to Mommaers, the dismay is the result of not feeling the Christmas event interiorly, and the whole vision is intended to respond to the fundamental question (which is especially present in Flemish and Rhineland mysticism): What good is it that Christ was born in Bethlehem if he is not also born in your own soul? I am grateful to John Arblaster for his help thinking about the meaning of this passage. These comments serve as a reminder of the need to take care in evaluating those elements of Hadewijch's work that seem to our ears to reflect certain psychological struggles. Even so, whether we read "depressed" or "completely dejected" or "dismayed," it seems clear that we are being given a glimpse of a moment of acute spiritual disorientation that Hadewijch herself associates with the experience of being drawn into a great and mysterious depth.

49. Hadewijch, *The Complete Works*, 291.
50. Hadewijch, *Mengeldichten*, 22, 26–30. Cited in Saskia Murk Jansen, in *The Measure of Mystic Thought: A Study of Hadewijch's Mengeldichten* (Göppingen: Kümmerle Verlag, 1991), 65. Jansen observes: "Hadewijch here describes the agony of loving and, as the love that binds the soul to God originates in God, she attributes her distress both to the act of loving and to the object of that love, God. This is a further example of the way in which Hadewijch uses the difficulty of distinguishing between the word *minne* meaning the emotion, and her use of the word to refer to the divine to enrich the content of her poetry." See also Steven Rozenski Jr., "The Promise of Eternity: Love and Poetic Form in Hadewijch's *Liederen* or *Stanzaic Poems*," *Exemplaria* 22, no. 4 (Winter 2010): 305–325.
51. Hadewijch, *The Complete Works*, 299. On the complex relationship of eros and abyss in medieval Christian mysticism and the challenges and possibilities of interpreting this language in the contemporary moment, see Grace M. Jantzen, "Eros and the Abyss: Reading Medieval Mystics in Postmodernity," *Literature and Theology* 17, no. 3 (2003): 244–264.
52. Hadewijch, *The Complete Works*, 311.
53. Hadewijch, *The Complete Works*, 312.
54. Hadewijch, *The Complete Works*, 344.
55. Hadewijch, *The Complete Works*, 344.
56. Hadewijch, *The Complete Works*, 356–357.
57. See Clark R. West, "The Deconstruction of Hell: A History of the *Resignatio and Infernum* Tradition," PhD diss., Syracuse University, 2013.
58. Georges Didi-Huberman, *Bark*, trans. Samuel E. Martin (Cambridge, MA: MIT Press, 2017), 66, 105.

Chapter 6

1. Agnes Martin, "Beauty Is the Mystery of Life," in *Agnes Martin: Writings/Schriften*, ed. Dieter Schwarz (Ostfildern-Ruit, Germany: Kunstmuseum Winterthur/Edition Cantz, 1992), 153.

2. Christopher Knight, "Survey of Agnes Martin's Powerful yet Meditative Work Draws a Straight, Vibrant Line to Zen," *Los Angeles Times*, April 29, 2016.

3. Frances Morris and Tiffany Bell, eds., *Agnes Martin* (London: Tate, 2015). See also Lynne Cooke, Karen Kelly, and Barbara Schröder, eds., *Agnes Martin* (New Haven: Yale University Press, 2011).

4. Gaston Bachelard, *Poetics of Space*, trans. Maria Jolas (Boston: Beacon, 1994), 183–210.

5. Karl Ove Knausgaard, *My Struggle: Book One*, trans. Don Bartlett (New York: Farrar, Straus, Giroux, 2009), 207.

6. Agnes Martin, cited in John Gruen, "Agnes Martin: Everything, everything is about feeling . . . feeling and recognition," *ArtNews*, September 1976.

7. Agnes Martin, "On the Perfection Underlying Life," in Schwartz, *Agnes Martin: Writings/Schriften*, 71. On the idea of "Free and Easy Wandering," which became important to Martin's thinking, see *Chuang Tzu: Basic Writings*, trans. Burton Watson (New York: Columbia University Press, 1964, 1996), 23–30.

8. Holland Cotter, "Agnes Martin at Pace," *Art in America* 77, no. 4 (April 1989): 257.

9. Arden Reed, *Slow Art: The Experience of Looking, Sacred Images to James Turrell* (Berkeley: University of California Press, 2017), 9. Also important to this discussion are Loetz Koepnick, *On Slowness: Towards an Aesthetic of the Contemporary* (New York: Columbia University Press, 2014), and Jonathan Crary, *Suspensions of Perception: Attention, Spectacle and Modern Culture* (Cambridge, MA: MIT Press, 2001), both of which place the question of what it means to see or behold within the larger social, political, and economic context of late capitalism.

10. James Elkins, *Pictures and Tears: A History of People Who Have Cried in Front of Paintings* (London: Taylor and Francis, 2001); T. J. Clark, *The Sight of Death: An Experiment in Art Writing* (New Haven: Yale University Press, 2008); Daniel Arasse, *Take a Closer Look*, trans. Alyson Waters (Princeton: Princeton University Press, 2013); Hanneke Grootenboer, *The Pensive Image: Art as a Form of Thinking* (Chicago: University of Chicago Press, 2020).

11. Nancy Princenthal, *Agnes Martin: Her Life and Art* (New York: Thames and Hudson, 2015); Eric Orr, James Leey Byer, *Zero Mass: The Art of Eric Orr* (Lund, Sweden: Propexus, 1990); Thomas McEvilley, "Negative Presences in Secret Spaces: The Art of Eric Orr," *Artforum* 20, no. 10 (1982): 58–66; Tracy Bashkoff, ed., *Hilma af Klint: Paintings for the Future* (New York: Guggenheim Museum, 2018); Jeffrey L. Kosky, *Arts of Wonder: Enchanting Secularity—Walter De Maria, Diller + Scofidio, James Turrell, Andy Goldsworthy* (Chicago: University of Chicago Press, 2013).

12. Princenthal, *Agnes Martin*, 101–110. Princenthal documents the wide and eclectic array of philosophical and spiritual influences that shaped Martin's thinking, including the Bible, Butler's *Lives of the Saints*, the life and teachings of Teresa of Avila,

and, crucially, the teachings of Lao Tzu and certain Buddhist teachers. Thomas McEvilley, "Grey Geese Descending: The Art of Agnes Martin," *Artforum* 25, no. 10 (Summer, 1987): 94–99, offers a perceptive analysis of the relationship between Taoism and Martin's conception of the grid.

13. Martin, quoted in Ann Wilson, "Linear Webs," *Art & Artists* 1 (October 1966): 48–49.

14. Agnes Martin, "Notes," in Schwarz, *Agnes Martin: Writings/Schriften*, 15.

15. On the relationship between Thomas Merton and Ad Reinhardt and the influence of apophatic thought on Reinhardt's work, see Arden Reed, "Ad Reinhardt's 'Black' Paintings," *Religion and the Arts* 19, no. 3 (2015): 214–229; see also Roger Lipsey, *Angelic Mistakes: The Art of Thomas Merton* (Boston: Shambala/New Seeds, 2006). Merton's writings on Zen Buddhism and Chaung Tzu were just beginning to emerge in the mid-to late 1960s (he died in 1968). See Thomas Merton, *The Way of Chuang Tzu* (New York: New Directions, 1965); Thomas Merton, *Zen and the Birds of Appetite* (New York: New Directions, 1968).

The rich and eclectic influences (Zen Buddhism, the *I Ching*, Christian mysticism, etc.) that shaped Cage's musical compositions of silence are well documented in Kyle Gann, *No Such Thing as Silence: John Cage's 4'33"* (New Haven: Yale University Press, 2010), 134–152. The sense of detachment or self-abnegation in Cage's approach to his composition 4'33" is evident from his comments in a 1973 interview: "I think perhaps my own best piece, at least the one I like the most, is the silent piece. It has three movements, and in all of the movements there are no sounds. I wanted my work to be free of my own likes and dislikes, because I think music should be free of the feelings and ideas of the composer" (16).

16. Martin cited in Wilson, "Linear Webs," 48.

17. Martin, cited in Gruen, "Agnes Martin."

18. William Seitz, *The Responsive Eye* (New York: Museum of Modern Art, 1963), 16; cited in Princenthal, *Agnes Martin*, 133–134.

19. Hilton Kramer, "An Art That's Almost a Prayer," *New York Times*, May 16, 1976, 23.

20. Rosalind Krauss, *The Originality of the Avant-Garde and Other Modernist Myths* (Cambridge, MA: MIT Press, 1985), 158–160. See also Rosalind Krauss, "Grids," *October* 9 (Summer 1979): 50–64.

21. Agnes Martin, "The Still and Silent in Art," in Schwarz, *Agnes Martin: Writings/Schriften*, 89.

22. David Albertson, "Cataphasis, Visualization, and Mystical Space," in *The Oxford Handbook of Mystical Theology*, ed. Edward Howells and Mark A. McIntosh (New York: Oxford, 2020), 347–368.

23. Charles Darwent, "Slight of Hand: Agnes Martin's Hermetic Paintings," *Modern Painters* (July/August 2005), 91–93.

24. Bachelard, *Poetics of Space*, 184.

25. Kasha Linville, "Agnes Martin: An Appreciation," *Artforum* 9, no. 10 (Summer, 1971): 72.

26. Bachelard, *Poetics of Space*, 184.

27. Simon Ortiz, "Culture and the Universe," in *Out There Somewhere* (Tucson: University of Arizona Press, 2002), 104–105.

28. Pseudo-Dionysius, *The Complete Works*, trans. Colm Luibheid (New York: Paulist Press, 1987), 136, 137, 139. I am grateful to my colleague David Albertson for drawing my attention to the significance of this language in the work of Pseudo-Dionysius.

29. Pseudo-Dionysius, *The Complete Works*, 137.

30. Pseudo-Dionysius, *The Complete Works*, 139.

31. John M. Connolly, *Living without a Why: Meister Eckhart's Critique of the Medieval Concept of Will* (New York: Oxford University Press, 2014).

32. Meister Eckhart, *The Complete Mystical Works of Meister Eckhart*, trans. and ed. Maurice O'C. Walshe (New York: Crossroad, 2009), 55.

33. Charlotte Radler, "Living from the Divine Ground: Meister Eckhart's Praxis of Detachment," *Spiritus* 6 (2006): 24–46, offers a fine analysis of how the dynamic process she calls "the praxis of detachment" (*abegescheidenheit*) functions in Eckhart's thought. Here one sees how the praxis of detachment allows the self to become undone and remade (again and again) in God, part an invitation to enter the "wayless way"—a simple, uncluttered, and radically free consciousness that Eckhart argued was available and open to all.

34. Eckhart, *The Complete Mystical Works*, 66–67.

35. Eckhart, *The Complete Mystical Works*, 117.

36. Eckhart, *The Complete Mystical Works*, 68.

37. Eckhart, *The Complete Mystical Works*, 69.

38. Marguerite Porete, *The Mirror of Simple Souls*, trans. Ellen Babinsky (New York and Mahwah, NJ: Paulist Press, 1993), 82. David Kangas, "Dangerous Joy: Marguerite Porete's Goodbye to the Virtues," *Journal of Religion* 91, no. 3 (July 2011): 299–319.

39. Porete, *The Mirror of Simple Souls*, 89, 108.

40. Porete, *The Mirror of Simple Souls*, 101.

41. Porete, *The Mirror of Simple Souls*, 102.

42. Porete, *The Mirror of Simple Souls*, 85.

43. Eckhart, *The Complete Mystical Works*, 56.

44. *Dekalog: One*. Directed by Krzysztof Kieślowski (Warsaw: Tor Studios, 1989).

45. Eckhart, *The Complete Mystical Works*, 59.

46. Simone Weil, *Waiting for God*, trans. Emma Craufurd (New York: Putnam's, 1952), 62.

47. Eckhart, *The Complete Mystical Works*, 60. Meister Eckhart has long been considered primarily a speculative mystic. But, as Charlotte Radler demonstrates, the role of love is central to his mystical vision. See "In Love I Am More God: The Centrality of Love in Meister Eckhart's Mysticism," *The Journal of Religion* 90, no. 2 (April 2010): 171–198.

48. Porete, *The Mirror of Simple Souls*, 168. Porete appears to draw here on the medieval life of Mary Magdalene: *The Life of Saint Mary Magdalene and of Her Sister Saint Martha: A Medieval Biography*, trans. David Mycoff (Athens, OH: Cistercian, 1989).

49. "Phenomenal: California Light, Space, Surface," Museum of Contemporary Art San Diego, September 25, 2011, through January 22, 2012. See Robin Clark, ed., *Phenomenal: California Light, Space, Surface* (Berkeley: University of California Press, 2011).

50. Wall text for Zero Mass, by Eric Orr. Light & Space, 12 March 2021–9 April 2022, Copenhagen Contemporary, Copenhagen.

51. Emily Dickinson, "We grow accustomed to the Dark—" (419), in *The Complete Poems of Emily Dickinson*, ed. Thomas H. Johnson (Boston: Little Brown, 1960), 201.

52. Dawna L. Schuld, "Practically Nothing: Light, Space and the Pragmatics of Phenomenology," in Clark, *Phenomenal*, 105–122; and *Minimal Conditions: Light Space and Subjectivity* (Berkeley: University of California Press, 2018), esp. 65–74. Both Schuld and Thomas McEvilley (in "Negative Presences in Secret Spaces") trace the deep philosophical-mystical sources that have informed Orr's work, resulting in what McEvilley calls an "esthetics of infinity."

53. Denise Levertov, "Eye Mask," in *Evening Train* (New York: New Directions, 1993), 41.

54. Matsuo Basho, *The Essential Basho*, trans. Sam Hamill (Boston: Shambala, 1999), xv.

55. Robert Hass, ed. *The Essential Haiku: Versions of Basho, Buson and Issa* (New York: Ecco, 1994), 189.

56. Carolyn Forché, "Prayer," in *Blue Hour* (New York: HarperCollins, 2003), 21.

57. David Ferry, "That Are Wild and Do Not Remember," in *Bewilderment: New Poems and Translations* (Chicago: University of Chicago Press, 2012), 101.

58. Gabriel García Marquéz, *Love in the Time of Cholera*, trans. Edith Grossman (New York: Vintage, 2003), 345.

59. Porete, *The Mirror of Simple Souls*, 162.

Chapter 7

1. Hadewijch, *The Complete Works*, trans. Mother Columba Hart (New York and Mahwah, NJ: Paulist Press, 1980), 57.

2. Casa de la Mateada was founded in fall 2013 under the auspices of a partnership between Loyola Marymount University in Los Angeles and La Universidad Católica de Córdoba in Córdoba, Argentina. It closed in 2018. During that time, over one hundred US students from thirteen universities participated in the program, living as a community in Córdoba, studying, working alongside their Argentine partners and friends, and reflecting on the meaning of solidarity and accompaniment. In addition, well over fifty Argentine faculty, staff, praxis partners, cooks, drivers, and friends of the program participated in and supported the work. Stories and a partial history of the program can be found at https://casadelamateada.wordpress.com/.

    The idea of "education for solidarity" is articulated by Rev. Peter-Hans Kolvenbach, S.J., in "The Service of Faith and the Promotion of Justice in American Jesuit Higher Education." Address given at Santa Clara University, October 6, 2000, https://www.scu.edu/ic/programs/ignatian-worldview/kolvenbach/.

3. Thomas Merton, *The Hidden Ground of Love: Letters*, ed. William H. Shannon (New York: Farrar, Straus and Giroux, 1985), 115.

4. In the history of Christian spirituality, the idea of the common life is often associated with the "Devotio Moderna" movement, the work of Geert Groote and the "Sisters and Brothers of the Common Life." See John Van Engen, *Sisters and Brothers of the Common Life: The Devotio Moderna and the World of the Later Middle Ages*

(Philadelphia: University of Pennsylvania Press, 2014). But the roots of the idea are older and can be found in the writings of Ruusbroec, Hadewijch, Porete, and others, where it connotes both something fundamental to the very life of God (the life of the Trinity is conceived of as an expression of the common life) and to the human experience of God as manifested in the shared life of community. The common life, the sharing of life with others, is understood to be the highest expression of the mystical life. See Rik Van Nieuwenhove, "Ruusbroec, Jordaens, and Herp on the Common Life: The Transformation of a Spiritual Ideal," in *A Companion to John of Ruusbroec*, ed. John Arblaster and Rob Faesen (Leiden: Brill, 2014), 204–236; James A. Wiseman, *Ruusbroec's Mystical Vision in "Die gheestelike brulocht" Seen in the Light of "Minne"* (Leuven: Peeters, 2018); Jessica A. Boon, "Trinitarian Love Mysticism: Ruusbroec, Hadewijch and the Gendered Experience of the Divine," *Church History* 72, no. 3 (September 2003): 484–503.

5. John R. Sachs, S.J., "Apocatastasis in Patristic Theology," *Theological Studies* 54 (1993): 617–640.

6. Carolyn Forché, *Blue Hour* (New York: HarperCollins, 2003), 7.

7. In the early morning of November 16, 1989, six Jesuit priests, their cook, and her daughter were murdered by the military at the victims' residence inside the José Simeón Cañas Central American University in San Salvador. The soldiers, members of the Atlacatl Battalion, entered the campus and the priests' residence. They ordered the priests—Fathers Ignacio Ellacuría, Ignacio Martín-Baró, Segundo Montes Mozo, Armando López Quintana, Juan Ramón Moreno Pardo, and Joaquín López y López—out of their dormitories and shot and killedthem. They also shot and killed Julia Elba Ramos and Celina, her fifteen-year-old daughter.

The events of this day and the time surrounding it have been the subject of extensive and ongoing research and scholarship. See Teresa Whitfield, *Paying the Price: Ignacio Ellacuría and the Murdered Jesuits of El Salvador* (Philadelphia: Temple University Press, 1994); Lucía Cerna and Mary Jo Ignofo, *La Verdad: A Witness to the Salvadoran Martyrs* (Maryknoll, NY: Orbis, 2014); Robert Lasalle-Klein, *Blood and Ink: Ignacio Ellacuría, Jon Sobrino, and the Jesuit Martyrs of the University of Central America* (Maryknoll, NY: Orbis, 2014); Joaquín M. Chávez, *Poets and Prophets of the Resistance: Intellectuals and the Origins of El Salvador's Civil War* (New York: Oxford University Press, 2017). See also Carolyn Forché's extraordinary and deeply personal account of the Salvadoran Civil War: *What You Have Heard Is True: A Memoir of Witness and Resistance* (New York: Penguin, 2019).

8. Hadewijch, *The Complete Works*, 344.

9. Benedicta Ward, trans., *The Sayings of the Desert Fathers: The Alphabetical Collection* (Collegeville, MN: Liturgical Press, 1984), 3.

10. Joseph F. Conwell, S.J., *Walking in the Spirit: A Reflection on Jeronimo Nadal's Phrase "Contemplative Likewise in Action"* (St. Louis: Institute of Jesuit Sources, 2004); Wilkie Au, "Contemplatives Even in Action: A Mysticism of Service," *Ignatian Service: Gratitude and Love in Action. Studies in the Spirituality of Jesuits* 40, no. 2 (Summer 2008): 17–21.

11. Walter Burghardt, S.J., "A Long, Loving Look at the Real," *Church* (Winter 1989): 14–18.

12. Joan Nuth, "*Acatamiento*: Living in an Attitude of Affectionate Awe—An Ignatian Reflection on the Unitive Way," *Spiritus* 10, no. 2 (2010): 173–191.

13. See: Charlotte Radler, "*Actio et Contemplatio*/Action and Contemplation," in *The Cambridge Companion to Christian Mysticism,* ed. Amy Hollywood and Patricia Beckman (Cambridge: Cambridge University Press, 2012), 211–222; Amy Hollywood, "Love of Neighbor and Love of God: Martha and Mary in the Middle Ages," in *Acute Melancholia and Other Essays: Mysticism, History and the Study of Religion* (New York: Columbia University Press, 2016), 253–259. This question continues to reverberate within contemporary thought and culture: Jennifer Summit and Blakey Vermeule, *Action and Contemplation: Why an Ancient Debate Still Matters* (Chicago: University of Chicago Press, 2018).

14. Evagrius of Pontus, *The Greek Ascetic Corpus,* trans. Robert E. Sinkewicz (Oxford and New York: Oxford University Press, 2003), 206.

15. Evagrius, *The Greek Ascetic Corpus,* 180.

16. The work of historian Peter Brown, in particular "The Rise and Function of the Holy Man in Late Antiquity," *The Journal of Roman Studies,* 61 (1971): 80–101, has had a significant impact on the work of reframing our understanding of the social reality of early Christian monasticism, especially in response to the immense pressures of living under the Roman Empire in Late Antiquity. Subsequent scholarship has revised and recast Brown's work in important ways (see the special issue of *Journal of Early Christian Studies* 6, no. 3 [1998] devoted to re-examining Brown's work). But the question of how to situate the world of early Christian monasticism within its social, cultural, religious, and political world has remained central to scholarship on this period: David Frankfurter, *Religion in Roman Egypt: Assimilation and Resistance* (Princeton: Princeton University Press, 1998); James Goehring, *Ascetics, Society and the Desert: Studies in Early Christian Monasticism* (London: Bloomsbury T & T Clark, 1999); Philip Rousseau, *Ascetics, Authority and the Church in the Age of Jerome and Cassian,* 2nd ed. (Notre Dame: University of Notre Dame Press, 2010).

17. Norman Russell, trans., *The Lives of the Desert Fathers* (Kalamazoo: Cistercian, 1981), 50.

18. Evagrius, *The Greek Ascetic Corpus,* 196.

19. Evagrius, *The Greek Ascetic Corpus,* 199. On the question of imageless prayer in Evagrius, see Columba Stewart, "Imageless Prayer and the Theological Vision of Evagrius Ponticus," *Journal of Early Christian Studies* 9, no. 2 (2001): 173–204; Demetrios S. Katos, "Humility as the Harbinger of Imageless Prayer in the Lausiac History," *St. Vladimir's Theological Quarterly* 51, no. 1 (2007): 107–121.

20. John Cassian, *Conferences,* trans. Colm Luibheid (New York: Paulist Press, 1985), 116, 138.

21. Evagrius, *The Greek Ascetic Corpus,* 197. Evagrius's sense of the complexity, ambiguity, and depth of memory and thoughts (*logismoi*) in the life of the monk suggests why discernment became so critical to the life of prayer. See Kevin Corrigan, "Thoughts

That Cut: Cutting, Lingering and Imprinting in Evagrius of Pontus," in *Evagrius and His Legacy*, ed. Joel Kalvesmaki and Robin Darling Young (South Bend, IN: University of Notre Dame Press, 2016), 49–72.

22. Evagrius, *The Greek Ascetic Corpus*, 195.

23. Evagrius, *The Greek Ascetic Corpus*, 194.

24. Evagrius, *The Greek Ascetic Corpus*, 195.

25. Evagrius, *The Greek Ascetic Corpus*, 107. See also Jeremy Driscoll, "Apatheia and Purity of Heart in Evagrius Ponticus," in *Purity of Heart in Early Monastic Literature*, ed. Harriet Luckman and Linda Kulzer (Collegeville, MN: Liturgical Press, 1999), 141–159.

26. Cassian, *Conferences*, 101.

27. Evagrius, *The Greek Ascetic Corpus*, 110.

28. Evagrius, *The Greek Ascetic Corpus*, 113.

29. Evagrius, *The Greek Ascetic Corpus*, 206.

30. Leslie Jamieson, *The Empathy Exams* (Minneapolis: Graywolf, 2014), 5.

31. T. S. Eliot, "Journey of the Magi," in *Collected Poems, 1909–1962* (London: Faber and Faber, 1974), 99.

32. On accompaniment, see Michael Jackson, especially his essay "Where Thought Belongs: An Anthropological Critique of the Project of Philosophy," in *Lifeworlds: Essays in Existential Anthropology* (Chicago University of Chicago Press, 2013), 253–269. Of particular importance in Jackson's work is his careful attention to the ethical-spiritual meaning of accompaniment, born of his work as an ethnographer and his awareness of the danger of assuming too intimate an understanding of one's subjects. He distinguishes between "identification" with the other (which, citing Paul Ricoeur, he deems to be "neither possible nor desirable") and "accompaniment," a more humble, open, and less intrusive way of being and walking with another that ensures (again citing Ricoeur) that "no one will have to live and die alone" (268).

Theresa Sanders, "Remarking the Silence: Prayer after the Death of God," *Horizons* 25, no. 2 (1998): 203–216, offers a beautiful account of the place of wordless prayer in the practice of solidarity. On the profound deconstructive work of contemplative practice, see Martin Laird, "The 'Open Country Whose Name Is Prayer': Apophasis, Deconstruction, and Contemplative Practice," *Modern Theology* 21, no. 1 (2005): 141–155.

33. Rev. Peter-Hans Kolvenbach, S.J., "The Service of Faith and the Promotion of Justice in American Jesuit Higher Education," https://www.scu.edu/ic/programs/ignatian-worldview/kolvenbach/.

34. Rainer Maria Rilke, *Duino Elegies*, Eighth Elegy. Cited in Pierre Hadot, "The Sage and the World," in *Philosophy as a Way of Life* (Oxford: Blackwell, 1995), 258. A. Poulin renders Rilke's words slightly differently: "He sees / all, himself in all, and whole forever." Rainer Maria Rilke, *Duino Elegies and the Sonnets of Orpheus*, trans. A. Poulin (New York: Mariner, 2005), 57.

35. Tracy K. Smith, "Everything That Ever Was," in *Life on Mars* (Minneapolis: Graywolf, 2011), 59.

36. Hadewijch, *The Complete Works*, 289.

37. Clarice Lispector, *Água Viva* (New York: New Directions, 2012), 8.

38. See J. Matthew Ashley's excellent essay, "Contemplation in the Action of Justice: Ignacio Ellacuría and Ignatian Spirituality," in *Love That Produces Hope: The Thought of Ignacio Ellacuría*, ed. Kevin F. Burke, S.J., and Robert Lasalle-Klein (Collegeville, MN: Liturgical Press, 2006), 144–165, esp. 149.

39. Ignacio Ellacuría, *Essays on History, Liberation, and Salvation*, ed. Michael E. Lee with commentary by Kevin F. Burke, S.J. (Maryknoll, NY: Orbis, 2013), 163.

40. Ellacuría, *Essays on History, Liberation, and Salvation*, 162.

41. Johan Baptist Metz, *The End of Time? The Provocation of Talking about God*, trans. J. Matthew Ashley (Mahwah, NJ: Paulist Press, 2004), 40. Matthew T. Eggemeier, drawing upon the work of Jon Sobrino, Simone Weil, and Sarah Coakley, deepens and extends Metz's work, especially through his careful attention to the significance of apophatic forms of spiritual practice for political mysticism, something he argues that Metz largely ignores. See "A Mysticism of Open Eyes: Compassion for a Suffering World and the Askesis of Contemplative Prayer," *Spiritus: A Journal of Christian Spirituality* 12, no. 1 (Spring 2012): 43–62.

42. Pope Francis, *Laudato Si': On Care for Our Common Home* (Mahwah, NJ: Paulist Press, 2015), §19.

43. Evagrius, *The Greek Ascetic Corpus*, 209.

44. Simone Weil, *Waiting for God*, trans. Emma Craufurd (New York: Putnams, 1952), 57.

45. Weil, *Waiting for God*, 64.

46. Simone Weil, *First and Last Notebooks*, trans. Richard Rees (Oxford: Oxford University Press, 1970), 71.

47. Weil, *First and Last Notebooks*, 97. Robert Zaretzky, *The Subversive Simone Weil: A Life in Five Ideas* (Chicago: University of Chicago Press, 2021), 52.

48. John Ruusbroec, *The Complete Ruusbroec*, English translation with the original Middle Dutch text, edited and with an introduction by Guido de Baere and Thom Mertens, vol. 1 (Turnhout: Brepols, 2014), 235.

49. Ruusbroec, *The Complete Ruusbroec*, vol. 1, 239.

50. Ruusbroec, *The Complete Ruusbroec*, vol. 1, 136.

51. Ruusbroec, *The Complete Ruusbroec*, vol. 1, 220.

52. Ruusbroec, *The Complete Ruusbroec*, vol. 1, 250.

53. Ruusbroec, *The Complete Ruusbroec*, vol. 1, 533–534.

54. Marguerite Porete, *The Mirror of Simple Souls*, trans. Ellen Babinsky (New York and Mahwah, NJ: Paulist Press, 1993), 107.

55. Ruusbroec, *The Complete Ruusbroec*, vol. 1, 217.

56. Hadewijch, *The Complete Works*, 332.

57. Ruusbroec, *The Complete Ruusbroec*, vol. 1, 258: "From this wealth derives the common life."

58. Hadewijch, *The Complete Works*, 57.

Bibliography

Acocella, Joann. "Rich Man, Poor Man: The Radical Visions of St. Francis." *The New Yorker*, January 14, 2013, 72–77.

Adorno, Theodor W. *Negative Dialectics*. Translated by E. B. Ashton. New York: Continuum, 1973.

Adorno, Theodor W. *Prisms*. Translated by Shierry Weber Nicholsen. Cambridge, MA: MIT Press, 1983.

Alaimo, Stacy. *Bodily Natures: Science, Environment and the Material Self*. Bloomington: Indiana University Press, 2010.

Alberti, Fay Bound. *A Biography of Loneliness: The History of an Emotion*. New York: Oxford, 2019.

Albertson, David. "Cataphasis, Visualization, and Mystical Space." In *The Oxford Handbook of Mystical Theology*. Edited by Edward Howells and Mark A. McIntosh. New York: Oxford, 2020, 347–368.

Aleixandre, Vicente. *A Longing for the Light: Selected Poems of Vicente Aleixandre*. Edited by Lewis Hyde. Port Townsend, WA: Copper Canyon Press, 2007.

Allen, Paula. *Flowers in the Desert: The Search for Chile's Disappeared*. 2nd ed. Gainesville: University Press of Florida, 2013.

Ammerman, Nancy T., ed. *Everyday Religion: Observing Modern Religious Lives*. New York: Oxford University Press, 2007.

Anderson, Elizabeth. "The Experience of Abandonment by God in Syriac Christian Ascetical Theology." *Spiritus* 20, no. 1 (Spring 2020): 79–104.

Arad, Yizhak. *The Operation Einhard Death Camps: Belzec, Sobibor, Treblinka*. Rev. and exp. ed. Bloomington: Indiana University Press, 2018.

Arasse, Daniel. *Take a Closer Look*. Translated by Alyson Waters. Princeton: Princeton University Press, 2013.

Arblaster, John, and Rob Faesen, eds. *A Companion to John of Ruusbroec*. Leiden: Brill, 2014.

Arsić, Branka. *Bird Relics: Grief and Vitalism in Thoreau*. Cambridge, MA: Harvard University Press, 2016.

Ashley, J. Matthew. "Contemplation in the Action of Justice: Ignacio Ellacuría and Ignatian Spirituality." In *Love That Produces Hope: The Thought of Ignacio Ellacuría*. Edited by Kevin F. Burke, S.J., and Robert Lasalle-Klein. Collegeville, MN: Liturgical Press, 2006, 144–165.

Athanasius. *The Life of Antony and the Letter to Marcellinus*. Translated by Robert C. Gregg. New York: Paulist Press, 1980.

Au, Wilkie. "Contemplatives Even in Action: A Mysticism of Service." *Ignatian Service: Gratitude and Love in Action*. Studies in the Spirituality of Jesuits 40, no. 2 (Summer 2008): 17–21.

Bachelard, Gaston. *Poetics of Space*. Translated by Maria Jolas. Boston: Beacon, 1994.

Bashkoff, Tracy, ed. *Hilma af Klint: Paintings for the Future*. New York: Guggenheim Museum, 2018.

Basho, Matsuo. *The Essential Basho*. Translated by Sam Hamill. Boston: Shambala, 1999.

Batchelor, Stephen. *The Art of Solitude*. New Haven: Yale University Press, 2020.

Bender, Courtney. *The New Metaphysicals: Spirituality and the American Religious Imagination*. Chicago: University of Chicago Press, 2010.

Benedictow, Ole J. *The Black Death, 1346–1353: The Complete History*. Woodbridge, UK: Boydel, 2004.

Bennett, Jane. *Vibrant Matter: A Political Ecology of Things*. Durham, NC: Duke University Press, 2010.

Berry, Wendell. "How to Be a Poet (to remind myself)." *Poetry*, January 2001, 270.

Besecke, Kelly. *You Can't Put God in a Box: Thoughtful Spirituality in a Rational Age*. New York: Oxford, 2014.

Bingemer, Maria Clara. "Seeking the Pathos of God in a Secular Age: Reflections on Mystical Experience in the Twentieth Century." *Modern Theology* 29, no. 3 (July 2013): 248–278.

Biss, Eula. *Notes from No Man's Land: American Essays*. Minneapolis: Greywolf, 2009.

Bitton-Ashkelony, Bruria. *Encountering the Sacred: The Debate on Christian Pilgrimage in Late Antiquity*. Berkeley: University of California Press, 2005.

Boman, Elizabeth S., ed. *Monastic Visions: Wall Paintings in the Monastery of St. Antony at the Red Sea*. New Haven: Yale University Press, 2002.

Boon, Jessica A. "Trinitarian Love Mysticism: Ruusbroec, Hadewijch and the Gendered Experience of the Divine." *Church History* 72, no. 3 (Sept. 2003): 484–503.

Bowles, Paul. *Their Heads Are Green and Their Eyes Are Blue*. New York: Harper Perennial, 2006.

Brakke, David. *Athanasius and the Politics of Asceticism*. Oxford: Clarendon, 1995.

Brennan, James P. *Missing Bones: Revisiting the History of the Dirty* War. Berkeley: University of California Press, 2018.

Brown, Peter. *The Making of Late Antiquity*. Cambridge, MA: Harvard University Press, 1978.

Brown, Peter. "The Rise and Function of the Holy Man in Late Antiquity." *The Journal of Roman Studies* 61 (1971): 80–101.

Burghardt, Walter. "A Long, Loving Look at the Real." *Church* (Winter 1989): 14–18.

Burton-Christie, Douglas, "Evagrius on Sadness." *Cistercian Studies Quarterly* 44, no. 4 (2009): 395–409.

Butler, Judith. "On Grief and Rage." *Pen America* 18 (May 8, 2015): 16–20.

Cameron, Sharon. *The Bond of the Furthest Apart: Essays on Tolstoy, Dostoevsky, Bresson and Kafka*. Chicago: University of Chicago Press, 2017.

Camus, Albert. *The Plague*. Translated by Stuart Gilbert. New York: Vintage, 1991.

Carlson, Thomas. *With the World at Heart: Studies in the Secular Today*. Chicago: University of Chicago Press, 2019.

Carson, Anne. *Decreation: Poetry, Essays, Opera*. New York: Vintage, 2006.

Carver, Raymond. *Where I Am Calling From: Selected Stories*. New York: Atlantic Monthly Press, 1998.

Cassian, John. *Conferences*. Translated by Colm Luibheid. New York: Paulist Press, 1985.

Celan, Paul. *Selected Prose and Poems of Paul Celan*. Translated by John Felstiner. New York: W. W. Norton, 2001.

Cerna, Lucía, and Mary Jo Ignofo. *La Verdad: A Witness to the Salvadoran Martyrs*. Maryknoll, NY: Orbis, 2014.

Cernuda, Luis. *Written on Water*. Translated by Stephen Kessler. San Francisco: City Lights Books, 1994.

Certeau, Michel de. *The Michel de Certeau Reader*. Edited by Graham Ward. Oxford: Wiley-Blackwell, 2000.

Certeau, Michel de. *The Mystic Fable*. Vol. 1: *The Sixteenth and Seventeenth Centuries*. Translated by Michael B. Smith. Chicago: University of Chicago Press, 1992.

Certeau, Michel de. *The Mystic Fable*. Vol. 2: *The Sixteenth and Seventeenth Centuries*. Translated by Luce Giard and Michael B. Smith. Chicago: University of Chicago Press, 2015.

Certeau, Michel de. *The Practice of Everyday Life*. 3rd ed. Translated by Steven Rendell. Berkeley: University of California Press, 2011.

Chase, Steven. *Nature as Spiritual Practice*. Grand Rapids: Eerdmans, 2011.

Chávez, Joaquín M. *Poets and Prophets of the Resistance: Intellectuals and the Origins of El Salvador's Civil War*. New York: Oxford University Press, 2017.

Christie, Douglas E. *The Blue Sapphire of the Mind: Notes for a Contemplative Ecology*. New York: Oxford University Press, 2013.

Christie, Douglas E. "The Eternal Present: Slow Knowledge and the Renewal of Time." *Buddhist Christian Studies* 33 (2013): 13–21.

Chuang Tzu. *Basic Writings*. Translated by Burton Watson. New York: Columbia University Press, 1964, 1996.

Clark, Robin, ed. *Phenomenal: California Light, Space, Surface*. Berkeley: University of California Press, 2011.

Clark, T. J. *The Sight of Death: An Experiment in Art Writing*. New Haven: Yale University Press, 2008.

Climacus, John. *The Ladder of Divine Ascent*. Translated by Colm Luibheid and Norman Russell. New York: Paulist Press, 1982.

The Cloud of Unknowing. Translated by James Walsh. New York: Paulist Press, 1981.

Coakley, Sarah. *Powers and Submissions: Spirituality, Philosophy and Gender*. Oxford: Blackwell, 2002.

Cobb, Edith. *The Ecology of Imagination in Childhood*. New York: Columbia University Press, 1977.

Cole, Henri. *Middle Earth*. New York: Farrar, Straus and Giroux, 2003.

Cole, Henri. *Nothing to Declare*. New York: Farrar, Straus & Giroux, 2015.

Cole, Teju. "In Dark Times, I Sought Out the Turmoil of Caravaggio's Paintings." *New York Times Magazine,* September 23, 2020.

Colegate, Isabel. *A Pelican in the Wilderness: Hermits, Solitaries and Recluses*. New York: Counterpoint, 2002.

Connolly, John M. *Living without a Why: Meister Eckhart's Critique of the Medieval Concept of Will*. New York: Oxford University Press, 2014.

Conway-Jones, Ann. "Exegetical Puzzles and the Mystical Theologies of Gregory of Nyssa and Dionysius the Areopagite." *Vigiliae Christianae* 75, no. 1 (2020): 1–21.

Conwell, Joseph F., S.J. *Walking in the Spirit: A Reflection on Jeronimo Nadal's Phrase "Contemplative Likewise in Action"*. St. Louis: Institute of Jesuit Sources, 2004.

Cooke, Lynne, Karen Kelly, and Barbara Schröder, eds. *Agnes Martin*. New Haven: Yale University Press, 2011.

Corrigan, John. *Emptiness: Feeling Christian in America*. Chicago: University of Chicago Press, 2015.

Corrigan, Kevin. "Thoughts That Cut: Cutting, Lingering and Imprinting in Evagrius of Pontus." In *Evagrius and His Legacy*. Edited by Joel Kalvesmaki and Robin Darling Young. Notre Dame: University of Notre Dame Press, 2016, 49–72.

Cotter, Holland. "Agnes Martin at Pace." *Art in America* 77, no. 4 (April 1989): 257.

Crary, Jonathan. *24/7: Late Capitalism and the Ends of Sleep*. London: Verso, 2014.

Crary, Jonathan. *Suspensions of Perception: Attention, Spectacle and Modern Culture*. Cambridge, MA: MIT Press, 2001.

Dailey, Patricia. "Children of Promise: The Bodies of Hadewijch of Brabant." *Journal of Medieval and Early Modern Studies* 41, no. 2 (Spring 2011): 317–343.

Darke, Chris. "Desert of the Disappeared: Patricio Guzmán on Nostalgia for the Light." *Sight & Sound* 22, no. 8 (August 2012): 34–37.

Darwent, Charles. "Slight of Hand: Agnes Martin's Hermetic Paintings." *Modern Painters*, July/August 2005, 91–93.

Daumal, Renée. *Mount Analogue*. Translated by Carol Cosman. Woodstock, NY: Overlook Press, 2004.

Davidson, Peter. *The Last of the Light: About Twilight*. London: Reaktion, 2015.

Davis, Robert Glenn. *The Weight of Love: Affect, Ecstasy and Union in the Theology of Bonaventure*. New York: Fordham University Press, 2017.

Deming, Alison Hawthorn, and Lauret Savoy, eds. *The Colors of Nature: Culture, Identity and the Natural World*. 2nd ed. Minneapolis: Milkweed, 2011.

Diamond, Cora. "The Difficulty of Reality and the Difficulty of Philosophy." *Partial Answers: Journal of Literature and the History of Ideas* 1, no. 2 (June 2003): 1–26.

Dickinson, Emily. *The Complete Poems*. Edited by Thomas H. Johnson. Boston: Little Brown, 1960.

Didi-Huberman, Georges. *Bark*. Translated by Samuel E. Martin. Cambridge, MA: MIT Press, 2017.

Digges, Deborah. *The Wind Blows through the Doors of My Heart*. New York: Knopf, 2010.

Diolé, Philippe. *The Most Beautiful Desert of All*. Translated by Katherine Woods. London: Jonathan Cape, 1959.

Drescher, Elizabeth. *Choosing Our Religion: The Spiritual Lives of America's Nones*. New York: Oxford University Press, 2016.

Driscoll, Jeremy. "Apatheia and Purity of Heart in Evagrius Ponticus." In *Purity of Heart in Early Monastic Literature*. Edited by Harriet Luckman and Linda Kulzer. Collegeville, MN: Liturgical Press, 1999, 141–159.

Duclow, Donald F. "The Hungers of Hadewijch and Eckhart." *The Journal of Religion* 80, no. 3 (July 2000): 421–441.

Dumm, Thomas. *Loneliness as a Way of Life*. Cambridge, MA: Harvard University Press, 2008.

Dyer, Geoff. *The Ongoing Moment*. New York: Vintage, 2007.

Edwards, Nina. *Darkness: A Cultural History*. London: Reaktion, 2018.

Eggemeier, Matthew. "A Mysticism of Open Eyes: Compassion for a Suffering World and the *Askesis* of Contemplative Prayer." *Spiritus* 12, no. 1 (2012): 43–62.

Elkins, James. *Pictures and Tears: A History of People Who Have Cried in Front of Paintings*. London: Taylor and Francis, 2001.

Ellacuría, Ignacio. *Essays on History, Liberation, and Salvation*. Edited by Michael E. Lee with commentary by Kevin F. Burke, S.J. Maryknoll, NY: Orbis, 2013.

Ellis, Fiona. *God, Value and Nature*. Oxford: Oxford University Press, 2014.

Enns, Diane. *Love in the Dark: Philosophy by Another Name*. New York: Columbia University Press, 2016.

Enríquez, Mariana. *Things We Lost in the Fire*. Translated by Megan McDowell. New York: Hogarth, 2017.

Espada, Martín, ed. *Poetry Like Bread*. Willimantic, CT: Curbstone Press, 2000.

Evagrius of Pontus. *The Greek Ascetic Corpus*. Translated by Robert E. Sinkewicz. Oxford and New York: Oxford University Press, 2003.

Fagenblat, Michael. *Negative Theology as Jewish Modernity*. Bloomington: Indiana University Press, 2017.

Faggen, Robert, ed. *Striving towards Being: The Letters of Thomas Merton and Czeslaw Milosz*. New York: Farrar, Strauss, Giroux, 1997.

Feitlowitz, Marguerite. *A Lexicon of Terror: Argentina and the Legacies of Terror*. New York: Oxford University Press, 1998.

Felstiner, John. *Poet, Survivor, Jew*. New Haven: Yale University Press, 2001.

Ferry, David. *Bewilderment: New Poems and Translations*. Chicago: University of Chicago Press, 2012.

Finney, Carolyn. *Black Places, White Spaces: Reimagining the Relationship of African Americans to the Great Outdoors*. Chapel Hill: University of North Carolina Press, 2014.

Flaubert, Gustave. *The Temptation of Saint Anthony*. Translated by Lafcadio Hearn. New York: Modern Library, 2002.

Forché, Carolyn. *Blue Hour*. New York: HarperCollins, 2003.

Forché, Carolyn. *What You Have Heard Is True: A Memoir of Witness and Resistance*. New York: Penguin, 2019.

Foucault, Michel. "Of Other Spaces." *Diacritics* 16, no. 1 (Spring 1986): 22–27.

Frank, Georgia. *The Memory of the Eyes: Pilgrims to Living Saints in Christian Late Antiquity*. Berkeley: University of California Press, 2000.

Franke, William. *On the Universality of What Is Not: The Apophatic Turn in Critical Thinking*. Notre Dame: University of Notre Dame Press, 2020.

Franke, William. *On What Cannot Be Said: Apophatic Discourses in Philosophy, Religion, Literature and the Arts*. Vol. 1: *Classic Formulations*. Notre Dame: University of Notre Dame Press, 2007.

Franke, William. *A Philosophy of the Unsayable*. Notre Dame: University of Notre Dame Press, 2014.

Frankenburg, Ruth. *Living Spirit, Living Practice: Poetics, Politics, Epistemology*. Durham, NC: Duke University Press, 2004.

Fuller, Robert. *Spiritual but Not Religious: Understanding Unchurched America*. New York: Oxford University Press, 2001.

Gadamer, Hans Georg. *Philosophical Hermeneutics*. Translated by David Linge. Berkeley: University of California Press, 2008.

Galilea, Segundo. *The Future of our Past: The Spanish Mystics Speak to Contemporary Spirituality*. Notre Dame: Ave Maria Press, 1985.

Gann, Kyle. *No Such Thing as Silence: John Cage's 4'33"*. New Haven: Yale University Press, 2010.

Garcia Marquez, Gabriel. *Love in the Time of Cholera*. Translated by Edith Grossman. New York: Vintage, 2003.

Gibbons, Reginald. *How Poems Think*. Chicago: University of Chicago Press, 2015.

Girmay, Aracelis. *Kingdom Animalia*. Rochester, NY: BOA Editions, 2011.

Gluck, Louise. *Faithful and Virtuous Night*. New York: Farrar, Straus and Giroux, 2014.

Glucklich, Ariel. *Everyday Mysticism: A Contemplative Community at Work in the Desert*. New Haven: Yale University Press, 2017.

Goehring, James E. "The Encroaching Desert: Literary Production and Ascetic Space in Early Christian Egypt." *Journal of Early Christian Studies* 1 (1993): 281–296.

Gowin, Emmett. *The Nevada Test Site*. Princeton: Princeton University Press, 2019.

Gould, Graham. *The Desert Fathers on Monastic Community*. Oxford: Clarendon, 1993.

Graham-Dixon, Andrew. *Caravaggio: A Life Sacred and Profane*. New York: W. W. Norton, 2010.

Grander, Forrest. *Be With*. New York: New Directions, 2018.

Gregory of Nyssa. *The Life of Moses*. Translated by Abraham J. Malherbe and Everett Ferguson. New York: Paulist Press, 1978.

Gregg, Robert C., and Dennis Groh. *Early Arianism: A View of Salvation*. Philadelphia: Fortress, 1981.

Grootenboer, Hanneke. *The Pensive Image: Art as a Form of Thinking*. Chicago: University of Chicago Press, 2020.

Gruen, John. "Agnes Martin: Everything, Everything Is about Feeling . . . Feeling and Recognition." *ArtNews*, September 1976, https://www.artnews.com/art-news/retros pective/what-we-make-is-what-we-feel-agnes-martin-on-her-meditative-practice-in-1976-4630/.

Gubar, Susan. *Poetry after Auschwitz: Remembering What One Never Knew*. Bloomington: Indiana University Press: 2003.

Guest, Tanis M. *Some Aspects of Hadewijch's Poetic Form in the "Strofische Gedichten."* The Hague: Martinus Nijhoff, 1975.

Gutierrez, Gustavo. *We Drink from Our Own Wells: The Spiritual Journey of a People*. Translated by Matthew J. O'Connell. Maryknoll, NY: Orbis, 1984.

Guzmán, Patricio. *Nostalgia de la luz* [Nostalgia for the light]. Icarus Films. 2011.

Hadewijch. *The Complete Works*. Translated by Mother Columba Hart. New York and Mahwah, NJ: Paulist Press, 1980.

Hadewijch. *Écrits mystiques des Béguines*. Translated by Jean-Baptiste Porion. Paris: Éditions du Seuil, 1954.

Hadewijch. *Poetry of Hadewijch*. Introductory essay, translation, and notes by Mariecke J. E. H. T. Van Best. Leuven: Peeters, 1998.

Hadot, Pierre. *The Philosophy of Everyday Life*. Edited by Arnold Davidson. Translated by Michael Chase. Malden, MA: Blackwell, 1995.

Hall, David D., ed. *Lived Religion in America: Toward a History of Practice*. Princeton: Princeton University Press, 1997.

Halpern, Sue. *Migrations to Solitude*. New York: Pantheon, 1992.

Han, Byung-Chul. *The Scent of Time. A Philosophical Essay on the Art of Lingering*. Translated by Daniel Steuer. Medford, MA: Polity, 2017.

Haraway, Donna. *Staying with the Trouble: Making Kin in the Chthulucene*. Durham, NC: Duke University Press, 2016.

Hart, Kevin. *The Dark Gaze: Maurice Blanchot and the Sacred*. Chicago: University of Chicago Press, 2004.

Hart, Ray L. *God Being Nothing: Toward a Theogony*. Chicago: University of Chicago Press, 2016.

Hass, Robert. *Sun under Wood*. New York: Ecco, 1996.

Hass, Robert, ed. *The Essential Haiku: Versions of Basho, Buson and Issa*. New York: Ecco, 1994.

Hayum, Andrée. *The Isenheim Altarpiece: God's Medicine and the Painter's Vision.* Princeton: Princeton University Press, 1990.

Helms, Mary W. "Before the Dawn: Monks and the Night in Late Antiquity and Early Medieval Europe." *Anthropos* 99 (2004): 177–191.

Hillesum, Etty. *An Interrupted Life.* Translated by Arno Pomerans. New York: Pantheon, 1983.

Hillgardner, Holly. *Longing and Letting Go: Christian and Hindu Practices of Passionate Non-Attachment.* New York: Oxford University Press, 2016.

Hodder, Allan. *Thoreau's Ecstatic Witness.* New Haven: Yale University Press, 2001.

Hole, Sam. *John of the Cross: Desire, Transformation, and Selfhood.* Oxford: Oxford University Press, 2020.

Hollywood, Amy. *Acute Melancholia and Other Essays: Mysticism, History and the Study of Religion.* New York: Columbia University Press, 2016.

Hollywood, Amy. "Love Speaks Here: Michel de Certeau's *Mystic Fable.*" *Spiritus* 12, no. 2 (Fall 2012): 198–206.

Holmes, Barbara. *Joy Unspeakable: Contemplative Practices of the Black Church.* 2nd ed. Minneapolis: Augsburg Fortress, 2017.

House, Freeman. *Totem Salmon: Life Lessons from Another Species.* Boston: Beacon, 1999.

Howe, Fanny. *Gone.* Berkeley: University of California Press, 2003.

Howe, Fanny. *The Wedding Dress: Meditations on Word and Life.* Berkeley: University of California Press, 2003.

Issa, Kobayashi. *The Spring of My Life and Selected Haiku.* Translated by Sam Hamill. Boston: Shambala, 1997.

Jabés, Edmond. *The Book of Margins.* Translated by Rosemarie Waldrop. Chicago: University of Chicago Press, 1993.

Jabés, Edmond. *The Book of Resemblances 2: Intimations: The Desert.* Translated by Rosemary Waldrop. Hanover, NH: Wesleyan University Press, 1991.

Jackson, Michael. "The Prose of Suffering and the Practice of Silence." *Spiritus* 4 (2004): 44–59.

Jamieson, Leslie. *The Empathy Exams.* Minneapolis: Graywolf, 2014.

Jansen, Saskia Murk. *The Measure of Mystic Thought: A Study of Hadewijch's Mengeldichten.* Göppingen: Kümmerle Verlag, 1991.

Jantzen, Grace M. "Eros and the Abyss: Reading Medieval Mystics in Postmodernity." *Literature and Theology* 17, no. 3 (2003): 244–264.

John of the Cross. *The Collected Works.* Rev ed. Translated by Kieran Kavanaugh and Otilio Rodriguez. Washington, DC: ICS Publications, 2010.

Jugrin, Daniel. "*Agnosia*: The Apophatic Experience of God in Dionysius the Areopagite." *Teologia* 67, no. 2 (2016): 102–115.

Kang, Han. *The White Book.* Translated by Deborah Smith. London: Portabello Books, 2017.

Kangas, David. "Dangerous Joy: Marguerite Porete's Goodbye to the Virtues." *Journal of Religion* 91, no. 3 (July 2011): 299–319.

Kars, Ayudogan. *Unsaying God: Negative Theology in Medieval Islam.* New York: Oxford University Press, 2019.

Katos, Demetrios S. "Humility as the Harbinger of Imageless Prayer in the Lausiac History." *St. Vladimir's Theological Quarterly* 51, no. 1 (2007): 107–121.

Keller, Catherine. *Cloud of the Impossible: Negative Theology and Planetary Entanglement.* New York: Columbia University Press, 2014.

Khawaja, Noreen. *The Religion of Existence: Asceticism in Philosophy from Kierkegaard to Sartre*. Chicago: University of Chicago Press, 2016.

Kierkegaard, Soren. *Concluding Unscientific Postscript*. Edited and translated by Howard V. Hong and Edna H. Hong. Princeton: Princeton University Press, 1992.

Kikuchi, Satoshi. *From Eckhart to Ruusbroec: A Critical Inheritance of Mystical Themes in the Fourteenth Century*. Leuven: Leuven University Press, 2015.

Kieślowski, Krzysztof. *Dekalog*. Warsaw: Tor Studios, 1989.

Kirk, Andrew. *Doom Towns: The People and Landscapes of Atomic Testing*. New York: Oxford University Press, 2017.

Knausgaard, Karl Ove. *My Struggle, Book One*. Translated by Don Bartlett. New York: Farrar, Straus and Giroux, 2012.

Koepnick, Loetz. *On Slowness: Towards an Aesthetic of the Contemporary*. New York: Columbia University Press, 2014.

Kosky, Jeffrey L. *Arts of Wonder: Enchanting Secularity—Walter De Maria, Diller + Scofidio, James Turrell, Andy Goldsworthy*. Chicago: University of Chicago Press, 2013.

Knight, Christopher. "Survey of Agnes Martin's Powerful yet Meditative Work Draws a Straight, Vibrant Line to Zen." *Los Angeles Times*, April 29, 2016.

Kramer, Hilton. "An Art That's Almost a Prayer." *New York Times*, May 16, 1976.

Krauss, Rosalind. "Grids." *October* 9 (Summer 1979): 50–64.

Krauss, Rosalind. *The Originality of the Avant-Garde and Other Modernist Myths*. Cambridge, MA: MIT Press, 1985.

Laird, Martin. *Into the Silent Land: A Guide to the Christian Practice of Contemplation*. New York: Oxford, 2006.

Laird, Martin. *An Ocean of Light: Contemplation, Transformation, and Liberation*. New York: Oxford University Press, 2019.

Laird, Martin. "The 'Open Country Whose Name is Prayer.' Apophasis, Deconstruction, and Contemplative Practice." *Modern Theology* 21, no. 1 (2005): 141–155.

Laird, Martin. *A Sunlit Absence: Silence, Awareness, and Contemplation*. New York: Oxford University Press, 2011.

Lang, Jessica. *Textual Silence: Unreadability and the Holocaust*. New Brunswick: Rutgers University Press, 2017.

Lanham, Drew. *The Home Place: Memoirs of a Colored Man's Love Affair with Nature*. Minneapolis: Milkweed, 2016.

Lanzetta, Beverly J. *Radical Wisdom: A Feminist Mystical Theology*. Minneapolis: Augsburg Fortress, 2005.

Lasalle-Klein, Robert. *Blood and Ink: Ignacio Ellacuría, Jon Sobrino, and the Jesuit Martyrs of the University of Central America*. Maryknoll, NY: Orbis, 2014.

Le Clézio, J. M. G. *Desert*. Translated by C. Dickson. Boston: Verba Mundi, 2009.

Lee, Felicia R. "Translating Flaubert, in the Gospel Tradition." *New York Times*, October 20, 2004.

Leopold, Aldo. *A Sand County Almanac: And Sketches Here and There*. New York: Oxford University Press, 1949.

Levertov, Denise. *Evening Train*. New York: New Directions, 1993.

Levertov, Denise. *This Great Unknowing: Last Poems*. New York: New Directions, 1999.

Levi, Primo. *Survival in Auschwitz: The Nazi Assault on Humanity*. Translated by Stuart Woolf. New York: Simon and Schuster, 1996.

Levinas, Emmanuel. *Totality and Infinity: An Essay on Exteriority*. Translated by Alphonso Lingis. Pittsburgh: Duquesne, 1969.

Lewis, Robin Coste. *Voyage of the Sable Venus and Other Poems*. New York: Knopf, 2015.

Limberis, Vasiliki M. *Architects of Piety: The Cappadocian Fathers and the Cult of the Martyrs*. New York: Oxford University Press, 2011.

Linville, Kasha. "Agnes Martin: An Appreciation." *Artforum* 9, no. 10 (Summer 1971): 141–155.

Lipsey, Roger. *Angelic Mistakes: The Art of Thomas Merton*. Boston: Shambala/New Seeds, 2006.

Lispector, Clarice. *Água Viva*. Translated by Stefan Tobler. New York: New Directions, 1973.

Lossky, Vladimir. *The Mystical Theology of the Eastern Church*. Cambridge: James Clark, 1957.

Lyster, William, ed. *The Cave Church of Paul the Hermit at the Monastery of St. Paul, Egypt*. New Haven: Yale University Press, 2008.

Madley, Benjamin. *An American Genocide: The United States and the California Indian Catastrophe, 1846–1873*. New Haven: Yale University Press, 2016.

Marcom, Micheline Aharonian. *The Daydreaming Boy*. New York: Riverhead, 2004.

Marion, Jean-Luc. *Negative Certainties*. Translated by Stephen E. Lewis. Chicago: University of Chicago Press, 2015.

Marno, David. *Death Be Not Proud: The Art of Holy Attention*. Chicago: University of Chicago Press, 2017.

Martínez, Rubén. *Crossing Over: A Mexican Family on the Migrant Trail*. New York: Metropolitan Books, 2001.

Martínez, Rubén. *Desert America: Boom and Bust in the New Old West*. New York: Metropolitan Books, 2012.

McEvilley, Thomas. "Grey Geese Descending: The Art of Agnes Martin." *Artforum* 25, no. 10 (Summer 1987): 94–99.

McEvilley, Thomas. "Negative Presences in Secret Spaces: The Art of Eric Orr." *Artforum* 20, no. 10 (1982): 58–66.

McGinn, Bernard. "The Abyss of Love." in *The Joy of Learning and the Love of God: Studies in Honor of Jean Leclercq*. Edited by Rozanne Elder. Kalamazoo: Cistercian, 1995, 95–120.

McGinn, Bernard. "The God beyond God: Theology and Mysticism in the Thought of Meister Eckhart." *The Journal of Religion* 61, no. 1 (1981): 1–19.

McGinn, Bernard. "Lost in the Abyss: The Function of Abyss Language in Medieval Mysticism." *Franciscan Studies* 72 (2014): 433–444.

McGinn, Bernard, ed. *Meister Eckhart and the Beguine Mystics: Hadewijch of Brabant, Mechthild of Magdeburg, and Marguerite Porete*. New York: Continuum, 1994.

McGinn, Bernard. *The Presence of God: A History of Western Mysticism*. 7 vols. New York: Crossroad, 1991–2020.

McGinn, Bernard, ed. *The Renewal of Mystical Theology*. New York: Crossroad, 2017.

McGuire, Geoffrey. *The Politics of Memory: Violence and Victimhood in Contemporary Argentine Culture*. Cham, Switzerland: Palgrave McMillan, 2017.

McGuire, Meredith B. *Lived Religion: Faith and Practice in Everyday Life*. New York: Oxford University Press, 2008.

McIntosh, Mark. *Mystical Theology: The Integration of Spirituality and Theology*. Malden, MA: Blackwell, 1998.

McIntosh, Mark A., and Edward Howells, eds. *The Oxford Handbook of Mystical Theology*. Oxford: Oxford University Press, 2020.

Meister Eckhart. *The Complete Mystical Works*. Translated and Edited by Maurice O'C. Walshe. New York: Crossroad, 2009.

Mercadante, Linda A. *Belief without Borders: Inside the Minds of the Spiritual but Not Religious*. New York: Oxford University Press, 2014.

Merton, Thomas. *Contemplative Prayer*. New York: Herder and Herder, 1969.

Merton, Thomas. "Day of a Stranger." *The Hudson Review* 20, no. 2 (Summer 1967): 211–218.

Merton, Thomas. *The Hidden Ground of Love*. Edited by William H. Shannon. New York: Farrar, Straus, Giroux, 1985.

Merton, Thomas. *Learning to Love: Exploring Solitude and Freedom: The Journals of Thomas Merton*. Vol. 6: *1966–1967*. Edited by Christine M. Bochen. San Francisco: HarperSanFrancisco, 1997.

Merton, Thomas. "A Life Free from Care." *Cistercian Studies Quarterly* 5, no. 3 (1970): 207–227.

Merton, Thomas. *The Other Side of the Mountain: The End of the Journey*. Edited by Patrick Hart. San Francisco: Harper, 1998.

Merton, Thomas. *Raids on the Unspeakable*. New York: New Directions, 1966.

Merton, Thomas. *Seeds of Destruction*. New York: Farrar, Straus, Giroux, 1981.

Merton, Thomas. *The Way of Chuang Tzu*. New York: New Directions, 1965.

Merton, Thomas. *Witness to Freedom: Letters in Times of Crisis*. Selected and edited by William H. Shannon. New York: Farrar, Straus, Giroux, 1994.

Merton, Thomas. *Woods, Shore, Desert: A Notebook, May 1968*. Santa Fe: Museum of New Mexico Press, 1982.

Merton, Thomas. *Zen and the Birds of Appetite*. New York: New Directions, 1968.

Metz, Johan Baptist. *The End of Time? The Provocation of Talking about God*. Translated by J. Matthew Ashley. Mahwah, NJ: Paulist Press, 2004.

Michaels, Anne. *Fugitive Pieces*. New York: Random House, 1996.

Milhaven, Giles. *Hadewijch and Her Sisters: Other Ways of Loving and Knowing*. Albany: State University of New York Press, 1983.

Millem, Bruce. "Four Theories of Negative Theology." *Heythrop Journal* 48 (2007): 187–204.

Milosz, Czeslaw. *Beginning with My Streets: Essays and Recollections*. New York: Farrar, Strauss and Giroux, 1991.

Milosz, Czeslaw. *The Collected Poems, 1931–1987*. New York: Ecco Press, 1988.

Mommaers, Paul. *Hadewijch: Writer, Beguine, Love Mystic*. Leuven: Peeters, 2004.

Mommaers, Paul. *Jan Van Ruusbroec: Mystical Union with God*. Leuven: Peeters, 2009.

Moorhead, Joanna. "Javier Sicilia: I have no more poetry in me." *The Guardian*, October 28, 2011, https://www.theguardian.com/lifeandstyle/2011/oct/29/javier-sicilia-mexi can-poet-son.

Morris, Frances, and Tiffany Bell, eds. *Agnes Martin*. London: Tate, 2015.

Morrow, Susan Brind. *The Names of Things: A Passage in the Egyptian Desert*. New York: Riverhead, 1997.

Morton, Timothy. *Dark Ecology: For a Logic of Future Co-Existence*. New York: Columbia University Press, 2016.

Morton, Timothy. "The Liminal Space between Things: Epiphany and the Physical." In *Material Ecocriticsm*. Edited by Iovino Serenella and Serpil Oppermann. Bloomington: Indiana University Press, 2014, 269–280.

Neuman, Andrés. *Fracture*. Translated by Nick Caistor and Lorenza Garcia. New York: Farrar, Straus and Giroux, 2020.

Neuman, Andrés. *Talking to Ourselves*. Translated by Nick Caistor and Lorenza Garcia. New York: Farrar, Straus and Giroux, 2015.

Niebuhr, Richard R. "The Strife of Interpreting: The Moral Burden of Imagination." *Parabola* 10, no. 2 (1985): 34–47.

Nixon, Rob. *Slow Violence and the Environmentalism of the Poor*. Cambridge, MA: Harvard University Press, 2011.

Nuth, Joan. "*Acatamiento*: Living in an Attitude of Affectionate Awe—An Ignatian Reflection on the Unitive Way." *Spiritus* 10, no. 2 (2010): 173–191.

Orr, David. *The Nature of Design: Ecology, Culture and Human Intention*. New York: Oxford, 2002.

Orr, Eric, and James Leey Byer. *Zero Mass: The Art of Eric Orr*. Lund, Sweden: Propexus, 1990.

Ortiz, Simon. *Out There Somewhere*. Tucson: University of Arizona Press, 2002.

Pak, Pyong-Gwan. "The Vernacular, Mystical Theology of Jan van Ruusbroec: Exploring Sources, Contexts and Theological Practices." Ph.D. diss. Boston College, August 2008.

Partnoy, Alicia. *The Little School*. Translated by Alicia Partnoy with Lois Athey and Sandra Braunstein. San Francisco: Midnight Editions, 1998.

Peck, H. Daniel. *Thoreau's Morning Work: Memory and Perception in* A Week on the Concord and Merrimack Rivers, *the Journal, and* Walden. New Haven: Yale University Press, 1990.

Pessoa, Fernando. *The Book of Disquiet*. Edited by Maria José de Lancastre. Translated by Margaret Jull Costa. London: Serpent's Tail, 1991.

Pessoa, Fernando. *The Book of Disquiet*. Edited by Jerónimo Pizzaro. Translated by Margaret Jull Costa. New York: New Directions, 2017.

Pizarnik, Alejandra. *The Galloping Hour: French Poems*. Translated by Patricio Ferrari and Forrest Grander. New York: New Directions, 1998.

Porete, Marguerite. *The Mirror of Simple Souls*. Translated and introduced by Ellen Babinsky. New York and Mahwah, NJ: Paulist Press, 1993.

Prevot, Andrew. "Divine Opacity: Mystical Theology, Black Theology and the Problem of Light-Dark Aesthetics." *Spiritus: A Journal of Christian Spirituality* 16, no. 2 (2016): 166–188.

Princenthal, Nancy. *Agnes Martin: Her Life and Art*. London: Thames and Hudson, 2015.

Pron, Patricio. *My Fathers' Ghost Is Climbing in the Rain*. Translated by Mara Feye Lethem. New York: Knopf, 2013.

Pseudo-Dionysius. *The Complete Works*. Translated by Colm Liubheid and Paul Rorem. New York and Mahwah, NJ: Paulist Press, 1987.

Radler, Charlotte. "*Actio et Contemplatio*/Action and Contemplation." In *The Cambridge Companion to Christian Mysticism*. Edited by Amy Hollywood and Patricia Beckman. Cambridge: Cambridge University Press, 2012, 211–222.

Radler, Charlotte. "Living from the Divine Ground: Meister Eckhart's Praxis of Detachment." *Spiritus* 6, no. 1 (2006): 24–46.

Radler, Charlotte. "In Love I Am More God: The Centrality of Love in Meister Eckhart's Mysticism." *The Journal of Religion* 90, no. 2 (April 2010): 171–198.

Rahner, Karl. *Theological Investigations*. Vol. 23. New York: Crossroad, 1992.

Reed, Arden. "Ad Reinhardt's 'Black' Paintings." *Religion and the Arts* 193 (2015): 214–229.

Reed, Arden. *Slow Art: The Experience of Looking, Sacred Images to James Turrell*. Berkeley: University of California Press, 2017.

Rigby, Cathy. "Spirits That Matter: Pathways toward a Rematerialization of Religion and Spirituality." In *Material Ecocriticsm*. Edited by Iovino Serenella and Serpil Oppermann. Bloomington: Indiana University Press, 2014, 283–290.

Rilke, Rainer Maria. *Duino Elegies and the Sonnets of Orpheus*. Translated by A. Poulin. New York: Mariner, 2005.

Rilke, Rainer Maria. *Letters of Rainer Maria Rilke, 1892–1910*. Translated by Jane Bannard Greene and M. D. Herter Norton. New York: W. W. Norton, 1969.

Rivera Garza, Cristina. *Grieving: Dispatches from a Wounded Country*. Translated by Sarah Booker. New York: Feminist Press, 2020.

Robertis, Carolina de. *Perla*. New York: Vintage, 2013.

Robinson, David M. *Natural Life: Thoreau's Worldly Transcendentalism*. Ithaca: Cornell University Press, 2004.

Roethke, Theodore. *Selected Poems*. New York: Library of America, 2005.

Rorem, Paul. *The Dionysian Mystical Theology*. Minneapolis: Fortress, 2015.

Rósiewicz, Tadeusz. *New Poems*. Translated by Bill Johnston. Brooklyn, NY: Archipelago Books, 2007.

Rozenski, Steven, Jr. "The Promise of Eternity: Love and Poetic Form in Hadewijch's *Liederen* or Stanzaic Poems." *Exemplaria* 22, no. 4 (Winter 2010): 305–325.

Russell, Norman, trans. *The Lives of the Desert Fathers*. Kalamazoo: Cistercian, 1981.

Ruusbroec, John. *The Complete Ruusbroec*. English Translation with the original Middle Dutch text. Edited and with an introduction by Guido de Baere and Thom Mertens. Vol. 1. Turnhout, Belgium: Brepols, 2014.

Ruysbroeck, John. *The Adornment of the Spiritual Marriage; The Sparkling Stone; the Book of Supreme Truth*. Translated by C. A. Wynschenk Dom. Westminster, MD: Christian Classics, 1974.

Sachs, John R., S.J. "Apocatastasis in Patristic Theology." *Theological Studies* 54 (1993): 617–640.

Saint-Exupéry, Antoine de. *Flight to Arras*. Translated by Lewis Galantière. New York: Harcourt, 1986.

Saenz, Jaime. *The Night*. Translated by Forrest Grander and Kent Johnson. Princeton: Princeton University Press, 2007.

Sanders, Theresa. "Remarking the Silence: Prayer after the Death of God." *Horizons* 25, no. 2 (1998): 203–216.

Savoy, Lauret. *Trace: Memory, History, Race, and the American Landscape*. Berkeley: Counterpoint, 2015.

Schalansky, Judith. *An Inventory of Losses*. Translated by Jackie Smith. New York: New Directions, 2018.

Schelvis, Jules. *Sobibor: A History of a Nazi Death Camp*. Translated by Karin Dixon. Oxford: Berg, 2007.

Schmidt, Leigh Eric. *Restless Souls: The Making of American Spirituality*. San Francisco: HarperSanFrancisco, 2005.

Schneiders, Sandra M. "Religion vs. Spirituality: A Contemporary Conundrum." *Spiritus: A Journal of Christian Spirituality* 3, no. 2 (2003): 163–185.

Schuld, Dawna L. *Minimal Conditions: Light Space and Subjectivity*. Berkeley: University of California Press, 2018.

Schuld, Dawna L. "Practically Nothing: Light, Space and the Pragmatics of Phenomenology." In *Phenomenal: California Light, Space, Surface*. Edited by Robin Clark. Berkeley: University of California Press, 2011, 105–122.

Schwarz, Dieter, ed. *Agnes Martin: Writings/Schriften*. Ostfildern-Ruit, Germany: Kunstmuseum Winterthur/Edition Cantz, 1992.

Schweblin, Samanta. *Fever Dream*. Translated by Megan McDowell. New York: Riverhead, 2017.

Sebald, W. G. *Austerlitz*. Translated by Anthea Bell. New York: Random House, 2001.

Sebald, W. G. *The Rings of Saturn*. Translated by Michael Hulse. New York: New Directions, 1998.

Seitz, William. *The Responsive Eye*. New York: Museum of Modern Art, 1963.

Sells, Michael A. *Mystical Languages of Unsaying*. Chicago: University of Chicago Press, 1994.

Sharlett, Jeff. *This Brilliant Darkness: A Book of Strangers*. New York: W. W. Norton, 2020.

Skloot, Floyd. *In the Shadow of Memory*. Lincoln: University of Nebraska Press, 2003.

Sluhovsky, Moshe. *Becoming a New Self: Practices of Belief in Early Modern Catholicism*. Chicago: University of Chicago Press, 2017.

Smith, Tracy K. *Life on Mars*. Minneapolis: Graywolf, 2011.

Smith, Tracy K. *Wade in the Water*. Minneapolis: Greywolf, 2018.

Snyder, Gary. *The Practice of the Wild*. San Francisco: North Point Press, 1990.

Solnit, Rebecca. *Hope in the Dark: Untold Histories, Wild Possibilities*. Chicago: Haymarket, 2016.

Sophrony, Archbishop. *St. Silouan the Athonite*. Younkers, NY: St Vladimir's Seminary Press, 1999.

Sorett, Josef. *Spirit in the Dark: A Religious History of Racial Aesthetics*. New York: Oxford University Press, 2016.

Sorrell, Roger D. *St. Francis of Assisi and Nature: Tradition and Innovation in Western Christian Attitudes towards the Environment*. New York: Oxford University Press, 1988.

Soseki, Musō. *Sun at Midnight*. Translated by W. S. Merwin and Soiku Shigematsu. San Francisco: North Point Press, 1989.

Speece, Darren Frederick. *Defending Giants: The Redwood Wars and the Transformation of American Environmental Politics*. Seattle: University of Washington Press, 2016.

Speece, Darren Frederick. "Seeds of Rebellion: The Fight over Sally Bell Grove and the Origins of the Redwood Wars." *California History* 94, no. 2 (2017): 4–21.

Stafford, Barbara Maria. *Ribbon of Darkness: Inferencing from the Shadowy Arts and Sciences*. Chicago: University of Chicago Press, 2019.

Steindl-Rast, David. "Man of Prayer." In *Thomas Merton Monk: A Monastic Tribute*. Edited by Brother Patrick Hart. Kalamazoo: Cistercian, 1983, 79–89.

Stewart, Columba. "The Desert Fathers on Radical Self-Honesty." *Vox Benedictina: A Journal of Translations from Monastic Sources* 8 (1991): 7–54.

Stewart, Columba. "Evagrius and the 'Eight Generic *Logisimoi*.'" In *In the Garden of Evil: The Vices and Culture in the Middle Ages*. Edited by Richard Neuhauser. Toronto: PIMS, 2005, 3–34.

Stewart, Columba. "Imageless Prayer and the Theological Vision of Evagrius Ponticus." *Journal of Early Christian Studies* 9, no. 2 (2001): 173–204.

Summit, Jennifer, and Blakey Vermeule. *Action and Contemplation: Why an Ancient Debate Still Matters*. Chicago: University of Chicago Press, 2018.

Storr, Anthony. *Solitude: A Return to the Self*. New York: Ballantine, 1998.

Taylor, Barbara Brown. *Learning to Walk in the Dark*. New York: HarperOne, 2008.

Taylor, Charles. *A Secular Age*. Cambridge, MA: Harvard University Press, 2007.

Taft. R. F. *The Liturgy of the Hours in East and West: The Origins of the Divine Office and Its Meaning for Today*. Collegeville, MN: Liturgical Press, 1986.

Taylor, Mark C. *Speed Limits: Where Time Went and Why We Have So Little Left*. New Haven: Yale University Press, 2014.

Tesson, Sylvain. *The Consolations of the Forest: Alone in a Cabin on the Siberian Taiga*. Translated by Linda Coverdale. New York: Rizzoli, 2013.

Thompson, Augustine., O.P. *Francis of Assisi: A New Biography*. Ithaca: Cornell University Press, 2012.

Thoreau, Henry David. *Walden*. Edited by J. Lyndon Shanley. Princeton: Princeton University Press, 1971.

Thoreau, Henry David. *A Week on the Concord and Merrimack Rivers*. New York: Penguin, 1998.

Tokarczuk, Olga. *Primeval and Other Times*. Translated by Antonia Lloyd-Jones. Prague: Twisted Spoon Press, 2010.

Tracy, David. *Fragments: The Existential Situation of Our Time*. Chicago: University of Chicago Press, 2020.

Turner, Denys. *The Darkness of God: Negativity in Christian Mysticism*. Cambridge: Cambridge University Press, 1995.

Uribe, Sara. *Antígona González*. Translated by John Plueker. Los Angeles: Les Figues Press, 2016.

Valance, Hélène. *Nocturne: Night in American Art, 1890–1917*. Translated by Jane Marie Todd. New Haven: Yale University Press, 2018.

Van Engen, John. *Sisters and Brothers of the Common Life: The Devotio Moderna and the World of the Later Middle Ages*. Philadelphia: University of Pennsylvania Press, 2014.

Van Nieuwenhove, Rik. "Ruusbroec, Jordaens, and Herp on the Common Life: The Transformation of a Spiritual Ideal." In *A Companion to John of Ruusbroec*. Edited by John Arblaster and Rob Faesen. Leiden: Brill, 2014, 204–236.

Vásquez, Juan Gabriel. *The Informers*. Translated by Anne McClean. New York: Riverhead, 2009.

Vauchez, André. *Francis of Assisi: The Life and Afterlife of a Medieval Saint*. Translated by Michael F. Cusato. New Haven and London: Yale University Press, 2012.

Vincent, David. *A History of Solitude*. Cambridge: Polity, 2020.

Voigt, Ellen Bryant. *Shadow of Heaven*. New York: W. W. Norton, 2002.

Waddell, Helen, trans. *The Desert Fathers*. London: Constable, 1936.

Wakefield, Ray. "Homeless Mystics: Exiled from God." In *Weltanschauliche Orientierungsversuche im Exil / New Orientations of World View in Exile*. Edited by Evelyn M. Meyer, Greg Divers, and Reinhard Andress. Leiden: Brill, 2010, 37–43.

Walcott, Derek. *Collected Poems: 1948–1984*. New York: Farrar, Straus and Giroux, 1986.

Ward, Benedicta, trans. *The Sayings of the Desert Fathers: The Alphabetical Collection*. Rev. ed. Collegeville, MN: Liturgical Press, 1984.

Warner, Michael, Jonathan Van Antwerpen, and Craig Calhoun, eds. *Varieties of Secularism in a Secular Age*. Cambridge, MA: Harvard University Press, 2010.

Watson, Gay. *A Philosophy of Emptiness*. London: Reaktion, 2014.

Webb, Chris. *The Sobibor Death Camp: History, Biographies, Remembrance*. New York: Columbia University Press, 2017.

West, Clark R. "The Deconstruction of Hell: A History of the *Resignatio ad Infernum* Tradition." Ph.D. diss. Syracuse University, 2013.

Weil, Simone. *First and Last Notebooks*. Translated by Richard Rees. Oxford: Oxford University Press, 1970.

Weil, Simone. *Gravity and Grace*. Translated by Emma Crawford and Mario von der Ruhr. London: Routledge, 2002.

Weil, Simone. *Waiting for God*. Translated by Emma Craufurd. New York: Putnams, 1952.

Wiesel, Elie. *One Generation After*. Translated by Lily Edelman and Elie Wiesel. New York, Schocken, 2011.

Wiseman, James A. *Ruusbroec's Mystical Vision in "Die gheestelike brulocht" Seen in the Light of "Minne"*. Leuven: Peeters, 2018.

White, Lynn Jr. "The Historical Roots of Our Environmental Crisis." *Science* 155, no. 3767 (March 1967): 1203–1207.

Whitfield, Teresa. *Paying the Price: Ignacio Ellacuría and the Murdered Jesuits of El Salvador*. Philadelphia: Temple University Press, 1994.

Wilson, Ann. "Linear Webs." *Art & Artists* 1 (October 1966): 47.

Wiman, Christian. *Hammer Is the Prayer: Selected Poems*. New York: Farrar, Straus and Giroux, 2016.

Wiman, Christian. *My Bright Abyss: Meditation of a Modern Believer*. New York: Farrar, Strauss and Giroux, 2013.

Winterson, Jeanette. *Weight: The Myth of Atlas and Heracles*. New York: Cannongate, 2005.

Wortley, John, trans. *The Book of the Elders: Sayings of the Desert Fathers: The Systematic Collection*. Collegeville, MN: Liturgical Press, 2012.

Yountae, An. *The Decolonial Abyss: Mysticism and Cosmopolitics from the Ruins*. New York: Fordham University Press, 2017.

Zambra, Alejandro. *Ways of Going Home*. Translated by Megan McDowell. New York: Farrar, Straus and Giroux, 2013.

Zaretzky, Robert. *The Subversive Simone Weil: A Life in Five Ideas*. Chicago: University of Chicago Press, 2021.

Zurita, Raúl. *Inri*. Translated by William Rowe. Grosse Pointe Farms, MI: Marick Press, 2009.

Index